Genre-Busting
Dark Comedies
of the 1970s

Genre-Busting Dark Comedies of the 1970s

Twelve American Films

WES D. GEHRING

Foreword by David L. Smith

McFarland & Company, Inc., Publishers

Jefferson, North Carolina

ALSO BY WES D. GEHRING AND FROM MCFARLAND: *Chaplin's War Trilogy: An Evolving Lens in Three Dark Comedies, 1918–1947* (2014); *Will Cuppy, American Satirist: A Biography* (2013); *Forties Film Funnymen: The Decade's Great Comedians at Work in the Shadow of War* (2010); *Film Clowns of the Depression: Twelve Defining Comic Performances* (2007); *Joe E. Brown: Film Comedian and Baseball Buffoon* (2006); *Mr. Deeds Goes to Yankee Stadium: Baseball Films in the Capra Tradition* (2004)

Frontispiece: Richard Dupont's sculpture "Going Around by Passing Through" captures the essence of the book—we pass through life going in circles ... killing time ... until time kills us... (© Richard Dupont and Artists Rights Society [ARS], New York).

All photographs are from the author's collection unless otherwise noted. (For uniformity, the films are arranged by when the picture was first reviewed in the *New York Times*.)

LIBRARY OF CONGRESS CATALOGUING-IN-PUBLICATION DATA

Names: Gehring, Wes D., author.
Title: Genre-busting dark comedies of the 1970s : twelve American films / Wes D. Gehring ; foreword by David L. Smith.
Description: Jefferson, North Carolina : McFarland & Company, Inc., Publishers, 2016 | "Foreword by David L. Smith—Preface and acknowledgments—Prologue—MASH (1970)—Catch/22 (1970)—Little Big Man (1970)—Harold and Maude (1971)—Cabaret (1972)—Slaughterhouse-five (1972)—Chinatown (1974)—Love and death (1975)—One flew over the cuckoo's nest (1975)—Annie Hall (1977)—Being there (1979)—All that jazz (1979)—Epilogue with notes on A clockwork orange (1971)—Filmography." | Includes bibliographical references and index.
Identifiers: LCCN 2016005839 | ISBN 9780786495429 (softcover : acid free paper) ∞
Subjects: LCSH: Comedy films—United States—History and criticism. | Tragicomedy—History and criticism.
Classification: LCC PN1995.9.C55 G425 2016 | DDC 791.43/617—dc23
LC record available at https://lccn.loc.gov/2016005839

BRITISH LIBRARY CATALOGUING DATA ARE AVAILABLE

ISBN 978-0-7864-9542-9
ISBN 978-1-4766-2251-4 (ebook)

On the cover: Boris (Woody Allen) dances with the Grim Reaper in the 1975 film *Love and Death* (United Artists/Photofest)

Printed in the United States of America

McFarland & Company, Inc., Publishers
Box 611, Jefferson, North Carolina 28640
www.mcfarlandpub.com

For the Future:

Michael
Emmett
Kadri
Lily
Ruby

Table of Contents

FOREWORD BY DAVID L. SMITH   1
PREFACE AND ACKNOWLEDGMENTS   3
PROLOGUE   5

 1. *MASH* (1/24/70)   11
 2. *Catch–22* (6/20/70)   34
 3. *Little Big Man* (12/15/70)   53
 4. *Harold and Maude* (12/21/71)   68
 5. *Cabaret* (2/14/72)   86
 6. *Slaughterhouse-Five* (3/23/72)   105
 7. *Chinatown* (6/21/74)   122
 8. *Love and Death* (6/11/75)   139
 9. *One Flew Over the Cuckoo's Nest* (11/20/75)   155
10. *Annie Hall* (4/21/77)   169
11. *Being There* (12/20/79)   184
12. *All That Jazz* (12/20/79)   198

EPILOGUE WITH NOTES ON *A CLOCKWORK ORANGE* (1971)   213
FILMOGRAPHY   219
CHAPTER NOTES   221
BIBLIOGRAPHY   232
INDEX   241

Foreword by David L. Smith

Madness is always fascinating, for it reveals the ungluing we all secretly fear: the mind taking off from the body, the possibility that the magnet that attaches us to a context in the world can lose its grip.

—Molly Haskell[1]

In writing this foreword I am reminded of a W.H. Auden cover blurb strongly praising *Agee on Film: Essays and Reviews by James Agee, Volume 1*.[2] Though many decades later, like Auden, I often find movie criticism by intellectuals without insight. That is why I don't bother reading many of the critics who write about movies. I am pleasantly surprised, however, to find myself not only reading Wes Gehring's latest book, but also consciously looking forward to his next one. His publishing is so regular that it seems he would run out of things to say. But here he is again and, as usual, what he says is always of profound interest and filled with extraordinary wit. This has placed him in a very select class.

Gehring picked his pivotal dark comedies by drawing from a genre-bending collage of seemingly different genres. And he has somehow managed to come up with most of my favorite black comedy heroes. Protagonists like Jack Crabb, Billy Pilgrim, Chance the gardener and R.P. McMurphy are just a few of the headliners who appear in Gehring's discussions of genre-crossing dark comedies. Many of the events portrayed in this selection of comedies border on horrific but the styles are light-hearted. This is a natural expectation when tragedy adopts the affecting language of comedy.

Gehring shows us how the theoretical separation of comic and tragic styles can be combined, and either genre can, on occasion, borrow the stylistic manner of the other to a striking effect. This is an unusual and fascinating book.

David L. Smith is a Ball State University emeritus professor and the author of many articles and texts on film and media in general. His latest book is Sitting Pretty: The Life and Times of Clifton Webb (*University Press of Mississippi, 2011*).

Preface and Acknowledgments

Most of us feel that we could never become extinct. The Dodo felt that way, too.[1]
—satirist Will Cuppy

There's rereading a book and then there's inhabiting it the way one is able to do in late childhood.[2]
—critic Dana Stevens

The same inhabiting phenomenon occurs when rescreening a beloved film. As noted at length in the forthcoming prologue, the catalyst for this book was exploring a new way to better understand the multi-faceted anti-genre American dark comedies of the 1970s. But it would be a major omission not to confess that this project was also an excuse to revisit several seminal movies and texts from my life-changing university film studies during the period before I found social and cinematic change were very much intertwined. This volatility was a great deal for a young mind to wrap itself around. Thus, besides feeling the period deserved a second look beyond greater understanding, the study could also serve as a measuring device for how far I had come. Of course, as Steve Martin suggests in his memoir, personal reflections on time past find one writing about someone one once knew.[3] Regardless, with age, thoughts of the past are ever more present … and complex.

Nonetheless, when one writes the acknowledgment section, there is always that fear that someone has been missed. So if anyone is overlooked, my profound apologies. Let me start with a *big* thank to my department chairman, Tim Pollard. Though I have served many excellent TCOM leaders over the years, none has ever been so generous with his support, both on this book and many other projects. And as with all my writing, Janet Warner supplied valuable editorial help, while Kris Scott was responsible for the computer preparation of the manuscript. Chris Flook was especially helpful with all of my technology questions. Two of the university's emeritus professors, David L. Smith and Conrad Lane, provided valuable discussions about the project, with David also contributing the foreword. Former BSU endowed chair (and award-winning filmmaker) Robert Mugge was also a most appreciated sounding board. And BSU's interlibrary loan staff—Sandy Duncan, Kerri McCellan, Lisa Johnson, Elaine Nelson, and Karin Kwiatkowski—managed to track down everything I requested.

Away from home, the New York Public Library's main branch at Fifth Avenue and Forty-Second Street—where the librarian makes like Jesse Owens in her exit at the start of *Ghostbusters* (1984)—is always an invaluable source. At this location I focus on the "tombs" section—looking at New York's many dead newspapers on microfilm. The other

3

pivotal Big Apple stop is the Performing Arts Library at Lincoln Center, with its critical period clipping files of film artists and individual movies.

I greatly appreciate the Estate of George Grosz for giving me permission to reproduce the paintings "The Relicts" (1921) and "Ballroom" (1929). The same thank you goes out to artist Richard Dupont for allowing me to reproduce a photograph of his sculpture "Going Around by Passing Through" for the book's frontispiece. It was during a random walk *around* New York's Columbus Circle that I spotted Richard's fascinating work. And its Brechtian title so fit the essence of the book in hand—essentially we go in circles as we pass through life—I knew I wanted it to lead off this text. (Fittingly, I was researching this book and power walking from the main library to Lincoln Center's Performing Arts Library, a back and forth I do whenever researching in New York.)

Saving the best for last, none of this would have been possible without the love, support, and *patience* of my family and friends. From nurturing parents, an encouraging muse (Cassie), and my film-loving daughters (Sarah and Emily), much can be accomplished.

Prologue

[Things] could be one hell of a lot better.... And don't tell me God works in mysterious ways. There's nothing so mysterious about it. He's not working at all.
—central character Yossarian in *Catch–22* (1961)[1]

This text examines twelve pivotal 1970s genre-crossing dark comedies frequently masquerading in other categories and scrutinizes that diversity in depth. The goal is a better understanding of cinema's modern (post–1967) dark comedy as it evolved into a complex *compound* genre, besides providing further pop culture insights into 1970s cinema. The study has the "American New Wave" or "New Hollywood" movement (approximately 1967 to 1979) as a *partial* catalyst. This Renaissance righting of the Hollywood ship, after the floundering 1950s, assumed a new direction from filmland's classic period of the early 1920s to the late 1940s. New Hollywood was the brief culmination of many events, from the TV-driven decline of the studio system, to cinema's "French New Wave." This latter screen movement started with Francois Truffaut's *The 400 Blows* (1959) and Jean-Luc Godard's *Breathless* (1960), and lasted until the mid–1960s.

Other key developments between derailing TV and the French New Wave, with regard to jump-starting the American New Wave movement, included the Supreme Court's 1948 decision (*U.S. vs. Paramount Pictures, Inc.*) to break up Hollywood's various theater chain monopolies and the post–World War II influx of provocatively realistic foreign films, beginning with 1940s Italian Neo-Realism (both of which precipitated the loosening of the censorship code). It also included the intellectually empty but expensive bloated blockbuster attempts to draw dwindling viewers away from their TV sets (see critic Manny Farber's "White Elephant Art vs. Termite Art"[2]), young college-educated baby boomers being drawn to engagingly topical 1960s "termite art" films, and the increasingly anti-establishment nature of the '60s (from civil rights to the forever escalating war in Vietnam).

Consequently, while the "American New Wave" school plays a part in the transition to this study's 1970 genre-crossing dark comedies, this work is in *no way* meant as a history of the movement, nor even a focus on its most important pictures, though several of the selections fit that description. However, these new, more complex dark comedies often ape three key differences from classic American cinema, differences the French New Wave baton passed onto the New Hollywood movement. First, instead of traditional admirable heroes, these films showcase anti-heroes—fascinatingly anti-establishment characters of a realistic, non-movie star status. Second, rather than normal chronological narratives, the movies are often about slice-of-life existence which revels in disjointed storytelling, like the randomness of life—less a narrative than a darkly comic cinematic mosaic. The sad truth is that all lives are metaphorical movie rough-cuts, with no chance for either reshooting or even a polished final cut. Third, in place of classic cinema's tidy upbeat conclusions, these counter-culture films end with a bittersweet honesty, from shattered dreams to death.

Despite this shared trilogy of themes, the genre-bending dark comedies about to be carefully examined harbor additional components not necessarily inherent to this New Hollywood, starting with a killingly off-kilter black humor tradition which predates cinema itself. Most fundamentally, the genre builds upon three interrelated hoary themes: the omnipresence of death, the inherent absurdity of the world, and man as beast.[3] Its often literary base is also represented by the fact that several of this text's focus dark comedies are adaptations from fiction. Interestingly, as a related sidebar to adaptations, the influential French New Wave movement actually railed *against* adaptations; the movement's architects felt film stories should be composed directly for the screen.

Ultimately, while there are many excellent studies of the American New Wave, especially Peter Biskind's *Easy Riders, Raging Bulls* (1998), these works spread themselves thin surveying dozens of movies without even precise period perimeters.[4] For example, besides my aforementioned time approximation of the New Hollywood era, one finds dates ranging from 1962 to 1980, to 1965 to 1976.[5] It is like "attempting to hit a moving target squared," or better yet, Peter Novick's tongue-in-cheek observation about writing history—trying "to nail jelly to a wall."[6] Consequently this book's ultimate investigation is a decade-tidy (1970s) examination of twelve genre-crossing dark comedies. The parallels among these movies will, I hope, provide insights into *both* an already complex, appropriately twisted genre, and the still turbulent New Hollywood decade which followed the 1960s. Because just as many early critics struggled with basic dark comedy, numerous later 1970s reviewers grappled with a further convoluted (anti-genre) version of the formula.

Before analyzing the traditional comedy components of these twelve films, this study explores smoke-screen genres that help defuse the more obvious in-your-face nature of most pre–1970s examples of black humor. For instance, using Hitler for humor in *The Great Dictator* (1940), or the nuclear Armageddon of *Dr. Strangelove or: How I Learned to Stop Worrying and Love the Bomb* (1964). Moreover, this collage of genres, or post-modern fragmentation, works on two levels. First comes the diversion stage which eases still tepid black humor fans into a new genre-bending phase of dark comedy.

Second and most paradoxically,

The title character (Charlie Chaplin) in *The Great Dictator* (1940).

the misdirection genre quickly morphs into a new and further reinforcement of the inherent black humor. That is, these seemingly standard genres rapidly go rogue, turning into what Robert Altman (see Chapter 1's *MASH*, 1970) sometimes called *anti-genre*. When these allegedly standard genres break their own formulas, it contributes to the chaos which is central to dark comedy—a cling-to-the-wreckage philosophy. For instance, two of this study's seminal examples would be *Little Big Man* (1970, see Chapter 3) and *All That Jazz* (1979, see Chapter 12), with the former usually labeled a Western and the latter a musical. But *Little Big Man* has viewers changing teams (rooting for the Native Americans against the bluecoats), while *All That Jazz* is ultimately a musical comedy about death. (Other anti-genre examples are dissected further in each of their chapters—which, naturally, also applies to all the other focus films/chapters.)

Regardless, much of my writing has studied various forms of comedy, with the catalyst coming decades ago by a statement from comedy theorist Jim Leach: "a genre which encompasses the visions of Jerry Lewis *and* Ernst Lubitsch is already in trouble.... [I]f a genre is defined too loosely [as with comedy] it ceases to be a literary tool"—encouraging a more ambitious examination of the comedy genres.[7] Thus, much of my life has gone into writing book-length studies on the following forms of film comedy: feel good populism (*à la* Frank Capra), dark comedy (the opposite of populism), screwball comedy (farce, and first cousin to black humor, best encapsulated in *Nothing Sacred*, 1937), romantic comedy, parody, and personally comedians.[8] While enjoying them all, I have always been particularly drawn to dark comedy, a genre which also bridges my career, from presenting a 1989 lecture on the subject at the University of Paris (back when the world was young), to my recent award-winning book *Chaplin's War Trilogy: An Evolving Lens in Three Dark Comedies, 1918–1947* (2014).[9]

So what are the dark comedy attractions for me? And don't kill the messenger, because these are fundamental modules of the genre. First, black humor is the bravest genre; it scrapes away all the institutionalized crutches which prop up most people. For example, just think of the religious jukebox of golden oldies on death: "It's God will," "She is in a better place," "God needed him more," *ad nauseam*. Black humor simply says this is it; there ain't no more, so deal with it. Do the right thing simply because it is the right thing to do, not for some promised heavenly reward and/or a damnation ticket threat to hell. For this genre, religion is a franchise driven by the *fear* of death, one of dark comedy's basic themes. And churches are the ideal business; one makes regular "travel" payments but there are *no* guaranteed arrivals. Yet, black humor is an equal opportunity institutional whistle blower.

For subjects like war, governments also play a variation of the same Orwellian head-in-the-sand comfort zone game. Plus, they, too, have their own grizzled tag lines: "Take our word for it, there is some [nebulous] threat; so just accept it" and "My country right or wrong," as in "Love it or leave it." Yet again, as Dalton Trumbo suggests in his anti-war novel *Johnny Got His Gun* (1939), some surviving "patriots" might toe the party line while the representatives for the dead have no voice in this lethal shell game. But true patriots clasp the duty of the seminal citizen: They ask questions like Socrates and memorize the notable words of celebrated Edward R. Murrow: "Never confuse dissent with disloyalty." To not guard freedom as such is *absurdity* (another pivotal dark comedy element). To debate is the guiding spirit of a non–fear-mongering American. The country was literally founded upon the belief in and need for continued inquiry. Thus, to blindly wrap one's self in the flag, ironically, is actually to be *un*–American. Nevertheless, this study is not here to make dark comedy converts, especially with the solace of God and/or Uncle Sam being a hard addiction to break, regardless of the truth. This book is merely sketching the basic black humor parameters of a genre after it had finally found a measure of 1960s acceptance.

Another reason drawing me to dark comedy is a firm belief in the First Amendment. How does this apply to the genre? It is best articulated by the famous defense lawyer Harold Price Fahringer: "Freedom is only meaningful if it includes all speech [and non-harmful activity], no matter who is offended by it. It would be a hazardous undertaking for anyone to start separating the permissible ... from the impermissible, using the standard of offensiveness.... Are we afraid to be free?"[10] There is that implication of fear again. I am reminded of Albert Brooks' sometimes dark comedy *Defending Your Life* (1991). After a deadly accident, he finds himself in an otherworldly waiting zone as his lawyer (Rip Torn) explains that all Earthlings are "little brains" ruled from birth by fear.

I am also drawn to another disturbing dark comedy truism, with which all other philosophies wrestle. In award-winning writer William Styron's slender volume on depression, *Darkness Visible: A Memoir of Madness* (1990), he draws from *The Myth of Sisyphus* and notes, "There is but one truly serious philosophical problem, and that is suicide. Judging whether life is or is not worth living amounts to answering the fundamental question of philosophy."[11] And suicide is one commodity that dark comedy knows only too well, and upon which it frequently centers its narrative, such as in *Harold and Maude* (1970, see Chapter 4).

An additional dark comedy appeal for this writer is the constant controversy associated with its ongoing reshaping. Just as the only constant in life is change, genres are gradually morphing into something else. For example, before Alfred Hitchcock's *Psycho* and Michael Powell's *Peeping Tom* (both 1960), horror films were more likely to be set in the past, *à la* ancient vampires, or Jack the Ripper's late 19th century London. Not that contemporary horror had never existed before (see Val Lewton's 1940s RKO "B" movies). Still, after 1960 the genre was much more likely to be concurrent.

Indeed, screwball comedy, with its sometime ties to dark comedy, chronicles an even more telling degree of change. For example, at first it was funny enough to just be screwy, such as the Carole Lombard character in *My Man Godfrey* (1936).[12] Later it became a more on-off proposition, as in Irene Dunne's calculating persona in *My Favorite Wife* (1940).[13] In the late 1930s, starting with *Topper* (1937, which became a minor movie franchise), being entertainingly nutty could also be the result of seeing a ghost, after Cary Grant and Constance Bennett are killed in the seemingly least painful of movie car wrecks. And through the years, the genre has found various other ways for people suddenly becoming comically unglued, with a particularly popular one involving suddenly encountering famous people, such as in two Julia Roberts vehicles, *Notting Hill* (1999) and *Runaway Bride* (1999).

So how is natural change different in dark comedy? Well, as in any genre, gradual transformations are taking place here, too. But keep in mind, black humor's stock in trade has always been *shock*. Now, it is one thing for screwball comedy to continue making people amusingly mad as a hatter over a ghost, only to later change the metamorphosis into being around prominent people. However, it is quite another thing to make one's mutation something ever more disturbing. For instance, it took two-thirds of the 20th century before even the most basic black humor components were broadly acceptable, including *Dictator* mocking Hitler, *thoughts* of killing a cheating spouse in *Unfaithfully*

Yours (1948), and *Strangelove*'s mushroom cloud. Moreover, these pioneering filmmakers made things more tolerable by minimizing and/or eliminating any on-screen violence. If this black humor formula had been allowed to effectively stay unchanged, this book would not have been necessary—controversy gone, case closed. But button-pushing dark comedy, by its nature, has become even more visually deadly, absurd, and hilariously cruel (man as beast), and the public storm clouds have repeatedly returned, for some viewers, and even reviewers. To illustrate, one major critic chronicled in this text was a pioneer in championing the 1960s emergence of the direct dark comedy approach. But she later immediately jettisoned any black humor merits to *All That Jazz* (1979), purely on the grounds of the heart surgery scene. And had she somehow missed the genre's groundbreaking use of just this sort of thing in *MASH* (1970)? Regardless, this text suggests, one early dark comedy transition still very much continues to work and/or deflect dark comedy's genre-bending, anti-genre route. However, keep in mind, there are also other simultaneously provocative new dark comedy techniques out there, from Quentin Tarantino's gross-out ("porn violence") approach in *Kill Bill 1* (2003), to a softer, dark comedy–lite style, like *Little Miss Sunshine* (2006). Moreover, the old school straight-up black humor continues, as in the Coen Brothers' 2004 remake of Ealing Studios' *Ladykillers* (1955).

A final personal allure to dark comedy is that while I cherish all things funny, something unique is at work with this genre. While some readers will find this explanation in bad taste (yet, after all, this is a genre once frequently referred to as "sick humor"), I find black humor's jusxtapositioning of something ugly with humor provocatively entertaining, because it pushes funny to the brink of one's greatest fear, death. And since this unflinching genre is all about honesty and nakedly approaching unanswerable questions, the thinking person ponders these things until the end (sometimes with mundane breaks for sheer insanity); dark comedy, ironically, amusingly challenges me to continue the waiting game.

As I age I find this tap-dancing at the edge of the abyss all very freeing, because I can finally deny what I call my "adult Santa Claus lie": there is no safety net of God and country. Or, as an elderly Kurt Vonnegut borrows from Gil Berman in *A Man Without a Country*, "If He were alive today, God would have to be an atheist…."[14] In the same vein, Vonnegut himself often said *Slaughterhouse-Five* was a failure, "because there is nothing intelligent to say about a massacre." Yet, if nothing else, dark comedy, even in this post-modern anti-genre collage, initially softens it for viewers. Nonetheless, the message remains the same: There is no message, and we remain alone in our angst. Or, as Samuel Beckett's Vladimir sarcastically tells Estragon in the theater of the absurd classic *Waiting for Godot*, which is generously referenced in the following pages, "No one ever suffers but you." In a 1971 revival of the 1953 play, critic Mel Gussow probably most succinctly defined Beckett's work: "We are born astride the grave. Birth-death, with a hyphen of life between."[15]

The anti-genre approach is also alive and well in the casting of these plays and films (like the twelve herein) about an absent and/or disinterested God, too. Tom Ewell, the comic actor best known for his Walter Mitty affair with Marilyn Monroe in *The Seven Year Itch* (1955), gives his greatest performance in a 1971 revival of Beckett's play.[16] The original production also starred Ewell, with vaudevillian Bert (*The Wizard of Oz*) Lahr. And more recent stagings have cast everyone from Robin Williams to Steve Martin. The anti-genre trick here is to soften this vision of mankind as fools, by presenting the human comedy with our dearest fools.

Keep in mind, however, that as the various versions of black humor thumb their noses at all forms of comforts—some need and/or find comfort in the lies, like "Things will be better in the next world," or "Corporate America cares"—the genre reserves the right to offend even its advocates. After all, what else would one expect of dark comedy, a position underlined earlier by the passionate First Amendment remarks of Harold Price Fahringer. Thus, Vonnegut once wrote:

> I have some good news for you and some bad news. The bad news is that the Martians have landed in New York City and are staying in the Waldorf Astoria. The good news is that they only eat homeless men, women, and children of all colors, and they pee gasoline.[17]

Even Mark Twain, as he slid into his final phase of life, what he called "the Damned Human Race," was fond of saying variations of the same axiom: "It'll be a hell of a heaven if everyone goes that thinks he will."

1

MASH (1/24/70)

Major Margaret "Hot Lips" Houlihan (Sally Kellerman) asks "Dago Red" (René Auberjonois), "I wonder how a degenerate person like [Donald Sutherland's "Hawkeye"] could have reached a position of responsibility in the Army Medical Corps." Looking up from his Bible, Dago Red casually replies, "He was drafted."

I was a draft age anti-war teenager when *MASH* opened during the Vietnam War, and the above exchange invariably generated *the* greatest laugh. I base this unscientific poll upon being drawn to the film multiple times in multiple theaters during its initial run. (Years later Ring Lardner, Jr., the film's Oscar-winning screenwriter, would also say the draft line got "the biggest laugh."[1])

Though Lardner and director Robert Altman adapted the movie from Richard Hooker's novel about a "Mobile Army Surgical Hospital" (MASH) during the Korean War (1950–1953), the film obviously targeted young anti–*Vietnam* War viewers like myself. And besides being the best genre-bending anti-war dark comedy since Leo McCarey crafted the Marx Brothers' *Duck Soup* (1933), Altman's movie had a key advantage over the earlier classic: period timing.[2] Unemployed Depression audiences, aware of the threat to America's core institutions, were afraid to embrace the iconoclastic values of these men from Marx. Thus, the team's seminal picture was initially a critical and commercial disappointment.

In contrast, *MASH* was shot at the end of the anti-establishment 1960s, with a young baby boomer audience questioning everything about foundation America. Weaned upon counter-culture literature (from J.D. Salinger's *The Catcher in the Rye*, 1951, to Kurt Vonnegut's *Slaughterhouse-Five*, 1969) and dissident films like *Bonnie and Clyde* and *The Graduate* (both 1967), as well as *Easy Rider* (1969), Hollywood's new passionately down-with-the-status-quo audience flocked to *MASH*. While some critical bastions of the past struggled with the movie—*Variety* complained that "surgeons and nurses in blood-soaked operating gowns like assembly butchers sent several viewers at studio screenings fleeing from the theater"—many pivotal critics lionized the picture.[3] For instance, *The New Yorker*'s Pauline Kael, under the title "Blessed Profanity," called the film "the best American war comedy since sound came in...."[4] Moreover, the movie generated monster box office numbers. This inexpensive (under four million dollars) production was second only to *Airport* (1970) as the top moneymaking movie of 1970.[5]

Ironically, *MASH*'s commercial success had even topped the sizable returns of that year's hit World War II biographical epic *Patton*, in which the mesmerizing Oscar-winning title performance by George C. Scott managed to bestow poetic nobility upon a warrior.

Additionally, other paradoxes linked these two diverse examinations of war. For instance, a second "reading" of *Patton* might also call this "good war" movie subtextually anti-war. That is, Scott's performance reveals a charismatically megalomaniac general only too willing now to fight our Russian ally, not to mention an ugly soldier-slapping scene in which Patton's behavior suggested that he equates cowardice with what would now be labeled posttraumatic stress disorder (PTSD). However, the most pertinent *MASH-Patton* paradox involves how the latter film indirectly assisted in making *MASH* more entertainingly provocative. Both movies were being shot simultaneously for Twentieth Century–Fox, and as Michael Murphy, who plays Hawkeye friend Me Lay Marston (of the New Era Hospital and Whorehouse) explains, "[The studio] had [pricey] *Patton* going on and they were paying more attention to *Patton* than they were to [Altman's low-budget] picture. So he kind of slipped through [cutting edge material]. He put the picture together [his way]...."[6] There were still post-production battles once the studio realized this was not the film it expected, especially the aforementioned bloody surgery scenes; however, a raucously positive San Francisco sneak preview helped keep the picture intact. (Fittingly, Altman, the anti-establishment director, would soon be known as an anti–Hollywood filmmaker, making pictures his way or no way.)

Of course, *intact* was not Altman's style when it came to genres, which makes *MASH* a perfect book opener for a genre-bending study of 1970 dark comedies. For example, *The New York Times* noted a key Altman "interest in film genres was candidly subversive. He wanted to explode them to expose what he saw as their phoniness"—a description which might have come from *Catcher in the Rye*'s Holden Caulfield.[7] Altman best describes this philosophy when discussing his anti–Western *McCabe & Mrs. Miller* (1971), made the year after *MASH*: wanting to drain the glamour from the Western by stripping it down to reality. Altman shared:

> I got interested in the project because I don't like Westerns. So I pictured a story with every Western cliché in it.... [In a general way the events in *McCabe and Mrs. Miller*] took place but not in the way you've been told. I wanted to look at it through a different window, you might say, but I still wanted to keep the poetry in the ballad.[8]

Watching *MASH*, one can see how Altman "explained" the basic conventions of the then-standard military service comedy. This genre had a long history in American cinema, with many major personality comedians actually doing their shtick in "uniform" comedies, including Abbott and Costello's *Buck Privates*, *In the Navy*, *Keep 'Em Flying* (all 1941), and *Buck Privates Come Home* (1947); Martin and Lewis in *At War with the Army* (1951), *Sailor Beware*, and *Jumping Jacks* (both 1952); and Bob Hope's *Caught in the Draft* (1941), *Let's Face It* (1943), *Off Limits* (1953), *The Iron Petticoat* (1956), and *The Private Navy of Sgt. O'Farrell* (1968). Yet, none of these films questions the military establishment, or even suggests the seriousness of a war situation. Indeed the Martin and Lewis pictures and Hope's *Off Limits* were all released during the Korean War, yet each one manages to ignore the conflict. For instance, Hope's movie has him as a prize-fighting manager who only enlists in the Army to keep an eye on a promising new boxer (Mickey Rooney) who has been drafted—with neither soldier (so-called) even leaving the States. The generic norm in all these pictures is simply an affectionate kidding of seemingly necessary military norms, such as basic training, elusive furloughs which complicate dating, tough sergeants, and general chauvinistic male bonding shenanigans. The velvet glove establishment nature of these "don't rock the boat" uniform comedies might best be captured in the tone of two Bob Hope routines. The first was part of a World War II–

oriented, March 1943 Oscar-hosting monologue: "The draft has hit the movie studios. In fact, when they give a new leading man a screen test, they don't bother with any long love scenes…. They just photograph him to show he can stand in a vertical position and the camera moves in for a close-up of the 4-F [unfit to serve] on his draft card."[9] A second Hope example comes from a 1950 Korean USO tour to entertain the troops: "They have so much rice in Korea…. After a wedding they throw the bride and groom at it."[10]

This is not meant to denigrate these still often funny films. In fact, *Sailor Beware* is arguably the best of all the Martin and Lewis teamings. Plus, the majority of these earlier service comedies, if they do manage to use an armed conflict for even a minimal backdrop—it's the "good war"—have comic escapism rather than dark comedy as the period audience's expectation. Exceptions to the norm were rare. Chaplin manages the trick with his watershed dark comedy *Shoulder Arms* (1918).[11] His Charlie the soldier starts out as a typical social comedy basic training bumbler (from which Abbott and Costello "borrow" material for *Buck Privates*), but Chaplin's World War I doughboy, via an extended dream sequence, soon morphs into a capable character directing dark comedy fun at the trench warfare horrors of that conflict. Chaplin also manages to play it both ways, *à la Shoulder Arms*, in *The Great Dictator*.

Another pioneering personality comedy which also unfurls its anti–military-related sequences in an honest black humor manner, *Duck Soup* begins with the Marx Brothers leading the cast in "This Country's Going to War," a big production number peppered with several musical styles and an inspired satire of how patriotism can be cranked up among the people to make armed conflict seem like a day in the country. Then the Marxes sharpen this putdown of unthinking jingoism by moving to the battlefront. After each comic cutaway the Marxes reappear in the combatant garb of another country in another time. The result is a macabre military fashion show of how misdirected patriotism has been "sold" with the shiny button pomp of a parade happily marching towards extermination.

Consequently, Altman's anti-genre penchant for exploding a service comedy was not without precedents. In fact, Chaplin's daughter Geraldine, later a periodic member of Altman's repertory company, would favorably link the subversive humor of the two directors:

> [Like my father's, Altman's vision] was so out of sync with the established way of thinking. He would laugh at things—if you tell a story that you think was tragic, he would see the [dark] humor in it. It wasn't cruel. It was the way he would read something and see it completely different…. My father probably would have enjoyed his films…. They're [both] funny in the right way. Funny in a critical way—of what the world is….[12]

That said, *MASH*'s incendiary undermining of the service comedy owes, as the following pages document, an equally important debt to the irreverent Marxes, as well as applying new interpretations to the standard shtick of some more traditional comedians.

MASH's first and most fundamental anti-genre attack on the service comedy is its blatantly ongoing anti-military perspective. This might best be summed up by Hawkeye's (Sutherland) response to Hot Lips' (Kellerman) comment about his casual negation of armed forces regulations: "[Your] kind of informality is inconsistent with maximum efficiency in a military organization." Hawkeye counters:

> Oh come off it, *Major*. You put me right off my fresh fried lobster, do you realize that? I'm going to go back to my tent; I'm going to put away the best part of a bottle of Scotch….

Elliott Gould's McIntyre (left) and Donald Sutherland's Hawkeye had their own thoughts about military service.

> And under normal circumstances, you being normally what I would call a very attractive woman, I would have invited you back to share my little bed with me [and] you might have come. But you really put me off. I mean you—you're what we call a regular army clown.

Naturally, as previously stated, any such anti-establishment statement and/or action also doubles as a core component of black humor. As Daniel O'Brien's Altman biography notes, though *MASH* "never explicitly condemns the Korean War or the then ongoing Vietnam conflict," the film is explicitly "anti-military."[13] Other exchanges in the afore-mentioned "regular army clown" spirit run rampant throughout the picture, such as the following disregard for Army protocol and ritual when Hawkeye and McIntyre (Elliott Gould) go to a Tokyo military hospital to operate on a Congressman's soldier son:

> CAPTAIN PETERSON [hostile tone]: You can't even go near a patient until Col. Merrill says it's okay, and he's still out to lunch.
> McINTYRE: Look, mother [head nurse], I want to go to work in one hour. We are the pros from Dover and we figure to crack this kid's chest and get out to the golf course before it gets dark. So you find the gas-passer [anesthetist] and you have him pre-medicate this patient. Then bring me the latest pictures on him. The ones we saw must be 48 hours old by now. Then call the kitchen and have them rustle us up some lunch.

The anti–armed forces, anti-war nature of the foundation novel *MASH* could not have found a more in-tune director for the film adaptation. Robert Altman, a decorated flyer in World War II, later observed,

I enlisted because I was going to be drafted. I don't think it was anything I would've chosen otherwise…. I didn't like the military. I didn't like anything about it…. I did not try to become a successful Army person, and I'm usually interested in being successful in whatever area I'm in. But the Army was never part of that. It wasn't anything I wanted.[14]

And unlike Vietnam, this was the "good war."

A second hamstringing of typical service comedies involves religion. If the genre mentions the institution at all, it receives reverential treatment, *à la* "There are no atheists in foxholes." Yet *MASH* attacks the church with the same fervor as it attacks the military. For example, when Hawkeye and McIntyre's tent mate Frank Burns (Robert Duvall) goes into prayer mode, Sutherland's character cracks, "Frank, were you on this religious kick at home, or did you crack up over here?" Moreover, in the spirit of the film, there is a seemingly spontaneous group mockery of Burns' religious nature when a camp parade suddenly passes his tent satirically singing "Onward Christian Soldier."

MASH's Father "Dago Red" Mulcahy (Auberjonois) is affectionately tolerated purely on his sweet milquetoast manner. Indeed, the character could literally be Casper Milquetoast the early 20th century anti-hero of the comic strip "The Timid Soul," from which the word Milquetoast is derived. (Cartoonist H.T. Webster frequently described his Dago Red–like underdog as "the man who speaks softly and gets hit with a big stick"—a comic bastardization of President Theodore Roosevelt's foreign policy, "Speak softly and carry a big stick.") Beyond Dago Red's less than dynamic demeanor being an indirect knock against religion, his periodic practical help trumps the importance of his theological calling. For example, note the following *MASH* exchange between Tom Skerritt's Duke Forrest and Dago Red during surgery, as Dago Red performs last rites over a soldier:

DUKE FORREST: Hey, Dago! Dago! Dago, I want you over here to hold this retraction. Now! Please, come on, now!
DAGO RED: Sorry, I'm coming.
DUKE FORREST: I'm sorry, Dago, but this man is still alive and that other man is dead, and that's a fact. Can you hold it with two fingers, Dago?

Dago Red exists not so much for comic relief (though there is that, too), but rather as a funny-sad commentary on the incongruous *lack* of purpose in *Catch-22* (1970). Moreover, these religious figures are not only lost in a war, they are ill equipped for life in general. Illustrating this is the famous *MASH* scene in which Radar (Gary Burghoff) places a mike under Major Houlihan's sexually active bed and her "Hot Lips" moniker is born during an unofficial camp "broadcast." Dago Red is clueless. He starts listening in with the boys, thinking it is the "Battling Bickersons," a reference to a Korean War-era American radio program about a forever-combative couple (Don Ameche and Frances Langford). Once Dago Red realizes the real nature of the "program," he embarrassingly staggers back to his tent.

Ironically, even when Dago Red stumbles upon a more traditional life or death "confessional" moment—the suicide thoughts of Captain Walt Waldowski, the "Painless Pole" dentist—he is paralyzed about what to do. And God does not bail him out, Hawkeye does. Though Auberjonois' Father can only reveal so much, Hawkeye paradoxically saves the day by actually embracing Waldowski's suicide plan. A fake farewell party, which doubles as a satirization of the Last Supper (borrowing from Luis Buñuel's *Viridiana*, 1961), manages to change the Pole's plan. Ultimately, Hawkeye's *pièce de resistance* involves even more entertaining blasphemy. Waldowski is the most well-endowed sexually driven man in the unit, and after he takes his "black capsule" (actually just a mild sedative), Hawkeye arranges for him to wake up with the mobile hospital's most attractive nurse—the fittingly nicknamed lieutenant Dish (Jo Ann Pflug). Hawkeye has created a new sexual interpretation to "raising the dead." The following morning a non–miraculously cured Waldowski is joyfully back to work.

A third *MASH* takedown of a basic service comedy component involves childish behavior—the most fundamental characteristic of the screen clowns, which formerly inhabited this genre. One might exemplify the phenomenon by Lou Costello's inability to acquire the nuances of marching (borrowed from Chaplin) in *Buck Privates*, or by Jerry' Lewis' hopeless attempts at calisthenics in *Jumping Jacks*. Moreover, since few do silly better than the Three Stooges, one might throw in their Army antics in *Boobs in Arms* (1940), or their photo shoot woes when dressed as Japanese soldiers in *No Dough Boy* (1944). Yet, as more than one critic has suggested, unlike the pointlessly delightful juvenile capers of earlier clowns, the *MASH* team brings cognitive meaning to childish activity.[15] Call it a planned comic catharsis after enduring bloody, sometimes 12-plus-hour surgery shifts near the front. In a rare somber moment of Richard Hooker's under-rated *MASH*, the novelist addresses the stress through which these doctors worked. Channeling his own surgery experiences through Hawkeye, Hooker has his unconventional character explains to some snobby new Army replacement doctors that slow, methodical, by-the-book medicine just does *not* work in a war zone:

> This is certainly meatball surgery we do around here, but I think you can see now that meatball surgery is a specialty.... We are not concerned with the ultimate reconstruction of the patient. We are concerned only with getting the kid out of here alive enough for someone else to reconstruct him … now and then we may lose a leg because, if we spent an extra hour to save it, another guy in the pre-op ward would die from being operated on too late.[16]

Despite the initial priggish nature of these new surgeons, one could initially cut them some slack given their rookie status in a near-combat setting. Yet, there was no forgiving the "regular army clown" tendencies of Duvall's Major Burns and Kellerman's Major Hot Lips. They stupidly and dangerously continued to proceed as if engaged in safe civilian surgical settings. Consequently, Hawkeye and McIntyre's pranks could assume a comically mean-spirited nature if they felt wounded soldiers were at risk. For example, the following dialogue comes after the sex scene which gave Hot Lips her nickname, and resulted in Burns being removed from the unit in a straitjacket:

> HAWKEYE: Morning, Frank [Burns]. Heard from your wife? A bunch of the boys asked me to, uh, ask you, Frank, what Hot Lips was like in the sack. You know, was she…
> BURNS: Mind your own business.
> HAWKEYE: No, Frank, you know, is she better than self-abuse? Does that—does that big ass of hers move around a lot, Frank, or does it sort of lie there flaccid? What would you say about that? … Would you say that she was a moaner, Frank? Seriously, Frank, I mean, does she go "oooh" or does she lie there quiet and not do anything at all?
> BURNS: Keep your filthy mouth to yourself.
> HAWKEYE: Or does she go "uh-uh-uh"?
>
> [Burns attacks Hawkeye with their commander looking on.]
>
> HAWKEYE: Get him off me! I've got glasses. Get him off me!
> DUKE FORREST [sarcastic]: What's going on, Frank? [Is] That [sexual] lesson one?
> HAWKEYE: Frank Burns has gone nuts! I'm wearing glasses, for God's sake.

McIntyre: Watch out for your goodies, Hawkeye. That man is a sex maniac; I don't think Hot Lips satisfied him. Don't let him kiss you, Hawkeye.

Concerning Burns and Hot Lips, author-critic Gary Shteyngart observed, "Satire always benefits when evil and stupidity collide."[17] One could also liken the behavior of Hawkeye, McIntyre, and Duke to stand-up comic Christopher Titus' dark comedy TV series *Titus* (2000–2002), based on his one-man show *Norman Rockwell Is Bleeding*. The premise of both are anchored in studies now showing that two-thirds of American families are dysfunctional—sort of civilian war zones. And Titus, living in the most extremely dysfunctional of settings (like our trio of *MASH* doctors), is better equipped to handle the next random firestorm of life better than someone tied to the old rigid norms of a "regular army clown" type.

Another way that *MASH* derails service comedies addresses how basic components of their personality clown population are altered from a mere scatter gun effect to a more specific anti-genre motivation. For instance, part of Bob Hope's persona, whether in a service or a civilian comedy, is a short, multi-purpose, high-pitched whistle. In a spoof of horror films, *The Ghost Breakers* (1940), Hope uses the whistle to designate fear. In contrast, during *The Lemon Drop Kid* (1951) Hope's egotistical Damon Runyon character finds his mirror image so handsome he cannot resist an admiring whistle. (This is the same picture in which he tells love interest Marilyn Maxwell, "Don't ever leave me, baby, you'd only suffer.") In contrast, *MASH*'s Sutherland's character uses the same Bob Hope whistle for a singular reason: Something has gone wrong, such as when he realizes the dentist is thinking of suicide. The whistle parallels the dark comedy mantra, "And so it goes," from Kurt Vonnegut's novel *Slaughterhouse-Five* (1969), which signified a resignation to yet another negative blindsiding of someone and/or something. For the late 1960s such dark comedy expressions captured the spirit of the time, a zeitgeist of sorts. To illustrate, the same year (1969) as Vonnegut's "so it goes," the Beatles' "Maxwell's Silver Hammer" (on their *Abbey Road Album*) was about someone destroying everyone with his little mallet. To paraphrase co-writer Paul McCartney's take on the tune's ironically upbeat tempo, "It epitomizes the downfalls of life ... my analogy for when something goes wrong out of the blue." The whistle is not in Hooker's novel, but given Altman's propensity for encouraging his actors to improvise timely material it was probably extemporized by Sutherland.

Some more personality comedian tweaking also occurs in both *MASH* the novel and the film, and involves Chaplin's Tramp and Harpo Marx. Again, an additional precise anti-genre service comedy meaning is brought to the Hooker-Altman setting. As with Hope's whistle, they are not credited *per se*, but the link is obvious. The *MASH* character involved this time is Gould's McIntyre. Upon his arrival at camp he is wearing a hooded parka and his responses to questions from Hawkeye and Duke are so minimal he might just as well be silent, *à la* the Tramp and Harpo. Yet the mysterious McIntyre's defining component is his seemingly magic parka pockets, from which assorted objects are easily procured—something Duke describes in the novel as "a regular perambulation [traveling] PX [Army post store]."[18] The topper to Gould's sorcery occurs when he is offered a homemade martini from Hawkeye and Duke's still in their spacious "Swamp" of a tent. When McIntyre requests an olive (since no martini is complete without one), his hosts explain some sacrifices are necessary, given their close proximity to the front. Without missing a beat, McIntyre produces an olive jar from his PX pocket and "happy hour" is complete.

For the student of screen comedy, this *MASH* moment immediately dovetails back to that memorable *Duck Soup* scene in which Harpo produces a blowtorch from his trenchcoat pocket. Despite the otherwise groundbreaking nature of the film, Harpo uses said torch in traditional multi-faceted ways. That is, Harpo's pockets are more likely to produce eclectic objects for random comic surprise, a trait seemingly borrowed from his comedy hero, Chaplin's Tramp.[19] Moreover, though Chaplin's *Shoulder Arms* is also a service comedy breakthrough, his pocket contents are also amusingly haphazard, such as sand doubling as period golf tees in *The Idle Class* (1921); assorted foods and accessories, including an egg, in *The Kid* (1921); and a banana in *The Circus* (1928).

In contrast, McIntyre's pockets are war-specific, keying upon a formula which makes the conflict more palatable: Liquid fun equals an emotional release, thanks to olive jars, beer, other liquor, and an ever-active can opener. Again, while getting sloshed in such situations might seem childish, it aids wartime survival and sanity. Another rationale for drawing the distinction between the varied aspect of Harpo's pockets to the *MASH*–McIntyre direct link to a watering hole on wheels involves a "big picture" look at two world views. The old-school comedian in a service comedy acts zany in a world presented as *sane*. At variance with this, *MASH*'s war setting is patently absurd, and as loopy as the band of Army surgeons often appear, that behavior allows them to bring a degree of sanity to a demented world.

The schtick of yet another Brother Marx, Groucho, can also be reframed for more war-directed settings, *Duck Soup* notwithstanding. The mustached one's signature peculiarity is his machine-gun patter, a saturation comedy device which allows the law of comic averages to find something funny in his high-speed verbal onslaught. These brilliantly entertaining riffs, however, are just as random as the contents of Harpo's pockets. Yet *MASH*'s Corporal "Radar" O'Reilly (Burghoff) brings uncommonly purposeful verbal saturation comedy to a military setting, just as deejay Robin Williams' speedy patter defuses the stress in *Good Morning, Vietnam* (1987). Yet unlike Groucho or Williams' inexplicable warp speed tongues, Hooker's novel provides a foundation for Radar's rapid chatter: "[U]nder certain atmospheric, as well as metabolic, conditions, and by enforcing complete concentration and invoking unique extrasensory powers, he was able to receive messages and monitor conversations far beyond the usual range of human hearing."[20]

Paradoxically, Altman's *MASH* is also able to reconfigure the seemingly unnatural use of saturation comedy in a realistic manner. The process is called "stacking sound" and/or "overlapping dialogue." For instance *MASH*'s episodic narrative is partially structured by twelve operating scenes, in which we hear "the constantly overlapping dialogue of doctors and nurses and the sounds of surgical tools from the several operations usually occurring at the same time."[21] Altman explained the process to me and several other University of Iowa (Iowa City) graduate students during a rambling preview-forum for his *Thieves Like Us* (1974), before it opened nationally. What follows is a paraphrasing of his comments:

> When you're in a bar you can barely hear the person sitting across from you for all the other conversations, plus the waitress taking and/or delivering orders, a band playing in the corner, or a sports bar TV blaring, the distant noises from the kitchen or the toilet, not to mention people interrupting and/or talking over each other. You're lucky to get half of what is being said. That is the reality of overlapping dialogue and sound. People rarely take turns talking in the real world, though that was the norm in classic Hollywood film.[22]

Like Altman's anti-genre philosophy, one might label this his "anti-traditional cinema dialogue" perspective. Though not entirely new to Hollywood—Howard Hawks pioneered the technique in films like *His Girl Friday* (1940)—Altman and his contemporaries pulled it to center stage in the 1970s. Ironically, while it initially seemed like a formalistic device in which the director draws attention to his cinematic bag of tricks, it ultimately reflects the real magpie world around us.

There is a legitimate formalistic application to overlapping dialogue: when an ending scene includes dialogue into that conversation before the new visual, or when dialogue from one sequence continues *after* cutting to a new scene. One such *MASH* example of the latter occurs when Hawkeye and Duke lobby Colonel Blake (Roger Bowen) for a chest cutter; this discussion continues on the soundtrack into the following surgery scene in which, fittingly, Hawkeye and Duke continue to discuss this need. Of course, such stacking sound saturation would not occur in a traditional service comedy, as the narrative needs to be realistically clear. Even those aforementioned inspired diatribes by Groucho depend upon no interruptions.

A fifth *MASH* sideswiping of the earlier Hollywood service comedies involves women. These films were invariably strafed with sexual innuendo, such as the pop-eyed salaciousness Robert Strauss brought to the subject in *Sailor Beware* and *Stalag 17* (1953), receiving an Oscar nomination for his suitably named "Animal" character in the latter. But censorship restrictions limited the subject to mere suggestiveness. Moreover, in some cases the military man idealized either the girl he left behind or the one he met in uniform, such as Chaplin yet again putting French peasant girl Edna Purviance on a pedestal in *Shoulder Arms* (1918).

Altman, a notorious womanizer in his day, possibly had his most anti-genre service comedy fun with this *MASH* category. Naturally, it also matched the tenor of the times, from the "free love" 1960s to the death of the censorship code. Thus, though both Hawkeye and Duke are married family men, they bed everything in sight. Sutherland's pickup line defense, especially if his potential lover is also married, is that he loves his wife and if she were there he would naturally be with her, but…. Behavior encouraged by folk rocker Stephen Stills' hit song "Love the One You're With," which was released the same year as *MASH*.

There is, however, a whole smorgasbord of unfaithfulness, from the married Burns bedding Houlihan and creating the "Hot Lips" escapade heard around the camp, a married Blake involved with the ever-so-lovely Lieutenant Leslie (Indus Arthur), and Waldowski, the "Painless Pole," putting a whole new spin on cheating stateside sweethearts. Though Painless is unmarried—the camp Don Juan is engaged to *three* girls back home—this qualifies as possibly the greatest service comedy spoof yet of "the girl left behind." Plus, McIntyre's character came with an already regionally famous nickname, which Hooker has Hawkeye explain to Duke:

> You know who we have been living with for the past week? … [T]he only man in history who ever took [someone in] the ladies' can of a Boston & Maine train. When the conductor caught him in there with his Winter Carnival date, she screamed, "He trapped me!" and that's how he got his name. This is the famous Trapper John….[23]

Though both *MASH* the novel and the film are laced with extracurricular sex, Altman definitely ratcheted it up in the adaptation of Hooker's book. However, in the director's defense, when critics sometimes called the movie anti-woman, Altman gave this measured response:

> Certainly after *MASH* [some] people said, "You're a misogynist." And I looked that word up and found out what it meant. But *au contraire* my answer was and is that I'm not mak-

ing this film to show you how I think things ought to be; I'm showing you the way I see them. And this is the way woman were treated…. This is what went on. The reality of that film was a reality of attitudes….[24]

Sally Kellerman was not bothered by her Hot Lips shower sequence, feeling the action was able to "liberate her [character] from being a 'regular army clown.'"[25] The perspective also defuses subsequent criticism of her nurse later suddenly becoming one of the boys. (As a footnote to the scene, Altman produced a very effective look of surprise from a nude Kellerman by simultaneously placing a naked Radar next to the camera.) This is also one more way Altman brought reality to his anti-genre philosophy, not to mention how even some of his aforementioned formalistic filmmaking (such as overlapping dialogue) played as something genuine.

Returning to the sexual card, if one needed a comparable qualifier on the subject for Hooker, the evidence is best found in his text. The novel was not without an occasional diplomatic softening factor, with regard to the principal characters. For instance, halfway through the book a new man in the unit requests pointers on camp conquests. Hawkeye is deemed the "big authority" and provides an abundance of tips, some of which are comically practical, e.g., "under no circumstances should you proceed more than ten yards north from the O[fficer's] Club [with a woman and a blanket,] because you might place the blanket on top of a [land] mine."[26] Still, when the sexual tutorial is over, Hawkeye begged off an any final advice: "Well, I don't really know. This is mostly theory with me."[27]

MASH's final subversive take on the service comedy occurs as it briefly has its key players abruptly embrace an antithesis genre. For example, after Hawkeye and McIntyre are put under temporary house arrest during their Tokyo trip, they simultaneously slip into film noir–tough guy dialogue without ever breaking character:

> McIntyre: They finally caught up with us, huh?
> Hawkeye: Where'd we fail?
> McIntyre: I don't know. I think it was the woman. Something tells me I've seen her some
>   place before.
> Hawkeye: She was the one in Tangiers.
> McIntyre: We don't blame you [to the M.P. guard].
> Hawkeye: You're [the M.P.] only doing your duty.

By playing this noir parody with such tongue-in-cheek seriousness, the duo complement the sober satire with which they grace the rest of the movie. Plus, as is demonstrated later in the text, noir and dark comedy have a great deal in common.

With Altman's extreme anti-genre fracturing of the service comedy formula embedded in MASH, moving on to the film's black humor base is a natural segue for a study about the genre-crossing fundamentals of dark comedy. Starting with black humor's first hat trick theme, the omnipresence of death, what could be more simpatico with "passing" than a war zone? Moreover, the genre-bending paragon-paradox of this dance with death is that as soon as the "lucky" man-child soldiers are patched up, they are gifted with a gun and Army fatigues to again play at authorized Russian roulette. Indeed, an ongoing war metaphor in both MASH the novel and film is gambling, whether it is the war-distracting, around-the-clock poker game in Painless' tent, or Hawkeye telling McIntyre during one particularly challenging surgery, "We're just going to have to shoot craps [and take a chance on this procedure]."

Altman's films often linked gambling to a flirting-with-death philosophy. He was fond of saying his father was one of the world's "worst gamblers": "I learned a lot about losing from him; that losing is an identity; that you can be a good loser and a bad winner; that none of it … has any real value … it's simply a way of killing time…."[28]

This Altman association of gambling with death is best represented by his *McCabe & Mrs. Miller*, which directly followed *MASH*. Fittingly, McCabe's (Warren Beatty) small-time gambler is a likable loser, which leads directly to his murder. Altman's fascination with gambler-related doom was ongoing, such as his ironic description of *California Split* (1974) as "a celebration of gambling," which is anything but a "celebration."[29] Though no one dies, that undoubtedly would have been the fate of Bill Denny (George Segal) had he not walked away. One would expect the same destiny for the Dostoyevsky character (Alexei) at the close of his 1867 novella *The Gambler* (which the novelist had written to pay off *his own* gambling debts).

Altman was 45 when he made *MASH*, was older than many other American New Wave era directors; his intrinsic gambler's "What the fuck?" attitude was emblematic of late 1960s disillusionment. Another period entertainer even older than Altman, yet seasoned with the same gambler's cynicism, was Rat Packer Dean Martin, whose first job was as a gaming club dealer. Martin's biographer described the *MASH*–like mindset this star projected via his hit TV variety show (1965–1974):

> His message was clear: All this fake-sincerity shit that was coming through … television, the newspapers, the pictures [movies], every politician's false-faced caring word and grin— it was all a racket. It was a message that appealed to the *menefreghismo* in every heart, [Italian for] "Fuck it all."[30]

This stance applies to the hollow title quotes of Douglas MacArthur and Dwight Eisenhower, *à la* the latter's "I will go to Korea," which were forced upon Altman's opening to *MASH*, as if that would somehow disguise the fact the film was obviously about Vietnam.

However one makes a gambler's connection to dark comedy's use of death, *MASH* showcases four basic lessons to be learned or reaffirmed from the genre's obsession with termination, or as Will Cuppy enthusiastically entitled his book, *How to Become Extinct*.[31] First, death itself is a terrible absurdity. How can a once vital, passionate, thinking individual suddenly be reduced to so much "garbage" in death? Yet that is a central black humor revelation-reminder. *Reminder*? Tom Stoppard's 1967 play *Rosencrantz and Guildenstern Are Dead* (sort of *Laurel & Hardy Meet Hamlet*) posits a disturbing question: "Whatever became of the moment when one first knew about death? There must have been one, a moment, in childhood when it first occurred to you that you don't go on forever. It must have been shattering—stamped into one's memory. And yet I can't remember it…. What does one make of that?"[32]

It means that despite Stoppard's Shakespearean Laurel and Hardy matching the flatliner mental status of the original duo Stan Laurel once described as "two minds without a single thought," we are as helpless before death as Stan and Ollie, living our lives as if we had no expiration date.[33] Yet, dark comedy acts as a reality check for its brave fans— people who can own the old axiom, "Life's a bitch, and then you die." Maybe the genre's candor about death might best be likened to a children's snow globe of some fragile miniaturized scene one dreams of inhabiting. Yet, it doubles as a locked-in syndrome, *à la* a *Twilight Zone* episode, or Jim Carrey bumping into the giant glass bubble which restricts him to *The Truman Show* (1998). Dark comedy, like shaking our personalized prison of a globe, underlines our under-glass mortality. Moreover, even the agitation does not emit a sound from those pretty tombs. Thus, death arrives quietly, like Carl Sandburg's description of the fog coming "on little cat feet."[34] While one might prefer to embrace Dylan Thomas' rebellion against the inevitable, "Do Not Go Gentle Into That Good Night," Sandburg's deathly quiet fog is not to be denied.[35]

Earlier in the text the observation was posited that death somehow reduces a vibrant life to so much garbage, a claim central to the dying of a particular character in Heller's *Catch–22* (1961), and effectively replicated in Mike Nichols' 1970 screen adaptation. While this scenario is played out fully in the following chapter, it represents the quintessential bridge to the jarring effect of death in *MASH*. That is, the disturbing *Catch–22* preposterousness of a wounded gunner's insides oozing onto the bomber's floor anticipates the traumatizing effect of that image abruptly played out tenfold in the surgery scenes in *MASH*. Then, tack on the jokingly casual conversations of the *MASH* doctors as they operate upon victims who already seem to have reached a similar "garbage" status, and then one has a sample of the genre's deathly whiplash wake-up call. Sutherland later shared that Altman was able to make the surgery scenes seemingly macabrely real by having actual

> bodies underneath the chunks of flesh we operated on. We put plastic and rubber bags on top of the real people—quite thick and glued on, so you could cut through the rubber, press down, and it would spurt blood.... We [also] had lessons in surgery [with doctors on the set]. I can [now] sew and double stitch, and do all the things with the scissors.... It all gets murky.... Blood is very sticky. And they used a kind of plasma.[36]

The second death instruction involves the casually random end-without-purpose unexpectedness with which death frequently appears—underlining both the world's absurdity and the insignificance of the individual. In *MASH* this might best be represented by the post-operation area death of a soldier. Robert Duvall's Major Burns blames the death on Bud Cort's orderly private. One of the unit's seemingly miraculous "meatball" surgeries had suddenly gone wrong. We don't know the soldier's name, nor his appearance—another blow for an individual's insignificance.

Moreover, Burns' pointless blaming of Cort's character is another example of an institution (the military) living up to its "regular army clown" anti-individual status. Not only has an essentially "unknown soldier" been wasted by war, the blaming of Cort's orderly has all but destroyed any sense of significance in this child-man soldier. Consequently, there are now *two* casualties. Additionally, if Burns is not preying upon the vulnerable and/or the naïve in destroying an innate sense of worthiness in a given person, he is wont to say that it was "God's will" that the young soldier died. No one has a *divine* source further negating the importance of a mere mortal for no perceivable reason. (In football this is known as "piling on.") It would now seem appropriate to recycle a portion of the *Catch–22* quote "Don't tell me God works in mysterious ways. There's nothing so mysterious about it. He's not working at all."[37] Along the same lines, Heller's aforementioned irony might just as well have been a reworking of Matthew 10:30, "'Not one sparrow ... can fall to the ground without your Father knowing it.' Of course, He doesn't do anything about it."[38]

Another tutorial to be drawn from black humor's fixation on death is the frequency of suicide to be referenced in the genre. *MASH*'s previously cited satirical Last Supper scene is the entry to the picture's mock suicide. Dark comedy dramatically demonstrates that the genre's disregard for life begins with the individual, even by the indirect manner of working oneself to death, *à la All That Jazz* (1979). While Hawkeye paradoxically puts together the fake suicide to save the Painless Pole, John Schuck's dentist, unlike Bud Cort's Harold in *Harold and Maude* (1971), does *not* know the situation is a sham. Indeed, actual suicide is the Pole's idea, with his comically inspired introduction of the subject when he asks for tips from *MASH*'s Swamp gang: "I'm kind of new at this [suicide]...."

Even though Hawkeye's clever ruse works, the quickness with which Schuck's depressed character had already put forward this suicide solution sadly symbolizes how easily people consider the option. Moreover, Sutherland's orchestration of the proceedings—though as a mercy mission—sardonically toys with the plus sides of suicide, including a catchy theme song summation, with its number one temptation-escape captured in the title "Suicide Is Painless," which acts as an ongoing refrain on the soundtrack.

Altman came up with the song title, which is sometimes called "Song from *MASH* (Suicide Is Painless)." It was originally written for Pfc. Seidman (Ken Prymus) to sing during the faux suicide of Schuck's dentist—the *Painless* Pole, making it a punning example of dark comedy, too. Initially meant as a throwaway song (during Altman's Iowa City visit, he described wanting a "stupid song"[39]), Altman let his poetry-writing teenage son Michael write the lyrics (with music by Johnny Mandel). Soon the director realized what a superlative overview the song provided for the whole anti-war film, and decided to use it as *MASH*'s theme—including the now iconic opening credits, with helicopters bringing in the wounded. In fact, it was eventually embraced as such a disturbingly topical song that it became a 1980s hit single in Great Britain, while it even made the American Film Institute's (2002) list of the country's top 100 movie songs, landing at number 66. (With an absurdity befitting dark comedy, in time Michael Altman's royalties for the song far eclipsed his father's salary for directing *MASH*.)

One might also push the envelope for a broader definition of the term "suicide." For instance, this text has established the endless killing-time poker game in Painless Pole's tent. A repetitiveness originating in seemingly interminable—waiting for the choppers to arrive—war can amount to its own form of suicide. One is reminded of Thomas Heggen's multi-faceted service comedy *Mister Roberts*, first published as a novel in 1946, adapted as a play by Heggen and Joshua Logan in 1948 and an Oscar-nominated Best Picture in 1955. The story involves an American cargo ship, the antiheroically named U.S.S. *Reluctant*, during the last months of World War II. The title character has supposedly wanted to see action and is finally transferred to a fighting ship. With the senseless dark comedy of war, his inevitable death occurs not while manning a battle post position, but rather while drinking coffee below deck. Yet the specter of suicide arrives in a last letter sent to his *Reluctant* replacement, which reads in part:

> I'm thinking now of ... all the guys everywhere who sail from Tedium to Apathy and back again—with an occasional side trip to Monotony.... But I've discovered ... that the most terrible enemy of this war is the boredom that eventually becomes a faith and, therefore, a sort of suicide.[40]

Interestingly, the play and film versions of *Mister Roberts* minimize any suicide over patriotic feelings (concerning the transfer) of the title character. However, in the original novel there is no second-guessing the darker meaning. While the quoted passage from Roberts' letter does not appear in the book—only some general small talk about the correspondence—the following conversation between his closest friends from the *Reluctant* spell it out:

Pulver spoke with sudden anguish: "Isn't that rough, Doc? You know how he wanted to get in the war? And then, as soon as he gets out there, he gets killed." His voice was almost pleading.

> The Doc nodded and chewed his lip. "That's funny," he said thoughtfully.
> "Funny?"
> The Doc looked up. "I don't mean funny, Frank," he said softly. He paused for a moment. "I mean that I think that's what he wanted."[41]

In Robert Match's *New York Tribune* review of the *Mister Roberts* novel, the critic might have been describing a softer 1940s take on dark comedy when he wrote, "Mr. Roberts' plight, the tragedy of the 'high-strung instrument in the low-strung role,' lies, like much of this book, somewhere between tears and laughter."[42] With a sad appropriateness, given that Heggen's novel was largely drawn from his own naval experiences during World War II, the writer took his own life in 1949.

The fourth and final lesson to be taken from dark comedy's addiction to death demonstrates people's callousness to shock. While many viewers initially tend to be disturbed, like the critics who left an early sneak preview of *MASH*, in-film black humor characters have a ho-hum complacency. *MASH*'s surgery scenes are Altman's contribution to horrific as the new normal. Despite macabre scenes, Pauline Kael's review described Hawkeye, McIntyre, and Duke as doing "their surgery in style, with humor; they're hip Galahads, saving lives while ragging the military bureaucracy."[43] With some distance in time, Peter Biskind perfectly captured these anti-heroes' unflappable laid-black humor amidst surreal surgeries with his own anti-establishment funny flippancy: "Like *Bonnie and Clyde*, *MASH* was a 'fuck you' from the cool to the uncool."[44] For anti-war draft age teenagers like myself, feeling angry and disenfranchised, Biskind's description of Hawkeye and company's "fuck you" demeanor laudably captures the tenor of the times—the "Hey, hey, L.B.J., how many kids did you kill today?" chants of our anti–Vietnam rallies. Moreover, for *MASH*, a mainstream movie, to embrace this attitude meant empowerment to us, too.

After this multi-faceted omnipresence of death, *MASH* is also a study in dark comedy's second fundamental theme—the inherent absurdity of the world. Nothing says ludicrousness better than war, particularly a decidedly unnecessary one. Yet the incongruity factor is decidedly squared when one acknowledges that man has been a strong contributor to the comic frightfulness of an unordered universe. *Pogo* cartoonist Walt Kelly encapsulates this nicely by derailing a famous axiom: "We have met the enemy and he is us." Thus, *MASH* demonstrates how the real foe is Uncle Sam, with the only adversary depicted being the military establishment, especially as personified by the aforementioned "regular Army clowns." Institutionalized absurdity, therefore, means man's chaos-making abilities can attain irrevocable steamroller proportions.

By *MASH* not showing actual fighting—only the casualties—its anti-war tone forms a bridge to the metaphorical civilian victims of the absurd world in general … still linked to institutions. Thus, while the movie's key focus is an anti-military stance, it also makes a similar dark comedy attack upon organized religion and standard medical protocol. Rigid rules and regulations, whatever the institution, create casualties. One does not witness the individual, internalized war most thinking human beings experience. Yet, 24/7 much of the world population qualifies as the "walking wounded." As Henry David Thoreau observed in *Walden* (1854), "The mass of men lead lives of quiet desperation. What is called resignation is confirmed desperation."[45]

Film Quarterly's review of Altman's film goes so far as to observe: "In short, [*MASH*] is not really about army life or rebellion or any of its other ostensible topics: it is about the human condition. And that's why it is such an exciting comedy."[46]

Regardless, the MASH units of the world represent safety values of diffusion. Thus, in the tradition of *Pogo*, one might scramble another classic axiom in the name of dark comedy: "All the world is a war zone."

MASH further accents the "life as war" nature of the civilian sector when it devotes considerable time near its close to a football game between Hawkeye's gang and another military unit. Ironically, from the film's 1970 opening through to today, the football sequence has either been attacked and/or gone underappreciated.[47] "Overlong tacked on slapstick without focused dark comedy" might serve as a condensed condemnation. Yet no other sport better captures the organized chaos of dark comedy as war. Before fleshing this out, one must backtrack to a central *MASH* element of absurdity—its disjointed narrative, a hallmark of the genre … and life. Though this is a basic component of Altman the auteur, it is also inherent to Hooker's hilarious novel, which reads like a rambling collection of short stories loosely connected by a war and core band of characters.

The lifelike nature of football, beyond its randomness and inherent violence, involves the chaos which suddenly breaks out among 22 players once the ball is hiked. Even professional cameramen sometimes lose track of the ball. The game's unsettling, explosive uncertainty makes football just the opposite of baseball, the methodical linear game linked to dark comedy's mirror opposite—populism.[48] This latter feel-good, Capraesque genre (think *Field of Dreams*, 1989) has a traditional one-thing-at-a-time narrative and does not move at life's—or football's—confusing warp speed. Comedian George Carlin's inspired routine on the semantic differences between baseball and football also gets at the latter sport's war-like links to dark comedy. Carlin's riff reads in part:

> Baseball is a 19th century pastoral game. Football is a 20th century technological struggle…. Baseball begins in the spring, the season of new life. Football begins in the fall, when everything is dying…. Football has hitting, dipping, spearing, piling on, late hitting, unnecessary roughness and personal fouls. Baseball has the sacrifice…. Football is rigidly timed and it will end even if we have to go to sudden death…. Baseball has no time limit…. In football … the quarterback … [or] field general [has] to be on target with his aerial assault riddling the defense … with deadly accuracy in spite of the blitz even if he has to use the shotgun. With short bullet passes and long bombs, he marches his troops into enemy territory … with a sustained ground attack. In baseball, the object is to go home, and to be safe.

The *MASH* football game embraces all of Carlin's war-like dark comedy ties to the sport. Though no one dies (Hot Lips does think someone is shot when a starter's pistol is fired to mark the end of a quarter), the game is full of casualties. And just like the flawed world of dark comedies, the *MASH* team does *whatever* it takes to win, including a sneaky play (making the center eligible to run), secretly including a professional NFL player (now an Army doctor) on their roster, and outright cheating—drugging the other team's star player with a hypodermic needle under a pile-up of players. The latter action also displays dark comedy's patented absurdity-incongruity by having the *MASH* player daintily apply a disinfectant to the star opponent's arm before inserting the syringe—after both a violent hit in the most atypical of medical settings. Moreover, given Altman's proclivity for realism and encouraging actors to improvise, this pioneering dark comedy game features American cinema's first mainstream use of the word "fuck." John Schuck, as Painless Pole, playing a *MASH* football lineman, ad-libs to his oversized opponent, just before the ball is hiked, "All right, Bub, your fuckin' head is coming right off!"

MASH's display of dark comedy's last major theme, after the all-pervasiveness of death and the inherent absurdity of the world, is revealing the beast-like nature of man. Beyond the obvious, war itself, which can legitimately be pigeonholed in the category of death, absurdity, and abominable behavior, it would still take an army of movie ushers to chronicle the genre's depiction of man's inhumanity to man and the insignificance attached to human life. Though no *MASH* beastly configuration approaches *Sweeney Todd: The Demon Barber of Fleet Street*, the killing character whose victims turn up as meat pie (a figure first appearing in British "penny dreadful" fiction of the 1840s), Hooker and Altman provide various cruel characters. In camp that dubious honor would go to Duvall's Major Burns, who's slow, overly by-the-book operating procedures lessens the number of wounded soldiers he can see and presumably save. Moreover, Burns is a master at causing unnecessary psychological grief among the surgical staff, such as the afore-mentioned incident with Bud Cort's Private Boone.

The pre-eminent *MASH* example of inhumanly cruel behavior nonetheless, involves the hospital chief whom Hawkeye and McIntyre encounter in Tokyo, Colonel Merrill

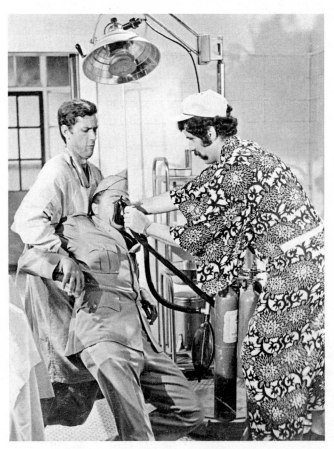

(J.B. Douglas). While the impetus for the trip was to operate on a Congressman's soldier son, Merrill's murderous policy involves not treating illegitimate children of American military personnel and Japanese civilians. Following the MASH duo's successful operation on the serviceman, they are made aware of such a baby in need of emergency surgery. Without a second thought, Sutherland's and Gould's doctors disregard this edict and proceed to save the baby's life. When Merrill attempts to stop said mercy mission, the iconoclastic MASH boys, with the willing assistance of the anesthetist (Michael Murphy), manage to gas the hospital chief into slumberland. Plus, for a blackmail insurance policy, they photograph the morning-after Merrill with some prostitutes.

Though the amusing Tokyo escapade might be the most iffy for viewers to believe, Altman, like pioneering comedy director Leo McCarey, knew enough to anchor most of what preceded it

Elliott Gould's McIntyre (right) does what he has to do to save a baby's life. Michael Murphy assists in the anesthetizing of the evil colonel.

in reality, thus making audiences more receptive to later exaggerations. Fittingly, the Japanese scenes were also the most blatantly anti-military, from the Merrill incident to Hawkeye and McIntyre's serviceman driver's only dialogue being an ongoing stream of "Goddam, goddam army!"—which is straight from Hooker's novel.[49] Furthermore, as if to underline this man-as-beast portion of the film, the MASH twosome spoof the concept by pretending to be Dr. Jekyll and Mr. Hyde while operating on the Congressman's son.

Such "fuck you" coolness also brings one full circle back to the chapter's opening dark comedy spin on the personality comedian. Great clowns endear themselves to us by what the French call *spirit d'escalier*—witty thoughts one only thinks to say on the staircase *after* the party. *MASH*'s black humor twist on the phenomenon is to focus the quips upon a specific anti-war perspective, instead of the normal comedian's any topic witticism. Plus, the same could be said for our pleasure in hearing comics say what we would never dare to utter. Except again, the norm is at best a scattergun-saturation comedy effect, while *MASH*'s monologues target specific anti-war topics. For example, when McIntyre becomes chief surgeon and the resulting party has him being carried about like the king of the O.R., he gets another dig in at "regular Army clown" Hot Lips by demanding of his blotto minions, "[Bring me] that one, the sultry bitch with the fire in her eyes! Take her clothes off and bring her to me!"

Since the goal of this text is to better understand modern dark comedy as it evolved into a complex compound genre in the 1970s, one might best process the preceding overview of *MASH* by a closer examination of director Altman, screenwriter Lardner, and novelist Hooker. A paraphrasing of Katie Arnold-Ratliff's perspective on art would suggest the *MASH* trio all embraced tactic number one: "Imagine the artist as a wager of war. Some stun with shock-and-awe maneuvers, while others pursue a subtler campaign, built on stealth subterfuge."[50]

MASH's critical and commercial success has come to be most associated with the emergence of Altman as a major New Age auteur whose maverick moviemaking strategies were a perfect marriage for an vignette style. Indeed, the episodic nature of the novel and screenplay had scared off numerous more established directors, including George Roy Hill, Stanley Kubrick, Sidney Lumet and Gene Kelly—how would one connect all those story snippets? Fittingly, Altman's solution to the problem is now considered his greatest contribution to the work—loosely linking the sequences with comic P.A. announcements. For instance:

Attention. Attention. Friday night's movie will be *The Glory Brigade* [1953]. Rock 'em sock 'em kisses you never got. It's Uncle Sam's combat engineers side by side with Greek hand bags. Showing the world a new way to fight as they use bulldozers like bazookas, bayonets like bazooka—bullets. Starring Victor Mature. That is all.

Not only did these loudspeaker announcements tie disparate parts together, such examples further increased *MASH*'s satire of the war, manufactured patriotism, the military, and old school cinema service comedies. Altman described this linking ironic commentary thus: "It's punctuation to me. For *MASH*, I had shot all this fragmented raw material and I knew I was going to have to have punctuation, cutaways. So I came up with the idea of those loudspeakers...."[51]

Other fundamental Altman movie mannerisms include a propensity to let the actors improvise, and a combination use of zoom shots and overlapping dialogue that creates a novel Greek chorus–like commentary in the same film frame. To borrow an overview originally applied to another artist, "[Altman] created a human reality on screen that you couldn't shake, couldn't deny, and could never, ever forget."[52] Of course, the freedom he gave his actors could backfire—Sutherland and Gould were initially so unhinged by Altman's unconventional style, they attempted to get him fired. One is reminded of the imposing improvising director Leo McCarey, whose casually unorthodox directing techniques so spooked Cary Grant that the actor attempted to get out of completing the classic hit screwball comedy *The Awful Truth* (1937, for which McCarey won his first Oscar).[53] Still, most actors sang the praises of Altman's collaborative nature, with Gould going on to star in several other Altman pictures.

Despite Altman being largely known as a TV director, with a modest under-the-radar movie career, his signing onto the project was fortuitous for all the reasons just noted. Moreover, he made other valuable contributions to the script, from the signature laugh line, "He was drafted," to "Hot Lips" Houlihan's lovemaking sequence with Burns being broadcast to the camp. Unfortunately, however, down through the years, Altman has puffed up his contributions to have been one big creative riff on his part. Screenwriter Lardner, Jr., beneficently noted in his memoir: "Bob ... was rather charmed by the idea that *MASH* had sprung much full-blown from his head. He suggested in several interviews that he had treated the script as a mere blueprint...."[54] Years later Lardner said he felt "90 percent of the movie is mine," though he regretted that Altman did not receive enough credit for what he did contribute.[55]

However one feels about Altman's error of ego, his real disservice to the *MASH* creative process involved the Hooker novel from which it was drafted. Sadly, the director disparaged the book from the beginning, which is parroted back in some of the film's reviews, such as the *New York Times* critique, "Based upon a barely possible novel of the same name...."[56] Worse yet, Altman later referred to the novel as "pretty terrible," as well as partially "racist."[57] The latter criticism was merely mirroring the period norm, just like Altman's defense about not being misogynist.[58] Even more hypocritically, the director recycles the racial references from the novel to the screen, from René Auberjonois' character retaining the nickname "Dago Red," to the film's secret NFL ringer of a black player-doctor (Fred Williamson) being called "Spearchucker" Jones.

Keep in mind that it was Lardner who found and so liked the novel in galley (pre-publication) form that he purchased the rights and eventually provided the cover blurb, "Not since *Catch-22* has the struggle to maintain sanity in the rampant insanity of war been told in such outrageously funny terms."[59] Moreover, period reviews of the novel, from the publications from which libraries make their purchasing decisions, were outstanding. For instance, *Booklist* declared: "Exuberant, unvarnished ... fiercely antimilitary, largely anticlerical, and always antisham.... The book is ... an entertaining manifesto in the rough for ... maintenance of sanity in an insane situation and environment."[60] The *Library Journal* called it "[h]ilarious, occasionally very serious, full of warm appealing eccentric characters; one could enjoy a very pleasant evening with this s*MASH*ing novel."[61] One might best sum up this praise with a pocket summary from *Publishers Weekly*: "To make life and death in *MASH* (Mobile Army Surgical Hospital) hilarious is not easy, but the pseudonymous Mr. Hooker has done it."[62]

In rereading the book after 40-plus years, I was amazed at how much of the film's ultimate source material was in the text. All the characters and their colorful quirks are alive and well between the covers. The majority of their basic comic misadventures are also showcased, including Hot Lips' shower incident, the football game, the "Onward,

Christian Soldier" parade of religious irreverence toward Burns, saving the suicidal Painless Pole via a mock suicide (with "the Last Supper"), and mysterious McIntyre producing an olive jar from his parka pocket when offered a Swamp tent martini. There were background tales on all the nicknames (from Hawkeye's dad loving the novel *The Last of the Mohicans*, to Hot Lips' sexual dalliance with Burns), the medical trip to Tokyo involving the whorehouse-hospital, the sick biracial baby and the evil Army administrator, dawn-to-dusk choppers carrying in the wounded, the surgeries mixed with humor (including the sequence in which Hawkeye and McIntyre operate in their Japanese golf duds), and more.

On top of these direct *MASH* novel-to-film zany character-driven sequences, the movie is also riddled with dialogue either exactly, or very similar, to discourse of how McIntyre received his Trapper John nickname: "When the [train] conductor caught him in there ["the lady's can"] with his Winter Carnival date she screamed, 'He trapped me!'" Likewise is McIntyre's sardonic reply to Colonel Blake asking him what was wrong with him for punching Burns for falsely telling Private Boone he was responsible for a patient's death: "I'm wondering the same thing, Henry. I hear the son-of-a-bitch got up. I guess I lost my punch." After Hawkeye has egged on Burns following the Hot Lips incident and the resulting fight ends with Duvall's character being washed out of the company, Duke asks Henry, "If I get into Hot Lips and jump Hawkeye, can I go home too?" Hot Lips' shower incident has her tell Henry in both novel and film that if something is not done she will resign her commission, to which he responds, "Resign your goddamn commission...." The often restated lines "regular Army clowns" and "We're the pros from Dover," the equally repeated condemnation "Goddam Army!," and countless other quotes are also represented in both media.[63]

Plus, as positive as screenwriter Lardner was about the novel, especially as compared to Altman, even he forgot a pivotal Hooker sequence being recycled into the film. In Lardner's memoir he states:

> [A]ll through the movie version [script], I was looking for ways to deal with story developments in visual rather than narrative terms. In the book, for instance, when Hawkeye realizes he has seen a new co-worker [*MASH* doctor] before but can't remember where or when, the answer comes to him undramatically after days of frustration. In the movie, Trapper John ... throws his "Dartmouth [football] pass" right into Hawkeye's arms, triggering his memory.[64]

Yet, a "Dartmouth pass" in Hooker's novel *does* rekindle Hawkeye's memory, as well as an entertaining relating of how his interception during a "blizzard" was the "single-handed" reason for Dartmouth's loss—all of which *was* in the movie![65]

MASH the novel even includes in abundance a litany of other blasphemous and/or macabre material which would have been ideal grist for more dark comedy. Two examples represent the diverse range of this background: Hooker's trio peddling autographed pictures of Jesus (a bearded McIntyre bearing a striking resemblance), and the wounded body parts of an American soldier seriously wounding his foxhole buddy. Plus, the clever text includes oodles of additional observations which would have been right at home in Altman's film, from Hawkeye's suggestion of a thank-you for Dago Red's medical assistance to the unit coming in the form of a "human sacrifice," to his charity towards a military chaplain who has come down with the clap: "I must do something to remedy the tragic results of his excessive libido before he returns to Kokomo, where he is betrothed to the bishop's daughter. Bishops, as a group, are opposed to gonorrhea...."[66]

Such absorbing *MASH*-the-novel diversity is suggested in yet another heartening critique of the book. *Kirkus Reviews* declared: that *MASH*'s characters "are irreverent, inventive and totally disarming.... But it isn't all games ... there is a real sense of the [medical] overview, frustration and pain present ... as the bodies poured in ... full of the worst, probably hopeless, cases. *MASH* is for ... those who remember the battles that were fought after the battle was over."[67]

The reason behind belaboring the noteworthiness of *MASH*-the-novel is twofold. First is that an injustice has been done, especially because a major perpetrator of this myth of mediocrity was Altman. In fairness to this talented filmmaker, I feel he and Lardner took an excellent novel and turned it into a great film. Yet, rare is the director whose *oeuvre* has had such a range of classics and abominable failures. Altman's filmography suggests his gift for improvising and just generally tweaking a story necessitates he have a strong tale with which to start. This is borne out with *MASH*, his greatest critical and commercial success. A friend and teaching colleague, award-winning filmmaker Robert Mugge (whose specialty is documentaries on musicians), made a recent intriguing observation on the subject. Given Altman's love of improvisation, Bob compared the director to an accomplished jazz musician whose extemporized notes were invariably superior when his riffing spontaneity started with a distinctive musical base.[68]

The second reason for dallying with the novel gets to the crux of this text—examining the compound nature and roots of 1970s dark comedy. As stated in the prologue, this genre transition during the so-called "Hollywood Renaissance" resulted from the most multifarious mulligan stew of post–1946 events. An excellent conduit for examining one such pivotal incident—the disgraceful McCarthy blacklisting of the post-war era—begs to ask why Lardner was so instantaneously attracted to Hooker's anti-establishment novel. Though the screenwriter's answer is not on record, beyond immediately seeing the book's movie possibilities, that Lardner was one of the blacklisted Hollywood Ten was certainly a factor. By refusing to discuss his political background with the House Un-American Activities Committee, unsubstantiated leftist accusations were made, with Lardner and nine others being cited for contempt of Congress. They were sentenced to one-year prison terms in 1950 and 1951. For Lardner, establishment Hollywood blacklisted him for nearly two decades. While many might call a *MASH* connection compelling but ultimately un-established, the following passage from Lardner's family memoir offers a legitimate link:

> The Hollywood blacklist lasted about fifteen years, seventeen in my case between screen-play credits. It had wiped out scores of careers and a few lives, but there were enough of us who survived it to create a whole new subversive threat to the content of American movies. The erosion so far is invisible to the naked eye, which is the way we prefer it.[69]

I would suggest that this "invisible erosion" is dark comedy.

Lardner would also have undoubtedly been bemused by parallels between the Hollywood Ten and Hooker's drafted doctors. The government forced the same one-year sentence–tour of duty on each iconoclastic group. Moreover, the screenwriter's family memoir also offers an additional potential insight as to how Hawkeye and company could maintain their mutinous mindsets without breaking. Lardner described his prison stay thusly:

> You think of it as a temporary inconvenience and start counting the days 'till it is over. You never really make the adjustment to a drastically different way of life with all its deprivations, and thus escape much of the gloom and frustration that come with the prospect of sustained confinement.[70]

A friend to both the screenwriter and his father, writer Lillian Hellman observed when she herself was threatened by HUAC, "I cannot and will not cut my conscience to fit this year's fashion."

Another *MASH* link for both Lardner and this text is the Korean setting. Though my generation embraced the film as an anti-war indictment of the Vietnam conflict, Lardner suffered through a blacklisting period greatly fanned by the Korean War (1950–1952). Celebrated historian Arthur M. Schlesinger, Jr., later explained:

> The Korean War had wrought a significant change in the public atmosphere. It had created a climate that transformed McCarthy's [communist-leftist witch-hunting] crusade from an eccentric sideshow ... into a popular movement. If communists were killing American boys in Korea should [alleged] communists be given the benefit of the doubt in the United States? ... A storm of near-hysteria blew up.[71]

An often neglected fact coupled to the McCarthy malignancy was the blacklisting brain drain it had on Hollywood. In other words, the 1950s were neither Hollywood's finest hour ethically nor artistically. How could it be, when talented people like Lardner, the Oscar-wining co-author (with Michael Kanin) of such "subversive" Katharine Hepburn–Spencer Tracey romantic comedies as *Woman of the Year* (1942), were banned. Thus, TV was not the only thing keeping movie attendance down.

As a postscript to other potential *MASH* factors which might have drawn Lardner to the novel, beyond that anti-establishment core, is the book's superabundance of baseball references. The screenwriter's father was the revered humorist and sports writer Ring Lardner, Sr., whose art often combined these two components. For example, two of the senior Lardner's pre-eminent works resulted in equally superlative Joe E. Brown baseball comedies, *Elmer the Great* (1933, from the Lardner–George M. Cohan play) and *Alibi Ike* (1935, from a Lardner short story).[72] His father's dual talents also had an impact upon Lardner, Jr., with his aforementioned Oscar winner being anchored in comedy and baseball. The heart of the movie's "opposites attract" scenario had sportswriter Spencer Tracy attempting to explain baseball to Katharine Hepburn's otherwise intellectual snob.

Most of Hooker's baseball asides do not make the movie, being merely shorthand accounts of camp events, like a description of McIntyre's first surgery being as smooth as Joe "The Yankee Clipper" DiMaggio going back for a fly ball.[73] However, while this study has already demonstrated that football best be the designated dark comedy sport, *MASH* the novel also uses baseball along anti-establishment lines. By illustration, on one occasion McIntyre makes small talk with a fellow New Englander on the Boston Red Sox's chances that year. The patient feels that without "the big guy" (Ted Williams had been recalled to active duty in Korea), the team had nothing. When McIntyre asks if having the legendary player in Korea was reassuring, he responds, "Are you kiddin,' Doc? I wouldn't wish this kind of thing [wasted war] on a dog. I'd feel much better if [Williams] was back over there [America] bustin' up a few ballgames for us."[74]

Regardless, *MASH*, the anti-establishment hit movie which so meshed with America's anti-war youth, was created by a trio of middle-aged men, with Lardner being the oldest at 54. Consequently, there was a great deal more dissent and frustration going on than merely being about the Vietnam War. Though Lardner had the most to be alienated about, Altman had gone unappreciated for years by old school storytelling Hollywood, and Hooker's decade-plus arduous wrestling match with the *MASH* material is best measured by his paraphrased confession, "Those in my unit, like most soldiers, were simply too young for these awful jobs."[75] One is both reminded that Vonnegut's struggle to get *Slaughterhouse-Five* on paper took over twice as long, and that his novel's subtitle is *The Children's Crusade.*

Pioneering dark comedies like Charlie Chaplin's *Monsieur Verdoux* (1947) and Preston Sturges' *Unfaithfully Years* (1948) overwhelmed a world predominantly not ready to acknowledge and/or recognize the innate existential nihilism of the genre—which argues life is without objective meaning or purpose. By the 1960s and '70s, however, the philosophy had moved to center stage. Dark comedy now had had two decades of multi-faceted disillusion upon which to build the genre's complex-compound foundation. While naysayers still existed, as they undoubtedly always will, the time was now right for people en masse to begin attacking the hypocritical status quo. A dark comedy epiphany was not to be denied. Indeed, the genre had already become so pervasive, at all levels of life, that even President John F. Kennedy had not been averse to using black humor privately. One instance would eventually prove to be most macabre. Shortly after his greatest accomplishment, averting nuclear war over Cuba in 1962, he allowed himself to think of it as a Lincolnesque moment. Kiddingly, he told his brother Robert, "Maybe this is the night I should go to the theater"—*à la* Lincoln attending a play as the Civil War ended, only to be assassinated.[76] Perversely, the story only becomes more nightmarish—dark comedy essentially being nightmares come to life—when the later assassinated Robert laughed and said, "If you go, I want to go with you."[77] Accordingly, such high-profile 1960s murders were just more grist for the increasingly twisted dark comedies of the 1970s.

Is it any wonder that *MASH* the movie generated a legion of positive reviews? Noting the preponderance of these critiques, the *New York Times* even couched its praise in the style of "a public notice": "*MASH* ... is so effective so much of the time that it's likely to be overpraised to the point that it can't possibly fulfill the extravagant hopes engendered by most of its notices.... [Still, it] is the last bleeding word on a film genre known as the service comedy."[78]

Newsweek placed the picture in the literary pantheon of dark comedy by comparing it to "[Jonathan] Swift's baby-munching in [the 1729 essay] 'A Modest Proposal.'"[79] The publication went on to state: "*MASH* is a remarkable achievement, and I confess com-

The only thing Hawkeye (Donald Sutherland, right) and McIntyre (Elliott Gould) were serious about was saving lives.

plete bafflement as to how the people who made it ever achieved what they did, a hyper-acute wiretap on mankind's death."[80] The *Monthly Film Bulletin* added:

> Because *MASH* is wildly, irreverently, scabrously, blasphemously funny, all to the accompa-niment of gouts [sic] of blood from Korean war-wounded, it has been hailed as the great anti-everything film.... If the Army (or the Establishment) then comes out badly in the film—as it does—it is simply because all authority has been proven conclusively to be use-less, irrelevant and even positively damaging....[81]

MASH's ability to squeeze subverse into silly paved the way for pictures like Harold Ramis' *Stripes* (1980), with reluctant soldiers Bill Murray yelling at his fellow G.I.s:

> We're not.... Spartans—we're Americans! That means that our forefathers were kicked out of every decent country in the world. We are the wretched refuse. We're the underdog. We're mutts. Here's proof. [Then, after touching a soldier's face, Murray says:] His nose is cold.

Ultimately, as *Film Quarterly* described *MASH*, "it is [simply] about the human con-dition."[82]

2

Catch–22 (6/20/70)

YOSSARIAN (Alan Arkin): Okay, let me see if I've got this straight. In order to be grounded,
I've got to be crazy. And I must be crazy to keep flying. But if I ask to be grounded, that
means I'm not crazy anymore, and I have to keep flying.
"DOC" DANEEKA (Jack Gilford): You got it, that's Catch–22.

Catch–22 (1970) follows the literary lineage of *MASH* (1970), yet another cinematic adaptation of an episodic anti-war novel (1961) not directly addressing Vietnam but quickly embraced by young protesters of the latter conflict. While 1968's *MASH* novel was written by a medical veteran of the Korean War, Richard Hooker, *Catch–22* author Joseph Heller was a World War II bombardier. Furthermore, besides being each writer's first and ultimately signature text, both novels involved long gestation periods. It was as if their prolonged incubations added validation to the anti–Vietnam War protesters, since neither book was a commercial success until embraced by these anti-establishment youth. Heller comprehended this argument when he said, "I don't think a writer's work of literature really influences people. It shapes them. It does confirm what they themselves might suspect."[1] Specifically, when *Catch–22* calls attention to the absurdities still inherent to what history now calls the "good war," it better highlights the senselessness of the Vietnam War.

Though the adaptations show similar patterns, the expectation levels and public responses were radically different. *MASH* director Robert Altman was essentially an under-the-radar filmmaker working on a low budget with an under-the-radar novel. In contrast, *Catch–22* director Mike Nichols was then the do-no-wrong director of a string of critical and commercial theater and film hits, culminating with his Best Director Oscar for the groundbreaking American New Wave film *The Graduate* (1967). Moreover, while the previous chapter documented how Hooker's novel was vastly superior to a negative reputation perpetuated by Altman, Nichols and screenwriter-actor Buck Henry were still reshaping a more multifaceted complex book with a sizable (thus, an increased nitpicking) audience. Consequently, Nichols had both the critics and the public counting on another home run, especially given an epic budget (six times that of *MASH*), and the resulting star-studded cast. Indeed, Nichols would later joke on the television talk show circuit that his assemblage of B-25 bombers was the sixth largest air force in the world, right behind France, and they had considered taking over Mexico—an area of which had doubled as the Mediterranean island for *Catch–22*, allegedly just off the Italian coast.[2] Regardless, during the film's post-production Nichols and his producer John Calley realized the director's golden boy status might soon be over. The two men attended a private *MASH* screening, purely because of the picture's similar subjects:

Right away…. Nichols got a tight feeling in his chest as Altman's darkly comic vision played out in front of him, recognizing that he had been blind-sided. "We were waylaid by *MASH*, which was much fresher and more alive, improvisational, and funnier than *Catch–22*. It just cut us off at the knees." So it came as no surprise to Nichols that *MASH* became a huge hit. Nor to Altman either, who was actually aware that he was chasing Nichols' tail. [Altman] had a banner up in his office that said, "Caught-22."[3]

Genre-bending components of *Catch–22* merit consideration. Like Altman, Nichols also squeezes anti-genre service comedy laughs out of the undisguised contempt for the military, which openly bleeds into black humor. For example, as the planes line up on the runway for the first mission, several flash pan camera movements reveal pilots giving a thumbs-up sign to the tower … only to end with Yossarian flipping off flight controller Danby (Richard Benjamin). Of course, one might also just record the multiple times a dead sober Yossarian freely and openly offers up variations of the following murder threat about his commanding colonel (Martin Balsam): "If he raises the number of missions again, I swear to God, I'll help you [Dobbs, played by Martin Sheen] kill him."

While there are a spattering of flagrant anti-military moments in both the novel and the film, *Catch–22* is even more potent at assailing the service comedy basic of honoring religion, another complement to dark comedy. Though Nichols' film does not savage the institution as exhaustively as *MASH*, there are innumerable examples, such as wheeler-dealer Lieutenant Milo (Jon Voight) speaking to the chaplain (Anthony Perkins): "As a matter of fact, Father, I know I can get my hands on an entire shipment of religious relics, blessed by the Pope himself. The Germans swiped them and put them on the open market. As I understand it, the stuff includes a wrist and collarbones of some of your top saints!"

Perkins' chaplain has neither purpose nor respect in the picture, a factor further accented in the novel by giving him an atheist for an assistant.[4] Perkins' character does not even serve any non-religious purpose, like *MASH*'s otherwise superfluous Father "Dago Red" (René Auberjonois), who occasionally helps in the operating room. Moreover, Perkins' figure merely makes the enlisted men nervous, while Colonel Cathcart's only need for the chaplain is a vanity project: write some snappy and effectively patriotic prayers in order to get the commander's picture in *The Saturday Evening Post*.

Perkins' character is such a cipher that he suggests a Walter Mitty … without even his intermittently soothing imagination. Gauge this religious fall from entertainment grace from even a peripheral service comedy, like director-writer Leo McCarey's multiple Oscar-winning *Going My Way* (1944, which was inspired by a hitchhiking serviceman using that expression when the director picked him up[5]). The military connection comes late in the picture, after Bing Crosby's Father O'Malley has already assisted a troubled young wartime female runaway. Crosby's priest then helps get an angry father to accept a marriage between said girl and his serviceman son.

Be that as it may, the sense of an inept Almighty which abounds in Heller's novel, such as the death of Kraft—"a skinny, harmless kid … who only wanted to be liked … had gone down in flame … on the seventh day, while God was resting"—permeates Nichols' adaptation, too.[6] Indeed, a less than competent Lord anticipates the thoughts of Woody Allen's czarist soldier in *Love and Death* (1975; see Chapter 8), "You know, if it turns out that there *is* a God, I don't think that He's evil. I think that the worst you can say about Him is that, basically, He's an underachiever."

A third anti-genre service comedy stance in *Catch–22* is giving a point to the engaging yet senseless silliness normally found in these films, such as Danny Kaye's hypochondriac soldier singing the punning patter song "Melody in 4F" from *Up in Arms* (1944). In contrast, there is the sheepishly amusing announcement by Danby that oh-so-bashfully suggests legitimate danger: "Weather conditions have improved tremendously over the mainland, so you [bomber flight crews] won't have any trouble at all seeing the target. Of course, we mustn't forget, that means that they won't have any trouble at all seeing you."

Another quintessential goofy component of service comedies is either the bad food and/or merely the lack of variety in the chow. For instance, Laurel and Hardy's *Block-Heads* (1938) begins with the duo as World War I soldiers. When their company is directed to go "over the top," Stan's orders are to stay behind to guard their Western Front trench. Well, actual scenes of fighting immediately go by, followed by the caption, "Armistice." Yet Stanley, the ever obedient numbskull, remains at his post for the next two decades, documented by the guard duty path he has worn into the ground *and* a mammoth pile of bean cans—a wonderful sight gag of army provisions. It is funny, yet there is no sub-textual meaning. Now contrast this inventive throwaway gag with the following *Catch-22* film dialogue:

> MILO: I want to serve this to the men. Taste this and let me know what you think.
>
> [Yossarian takes a bite.]
>
> YOSSARIAN: What is it?
> MILO: Chocolate covered cotton.
> YOSSARIAN: What are you, crazy?
> MILO: No good, huh?
> YOSSARIAN: For Christ's sake, you didn't even take the seeds out.
> MILO: Is it really that bad?
> YOSSARIAN: It's cotton!

Besides supplementing the dark comedy absurdity criticism soon to follow, the sequence has a basic service comedy anti-genre element. Beyond the silliness of passing off chocolate-covered cotton as food, the scene encapsules the extremes to which Milo will go to make money on the war. The episode is a throwback to Chaplin's pioneering dark comedy on war as big business, *Monsieur Verdoux* (1947). Here war profits justify *anything*. To illustrate, shortly before the ending, Verdoux (Chaplin) meets a young woman whose life he once spared, unbeknownst to her. Now she is rich from a marriage to a munitions manufacturer, and Chaplin's title character states, "That is the business I should have been in. It will be paying big dividends soon [with the approaching war]!"

One can see the direct link between Chaplin's seminal pronouncements about the murderous money-driven institutionalized link between corporations and warring governments and *Catch-22*. Milo is the perfect example of this phenomenon, with or without the zaniness of the chocolate-covered cotton. His creation of "M and M Enterprises" turns World War II into the most profitable of businesses, and the source of methodical absurdity—moving easily from anti-genre service comedy to purely dark comedy, such as taking the camp's parachutes because he can obtain a good price on silk ... sharing the wealth *if* the flyers do not need a parachute.

Though *Catch-22*'s anti-genre shish-kebabing of service comedies could go on forever, one might close with sexual relationships. Standard service comedy comics are virginally "as pure as the driven snow." But unlike Mae West's sexual close to this axiom, "until they drifted," these old school comedies end up with equally wholesome young women, like Jerry Lewis' girlfriend in *Sailor Beware* (1951). Earlier, Eddie Bracken, the

1940s prototype for Lewis, courts an equally upright girl next door in satirist Preston Sturges' service comedy *Hail the Conquering Hero* (1944).

Divergences from this abound in *Catch–22*. The most innocent is naïve Nately (Art Garfunkel), whose equally pure voice as part of Simon and Garfunkel graces the soundtrack of the groundbreaking *The Graduate*. Nately falls in love with a whore ... who does not even care for him, beyond an escape to America. And Yossarian's love interest is a worldly yet seemingly decent woman in white who still ends up working in Nately's M and M Enterprises whorehouse. As with *MASH*, one talks in terms of lust, not love. Service comedy variations from this new norm were rare prior to the 1970s, such as the squeaky clean wannabe soldier Eddie Bracken ending up with trampishly patriotic Betty Hutton in *Miracle of Morgan's Creek* (1944).

This anti-genre service comedy façade for *Catch–22*, as already demonstrated, is the consummate gateway to the picture's black comedy nucleus. As with *MASH*, war provides the ultimate setting for the genre's first core theme—the pervasiveness of death. Nichols' film even ratchets up the subject by centering upon aerial combat, versus the *MASH* unit not being on the front lines. The death engine which drives *Catch–22* is Yossarian's fear and anger over the ever-mounting number of missions one must fly before being rotated back to the States, *à la* the chapter's opening examination of the meaning for Catch–22. Therefore, death percolates through every film frame, regardless of the setting. For instance, even at the dinner mess it is the focal point of the conversation:

> YOSSARIAN: Those bastards [the enemy] are trying to kill me.
> MILO: No one is trying to kill you, sweetheart. Now eat your dessert like a good boy.
> YOSSARIAN: Oh, yeah? Then why are they shooting at me, Milo?
> MILO: They're shooting at everyone, Yossarian.
> YOSSARIAN: And what difference does that make?
> DOBBS: Look, Yossarian, suppose, I mean, suppose everyone thought the same way you do?
> YOSSARIAN: Then I'd be a damn fool to think any different.

Both the novel's and the film's central personification of death hinge upon the fate of tail gunner Snowden (Jon Korkes). In each medium's disjointed telling of the story, both Yossarian and the reader-viewer are privy to a bit more information with each Snowden sequence. The scenario is evocative of so many dark comedy Everyman anti-heroes, because what often seems to be successive insights and/or clues are really misdirections, such as Jake Gittes' (Jack Nicholson) scenes involving some spectacles and whether a servant says "glass" or "grass" in *Chinatown* (1974, see Chapter 7). Consequently, there is a series of *Catch–22* flashbacks in which Yossarian is repeatedly asked by his pilot to help wounded gunner Snowden. In each sequence the bombardier does more to assist the gunner, from finding a non-fatal injury to bandaging it. Yet, in the last flashback a fatal chest and stomach wound suddenly becomes apparent as poor Snowden's insides ooze to the plane's floor. Heller observed in the novel:

> [T]hey were all out to bump him off. That was the secret [drawn out over time] Snowden had spilled to him on the [bombing] mission to [the enemy held French city of] Avignon—they were out to get [Yossarian], and Snowden had spilled it all over the back of the plane.[7]

Snowden's terrible secret goes deeper, as briefly touched upon in the previous chapter. When ephemeral life leaves the body it becomes, in Heller's words, so much "garbage," which will "rot like other kinds of garbage."[8] Beyond any existential emptiness is Kafka's simple truism, "The meaning of life is that it stops." One might even double count death as part of another fundamental dark comedy theme—absurdity. That is, how can a once vital, passionate, thinking human being suddenly be reduced to refuse?

Man struggles with the disconnectedness of life. We need a comfortingly orderly fantasy in which, if there must be death, it must have some meaningful continuity attached. Such a perspective represents a societal power and/or comfort franchise. As novelist Philip Roth has suggested, the church and government "imposes fantasy on the populace" throughout history.[9] Therefore, another aspect of disturbing dark comedy is how death arrives with random end-without-purpose casualness. For example, one of *Catch-22*'s minor characters is the prankish McWatt, whose off-duty time often involves buzzing the camp and/or the nearby beach area. During one such stunt he come in low

> over the bobbing (off-shore) raft on which blond, pale kid Sampson ... leaped clownishly up to touch [the aircraft] at the exact moment some arbitrary gust of wind, or minor miscalculation of McWatt's senses dropped the speeding plane down just low enough for a propeller to slice him half away.[10]

For a brief surreal moment the now ironically named Sampson's bottom half disgustingly defies death and remains standing, before toppling into the sea. Not surprisingly, this also results in yet another example of dark comedy suicide, as the shocked McWatt flies his plane into a mountain.

Such cruel randomness, often sardonically during a fun (lowering of an audience's guard) moment, *à la* Kid Sampson's pontoon playfulness, exhibits the individual's insignificance in dark comedy. This again confirms the genre's connection between death and incongruity. Nichols, who struggles with differentiating between comedy and tragedy, feels that a director is saying to his audience:

> "This [actually or metaphorically] happened to me; did it happen to you too?" ... The impulse is strong to say to whoever is watching, "You, too?" So I don't think of the [dark] humor [in my work] as being manipulative but almost as a way of checking with other people. "Do you experience things as I do? Is it like that for you?"[11]

Fittingly, for this struggling Everyman mindset, despite Nichols' many deepdish influences, including Edward Albee, Thomas Mann, and Federico Fellini, he is not shy about acknowledging the impact of Walt Kelly's comic strip *Pogo*, whose signature axiom is the aforementioned line, "We have met the enemy, and he is us."[12]

This *Pogo* connection makes for a first-rate transition to appraising *Catch-22*'s second essential dark comedy thesis: absurdity. Kelly's seminal dictum suggests that man-made insanity is the result of both general species incompetence and its perpetuation in human institutions. Yet, one might best begin discussing this subject by scrutinizing this chapter's earlier reference to the disjointed narrative of *Catch-22*. This is a situation synonymous with dark comedy in general, and specifically this study's focus films—which are often adapted from equally fragmented and seemingly jumbled literary works. As briefly reported in the prologue, even though the influential French New Wave demanded slice-of-life original work for film, versus American New Wave's openness to other source material—the end result was often similar: provocatively disordered yet true-to-life storylines.

The American adaptation perspective makes for a richer cinematic amalgamation of anti-establishment absurdity components in society predating either New Wave movement, since the French preferred a total break with post–1950 literary developments. Of course, this is not to say that French filmmakers were not cognizant of, and/or influenced by postmodernism fiction. However, metaphorically to demand one must artistically recreate the wheel for each film seems limiting. Moreover, by the American directors and screenwriters often drawing upon the period's pre-existing disjointed dark humor novels, though still not always fully understood and/or appreciated, it helped make the dark comedy films to follow more accessible than, say, the trailblazing *Monsieur Verdoux*, which so blindsided all but the most astute back in 1947. Indeed, these later novels helped provide a sort of *CliffsNotes* assistance to new dark film comedy viewers. For example, the *New York Times*' Vincent Canby's review opened with a qualified rave: "Mike Nichols' *Catch–22* ... is the most humane—oh, to hell with it!—it's the best American film I've seen this year. But there's a catch: I'm not sure that the movie will make complete sense, or that it can be fully appreciated, unless one has read and admired the book."[13] Yet, later in the same critique, Canby adds:

> The first time I saw it.... I laughed often ... [but] I was somewhat confused.... Having read the novel when I saw the film the second time, I was able to not only make bridges in the continuity ... but also to marvel at how closely ... the novel's mood of triumphant madness [is maintained].[14]

Of course, even at this late date (1970) there were critics who perfectly described the genre but were oblivious to its meanings. For instance, *The Hollywood Reporter*'s John Mahoney complained:

> We are not given a balance to that madness [of life's basic absurdity] ... the film of *Catch–22* says that people are no damn good, that everything is a hype, that man can be corrupted for a cookie, that nothing is beneath his dignity and that none may rise above that low if the price is right, that man is irredeemable [in this illogical world].[15]

One wants to pencil in, "And your point is?" Granted, dark comedy is a very big tent. Yet, in making such a statement as late as 1970, when for some pop postmodernism was already flirting with being a cliché, one is tempted to either recycle that old axiom, "There's no monopoly on philistinism," or quote the pioneering dark comedy essayist-critic Will Cuppy, "Never call anyone a baboon unless you are sure of your facts."[16] Indeed, one need not agree with the philosophical tenets of a given genre, but to belittle its mere right to exist, especially when a critic is supposed to be more of a teacher-guide than a judge, merits a volley directly from a classic work of absurdity first performed 15 years prior to the aforementioned review: Samuel Beckett's *Waiting for Godot*, where the play's timeless hoboes are machine-gunning negative patter:

VLADIMIR: Moron!
ESTRAGON: Vermin!
VLADIMIR: Abortion!
ESTRAGON: Morpion!
VLADIMIR: Sewer-rat!
ESTRAGON: Curate!
VLADIMIR: Cretin!
ESTRAGON [with finality]: Critic![17]

Regardless, absurdity comes in many *Catch–22* forms, beyond the phrase itself. The film adaptation, like the novel, is a compendium of the many figures which are interwoven through part or parcel of an existence, meriting the eternal question, "To what purpose?" Each chapter in the text is essentially about another eccentric individual in Yossarian's unit, with Alan Arkin's bombardier periodically wandering through each section. Though the film's flashbacks are initially a challenge to follow, Yossarian has more of a unifying presence here than in the novel. *Catch-22*'s character collage is not unlike the various figures who occupy the boarding house in Christopher Isherwood's novella *Goodbye to Berlin* (1939), the foundation for *Cabaret* (1975, see Chapter 5). Like *Catch-22*, this musical is essentially a collection of related character studies often including the cabaret singer Sally Bowles. Along similar lines, the loose structure of both *MASH* the novel and *MASH* the film might be described as an anthology of Hawkeye sketches, with periodic appearances by Swamp tent gang members McIntyre and Duke. And Arthur Penn's 1970 adaptation of Thomas Berger's novel *Little Big Man* (1964, see Chapter 3) has the 121-year-old Jack Crabb taking the viewer-reader on yet another short story–like compendium of the Old West, including encounters with everyone from legends (such as Wild Bill Hickok and General Custer) to fascinating composite characters (from Dustin Hoffman's title figure, to Chief Dan George's scene-stealing Old Lodge Skins).

Such tales are not diminished by their episodic nature but rather enhanced by replicating life's random catch-as-catch-can nature. Where acknowledged or not, a subtext to most dark comedy artists' work is to remind us of the messy chaos that passes for existence. Plus, good, bad, or indifferent, the figures which come one's way help to distract us from life's endless waiting ... and the attempts to make sense of this absurdity. Yossarian is like the aforementioned Estragon and Vladimir from *Waiting for Godot*, who are in eternal pause mode. And who or what is Godot? Frequent "readings" through the years have ranged from an indifferent God, to film noir's "Big Sleep" (death). Such ambiguous thoughts on the subject are not unlike a paraphrased recycling of Heller's comments to begin the chapter, "Writing does not shape the reader-viewer, it confirms what the audience might suspect." Beckett, when asked who or what Godot means, said, "If I knew I would have said in the play." This implies, like Heller, that in a non-traditional narrative, meaning is even more in the audience's hands.[18] For me, the previously suggested confirmations are one and the same; such an apathetic Father is *no* Father at all, and Godot, if not God, represents the eternal dirt nap which follows the farce called life. Intriguingly, while Heller later confessed to "not being familiar with Beckett when he wrote *Catch-22* ... I have since been amazed by certain very striking similarities [between our work]."[19]

Divertingly, with the preponderance of sex to be had and obsessed over in dark comedy in general, and *Catch-22* in particular, absurdity as a waiting game is often synonymous with death. For example, intercourse represents an absence of self-control, consistent with man's plight in black humor. This breakdown is most comically presented in the bug-eyed panting of Yossarian and his *Catch-22* company after they meet the sexy companion of visiting General Dreadle (Orson Welles)—completely ignoring a life-or-death bombing briefing. One is also reminded of Major King Kong (Slim Pickens) happily straddling a falling, phallic-shaped atomic bomb called Lolita, whooping his way to world oblivion in *Dr. Strangelove or: How I Learned to Stop Worrying and Love the Bomb* (1964). As Luis Buñuel, the most acclaimed foreign director of black comedy, has observed, "In a rigidly hierarchical society, sex—which respects no barriers and obeys no laws—can at any moment become an agent of chaos [absurdity]."[20] Indeed, *Catch-22*'s most spellbinding mix of absurdity-sex-death fittingly plays itself out in a brothel. It is a dialogue between naïve Nately and the old man who resides there. Though technically a conversation, it plays out as more of an absurdly truthful civic lesson on history:

NATELY: Don't you have any principles?

OLD MAN: Of course not!

NATELY: No morality.

OLD MAN: I'm a very moral man, and Italy is a very moral country. That's why we will certainly come out on top again if we succeed in being defeated.

NATELY: You talk like a madman.

OLD MAN: But I live like a sane one. I was a fascist when Mussolini was on top. Now that he has been disposed, I am anti-fascist. When the Germans were here, I was fanatically pro–German. Now I'm fanatically pro–American. You'll find no more loyal partisan in all of Italy than myself.

NATELY: You're a shameful opportunist! What you don't understand is that it's better to die on your feet than to live on your knees.

OLD MAN: You have it backwards. It's better to live on your feet than to die on your knees. I know.

NATELY: How do you know?

OLD MAN: Because I am 107 years old. How old are you?

NATELY: I'll be 20 in January.

OLD MAN: If you live [which he does not].

The *pièce de resistance* of absurdity for this sequence is *Catch–22* director Nichols casting Marcel Dalio as the Old Man. Dalio had teamed so significantly with Jean Gabin as prisoners of war in Jean Renoir's revered anti-war film *Grand Illusion* (1937). This was copybook casting on two absurdity levels, beyond both films being singular anti-war pictures. First, Renoir inimitably anticipates the absurdity of the Holocaust to come by chronicling the friendship which develops between the two escapees—the gentile Gabin and the Jewish Dalio. Second, there is the funny-tragic insanity of the last sequence, when the duo approach the freedom of the border between Germany and neutral Switzerland. Until that point German soldiers had been firing upon them. Absurdly, however, once the pair had reached that invisible arbitrary man-made borderline between the two countries, the firing stopped, and war had been reduced to a bizarre "olly olly oxen free" children's game of hide and seek.

Nevertheless, before leaving dark comedy's waiting trilogy of absurdity-sex-death, one must return to yet another Heller-like sequence from *Waiting for Godot*:

VLADIMIR: What do we do now?

ESTRAGON: Wait.

VLADIMIR: Yes, but while waiting?

ESTRAGON: What about hanging ourselves?

VLADIMIR: Hmm. It'd give us an erection.

ESTRAGON [highly excited]: An erection!

VLADIMIR: With all that follows. Where it [semen] falls mandrakes grow [a plant root of the past resembling a person and thought to produce a sleeping potion]. That's why they shriek when you pull them up....

ESTRAGON: Let's hang ourselves immediately! [implying that either one might never awake from this mandrake sleep, or the semen would again start the absurd cycle].[21]

Curiously, *if* any conventional comforting humor comes from this New Age absurdity, be it Vladimir and Estragon, or Tom Stoppard's title characters in *Rosencrantz and Guildenstern Are Dead* (a 1960 "theater of the absurd" play), it has roots in an old age source—traditional personality comedy. (Bert Lahr, the Cowardly Lion in the 1939 *The Wizard of Oz*, later played Estragon to critical acclaim in the first production of *Godot*.) In any event, Estragon and Vladimir, and Rosencrantz and Guildenstern, are couples that have Laurel and Hardy written all over them. Each is an amusingly bickering, dim-witted duo caring for each while stumbling through a disturbing world distracted (protected?) by minutiae. As it happens, *Waiting for Godot* even has sketch material, such as a hat-switching routine, which is a variation of a piece Leo McCarey first created for Laurel and Hardy in the 1920s, and later recycled in his Marx Brothers film *Duck Soup* (1933).[22] Kurt Vonnegut (see Chapter 5's *Slaughterhouse-Five*, 1972) directly addresses this Laurel and Hardy–absurdity factor in his dark comedy novel *Slapstick* (1976). After a dedication to the comedy team, in which he describes them as "two angels of my time," the book's prologue opens:

> This is the closest I will ever come to writing an autobiography. I have called it *Slapstick* because it is grotesque, situational poetry—like the slapstick film comedies, especially those of Laurel and Hardy, of long ago. It is about what life *feels* like to me. There are all these tests of my limited agility and intelligence. They go on and on. The fundamental joke with Laurel and Hardy ... was that they did their best with every test. They never failed to bargain in good faith with their destinies.... There was very little love in their films.... It was yet another test—with comical possibilities, provided that everybody submitted to it in good faith ... perhaps because I was so ... instructed by Laurel and Hardy during my childhood.... I find it natural to discuss life without ever mentioning love. It does not seem important to me.[23]

The optimum word for Vonnegut's take on Laurel and Hardy is their innate decency in the face of absurdity. Even when the couple's instinctive courtliness is pushed to anger, another McCarey-authored mannerly sketch kicks in. Often referred to as a deferential "tit for tat" routine, the duo politely take turns with their adversary in administering comic carnage. In fact, such a courteous form of vexation constitutes yet another degree of absurdity. In contrast, absurdity weighs more heavily on Yossarian because while he has Laurel and Hardy's instinctive morality, his greater intelligence makes it difficult for him to be distracted by abominations from life's trivialities. Moreover, besides the "catch–22" anxiety-danger this produces, Yossarian's civility creates other threats. For instance, when Nately is killed on an absurdly pointless mission (compounded by being a victim of a twisted form of friendly fire), Yossarian attempts to do the right thing by telling "Nately's whore" (Gina Rovere) what happened. Suddenly Arkin's character is caught in a game of "kill the messenger," with the prostitute eventually stabbing him in the back, though the movie does not initially make the attacker's identity clear.

One could list innumerable examples of *Catch–22* absurdity, but the signature anti-war example involves Yossarian doing a favor for Gilford's "Doc" Daneeka. Unknowingly, a family has arrived too late to see their dying son, and Doc wants Yossarian to substitute for the lad. When Arkin's bombardier protests that the flyer's relatives will recognize he is not their boy, Gilford's character, who is sentimental about parents yet cynically insightful about the absurdity of war, tells Yossarian, in the words of Heller, "one dying boy is just as good as any other, or just as bad ... all dying boys are equal."[24] Sometimes absurdity can be touched by a poignant truthfulness, like traditional American humor's "wise fool," whose gibberish is sometimes sprinkled with wisdom.

H. Wayne Schuth's study of Mike Nichols would prefer to interpret the dying flyer scene as a Yossarian dream, in order to explain why parents would not recognize their son.[25] Yet, this is too much an "old school" elucidation of the sequence, *à la* Luis Buñuel and Salvador Dali's pioneering surrealistic dark comedy *Andalusian Dog* (1929). At this late date there is no reason to wrap cinematic absurdity in any kind of reverie or trance.

Even before black humor moved to center stage during the chaotic 1960s, the genre's showcasing of absurdity via the dream or the nightmare had become the day-to-day norm. One need only turn on the news. However, if forced to critique a *Catch–22* sequence as a not-to-be-believed dream absurdity, the logical choice would be the film's conclusion. Yossarian has decided not to take his commanders' sell-out offer to go home in return for praising their ludicrous leadership. Instead, he joyfully jumps out of a hospital window, runs to the nearby sea and, in order to escape the war, begins paddling to Sweden in a rubber dinghy! This over-the-top happy ending, bolstered by upbeat John Philip Sousa music played by a marching band on the base runway, has metaphorically jumped the tracks of reality. Dark comedies normally end with a scary finality, *à la* the close of *Dr. Strangelove,* or with such an exaggeratedly ecstatic conclusion the filmmaker is satirically saying, "This will never happen." Groundbreaking examples of the latter would include the orange grove paradise W.C. Fields slaps on the end of *It's a Gift* (1934), or Preston Sturges' miraculous finale to the aptly titled *Miracle of Morgan's Creek* (1944). In modern dark comedy, Yossarian's exit could be compared to Terry Gilliam's dazzling euphoric close to *Brazil* (1985, described at the time as "*1984* on acid"). Regardless, *Brazil's* dark comedy anti-hero (Jonathan Pryce) only ends up exhilarated because it is all in his mind, having reached the proverbial "mad as a hatter" category. His lunacy gives him the gloriously ironic illusion that he is escaping. The same scenario could be applied to Yossarian.

If *Catch–22's* dying boy sequence is the picture's ultimate moving scene, the most disturbingly ongoing situation involves "Doc" Daneeka's identity being linked to McWatt's suicide crash, after accidentally slicing Kid Sampson in half. "Doc" "hated to fly [and] felt imprisoned in an airplane."[26] Yet, Gilford's character needed time in the air each month to qualify for flight pay. Accordingly, an arrangement with McWatt had been made to put "Docs'" name on the flight log whenever he was airborne. Unfortunately, when McWatt flew his plane into a mountain, "Doc" technically died, too, since he was listed as onboard. Hence, for the rest of the film "Doc" is essentially invisible, with people mourning his passing, even when he is standing next to them. This is an absurd exaggeration, yet in today's forever proliferating bureaucracy, is it really? For example, "identity theft" has become a cottage industry, and Heaven forbid if you lose a credit card or someone obtains your Social Security number. Like "Doc," one might just as well be invisible. You are equal parts computer chip and flesh and blood—one might define it as a new variation on being a "clockwork orange."

Even "Docs'" absurdity dilemma comes full circle back to Yossarian's decency parallels with Laurel and Hardy. It was Arkin's character who persuaded McWatt to put "Doc" on his flight log. Yossarian, like Stan and Ollie, had not only done the dependable thing and failed, he made things worse. Again, in this dark comedy world of absurdity, honorable intervention proves a liability. Ironically, this is one more way, though inadvertently, that the institution of religion fails modern man. Every major creed preaches some form of "Do onto others," yet people are more likely to follow the dark comedy creed of Paul Muni's title character gangster in *Scarface* (1932): "Do it first, do it yourself, and keep on doing it."

This is a natural segue to dark comedy's third crucial theme—man as beast. Though this overlaps with the genre's two other key suppositions, the omnipresence of death and absurdity, examples of man at his most frightening abound in *Catch–22.* And that is the point, in part, of the more complex 1970s dark comedies. Pioneering works of the genre often suggested the pervasiveness and/or possibilities of universal evil, yet the phenomenon tended to fixate on a charismatic offender, such as Chaplin's title character in *Monsieur Verdoux*, or Dennis Price's avenging Duke of Chalfont in *Kind Hearts and Coronets* (1949). In fact, in the latter film, one might even call Price's character a semi-title character, since the film's name is derived from a line of Lord Tennyson's poem "Lady Clara Vere de Vere" (1842): "'Tis only noble to be good. Kind hearts are more [rare] than Coronets...."[27] Regardless, in a novel-film such as *Catch-22*, despicable men stumble over themselves.

The assortment of depraved types from Nichols' adaptation of *Catch-22* might range from Jon Voight's "war as big business" Milo Minderbinder to Charles Grodin's rapist-murderer Aarfy Aardvark. Voight's character is frightening because he does not even recognize the nefarious, fascist-like nature of what he is doing. Milo merely represents an ugly variation of the capitalistic Yankee go-getter. Fundamentally, what could be more American? Heller has Milo state, "The business of government [whatever its activities] *is* business. [President] Calvin Coolidge said that ... so it must be true."[28] In contrast, Grodin's figure realizes the heinous nature of his crimes but does them because he knows he can. His Aarfy also compartmentalizes his actions, *à la* a Jekyll and Hyde, because for the majority of the movie he seems to be a cultured patriarchal figure. One could argue their natures are in their names. Voight's Minderbinder sounds like "mindbender," someone whose profit margin mentality depends upon, to quote a later John Lennon song-

Catch-22's extreme opposites: Jon Voight's Minderbinder (left) cashed in on war as big business. And Anthony Perkins' chaplain was lost and unneeded.

album, playing *Mind Games* (1973). And Grodin's beastly side is reinforced by having an animal name, despite its comic sound: the aardvark.

The aardvark–Grodin character connection has a coincidentally darker fitting link to the aforementioned black humorist Will Cuppy, given that the satirist's nature of skewering human behavior under the guise of natural history –short tongue-in-cheek animal essays or "studies." Moreover, in one collection of these pieces, whose title *How to Tell Your Friends from the Apes* foreshadows *Catch–22*'s message that humanity is not to be trusted, there is a book-closing critique of the aardvark, as if to suggest being especially wary of a creature with such an innocuous-sounding name. And keep in mind that Grodin's character was seemingly the least likely of the *Catch–22* cast to commit a rape-murder, with his justification for the latter act being to keep the victim from saying bad things about him.[29] With that in mind, listen to Cuppy's description of the aardvark:

> Of their mental operations it would be kinder to say nothing. They have lucid intervals and certain beliefs which cannot be gone into here.... They are afraid of being laughed at or sneered at.... We could do without Aardvarks.... The N'jemps [tribe] of Legumukum have a popular saying, "Don't be an Aardvark."[30]

This is not to suggest that Heller borrowed the name from Cuppy; it is merely an interesting coincidence that a best-selling dark comedy humorist whose fans included President Dwight David Eisenhower and Edward R. Murrow (who read Cuppy essays over the air at CBS) was an influential satirist when Heller was preparing *Catch–22*. Nonetheless, in any final analysis of Milo and Aarfy's evil, there is at least a transparency to Milo's demonic nature, while the only possible protection from Aarfy's unexpected maliciousness would necessitate warning subtitles swirling about his head.

Despite these Milo and Aarfy parameters, *Catch–22* provides an even more monstrous duo. It comes in the form of Yossarian's two supervisors, Martin Balsam's Colonel Cathcart and Buck Henry's punningly titled Colonel Korn. Whereas Milo and Aarfy were about destroying individuals, these two other Yossarian adversaries wanted something worse—to *defeat* him. That is, the only way Arkin's character could get out of flying more missions was a two-part arrangement. What follows is the core of the part Balsam and Henry's characters proposed:

> COLONIAL KORN [speaking to Yossarian]: All you have to do is be our pal.
> COLONEL CATHCART: Say nice things about us.
> COLONEL KORN: Tell the folks at home what a good job we're doing. Take our offer, Yossarian.
> COLONEL CATHCART: Either that or a court-martial for desertion.

It is one thing to be diplomatically agreeable at home about the war effort, but the "be our pal" portion of the contract smacks of the disturbing close to George Orwell's *1984* (1949), in which the totalitarian "Big Brother" wants rebel protagonist Winston Smith to be a pal, too. While *1984*'s double whammy of defeat and destruction occurs at the close ("[Smith] had won the victory over himself. He loved Big Brother"), a more troubling summary arises earlier in the text: "We do not merely destroy our enemies; we change them."[31]

Everyone is eventually destroyed by death, but to maintain a quintessential principle against all odds is the only modest victory you wrest from life. This is one request too much for Yossarian. *Catch–22*'s happy (wink wink) conclusion is yet another example of a dark comedy anti-hero's personal victory only being a fantasized one. This explanation is in the Orwellian spirit of what Heller had in mind for Yossarian's interrogation scenes. However, the author confesses to having drawn this similarly disconnecting scenario from an actual American moment of infamy—the communist witch-hunting of the 1950s:

> The thing that inspired [Yossarian's problem] was the congressional hearings that were going on then [during the book's gestation span]—this was the period of [Senator Joseph] McCarthy and the House Un-American Activities Committee [causing Hollywood black-listing]. We had state committees as well as loyalty oaths. [And] Kafka's *The Trial* was [also] very much present [too]. It's [the waiting and] the idea of being charged with something and not knowing what it is....[32]

Again, being inclusive of such mutinous mandates broadens the satirical foundation of these many-sided 1970s dark comedy films, especially given that *Catch-22* was published in 1961, years before the Vietnam conflict polarized society. While this American New Wave–influenced black humor was also impacted by the earlier French New Wave (including making self-awareness of the camera another movie character), the former cinema development encompassed a more sweeping anti-establishment base, given its frequent literary foundation. Thereby with *Catch-22*, the "Hell no, we won't go to war" generation had more pre-existing artistic fodder for the anti–Vietnam crusade. These previous travesties, such as nuanced dangers of McCarthyism in both *MASH* and *Catch-22*, provided further corroboration for the insurrectionary early 1970s. Moreover, the veteran iconoclasts upped the ante when they joined this later irreverence. Here is Heller on the anti–Vietnam War movement, in 1970:

> I am in total sympathy with the students. I think indifference and stupidity of the government administration has made it necessary to move from peaceful dissent to acts of violence. I hold the [Nixon] administration guilty, [President] Nixon and [Vice President] Agnew particularly guilty for the shooting at Kent State [where four non-violent student protester were killed by the National Guard]. Agnew has been inciting to riot in every speech he makes; they are almost paraphrases of the Nazi speeches of Germany ... the "rotten apples" that have to be separated from our society.... I think that any other course than this [violence] at this time would result in a loss of freedom in this society. The war is illegal....[33]

Again, to better connect art with history is to know the artist's perspective on the work and/or its repercussions.

Both *Catch-22* the novel and the film initially met with distinctly mixed reviews. There were two *New York Times* critiques of the book, in back-to-back issues. On October 22, 1961, a review with the punningly apt title "Bombs Away" stated, "*Catch-22* has much passion, comic and ferment, but it gasps for want of craft and sensibility...."[34] The very next day another reviewer opined, "Wildly original, brilliantly comic, brutally gruesome, it is a dazzling performance that will probably outrage nearly as many readers as it delights."[35] Heller shared in his 1998 memoir:

> There were reviews that were good, a good many that were mixed, and there were reviews that were very bad, very bad, almost venomously spiteful, one might be tempted to say (and I am the one that says it).... [For example,] *The New Yorker* [critic] decided "...Heller wallows in his own laughter and finally drowns in it."[36]

Sure enough, "Heller remained bitter about the reception of *Catch-22* to the end, remembering too many of the slights that go with the job, the bad reviews, the slow fuse of appreciation...."[37]

Along similar lines, Nichols' *Catch–22* received the most disparate of reviews. Two earlier noted critiques gauged the range in their titles, from the *New York Times'* heading, "A Triumphant *Catch*" to *The Hollywood Reporter's* label, "*Catch–22* Brilliant Bits; Cynical and Bitterly Cold."[38] *Newsweek* magazine's patently diverse review with wannabe positive observations perceptively commented on the added adaptation difficulty in separating *Catch–22* the novel from the film:

> If American movie audiences in 1961 [when the novel was published] weren't ready to hear that war was idiocy, that patriotism was bullcrap and that profit was a stronger sustaining principle than principle, neither were American moviemakers ready to solve the artistic problems of putting such a book on the screen [in 1970].[39]

The *New York Times'* Vincent Canby addressed this literary-related complexity which makes these blackest-of-the-black 1970s dark comedies harder to scrutinize when he wrote that an existential work like *Catch–22* "makes underground literary critics out of men who, when they signed on for their jobs, thought that all they had to do was to sit in the dark, facing forward, with their eyes propped open."[40]

Moreover, it was even difficult to keep Heller quotes and/or references out of *Catch–22* film reviews. The preeminent example of this occurs in *Time* magazine's positive rambling, *à la Catch–22*, critique of the picture, which also exhibits more illustrations of the added difficulty deciphering these New Age black comedies: "I [Heller] wrote it during the Korean War and aimed it for the one [Vietnam] after that."[41] Though this is evocative of *MASH* using the Korean War as a platform against the Vietnam conflict, the *Time* piece notes other Heller institutional targets, from General Motors' "Engine Charlie" Wilson to the Cold War.[42] Indeed, Heller's memoir even added "Babbittry"—that narrow-minded, self-satisfied society associated with Sinclair Lewis' *Babbitt*, his 1922 satirical novel of middle-class America—to *Catch–22's* list of targets.[43]

Like Heller's earlier comments on the scope of negative reviews for the novel, Nichols' picture also had some "very bad" notices, such as Roger Ebert's *Chicago Sun-Times* comment, "Mike Nichols' *Catch–22* is a disappointment ... he tells us war is evil and causes human suffering. We already know all that; we knew it from every other war movie ever made."[44] And there were "venomously spiteful" reviews, too, like *Variety's* observation, "The [film's] resultant artistic sludge is ... a downer from start to finish."[45] *Variety* did, however, admit the film might receive a box office response "from the under–30 [anti-war] audience," which it did.[46] The majority of the pundits gave the highest kudos to Arkin, with *Newsweek*[47] being the most eloquent:

> Its [*Catch–22*] most valid claim to greatness is Alan Arkin's performance as Yossarian. Incredible demands are made on Arkin to play an impossible mix of styles and attitudes but he fulfills them all. He's in acute pain as the only man who notices that there's a war going on and that live people are being made dead under deplorable circumstances ... [There's a signature scene when] Yossarian impersonates a dying soldier for someone else's mother, father and brother, and they never notice that he's a stranger. At moments such as these the insanity is miraculously intact.[48]

This is one of the film's two defining scenes, a close second to Yossarian's eventual realization of Snowden's fate, with Arkin's ineffably haunting response to the dying man-child—the tenderly repeated, "There, there." I am reminded of a description once applied to another performance in a review aptly titled "After Darkness": "[There was] a civil war inside him. Though he strives to be self-contained, the container keeps leaking...."[49]

In Heller's daughter Erica's biography of her father, *Yossarian Slept Here* (2011), she shared how Nichols had arranged a private screening for Heller's family. In a theater off Times Square they were greeted by Nichols, and then a rather dramatic viewing arrangement ensued after the novelist and director had a brief chat. Erica's father sat alone in the front row, Nichols stood in the back, and the Heller family sat somewhere in the middle:

> My father was uncustomarily nervous. Although Buck Henry had written the screenplay, this was still Dad's baby, and he was about to see whether it had made it across [filmland's] Santa Monica Freeway in one piece.... When the lights came back on, my father sat and conferred with Nichols. He looked relieved: the patient would live. On the cab ride home, Dad started to cry. He was so elated, he put two Stim-U-Dents [plaque removers, instead of gum] in his mouth by mistake.[50]

In an article at the time, Heller further fleshed out the experience:

> "I was prepared not to like the movie. It's a matter of vanity. My feeling is that complex novels don't make good movies...." When the screening was over, Mr. Heller got up and saw Mr. Nichols heading out of the theater and he figured that Nichols figured that Mr. Heller did not like what he had done to his book. "I caught up with him and took him by the arm and said I guess maybe it's the best movie I ever saw." That broke the ice and we [all] went out and had a sandwich.[51]

Heller even suggested Nichols had improved upon the text. For example:

> At the end of the movie, Yossarian goes out in the ocean, with a little paddle and a [tiny] rubber raft, to [attempt the impossible and to] row to Sweden. That's not in the book but it's exactly the effect I tried to create with the ending of the novel. Nichols was not trying to make an easy commercial movie. I was very glad that he didn't go for an easy froth of comedy and sex [like *MASH*?]. He went for the somber parts of *Catch–22*. I never thought of *Catch 22* as a comic novel....[52]

Heller's serious close to these thoughts are reminiscent of a *Time* review line applied to *MASH* which always seemed more applicable to *Catch–22*: "'And if I laugh at any mortal thing, / Tis that I may not weep,' wrote Byron. That philosophical fragment accounts for the duality of all black farce; looking between the cracks, one catches glimpses of hell."[53]

Within a year of its publication, Heller's book was a money tree which was forever green. Moreover, revisionist criticism soon canonized it as a 20th century magnum opus. Nichols' adaptation, even with Heller's praise, was a major box office disappointment, given its huge budget—$20 million ($120 million in 2015 dollars) versus film rentals of $12,250,000.[54] In contrast, *MASH*'s minuscule budget garnered $36,720,000 in rental fees.[55] Consequently, while *Catch–22*'s turnstile numbers were actually respectable for the period, parent studio Paramount took a financial bath. Also, in contrast to Heller's novel, Nichols' adaptation has yet to experience the prompt pivot to seminal status. That being said, the film immediately developed a cult following, which has continued to grow.

Still, why the slow appreciation of the movie? First, one must expand upon a previously suggested axiom, "To whom much is given much is expected."[56] Only in his late thirties, Nichols had already become an award-winning juggernaut, having won a Grammy for Best Comedy Album (*An Evening with Mike Nichols and Elaine May* 1961, a recording of their 1960 Broadway debut of the same name; see following chapter); Nichols had three Tonys for Best Director (*Barefoot in the Park*, 1964; *The Odd Couple*,

1965; and *Plaza Suite*, 1968), and the Best Director Oscar for *The Graduate*. Consequently, several critics felt that even with such a difficult book to adapt, magician Nichols would pull it off. And when they panned the movie it was more of a pan of the director. This development is best represented by Ebert's critique:

> [Nichols] fails to do justice to the Heller novel. That was almost inevitable, I guess; there was something of a juggling act in Heller's eccentric masterpiece ... which took him seven years of rewriting to get all the pieces in the air at the same time. For Nichols to pull off the same trick ... [with] so many more pieces than a novel, looked impossible. Still, I thought Nichols would pull [it] off....[57]

As the scatological satirist Nathanael West has taught us in novels like *Miss Lonelyhearts* (1933) and *The Day of the Locust* (1939), there is another darker side to viewers and critics, knocking a work besides expecting more from the artist. Sometimes peo-

Mike Nichols, renaissance man.

ple seem to enjoy tearing down, after a point, the very successful, whether the virtuoso stumbled or not. For example, even before Nichols' *Catch–22*, the usually sensitive Oscar-winning writer William Goldman performed such a number on Nichols. In Goldman's *The Season: A Candid Look at Broadway* (1969), penned a year prior to the release of Nichols' *Catch–22*, the multi-talented writer simply sandbags the director. Even his essay title on Nichols, "Culture Hero," hints at the iconoclasm which follows.[58] Substantial success just breeds loathing, as the notable Chicago columnist cynic Mike Royko once wrote: "Hating the Yankees is as American as pizza, unwed mothers and cheating on your income tax."[59]

A second reason for the slow recognition of Nichols' *Catch–22* can be derived from some perceptive paradoxical praise of the novel:

> What I think most of us who love *Catch–22* love most is precisely what, from a Flaubertian [forerunner of naturalism] position, is wrong with it. Its looseness, its unruliness, its extravagance ... its emotional waywardness, its impatience with the niceties ... its devil-may-care clumsiness, its hysteria, its tomfoolery, its brutality ... [and] its *apparent* form-lessness.[60]

That quote might also have italicized "tomfoolery" in examining any complaint about "formlessness." There is a general tone to many *Catch-22* reviews, as well as most films examined in this text (especially see the following chapter on *Little Big Man*, 1970), that narrative "looseness" is from broad vaudeville-like humor mixed with tragedy. Yet, that mingling was a major reason for the earlier commentary on *Waiting for Godot*! Black humor and life—a clear redundancy—*is* an amalgamation of unsubtle humor and dead seriousness. *New Yorker* critic John Lahr championed this in *Notes on a Cowardly Lion*, his inspired 1969 biography of his Estragon-playing father Bert Lahr: "He lived with silences; his understanding of language was commensurate with Beckett's precise, philosophical use of it. His appreciation of the playful potential of words went back to his burlesque days and his use of the malaprop[ism]...."[61]

As Oscar-winning actor Colin Firth once described his take on life, "You're a bit part in [an unstructured] farce. You're not the star of some big tragedy. If you lose your sense of the absurd, you're likely to become miserable."[62] Instead of complaining about a disordered chronicle, one might best embrace the expression "beautiful confusion," used to described the narrative of Federico Fellini's meandering masterpiece *8½* (1963), one of Nichols' favorite films.[63] Indeed, if *Catch-22*'s director had gone a smaller black-and-white avant-garde route, *à la 8½*, this adaptation of Heller's novel would have immediately been an art house hit ... a standing towards which its current cult status now leans. Moreover, to many reviewers, like *Variety*'s Arthur D. Murphy, whose negative critique had all guns smoking, *Catch-22*'s huge budget needed to be equated with the most linear of storylines.[64] *Little Big Man* director Arthur Penn would catch the same sort of flack on his expensive, serpentine epic. It was almost as if formlessness was only okay for modestly priced sleepers like *MASH*.

Another rationale for the delayed acknowledgment of the unique qualities of Nichols' *Catch-22* is a paradoxical link to the previous complaint: The movie's only praise was sometimes credited to just being a partial compendium of the novel's best bits. For instance, the *New Yorker* critic felt the film was only successful as it related to Heller, "who invented Yossarian."[65] Yet, if the film's just delineated disjointedness was a major problem in 1970, how can the same "formlessness" of the novel have, by that time, been bestowed with pantheon status? Moreover, there is added irony in the fact that the Henry script has made the story more accessible to the *Catch-22* fan by further interweaving Yossarian into the individual character studies. No, the real reason for this early deflection of the picture seemingly not receiving kudos beyond the novel's superlative sequences gets to the heart of these complicated modern comedies. Specifically, just as earlier critics often had difficulty just grasping the concept of black comedy, 1970s reviewers were often incapable of fully comprehending the genre's almost impenetrable evolution. As communicated in the prologue, this was one of the sparks for this text.

Dark humor-shock comedy, by its very nature, must become increasingly disturbing and convoluted. Accordingly, that is the rationale for these films often having multi-genre smokescreens, as well as one or more of these camouflaging genres going rogue with their quintessional components. Furthermore, as to Nichols' *Catch-22* being merely Heller's greatest hits, nothing could be more erroneous. Yes, some of the novel's comic nightmares are repeated, such as the essential routine of Yossarian doubling as the dying flyer. But there is such an epic comedy-tragedy mosaic of Heller material that Nichols and Henry were able to reconstitute their own dark comedy collage, including the seemingly exuberant freaky false ending admired by Heller himself.

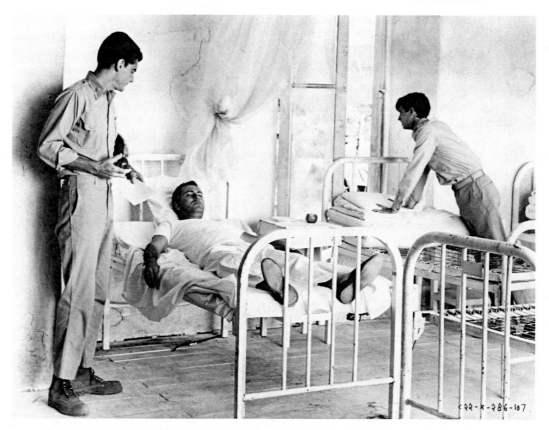

Shortly before Yossarian's (Alan Arkin, center) happy ending which was all in his mind, with Richard Benjamin (left) and Anthony Perkins.

Catch–22 is one of this study's intricate 1970s dark comedy films which did not fully receive the immediate critical and/or commercial commendation it deserved. Other examples include the pricey, epic adaptation of *Little Big Man*, and the almost invisible commercial screen presence of George Roy Hill's reconfiguration of Vonnegut's *Slaughterhouse-Five* (1972). Yet they all share an observation made by period photojournalist Diane Arbus, whose work was "characterized as blackly comic."[66] Committing suicide the year after *Catch–22*, Arbus had said that all life was bizarre "if you [took the time to] scrutinize reality close enough, or if some way you really really get to it...."[67] Arbus obviously got too close, while Yossarian either had a happy unhinging, or bizarre catharsis.

For this writer, the *Catch–22* screen version honored the novel. As with Altman and Lardner's *MASH*, Heller's solid if loopy novel enabled Nichols and Henry an excellent foundation from which to further creatively riff. And while Altman denigrated the *MASH* novelist, it meant a great deal to Nichols that Heller enjoyed the adaptation.

An elephant-in-the-room factor briefly touched upon in the prologue merits addressing: that old bugaboo about only poorly adapted work makes for good movies, or as film professor/author J. Dudley Andrew states:

[Major film theorist Béla] Balázs counsels the adaptation of mediocre works which are more likely to have within them the possibility of cinematic transformation. [Balázs] can point to innumerable cheap novels and plays which have made magnificent films because the adaptor saw within them a truly cinematic subject....[68]

While Andrew and Balázs are academics focused upon artists, one could argue that the preceding quote is less a creative tip than a warning about avoiding the wrath of fans and aficionados who cry "Foul!" if anything is changed in the adaptation of a particularly popular work they admire. However, this text will continue to assert that in refashioning an exceptional novel, everyone can win if the moviemaker is an exceptional talent, too— in view of the fact that potentially even more new perspectives surface. Unaffectedly, one does not have to accept another stance but it will undoubtedly make the viewer re-examine his interpretation by having a new frame of reference. Both Heller and Nichols see *Catch-22* as meaning more than the insanity of war, with the novelist's positions already presented. In contrast, Nichols equated Yossarian's dilemma with how some Jews managed to survive Nazi concentration work camps—by drawing a line: "Beyond *this* point I will not go."[69] With Yossarian it meant no more bombing runs. Yet, in the Nichols milieu, decisions are often movie-ending dead ends, such as Yossarian's "escape" into a soothing insanity. Plus, some Nichols reality-based wrap-ups would range from the "what do we do now?" runaway couple (Dustin Hoffman and Katharine Ross) ending of *The Graduate*, to Meryl Streep's title character activist in *Silkwood* (1983) dying under suspicious circumstances on her way to share provocative evidence with a reporter.

With Nichols' Chicago-based entertainment beginnings, a fitting dark comedy close to this chapter might again return to Mike Royko: "The Chicago Cubs, like life itself, are a losing cause. That's why we have cemeteries. And Wrigley Field."[70]

3

Little Big Man (12/15/70)

> When Old Lodge Skins (Chief Dan George) does not succeed in willing his own death at the movie's end, he tells his surrogate grandson Little Big Man–Jack Crabb (Dustin Hoffman), "Am I still in the world? I was afraid of that. Well, sometimes the magic works, sometimes it doesn't."

Following *MASH* and *Catch–22*, director Arthur Penn's *Little Big Man* was the third film adaptation of an episodic anti-war novel to appear on 1970 movie screens. Drawn from Thomas Berger's Mark Twain–like panoramic revisionistic look at the American West, the film's near-culmination is the genre's most high-profile event, short of the Gunfight at the O.K. Corral: the 1876 Battle of the Little Bighorn. The narrator of this rambling, picaresque tale is the 121-year-old Jack Crabb, allegedly the sole white survivor of the aforementioned battle, though his life has had him alternately living with Indians and settlers. Once again an anti–Vietnam War message is an intrinsic part of the film, though the Western facade at first might seem to distance it more than the Korean and World War II backdrops of the other two-thirds of this 1970s trilogy, *MASH* and *Catch–22*. Ironically, however, *Little Big Man* quickly becomes much more than a subtextual visceral attack on America's involvement in Southeast Asia. For example, *The New Yorker* observed:

> The massacres of the helpless Indians on the screen are, of course, like the massacres of Vietnamese villagers and this makes a powerful emotional connection ... [Penn uses] the violence to stand in for a demostration that white Americans have been racists throughout history....[1]

In a *Positif* interview shortly after the film's release, director Penn bluntly seconds this verdict, as well as underscoring the significance of Berger's gift:

> *Little Big Man* is a film about genocide. As for Berger's humor, I'd say it's a confirmation of his talent. You get the feeling that his novel was written with a scalpel. In order to tell the story of genocide he had to use sharp wit, something we emphasized in the film.... But in addition to genocide Americans did something more than just kill. What's even sadder is that they also signed treaties. They pretended to be honest and claimed they could be trusted, and made deals along the lines of "As long as grass shall grow ... and the sky be blue, this land shall be yours."[2]

This chronicle of lies has even resulted in a phrase entering the American language two centuries before, to be an "Indian giver"—someone who gives gifts and later wants them back. One could argue it rates inclusion with other expressions at home in dark comedy, such as Joseph Heller's "Catch–22" and Kurt Vonnegut's "and so it goes."

Penn had another motive for doing *Little Big Man*. He wanted to demolish the Native Indian myths perpetuated for years by American pop culture. Even a year before the film's release, in an interview entitled *"Little Big Man*: History Rewritten," the director said, "One thing this film will do is show the Indian's side in the West. There has been so much [negative] nonsense about the Indian in Westerns that it's time someone showed how he was wronged by history."[3]

Soon after the movie's opening, in an interview for *L'Express*, Penn elaborated on this righting of the West with regard to myths about whites in general:

> The cowboys, the hired killers, and the well-meaning priests we see in most Westerns never really existed. For Indians back then substitute the Vietnamese today. The younger generation is tired of us not addressing their issues. *Little Big Man* speaks to those people who want to know why America is always lying to them.[4]

For "the younger generation," of which I was then a part, this was once again more anti-establishment validation from a prominent older artist, *à la* the previous chapters' Robert Altman and Mike Nichols. If Penn's perspective seems extreme, he himself might have fallen back for substantiation from Hollywood's definitive cowboy during its golden age, Gary Cooper. A year before the actor's death, entertainment columnist and author Joe Hyams wrote:

> [Cooper] told me in an interview that the only Western he'd ever do again was something with historical value. "I doubt anyone will want to make that kind of picture.... The public has been fed a false concept of the West for so long I don't think they'll accept anything authentic.... Youngsters growing up today have no real concept of American history from 1850 to 1900."[5]

Karl Malden in the foreground of the game-changing *Cheyenne Autumn* (1964), linking the bluecoats' massacre of Native Americans to the Holocaust.

Four years after Cooper's comments, John Ford, the acclaimed Western director who was responsible for more movie Indian deaths than anyone else in Hollywood history, also did an about-face when he made the history-based *Cheyenne Autumn* (1964). Said film focuses upon the title tribe's tragic death march back to their original settlement after being relocated by the often brutal American cavalry. By making one of the officers a murderous German American (Karl Malden), Ford is suggesting that the massacre of the American Indians be equated with World War II's Holocaust. Fittingly, this Western addressing American genocide greatly influenced Penn, with the director also further broadening the scope of racist American, *vis-à-vis Little Big Man*, by stating in a *Films and Filming* interview that this "early history with the Indians [could also be] carried forward now in the case of the blacks [and slavery]."[6]

The film's gender-bending anti-genre ingredients—the camouflaging of the black humor—warrant examination. One must begin with the anti–Western aspects of the picture. The pioneering Rosetta Stone of Western narratives remains John G. Cawelti's *The Six-Gun Mystique*, published the year after *Little Big Man*'s release.[7] Cawelti's study maps numerous sagebrush scenarios, from the obvious, such as the outlaw plot and the marshal story, to the more multi-faceted communication-transportation tale, including yarns involving wagon trains, stagecoaches, the Pony Express, stringing telegraph lines, and building the transcontinental railroad. Yet, arguably, the signature Western type is the cavalry vs. Indian saga. Thus, what makes *Little Big Man*'s anti-genre blitzing of the Western so provocative is both taking on this long-honored narrative, and so completely turning it into a 180-degree example of topsy-turvy–dom. Prior to Penn's film, the American cavalry, after their crushing Battle of the Little Bighorn defeat, had been overwhelmingly venerated in saving the West from the savage Native Americans; this included deifying General George Armstrong Custer, who died with all his command at said battle. Probably the most romanticized Hollywood take on this massacre was *They Died with Their Boots On* (1941), with a flamboyant Errol Flynn playing Custer. Yet, regardless of Custer, soldier blue cavalry stories were usually bathed in idealized, even sentimentalized hues. There were occasional cracks in this veneer. For instance, in Glenn Frankel's fascinating study *The Searchers: The Making of an American Legend* (2013), he notes the bipolar nature of Ford's famous Cavalry Trilogy, in which *Fort Apache* (1948, with Henry Fonda playing a glorified yet unsympathetic Custer-like character) and *She Wore a Yellow Ribbon* (1949) showed respect and even admiration for some of the Indian characters. By contrast, *Rio Grande* (1950) was riddled with racism."[8]

In the 1950s there were so many Westerns on TV that Bob Hope joked about brushing the hay off his set before turning it on. Uplifting cavalry tales were front and center; they included *Boots and Saddles* (1957–1958) and my favorite, *The Adventures of Rin Tin Tin* (1954–1959), about a small boy orphaned in an Indian raid, who was then adopted, with his dog, by the cavalry at Fort Apache, Arizona. According to TV historians Tim Brooks and Earle Marsh, *Rin Tin Tin* was full of violent action, "including gunfights, rampaging Indians, and the like."[9] Even today, popular British history–oriented comedian Eddie Izzard enjoys using the old metaphor about the "American cavalry riding to the rescue" to help win World War II.

Regardless, *Little Big Man* was quite the iconoclastic statement when it had audiences rooting for Old Lodge Skin's tribe, "the Human Beings," against Custer and his men. *Little Big Man*, with groundbreaker dramas like *Cheyenne Autumn* and *Soldier Blue* (1970), asked viewers, via its anti-genre, anti–Western format, to completely change teams.

Little Big Man also radically expanded the anti-establishment playing field for young adults like myself. Whereas *MASH* and *Catch–22* took on the anti-war status quo in a generalized manner, Penn's film more pointedly suggested specific troubling period events, such as the 1968 My Lai Massacre in Vietnam and the 1969–1971 Occupation of Alcatraz by the group of Indians of All Tribes. The former horrific incident, often considered the most appalling episode of a heinous war, involved the mass murder of between 300 and 500 unarmed South Vietnam civilians (our allies) by U.S. Army soldiers. It provoked international disgust after it became public knowledge in late 1968.

My Lai was reminiscent of common U.S. cavalry genocide tactics during the frontier Indian Wars, when warriors were first lured away from unprotected Native American camps, a variation of which occurred in a Custer-led massacre of women and children at the Battle of Washita River in 1868. In contrast, the Occupation of Alcatraz pertains directly to Penn's aforementioned "Indian giver" lies. That is, 1868's Treaty of Fort Laramie promised the Sioux Tribe that all abandoned and/or surplus federal property would be returned to Native Americans. Since the Alcatraz Island penitentiary was essentially out-of-use federal land by 1963, Sioux activists decided to turn the occupation into a *cause célèbre* test care. Though the protesters would eventually be evicted peacefully, the civil rights–like action had a direct impact on both future federal Indian policy and Native American activism. Many celebrities, such as Jane Fonda and Marlon Brando, further fueled awareness by becoming involved. For a time Brando would be the main financial underwriter for A.I.M. (the American Indian Movement), as well as controversially declining his Best Actor Oscar for *The Godfather* (1972) with a statement which said, in part, "[The reason for this action is] the treatment of American Indians today by the film industry ... and on television in movie reruns and also with the recent [1973] happenings [Indian protests] at Wounded Knee."[10]

A second anti-genre smokescreen for *Little Big Man*'s dark comedy is the treatment of the picture as a spoof of the "profile film," a second cousin to the biography movie for critic-filmmaker Francois Truffaut. While there never was an actual Jack Crabb, Berger and Penn spin a quasi-autobiographical tale which is closer to the truth than found in many pre–1970 Western films. Berger and Penn then derail one's expectations for the profile picture with a healthy dose of Southwestern humor.

This branch of homegrown humor, born of the American frontier, has been defined by humor scholar John Gerber as a contrast with the New England "Uncle Sam" Yankee: The Southwesterner is amoral where the Yankee is moral, impractical where the Yankee is practical, shrewd as opposed to displaying Yankee common sense, interested in either upsetting the norm or moving on versus Yankee contentment, and suspicious of authority where the Yankee is trustful.[11]

This makes Crabb a second cousin to Mark Twain's Southwestern-influenced rough-and-tumble Huck Finn, with much humor also drawn from a search for freedom hiding behind comic physical discomfort, casual amorality and autobiographically plain but "wise fool" language. However, unlike many Southwestern figures, Huck and Jack are more likely to be the victims of frustration than its cause. Humor historian Walter Blair also emphasizes this figure's gutsy, often first-person vernacular English, including loads of local color.[12] A pivotal example of Jack echoing Huck occurs when Crabb leaves the Reverend and Mrs. Pendrake, after his first extended period with the Indians. Jack's letter explains, in part:

I got to go off now but it ain't your fault, for you been mighty kind. The trouble is I don't think I can ever be civilized ... for I can't get onto your ways, though I know they is the right ones.... I promise never to reveal my connection with you so you won't be disgraced.[13]

Compare this to Twain's close to *The Adventures of Huckleberry Finn*:

If I'd knowed what a trouble it was to make a book I wouldn't a tackled it and ain't a-going to no more. But I reckon I got to light out for the Territory ahead of the rest, because Aunt Sally she's going to adopt me and sivilize [sic] me and I can't stand it. I been there before.[14]

One could almost argue that Jack Crabb's misadventures out West constitute Huck's continuing saga after he left "out for the Territory." However, if this position is taken, one must admit the language perspective of Jack does embrace, at times, a more self-serving Southwestern humor approach to the world than Huck's humor. Of course, Twain's figure would no doubt have evolved in that direction, too, had he lived 121 years. Novelist Berger admits, "Crabb is not always uniform [in his speech], using 'brought' and 'brung,' say, or 'they was' and 'they were' interchangeably.... If he wishes, [Crabb will] speak well, and sometimes may only to elicit a gratuity. It is clear his habitual idiom is a product of self-awareness."[15]

Nonetheless, Crabb never approaches the sneaky nature of an American Southwestern figure like Johnson J. Hooper's much applauded Simon Suggs, whose favorite axiom was, "It is good to be shifty in a new country."[16] Crabb's perspective is more along the practical side of Will Rogers' title figure in the John Ford–directed *Judge Priest* (1934): "The first thing I learned in politics is when to say ain't."[17]

Both Jack and Huck learned young about hypocrisy, and each reluctantly embraced a principle (though it took Crabb 121 years)! Huck saved the runaway slave Jim, though by doing so he fully expected eternal damnation, since Southern preachers and federal law then dictated returning "property." Crabb's cause of frustration, like some of the comments already noted by Penn, was to set the Western record straight. For example, at the end of the novel, Berger has his character ask himself, "Why now?" Crabb's response essentially boils down to getting tired of how Indians were being portrayed on TV Western shows. "It gets on my nerves to see Indians being played by Italians, Russians, and the like ... [with] lumpy arms ... [and features] like gangsters.... [Before,] who would ever have believed me? But I am now too old to care. So if *you* don't, you can go to hell."[18]

Given this common ground between Berger's Crabb and Penn, is it any wonder that *Focus on Film* could extol how the director's adaptation has "astonishing fidelity to the sprawling density of the book's structure"?[19] This also once again underscores a basic theme of the text: A rich literary foundation greatly augmented the power of these more complex gender-bending dark comedies of the 1970s.

Penn was also on the same page with the Southwestern humor slant. He told one interviewer, "I don't think of this picture as a Western. It's more of a picaresque tale of one man's life on the frontier, told from an ironic point of few."[20] And the picaresque tale has so much in common with Southwestern humor, especially the meandering plot, and the satirically common first-person voice.

With these anti-genre uses of the Western and the profile picture as the thinnest of covers for *Little Big Man*'s inherent dark comedy nature, the latter genre basics once again merit perusal. The first crucial theme is death. As with *MASH* and *Catch-22*, *Little Big Man*'s frontier Indian Wars backdrop is a consummate setting for the pervasiveness of death. Yet, unlike the first two pictures, *Little Big Man* goes beyond the military victims of battle. Penn's picture probes the civilian casualties of war, what today's vernacular minimizes with phrases like "collateral damage" and "friendly fire." Moreover, he pushes the death envelope further by revealing how these civilians were not accidental fatalities but genocidal targets. As this mass murder context is probed, *Little Big Man* comes to have most in common with Kurt Vonnegut's *Slaughterhouse-Five* (1972). But whereas this latter picture scrutinizes the non-strategic 1945 firebombing destruction of a single city, Dresden, Germany, *Little Big Man* analyzes the attempted genocide of an entire race. (Interestingly, both Penn and Vonnegut were American soldiers caught in Germany's surprise Battle of the Bulge campaign in 1944 and 1945, which just preceded—helped precipitate?—Dresden's firestorm eradication.) Logically, Penn's wartime experiences are pertinent to death in his dark comedies:

> I saw enough violence during [World War II] to make me think it wasn't something we could ignore or sanitize. In those [movie] days there were rules from the Hays [censorship] office that said you couldn't have someone shoot a gun and someone else get hit in the same shot. There had to be a cut between. I thought the hell with that. Remember, this was during the [Vietnam] war we were watching on television. We were seeing young men in body bags ... [As with the TV coverage, my film] violence grew out of what was happening to [the tale's subjects]. The violence was never a central part of the story, unlike the work of people like [Quentin] Tarantino.[21]

Along related lines, *The Hollywood Reporter's Little Big Man* review praised a film "that looks like the 6 p.m. news footage of Vietnam."[22] Plus, as the TV coverage of the war escalated, there was an increased focus upon civilian victims, especially after the My Lai Massacre. CBS news anchor Walter Cronkite eventually introduced nightly "us versus them" body count screen graphics, which were interpreted in multiple ways. For example, since there were invariably more dead North Vietnam soldiers and/or allegedly collaborating citizens, conservatives could claim the U.S. was winning the war of attrition, especially because there were few conventional battles. In contrast, liberals could maintain CBS was pressuring the powers that be with a daily reminder of this war's horrific cost.

Penn's presentation of *Little Big Man* aped period TV reportage in its ever-expanding depiction of Indian women and children being killed. Indeed, despite what one critic described as the large-scale "terrifying realism [of] the massacre of the Indians," the film's most appalling death was the single shooting of Little Big Man–Crabb's poignantly named wife Sunshine (Amy Eccles) as she and her baby attempt to escape a senseless cavalry attack.[23]

As the censorship code essentially ended in the 1960s, allowing filmmakers like Penn to be more explicit with their depictions of death, there was often criticism suggesting they were exalting violent death. Penn best articulated his position in an interview almost exactly a year after *Little Big Man*'s release. Confessing his *need* to elevate violence, he argued it was never gratuitous but "only violence directed against brutality. My films themselves are never brutal... [Moreover,] life is violent."[24] In brief, Penn attempted to attach a satirical social meaning to the randomness of the violence and death in his movies, while the aforementioned Tarantino's modus operandi is to ratchet up these erratic acts without any message. For instance, in his signature dark comedy *Pulp Fiction* (1994), there is a sequence in which John Travolta's hit man accidentally shoots an off-screen character in the face. The causal shock effect response to the incident is more typical of black humor's indiscriminate "and so it goes" attitude, *à la* the *Catch–22* scene in

The title character in *Little Big Man* (Dustin Hoffman) and Sunshine (Amy Eccles).

which Hungry Joe is unexpectedly cut in half by a plane. Nevertheless, Penn walks a thin line between satire and pure black humor nihilism, and *Little Big Man* is equally laced with the latter, too, such as the comically senseless demise of Wild Bill Hickok (Jeff Corey).

Getting beyond the actual death scenes, Old Lodge Skins best expresses the clash between the two cultures which invites the subject of genocide. When Dustin Hoffman's title character asks him if he hates the white man, Chief Dan George's Old Lodge Skins responds, in part:

> The Human Beings [his tribe], my son, they believe everything is alive. Not only man and animals. But also water, earth, stone.... That is the way things are. But the white man, they believe *everything* is dead. Stone, earth, animals. And people! Even their own people! If things keep trying to live, white man will rub them out. That is the difference.

These words become more prophetic daily, especially now as applied to the environment and killing Earth. Not surprisingly, however, Old Lodge Skins' thoughts lead to the inevitable dark comedy question, "to be or not to be." Thus, when Little Big Man asks Old Lodge Skins why he wants to die, the character responds with touching "Human Being" irony: "Because there is no other way to deal with the white man, my son.... There is a limitless supply of white men. But there has always been a limited number of Human Beings. We won today [at Little Bighorn but] ... we won't win tomorrow."

In Berger's novel, Little Big Man–Crabb expresses his own distressing take on the deadly white world when he once again pinballs from the Human Being tribe back to "civilization":

> There was already so many white men around Laramie you could hardly breathe, and I didn't sleep well in them rectangular barracks, on account of having been trained by [Indians] to favor the circular dwelling. I think I mentioned their feeling about circles, the circle of the earth and so on. They was set against the ninety-degree angle, which brought continuity [life] to a dead stop…. Now I was going back to a whole world of sharp corners….[25]

As academic author Brooks Landon observes, when Crabb–Little Big Man opens the novel with the claim, "'I am a white man and never forget it,' he refers to his personal curse more than to a matter of racial pride."[26] And the tall tale that follows is perfectly in line with that old adage about good fiction: "the lie that tells the truth."

Little Big Man's dark comedy use of death's omnipresence embraces one of the most primal theories of comedy: black humor by way of modern cinema shock. For instance, Penn's General Custer (Richard Mulligan) casually observes late in the movie, "Nothing in this world is more surprising than the attack without mercy." Naturally, there is nothing inherently new about stupefyingly designed acts of mass murder. For example, the Old Testament could double as history's first *CliffsNotes* guide to genocide. Yet the increasingly complex dark comedy mixes it with broad humor and constantly underlines that incredulity factor, from the aforementioned Custer comment, to Christian Slater's *Heathers* (1989) character observing, "The [deadly] extreme always seems to make an impression." Critics even try to fine-tune this surprise-shock syndrome, as demonstrated by the following *Variety* review excerpt on *Pulp Fiction*: "When [Tarantino] characters draw guns, as they so frequently do, one never knows if they're going to blow others' heads off, make funny speeches (they often do both), have the tables turned on them or make an honorable, peaceful exit."[27]

This "bolt from the blue" component makes an ideal segue to *Little Big Man*'s application of dark comedy's second paramount theme—absurdity. As with Joseph Heller's book *Catch-22* and Mike Nichols' screen adaptation, both *Little Big Man* the novel and film took some initial criticism for mixing the proverbial vaudevillian shtick with serious—to the point of death—material. For example, the *New York Times* critique of the novel, with its jokingly sad review title "Heaped Forked Tongue" (an inept attempt to capsulize its anti-mingling philosophy), suggested that one cannot blend "burlesque heroes [like] Old Lodge Skins … [who represents] the genuine article."[28] Along similar lines, *Variety* lambasted the film adaptation as "a sort of vaudeville show … loaded with sketches of varying degrees of serious and burlesque humor … climaxed by the…. Little Bighorn [battle]."[29] Yet Penn, like Nichols, was a fan of Samuel Beckett and the theater of the absurd (see previous chapter), and recognized that life is a bittersweet blend of buffoonery and gallows humor. Also, keep in mind that Penn's first job in television was holding cue cards for Milton Berle. No wonder Penn has said, "I see life as both tragic and comic. Making my films funny stops them from becoming too pedantic, which is why I like Beckett so much."[30]

Because the absurdity factor of both the print and screen versions of *Little Big Man* is so exceptionally rich, it is important to note *Focus on Film*'s observation, "Penn's film [is marked by] astonishing fidelity to the sprawling density of the book's structure…."[31] A gifted director has benefitted from adapting a strong work of fiction; one can now focus on the movie as a faithful variation of the original text. Of all the story's superlative examples of absurdity, potentially the most multifarious involves huckster Allardyce T. Merriweather (Martin Balsam). Both his diddling and dark comedy's low opinion of humanity are encapsulated in this dissertation upon the absurd extremes of gullibility: "Listen to me, a two-legged creature will believe anything, the more preposterous the better. Whales speak French at the bottom of the sea. The horses of Arabia have silver wings. Pygmies mate with elephants in darkest Africa. I have sold all those propositions...."

A second level of absurdity channeled through Merriweather takes a broader dark comedy perspective on his "trade." Con artist, confidence man, grifter, huckster, diddlers—whatever the name, the type has been around as long as there have been people.[32] In his comic 1844 essay on the phenomenon, "Diddling: Considered as One of the Exact Sciences," Edgar Allan Poe observes, "To diddle is [Man's] destiny.... This is his aim—his object—his end. Perhaps the first diddler was Adam."[33] Poe's work appears early in what might be called *the* huckster time and place: nineteenth-century America—the world of Merriweather. Literary historian Susan Kuhlmann ironically describes the era's con man as the "individualization of manifest destiny ... the belief that a free man may be whatever he claims he is (however absurd), may have whatever skills he can win."[34] Kuhlman goes on to suggest that the characteristics of these who "opened" our country—resourcefulness, adaptability, nomadic tendencies, and a desire to get ahead—also describe the con man. However, from a black humor perspective, might one not also describe American "Merriweatherism" as the catalyst for the preposterous stealing of the West and declaring genocide upon its original inhabitants? Moreover, while most cultures past and present have had confidence men, there is recognition, even outside this country, of nineteenth-century America's special affinity for this cockamamie con artist mentality.[35]

A third position of Merriweather absurdity involves his proclivity for ever-vanishing bits of his anatomy each time Crabb re-encounters him in this lengthy tale. *The New York Times* amusingly described him as the "patent-medicine salesman who loses parts of his body (an ear, a hand, a leg) the way other people lose small change."[36] (Eventually the whittling down of Merriweather also includes losing an eye and his scalp.) *Newsweek's* "How the West Was Lost" review takes a symbolically covert big picture exposition which complements the previous point: ["Balsam's] moral cynicism and missing limbs embodies all the destructiveness—and self-destructiveness—of the American commercial ethic."[37] The review was signed "P.D.Z."—a period pseudonym attached to critiques linking a movie to a "message of corporate menace." According to *Show* magazine, "[Merriweather] embodies the wages of greed, literally giving up a hand, an eye, a scalp, a leg, anything in his pursuit of the dollar.... He has become as phony (hooks, peg legs, etc.) as his value system...."[38] Once again, as with *Little Big Man's* expanded dark comedy use of death to the disturbing domain of genocide, this augmentation of absurdity makes for a more substantial indictment of American history.

Another degree of troubling Merriweather black humor absurdity is the reality that Balsam's character never really gets the broader ramifications of his acts, as was the case with *Catch-22's* Milo Minderbinder (Jon Voight). In fact, each time Hoffman's character meets the ever-diminishing Merriweather, he is as happy as his name. Ironically, this also constitutes simple physical comedy absurdity, since who remains cheery as he continues to be trimmed down? Consequently, in his own way, Merriweather is as vapid as the genre's generally vacuous human herd. In the spirit of this stupidity, while the Indian

Wars–related Merriweather is in the tradition of the more sneaky Southwestern humor characters, his attitude, coupled with his shrinking condition, is reminiscent of a signature idiot from another school of American humor—the New England Yankee.

This earlier version of Merriweather, from the world of the capable crackerbarrel Yankees, is a figure named Birdofredum Sawin. The two are ultimately so "big picture alike" that a brief background of Sawin would be helpful. He is a character created by liberal humorist and later diplomat James Russell Lowell. In his satirical work *The Biglow Papers* (1848), Lowell juxtaposes the principled anti-war Yankee Hosea Biglow against the Merriweather-like Birdofredum. The foolish, short-sighted jingoism of the ironically named Birdofredum underlines the adept insightfulness of the balanced—note the first name—Biglow. Moreover, by putting Biglow and Sawin on opposite ends of a political issue, the position of Biglow is reinforced all the more. For example, he opposed the Mexican War (1848), another controversial conflict in American history. Though Mexico was not without blame in the conflict, historians agree that "the central cause was nevertheless the readiness of Americans to resort to arms to fulfill their [hawkish] Manifest Destiny."[39] In contrast, Birdofredum is an often wounded soldier still parroting rhetoric to the glory of war—the Mexican War—which American expansionists were using to annex and steal the provinces of New Mexico and California: "I've lost one eye but that's a loss it's easy to supply out o' the glory that I've gut, for that is all my eye; An' one is enough, I guess, by diligently usin' it...."[40]

Like the later Merriweather, the misguided Birdofredum gaily goes on to lose an arm, the fingers of his other hand, and a leg, all in the name of extreme flag-waving nationalism, *à la* the Vietnam War. This loss of limbs provides Lowell with further satire related to his character's full name, Birdofredum *Sawin*: The sawing-off of body parts never ceases. Merriweather and Birdofredum morph into dark comedy Ahabs, destined to forever lose limbs to a great white whale called war. Again the absurd comedy-tragedy of Merriweather's repetition of Birdofredum is an inability to think beyond the axiom of "my country, right or wrong." Regardless, whether *Little Big Man* author Berger was aware of this literary link in his tapestry of frontier dark comedy, Penn's film is all the richer for both recognizing the significance of Merriweather and intertwining him throughout this equally epic adaptation.

As previously suggested, while Merriweather was a unique example of *Little Big Man* absurdity, the picture oozes insanity, beginning with our title character. Most illogical was the hundred-odd years it took him to finally tell the true story, or at least a closer facsimile, of the American West. For much of his saga he seems merely a bystander to history, like the Berlin-based central characters of *Cabaret* (1972, see Chapter 5), who are busy with other things as the Nazi party slowly comes to power. In fact, in Christopher Isherwood's short story–like collection of a novel, *Goodbye to Berlin* (1935), on which *Cabaret* is based, the narrator says at the beginning, "I am a camera...."[41] Along these same lines, the 100-plus-year-old survivor (Marcel Dalio) of *Catch–22* also comes to mind.

Being a historical onlooker implicates one in nefarious business, whether it is the genocide of Jews or Native Americans. But rather than being one of these passive collaborators, Crabb is more a bumbling fifth columnist. Beyond his history-rewritten revelations, there are many mitigating factors in his favor, all of which have an absurd twist. For example, with an assist from tall tale Native American magic, Hoffman's character leads the now blind and elderly Old Lodge Skins to safety through Custer's 7th Cavalry surprise attack on a Cheyenne camp. Paradoxically, however, Crabb's greatest act of dissent, with regard to genocide, simply involves telling the truth. He has become a scout, of sorts, for Custer on the eve of the Little Bighorn battle. He honestly reports to the general that a Native American force of overwhelming numbers is hidden within the Little Bighorn valley. Yet, fittingly, his report comes with attitude: "And when [the Indians] get done with you, there won't be nothing left but a greasy spot.... You go down there, if you've got the nerve." But the buffoonish Custer decides to use Crabb as a reverse barometer:

> Still trying to outsmart me, aren't you, mule-skinner [Crabb]? You want me to think that you don't want me to go down there but the subtle truth is you really *don't* want me to go down there.

Berger's original truth, wrapped in exaggerations of actual events to which the film closely adheres, is heavy with absurdity. Thus, in the interest of time, the innumerable examples will be epitomized by one more character—Old Lodge Skins. Remember, this is the figure that *New York Times* critic George P. Elliott earlier claimed was one of the story's "real heroes," not to be confused and/or mixed with lesser vaudeville comedy characters. Now there is no debating that Chief Dan George's figure is the genuine article, besides stealing every scene he is in. Nevertheless, as *Newsday*'s Joseph Gelmis so aptly describes Old Lodge Skin, "[He's] a sage who is also a clown."[42] This populist Indian is constantly sharing vaudevillian-like riffs with Hoffman's character, such as Old Lodge Skins' description of an additional wife:

> My new snake wife cooks dog very well.... She also has a very soft skin. The only trouble with snake women is they copulate with horses, which makes them strange to me. She says she doesn't. That's why I call her "Doesn't Like Horses." But of course, she's lying.

An additional bit of Old Lodge Skins' absurdity is that when he is not busy being a "sage" or a "clown," he is capable of the most affectionate parental warmth, such as his naming of the young Crabb: "This boy is no longer a boy. He's a brave. He is little in body but his heart is big. His name shall be 'Little Big Man.'" Because of this, more than one critic also likened him to a "Jewish mother."[43]

Evidently there was a great deal of legitimacy to Chief Dan George being part "Jewish mother." In the *New York Times* article "Dustin Calls Him Grandpa," George, who did not start acting until 1960, said he got along wonderfully with his co-star: "One day he told me, towards the end of shooting, 'I never did have a grandfather.' Then he asked me if he could call me grandfather, and I said, 'Any time, son. I already have 36 grandchildren—I might as well have 37.' And he did call me that, and whenever he sees me or writes to me, he calls me that."[44]

There is another telling example of Chief Dan George's closeness to the part in the same article: "[In the scene] where I go up on the mountain to die, [Penn] never told me how to do it. That was my *own* song, my *own* dance, and my *own* way of talking to the great white spirit. Those things were all my idea."[45]

George was not the only one improvising in this scene. As much as Penn embraced Berger's novel, the director changed the conclusion. In the book, Old Lodge Skins dies at the end, whereas Penn's cinematic rescue provides room for the chief's wonderfully absurd line about getting his death exit clairvoyance wrong. Penn felt that letting Old Lodge Skins live would avoid letting sadness into the film.... The film would have become dramatic, even melodramatic, instead of picaresque. I also wanted to show that not only were the Indians going to be destroyed, but they were also condemned to live [a restricted life on various reservations].[46]

The last part of that "condemned to live" quote has broader dark comedy ramifications, starting with Crabb. At 121 years of age, he is living a variation of what is known as the "locked-in syndrome," a prisoner of his own body. Thus, his need to tell his tall tale–like history might be likened to the real-life story of Jean-Dominique Bauby and his hauntingly poetic memoir *The Diving Bell and the Butterfly* (1996). In late 1995, Bauby suffered a stroke so severe that he was left permanently paralyzed and speechless—a victim of the "locked-in syndrome."[47] With his mental faculties remaining intact, Bauby's only means of communication was by blinking when the correct letter was spoken by an assistant slowly going through an abbreviated "alphabet" (most frequently used words) *over* and *over*. Bauby's feat of "writing" this modern classic, based upon imagination, memory, and persistence, might seem miles away from Crabb's oral history—told in flashback to a framing device academic. But the "locked-in syndrome" doubles as a powerful metaphor for the dark comedy of life. We are all prisoners of some such affliction, and are often in need of a storytelling catharsis. Crabb's controversial story-tall tale builds upon imagination, memory, and persistence. And even in a dark comedy, man continues to try to make sense of things ... how absurd is that?

Moving to the multiple complexities inherent in modern black humor's third major element—man as beast—in *Little Big Man*, the examples are again limitless. Not surprisingly, one might merely go back and reconfigure the genre's fascination with death. For instance, the ease with which Custer could kill makes him a monster, just as white America's overwhelming acceptance of Native American genocide qualifies as man as beast on a "manifest destiny" scale. The "savages" are white and the story's focus tribe members are called "Human Beings." And each time Little Big Man returns to "civilization" as Crabb, he witnesses yet another example of human depravity. From the novel: "No matter what we do, the white man will cheat us. If we plant potatoes, they will steal them. If we try to hunt buffalo, they will scare the game away. If we fight, they will not make war properly."[48]

However, one could take the devilish perspective on mankind in a different direction, and focus on two women who systemically appear in Jack Crabb's odyssey: Caroline (Carole Androsky), his sister, and Louise (Faye Dunaway), the wife of the rotund Reverend Silas Pendrake (Thayer David), who adopts Hoffman's young teenage character after his first sojourn with the tribe. His sister's ogre-like tendencies begin with Caroline's greatest concern after her parents' massacre: that the Native Americans did *not* rape her. And when the kidnapping tribe continues to have no sexual interest in the man-like Caroline, she abandons her little brother. Much later, when Jack is working for huckster Merriweather, his sister is part of a mob which tars and feathers them. Their next encounter has her attempting to make Jack into a killer gunslinger named the Soda Pop Kid—a Keatonesque sequence which best demonstrates Hoffman's talent for broad humor. But after he sees a gunman's death, when his friend Wild Bill Hickok kills in self-defense, Jack "Soda Pop Kid" Crabb gives up his hilarious wannabe shootist ways, and Carolina disowns him yet again. Berger optimally summarizes Hoffman's post–cowboy-attired-dude thoughts on Caroline:

> Funny how members of your own family, even when you haven't been especially close ... can drive the knife home with perfect accuracy.... She found me more satisfying as a

Dustin Hoffman's big boy getting a most provocative bath from his new stepmother Faye Dunaway.

derelict.... The Cheyenne would have been depressed to see a fellow tribesman gone to rot; they would have believed it reflected discredit upon all Human Beings. On the contrary, an American just loves to see another who ain't worth a damn. And my sister proved no exception.[49]

Fittingly, even when pivoting upon an individual seemingly so remote from an obvious monster like Custer, one still finds a beast-like persona.

In contrast to the eventual devastatingly broad disillusionment in "civilized" humanity caused by his sister, there is the radically different relationship with his sexy surrogate mother Louise. To young Jack, she is a proper beautiful lady on a pedestal. In fact, she is so respectable, Berger had the teen reflecting that, if men looked at her in a carnal manner, she "acted as if they were standing in horse manure about ten feet below her location."[50] Hoffman's figure adjusted to this genteel religious setting, though Louise's bathing of the boy had more than a little pedophilia about it. However, she bought Jack nice things and spoiled him with drugstore soda, made all the more enchanting by the toy elephant head spigot from which if flowed. Unfortunately, this is where his romantically glorified Louise, wife of the good the Reverend Pendrake, took a tumble off that pillar of piety. While Dunaway's character thinks she has the youngster occupied, he discovers that in the backroom the druggist is doing more than filling a prescription with Louise. After this bitter enlightenment, Crabb observes, "That was the end of my religion period. I ain't sung a hymn in 104 years." Hoffman's character learns yet again, like Huckleberry Finn or his modern model—J. D. Salinger's Holden Caulfield (*The Catcher in the Rye*, 1951)—that it is a phony man-as-beast world. Appropriately, the next time Crabb encounters Louise, she is a whore, though Dunaway's prostitute still attempts to dress up the situation with some comic understatement: "Well, Jack. Now you know. This is a house of ill fame. And I'm a fallen flower. This life is not only wicked and sinful. It isn't even any fun."

So how did audiences react to yet another adaptation of a monumental episodic anti-war, anti-genre novel, *à la* Mike Nichols' *Catch–22*? Penn's picture was embraced by more critics and larger audiences, but some comparisons were inevitably made, usually to the detriment of both movies. For example, *The New Yorker* said that *Little Big Man* was Penn's big film "in the way *Catch–22* was Mike Nichols' big one. Arthur Penn stays within a smaller range but you come out of this ten-million dollar movie feeling that Penn, like Nichols, got into something complex he couldn't bring off."[51]

This was a minority report. More critics were now both appreciably conscious of black comedy and grasping its growing complexity. There were fewer piecemeal reviews like Charlie Chaplin suffered through with *The Great Dictator* (1940) and *Monsieur Verdoux* (1947).[52] For instance, he invariably received kudos for his ballet-like globe sequences in the former picture, even though most reviewers struggled with embracing a narrative which used Hitler as a dark comedy subject. Regardless, for every *New Yorker* critic who still could not understand the complex chaotic scope of black humor, there were more critiques like the following *Films and Filming* overview: "In the long run, the winning thing about *Little Big Man* is its refusal to toe any line. It mocks the Western myth, as Arthur Penn has done before more seriously in *The Left Handed Gun* [1958]. It also has a tendency to gawp [satirically stare with astonishment] at history."[53] *Newsday*'s Joseph Gelmis closed his positive review by scrutinizing what was, for him, the signature scene:

> When [Old Lodge Skins] lies out to await death, all he gets is rain in the face. It is the moment that reveals what *Little Big Man* is really about: Every tragedy is also a potential comedy. The man outside, or in the middle in this case, observes both the laughter and the tears simultaneously. *Little Big Man* runs two-and-a-half hours. I loved every minute.[54]

After favorably comparing the film to the dark comedy of Jonathan Swift, *Time* magazine asked, "[W]hy should *Little Big Man* be counted as a rambunctious triumph? Because in its 360° scope of slaughter and laughter, the film has contrived to lampoon, revere or revile the length and breadth of the entire frontier.... The '70s has its first great epic."[55] Maybe *Time*'s capsule review said it best: "reality lost in myth."[56] And not surprisingly, young critic Roger Ebert, still part of the under-thirty crowd most drawn to the films, called it "an endlessly entertaining attempt to spin an epic in the form of a yarn.... It is the very folksiness of Penn's film that makes it, finally, such a perceptive and important statement about Indians, the West, and the American dream."[57] Pauline Kael wrote of counterculture movie fans:

> The young, anti-draft, anti–Vietnam audiences that were "the film generation" might go to some of the same pictures that the older audience did but not to those only. They were willing to give something fresh [like dark comedy] a chance, and they went to movies that weren't certified hits.[58]

In this case, however, *Little Big Man* became one of those "certified hits." Released late in 1970, it would be the #2 grosser of 1971 (after *Love Story*), just as *MASH* occupied the same commercial slot (after *Airport*, 1970).[59] And even though the third part of this 1970 anti-war trilogy, *Catch–22*, lost money because of a huge budget, it was still one of the ten top-grossing movies of the year.[60]

Dark comedy and anti–Vietnam films had very much gone mainstream. Yet what was possibly most fascinating about *Little Big Man*'s critical and commercial success was the fact that it was the last film in this trilogy. That is, the huge success of *MASH* was sometimes noted as an additional factor in follow-up *Catch–22* not receiving more immediate acclaim. So why did the *third* variation on this anti–Vietnam theme return to near–*MASH* ballyhoo? Undoubtedly much of it had to do with this chapter's opening hypothesis about *Little Big Man*'s audacity in indicting the bulk of U.S. history with racism and genocide, instead of a narrow anti–Vietnam period metaphorically subtextualized in two other wars (Korea and World War II).

That being said, one could also argue that Berger's novel and Penn's personal demons made for a perfectly complex dark comedy marriage. This director was forever creatively angry about lies and being backed into a corner. While this chapter has already chronicled his rage about the Western truths so long presented as fact, this was hardly a singular passion for him. Like Joseph Heller saying *Catch–22* had a great deal to do with McCarthyism, all of Penn's work was fueled to some degree by creatively coming of age during those witch-hunting years. The period had made it dangerous to express some ideas, and for Penn, "The whole damned society was incapacitated.... How that drunken fool [McCarthy] was able to bring the country to its psychological knees was one of the most irritating things I've ever encountered."[61] It was time to speak out.

Yet again, while older directors like Penn helped validate my protesting anti-war generation, like all great artists he was also validating himself. Ironically, Penn generously also credits 1960s dissent for helping him find his own voice.[62] This is another multi-layered example of the intricacies of the 1970s dark comedy. Berger's novel was also an excellent anti-genre work for Penn with which to work: "The Western is the most highly specialized of American genres.... The genre is so identified with the set of conventions that define it that any significant departure from them is met with resistance."[63] Therefore, an anti–Western is arguably the most provocative anti-genre with which to work, and probably explains why Penn's short filmography starts with a Western, *The Left Handed Gun*, and periodically returns to the genre, from *Little Big Man*, to *The Missouri Breaks* (1976). In fact, revisionist studies of Penn's *Bonnie and Clyde* (1967) sometimes treat it as black comedy quasi–Western.

Like most artists, especially ones working in dark comedy, Penn saw himself as an outsider, struggling to say that what he thought and did belonged to him. This is also at the heart of his work. And though much has been written here about his shish-kebabbing of the Western, the secret key to his characters is in his much-honored direction of *The Miracle Worker* on Broadway (1959) and on the screen (1962):

> Helen Keller is *literally* what other Penn protagonists are only metaphorically—blind, groping, stumbling, inarticulate. She is the ultimate outsider, an outcast from life itself, with nothing but the most physical, animal-like behavior at her disposal to make herself recognized.[64]

It might have been written by Beckett ... to describe Jack Crabb.

4

Harold and Maude (12/21/71)

> *Harold and Maude* has all the fun and gaiety of a burning orphanage.[1]
> —*Variety* (1971)

This opening to *Variety*'s review of *Harold and Maude* (1971) was brutal, especially because the publication was the entertainment industry's bible. This show business journal was once so significant it was even well known for creating its own jargon, "Varietyese," such as the example used in the musical biography of George M. Cohan, *Yankee Doodle Dandy* (1942): "stix nix hix pix," meaning country audiences disliked rural-based movies.

Why did *Variety* and many other *Variety*-influenced period reviews so savage the picture—particularly since it would eventually be anointed a cult classic, and even recover from its initial minimal revenues? Maybe the greater question is how did this text's previously probed dark comedies (*MASH*, *Catch–22*, and *Little Big Man*, all 1970) open with mixed to magnificent reviews, and fair to fantastic box office returns? Black humor seemed to have arrived in the New American Cinema era, or at least become more widely accepted. Why the regression with *Harold and Maude*?

Several factors come into play. First, unlike the opening trilogy, the Hal Ashby-directed, Colin Higgins-written *Harold and Maude* begins with dark comedy. Teenage title character Harold (Bud Cort) appears to hang himself—jokingly replicating an early name for the genre, "gallows humor." In contrast, the aforementioned film trio ease into the black humor, and are initially camouflaged by other genres, though their basic components are soon snapped, too. For instance, *MASH* starts with a personality comedy slapstick theft of a Jeep. For all one knows, the viewer might just have entered the updated service comedy world of Abbott and Costello's *Buck Privates* (1941). Admittedly, *Harold and Maude* also periodically performs its own anti-genre disguises and distractions from dark comedy (to be analyzed shortly). Yet the fact remains, the Ashby picture commences with a jolt, and never lets up—chronicling a romantic relationship with a sixty-year age difference.

Second, unlike the earlier threesome, which eventually make their dark comedy more palatable by feeding upon the period's growing anti–Vietnam War viewpoint, Harold's actions are given no immediate backstory catalyst. Though a nihilistic genre whose message is "There is no message," hardly requires a justification, a cause is advantageous during an age (the early 1970s) when one aspires for a more sweeping acceptance of dark comedy. Ironically, an anti-war conviction even beyond Vietnam, to the point of encompassing the Holocaust, is also part and parcel of *Harold and Maude*; it just takes time to narratively unfold. This, too, will be scrutinized.

And, while the previous triad focused their anti-establishment ethos upon the easier target of an unpopular war (though obviously other illustrations of mankind's inhumanity surface), dissimilar *Harold and Maude* more systematically skewers society's monstrosities. This methodical approach involves Harold's periodic forced interaction with different high-profile branches of the establishment: General Victor Hall (Charles Tyner), a priest (Eric Christmas), a psychiatrist (George Wood) and, most damning, a luxuriously wealthy matriarchal mother, Mrs. Chasen (Vivian Pickles), who almost steals the picture from Cort and Ruth Gordon (Maude). By pummeling the military, the church, the medical complex, and family, *Harold and Maude* arguably remains the most comprehensive investigation of dark comedy in the canon.

In *Harold and Maude*, the first genre to be discombobulated is the coming-of-age picture. While a bulwark of this film category is often the dysfunctional family, no one does this parental train wreck better than *Harold and Maude*. Harold is so estranged from his abominable mother,

Harold (Bud Cort) and Maude (Ruth Gordon) initially met over their fondness for attending the funerals of strangers.

and life in general, he stages elaborate sham scenes of self-destruction in order to upset her:

> PSYCHIATRIST: Tell me, Harold, how many of these, eh, "suicides" have you performed?
> HAROLD: An accurate number would be difficult to gauge.
> PSYCHIATRIST: Well, just give me a rough estimate.
> HAROLD: A rough estimate? I'd say [*pause*] fifteen.
> PSYCHIATRIST: Fifteen?
> HAROLD: That's a rough estimate.
> PSYCHIATRIST: Were they all done for your mother's benefit?
> HAROLD: No, no, I would not say "benefit."

The most telling of these mock suicides, with regard to Harold's legitimate repugnance for his mother, occurs when she decides to enroll him in a computer dating service. Being the personification of self-centeredness, Mrs. Chasen not only begins to fill out the survey in his presence, she quickly morphs into answering the questions for herself. For instance, Mrs. Chasen's response to the inquiry, "Do you sometimes have headaches or backaches after a difficult day?" is "Yes, I do indeed." She is so oblivious to Harold that she does not see what her seated son is doing. While she prattles away stating and answering printed queries, with her eyes never leaving the survey, Cort's teenager has produced a gun and looks to shoot himself in the head. Paradoxically, at approximately the point where Mrs. Chasen replies, "Yes, indeed ..." to the question, "Does your personal religion or philosophy include a life after death?" Harold points the weapon at his mother. After a slight pause, however, he turns the situation into another fake suicide, though his discharge of the weapon knocks both Harold and his throne-like chair over backwards. By this point Mrs. Chasen has become so used to these mini-melodramas that she runs her admonishment of him into the next (now ironically phrased) question, "Harold, please! 'Do you have ups downs without obvious reasons?' That's you, Harold!"

Another aspect of the anti-genre coming-of-age factor applied to *Harold and Maude*, after teenager Harold's loathing of his mother, is his sexual awakenings being triggered by a woman of eighty. The relationship with Maude does lead to growth towards maturity for him, a given in the genre. Yet again, it is hardly the norm for this to be prompted romantically by an elderly lady. This is validated in the movie by Harold's psychiatrist telling him, "A very common neurosis, particularly in this society, whereby the male child subconsciously wishes to sleep with his mother. Of course, what puzzles me, Harold, is that you want to sleep with your grandmother." This anti-genre abnormality is further authenticated by references in other films, such as Cameron Diaz's vapid character in *There's Something About Mary* (1998) ironically saying *Harold and Maude* is the "greatest love story of our time." Indeed, given the childlike appearance and nature of Cort, not unlike his timorous *MASH* character Private Boone, one could conceivably argue that the bizarre "romance" of *Harold and Maude* is pedophilistic.

Another anti-genre coming-of-age factor in *Harold and Maude* even dovetails into a more darkly comic connection than pedophilia. That is, plausibly the most common black humor target addresses war and/or the military. And the closest thing Harold has to a father figure is his uncle, General Victor Hall. Like sticking Harold with a flippantly insensitive mother, having a career pro-war military man fill a supporting parental role profoundly compounds this man-child's dysfunctional family. This configuration pushes the situation to the macabre world of a Charles Addams *New Yorker* cartoon, much darker than the watered-down variations which subsequently appeared in multiple media as *The Addams Family*. This scenario is ably assisted by the actor (Charles Tyner) playing Uncle's Victor being best known as Boss Higgins, the sadistic prison guard in *Cool Hand Luke* (1967).

In *Harold and Maude* the uncle's misguided patriotism is treated as a joke, underlined in the movie's two best sight gags. Before his mother has Harold visit General Hall, she praises his uncle's wisdom: "After all, he was General MacArthur's [America's Pacific theater commander-in-chief during World War II] right-hand man." Thus, the first comic pay-off occurs when Harold visits his uncle's military base office and the viewer realizes the uniformed general has neither a right hand nor a right arm. This laugh is then topped after Hall gives Harold a pep talk, saying that in

> the military, "You'll walk tall with a glint in your eye and a spring in your step and a knowledge in your heart that … you are serving your country, just like Nathan Hale. That's what this country needs, more Nathan Hales. I think I can see a little Nathan Hale … in you."

At this point, Hall looks at a painting of Hale in his office and goes into a stiff military posture, which involves somehow activating a mechanical device which results in his starched-flat empty right sleeve saluting the picture.

A limb-less, clue-less general caustically called Victor is reminiscent of *Little Big Man*'s struggling huckster Allardyce T. Merriwether and his own sardonically upbeat name, despite a similar disadvantage of lost body parts. And just as Merriwether was compared to James Russell Lowell's one-eyed jingoistic fool with an equally ironic name, Birdofredum Sawin, the same link could be made to Uncle Victor.[2] In fact, Birdofredum and Victor have even more in common, given that they are both imprudently patriotic soldiers whose ongoing anatomical trimmings represented unjust conflicts (the Mexican and Vietnam Wars) and did nothing to dampen their absurd zeal for something approaching that ill-founded axiom, "My country, right or wrong." Moreover, Uncle Victor has so jumped the tracks he has willingly turned himself into a sort of flag-waving "clockwork orange"—part mechanical, part human.

Harold and Maude also has another twisted anti-genre distraction, in addition to its dismantling of the coming-of-age picture. Again, even though the film's dark comedy is immediately front and center, the viewer is frequently diverted by its engaging perversion of screwball comedy.[3] A triangle format is central to this genre, with a childlike antiheroic male riding the apex of the configuration. At one corner of the triangle base is a controlling fiancée or wife who acts more like a martinet mother than a romantic partner. At the opposite corner in a whirlwind of a life force woman who represents freedom and fun. This latter figure is the screwball heroine who rescues the male from a rigid lifestyle. For instance, in Howard Hawks' template for the genre, *Bringing Up Baby* (1938), Cary Grant plays a professor assembling a giant brontosaurus skeleton. This symbolizes the lifeless future he faces as an academic engaged to a suffocating woman assistant aptly named Swallow.

Grant's screwball rescuer is a daffy free spirit played by Katharine Hepburn. The Baby of the title, a leopard in Hepburn's possession, represents the "life" she can bring to his world. Fittingly, the film ends with Grant realizing he loves the lively Hepburn just after she has caused his rigid metaphorical alter ego brontosaurus skeleton to collapse. Cinema has still never seen a more symbolic bit of slapstick.

In the post–New American Film era, the signature screwball comedy is writer-director Steve Gordon's *Arthur* (1981), a different slant on the danger of a rigid male lifestyle. Dudley Moore plays a wealthy, wonderfully engaging man-child threatened by another deadly Swallow-like fiancée and a nine-to-five job working for her financial fascist father. Unlike Grant, Moore's character is enjoying life to the fullest, but an arranged marriage to a clone of her dictator dad looks to change that. However, another screwball deliverance is made possible by the arrival of Liza Minnelli's free-thinking blue collar heroine.

As an important addendum to these examples, and to the genre in general, screwball comedy plays best in the escapist world of high society. A period critique of René Clair's fantasy screwball comedy *I Married a Witch* (1942) tellingly describes the condition with the phrase "caviar comedy," while the ever-insightful modern critic-historian Richard Schickel simply observed that "screwballism was purely a disease of the wealthy."[4] The titles of two other celebrated examples of the genre express this ambience quite effectively: Mitchell Leisen's *Easy Living* (1937) and George Cukor's *Holiday* (1938). Moreover, given this money backdrop, the genre relationships which develop are often described as implosive, with the screwball couples frequently coming from different social classes. That is, with this version of American farce having been born in the Great Depression, when American society as we know it was on the proverbial ropes, "implosive" meant the classes were capable of coming together peacefully in an allegorical love affair.

The anti-screwball comedy genre aspect of *Harold and Maude* metastasizes again from Pickles' provocative Mrs. Chasen. If one constructs the zany comedy's triangle structure, she represents the constraining fiancée-wife figure. Ruth's Maude is the "force of nature" woman who suddenly shakes things up. Thus, yet another aspect of this bastardization of the screwball configuration (beyond Mrs. Chasen literally being Harold's mother) is that Maude never plans to be the anti-hero's lover, as is screwball comedy's norm for this freeing figure. She is a lifestyle master instructor, not a mistress. Instead, it is Harold who takes the romantic initiative, which is *not* the genre standard. Moreover, it further accents his child-like nature—the little boy infatuated by a special teacher—which also denotes an anti-genre depiction of the conventional screwball male.

Perhaps the preeminent later example of a dark comedy exploiting an anti-genre use of screwball comedy would be the John Cleese-Charles Crichton–written *A Fish Called Wanda* (1988, with Crichton doubling as director). As a related footnote, Cleese had pulled Crichton out of retirement after the filmmaker's distinguished career at London's Ealing Studio, which specialized in dark comedies following World War II. Anyway, *Wanda's* anti-genre topsy-turvydom of screwball comedy has a rigid male (Cleese), a stereotype of reserved woodenness for which the British have a gift, whose browbeating wife and dryly inflexible law career have made him as stiff as Cary Grant's brontosaurus bones. The anti-genre component arrives in the independent-minded Jamie Lee Curtis character, whose motives are neither to liberate nor love Cleese's barrister but rather to use him in the commission of a robbery. And even at the film's conclusion, when Cleese has been sufficiently loosened up and is in a criminally comic-driven relationship with Curtis, her romantic (versus money) motives remain suspect.

Moving beyond *Harold and Maude's* compounding use of anti-genre components, it is the most multi-faceted dark comedy thus evaluated in this study. The film builds upon the aforementioned assault on multiple establishment institutions: the military, religion, modern medicine, and family. Like all great art, these picture perceptions are often more relevant today. For example, given the ongoing revelations about pedophile priests in recent years and the Roman Catholic church's systematic cover-ups, a certain observation by Harold's priest has even more sardonic bite today. The sequence is prompted by the Church Father learning that Harold plans to marry a woman 60 years his senior: "I would be remiss in my duty, if I did not tell you [Harold] that the idea of … intercourse—your firm, young [*pause*] body [*pause*] comingling with [*pause*] withered flesh [*pause*], sagging breasts [*pause*], flabby b-buttocks [*pause*] makes me want [*pause*] to vomit."

Along similar lines, today's continuing failure of the United States Department of Veteran Affairs to adequately address the medical needs of our military personnel gives added dark comedy bite to the *Harold and Maude* scene in which Uncle Victor has taken the teenager to visit an old soldiers' home. The purpose is for the general to have a fitting backdrop in which to rhapsodize yet again about the benefits of military life, while old and/or handicapped veterans collapse behind them without anyone coming to their aid.

Director Ashby later expanded upon the Veteran Affairs' lack of attention and concern for disabled military men in his multi–Oscar-winning drama *Coming Home* (1978). This anti–Vietnam War melodrama featured Jon Voight in an Academy Award–winning performance as a paraplegic veteran, inspired, in part, by Ron Kovic's Vietnam experience as chronicled in his ironically titled 1976 memoir *Born on the Fourth of July*. The autobiography would later also become a multi–Oscar-winning picture, with a script by Kovic and Oliver Stone, and Tom Cruise playing the "born on the Fourth of July," paraplegic, anti–Vietnam War veteran.

In Ashby's *Harold and Maude* one could also link the teenager's less than compassionate psychiatrist to veterans past and present not getting adequate counseling subsequent to experiencing post traumatic stress disorder. Keep in mind, Harold discovers he "enjoyed being dead" (staging suicides) *after* surviving a chemistry lab explosion at school. If this link seems thin, it is also assisted by having the same actor, George Wood, play both Harold's therapist and the uncaring, football-driven General Hammond in *MASH*, a movie also featuring Bud Cort. Moreover, *Harold and Maude*'s suggestion of an apathetic Veteran Affairs-medical care backdrop, *à la* armless Uncle Victor, might be summarized by a signature scene in *Catch–22*. The sequence in question concerns Yossarian (Alan Arkin) observing two perverse nurses in the Army hospital laughingly switch the IV drip bottle with the urine bottle on a patient entirely encased in white, like a mummy. Besides symbolizing nonchalant military medicine's heartlessness and/or incompetency squared, the unidentifiable figure in white could represent all neglected veterans, like a depraved twist on the Tomb of the Unknown Soldier.

In *Harold and Maude*, dark comedy's first basic element—death and/or its implication—has never been more omnipresent. Harold's mock suicides cover a wide spectrum, starting with those solely to upset his mother: hanging, slashing his throat, and drowning. These mini-plays of self-destruction then expand to both disturb his mother and unnerve a series of computer dates: appearing to cut off his hand (inspired perhaps by Uncle Victor), self-immolation, and hari-kiri.

The latter two illustrations have additional dark comedy ramifications of a provocative nature. Since *Harold and Maude* eventually gets around to Cort's character attempting to avoid the Vietnam draft, any depiction of self-immolation would have a specific reference point for period audiences. That is, in 1966 Buddhist monk Quang Duc became famous when a BBC photographer caught him setting himself on fire. The monk was protesting the South Vietnam government which America was propping up, in colonial-like fashion, during what was essentially a Vietnamese civil war. There had been several other self-immolation acts of suicidal protest, dating back to the early 1960s. But Quang Duc was caught on film and was a more shockingly vivid acknowledgment of America's mistake in being there. Consequently, having Harold light himself up was dark comedy death at its most visceral. Such a disturbing image used for comic purposes undoubtedly contributed to that *Variety* opening review about the film having "all the fun and gaiety of a burning orphanage."

Though the distance of time has lessened the image's numbing effect, Ashby has offered the viewer some relief by shooting the scene in long shot, as viewed through a picture window of Mrs. Chasen's family mansion. Yet this is not necessarily a compromise by the filmmaker. While Ashby was a master editor, having won an Academy Award for cutting his mentor Norman Jewison's *In the Heat of the Night* (1967), the self-immolation scene in *Harold and Maude* creatively gets around the need to edit. Through the imaginative use of the screen's background and foreground, a single shot showcases the whole event. While what appears to be a burning monk-like Harold is in the distance, Mrs. Chasen and the computer date witness this frighteningly funny (to the viewer) event in the foreground—which is then comically topped by Cort's character casually strolling into the film frame. Through this use of deep focus, Ashby has eliminated the need to edit. As if to congratulate himself on this tight filmmaking and/or Harold on another superb mock suicide, the scene ends with the teenager's only example of direct address. With his smiling nod at the camera (the audience), entertainingly breaking the fourth wall, he further bonds with the viewer by suggesting he is the only cast member aware that there is a movie going on.

This alliance between Harold and the viewer further implicates the audience in all the implied death with which Harold surrounds himself. Beyond his ongoing exercises in suicide, the teenager is most comfortable among iconic symbols of death. These include driving a hearse (salvaged from an automobile graveyard), attending the funerals of strangers, and having picnics with Maude at the massive military burial ground in Golden Gate National Cemetery, in San Bruno, California. This setting, like Arlington Cemetery in Washington, D. C., has many thousands of identical white grave markers. Ashby accents this ocean of death by eventually pulling the camera back ad infinitum without ever escaping all those neatly arranged white crosses. Ironically, a military protocol of equality—all markers are the same size, regardless of the veteran's rank—also sends an unintended negative message. Individual lines and markers are reduced to pretty geometrical patterns (not unlike the decorative designs of Busby Berkeley movie choreography), resulting in mesmerizingly lifeless mosaics.

Another initial response to suicide-staging Harold is to return the viewer to the absurdist world of Samuel Beckett's 1953 play *Waiting for Godot*. Like Vladimir and Estragon, Harold is essentially playing a waiting game. But because his existentialistic figure has anticipated that Godot/God is never coming, and that the only inevitable given is death, Harold quite literally "kills time" by producing mini-sketches of self-destruction. He is a walking metaphor for the disillusionment of the late 1960s. Then after Maude inspires him to live life to its fullest, the specter of the Vietnam War surfaces again. His mom wants him in the military and Uncle Victor is to facilitate the process.

Ironically, images of death will now come to his rescue. Maude agrees to assist him in a plan to convince the general that his nephew is too unstable to join the military. The death-driven strategy is a success, with Harold deftly avoiding Yossarian's Catch–22 dilemma by implementing his scheme *before* being in uniform. So what deadly diagram did the two hatch? First, Harold seemingly embraces the military scenario by encouraging his Uncle Victor to dredge up old war stories of battle deaths. Second, Cort's character enthusiastically asks the general if the military will teach him diverse ways to kill, too, with Harold acting out assorted—or is that sordid?—termination techniques, such as bayoneting an enemy. A now emotionally excessive Harold asks if as a soldier he would be able to take trophy kills, such as the "eyes" and "privates" (genitalia) of the enemy. By way of an example, the boy produces a shrunken human head. Suddenly an anti-war placard-waving Maude appears and takes the trophy head. Harold goes ballistic: Grabbing his mentor's sign, he begins chasing her down a chiseled-out-of-rock staircase towards the nearby sea. Uncle Victor and Harold eventually catch her on a stone landing above an ocean inlet. As the boy is on the brink of doing bodily harm to Maude, she slips through a hitherto unseen opening in the landing and seemingly falls to her death. Harold's Keystone Cops–like chase appears to have ended in murder, comically topped by an appalled Uncle Victor accidentally saluting the action with his malfunctioning starched empty sleeve.

All mention of Harold being drafted and/or forced to enlist evaporates, and now the child-man can concentrate on romancing Maude. However, after giving her a lovingly private birthday party, she thanks him for such a tender farewell and casually reveals she has taken an unspecified drug which will render her dead by midnight. Throughout a courtship which has lasted barely a week, Gordon's character had periodically given veiled hints that it would "all be over" with this birthday. Now Harold, who has constantly played at death, must face the real thing.

The teenager manages to orchestrate a frantic but fruitless trip to a hospital in which he is banished to the solitude of an Edward Hopper–like waiting room, while editor Ashby simultaneously cross-cuts these scenes with an anguished Harold driving an ever-accelerating Jaguar (which he had earlier converted to a second hearse) towards an undisclosed destination. Eventually the pasty-white Harold, whose complexion has been cadaver-like throughout the movie, drives his sports car off an oceanside cliff. Is this yet another mock suicide, or now, with genuine grief as an incentive, has Harold decided to truly take his own life? Ashby has muddied the answer by shooting the cliff exit in long shot, making unclear whether Harold is at the wheel. And just as the director's cross-cutting has created a classic example of dark comedy's affinity for the confusion of a disjointed narrative, Ashby adds to the mystery by briefly holding the airborne car in a freeze frame, after it has begun to fall towards the rocky beach below. This formalistic (self-conscious filmmaking) method creates expanded time for viewers to further ponder the puzzle. Paradoxically, Ashby had originally planned to formalistically expand the time during the car's fall by shooting it in slow motion. But a camera jammed and Ashby decided to go with the freeze frame.[5] To paraphrase an army of filmmakers past and present, "Sometimes the best things are purely accidental."

Even after the car crashes on the beach, Ashby further toys with the audience by holding the shot on the wrecked mini-hearse, before slowly panning up to the clifftop. Harold is standing there with the banjo Maude has given him; he begins to play as Cat Stevens (now known as Yusuf Islam) sings the upbeat song "If You Want to Sing Out, Sing Out" on the soundtrack. Despite Maude's real suicide, and Harold performing one final fake exit, because of his lover-teacher's positive role model the picture manages to end on a seemingly positive note. The movie anticipates a "dark comedy lite" development of the early 21st century.[6]

Granted, the genre has continued to push the shock effect for what registers as black humor, such as the Coen Brothers' *No Country for Old Men* (2007). Yet, while this propensity for an ever-escalating demonstration of the comically macabre definitely is not going away, in recent years a curious new wrinkle has emerged. One might call this a gentler form of dark comedy that eventually dovetails into a feel-good conclusion—a development normally contradictory to the genre. Prime examples of this softer side of black humor would include Curtis Hanson's *Wonder Boys* (2000), Wes Anderson's *The Royal Tenenbaums* (2001), Burr Steers' *IGBY Goes Down* (2002), Jonathan Daygon and Valerie Faris' *Little Miss Sunshine* (2006), and Christine Jeffs' *Sunshine Cleaning* (2009). Unlike the purposefully not-to-be-believed quick fix of *Catch–22* conclusions, these dark comedy lite pictures have at least one foot in reality.

Of course, if Harold is over his dark comedy obsession with death, why the final fake "cliffhanger," to pun the Jaguar episode? One could call it the teenager's final catharsis-cleansing in order to move on. After all, this time he is doing it for himself, with neither a mother nor a computer date for an audience. Moreover, he is ritualistically destroying a symbol of death with which he had formerly chosen to define himself—a hearse. Finally, the last image of banjo-playing Harold even adds, in a subliminal manner, to the life-affirming influence of Maude. To illustrate, the movie appeared at a time when Steve Martin was first emerging as a banjo-playing stand-up comic, and he was prone to claim that playing that instrument gave him "happy feet," a funny image which further suggests that Harold is now going to be all right ... or at least closer to normal. Indeed, the phrase "happy feet" fits in with the importance Maude placed upon music making one come alive: "Dear me, everybody should be able to make some music. That's the cosmic dance."

I have purposely saved Maude for last in discussing death in this movie. She is easily the most compellingly complex character on the subject in the Ashby menagerie. Despite her pep talk mentality—"Go team, go! Give me an L. Give me an I. Give me a V. Give me an E. L-I-V-E. *Live*! Otherwise, you got nothing to talk about in the locker room"— she is essentially a dark comedy philosopher whose metaphorical degree is anchored in death. The attentive viewer notes the fleeting revelation that Maude has a concentration camp number on her arm. This bundle of life has survived the Holocaust. Thus, like Yossarian on Prozac, she is constantly aware of how quickly life can end. For example, when Harold tells her she is upsetting people by randomly taking things, Maude explains, "I'm merely acting as a gentle reminder; here today, gone tomorrow, so don't get attached to things...."

Like Chaplin's close to *The Pilgrim* (1923), or Jean Renoir's conclusion to *Grand Illusion* (1937), Gordon's Maude also realizes mankind's arbitrary absurdity in both creating boundaries between countries, and the countries themselves, given that rival nations fuel the nationalism which leads to war. Consequently, when Cort's Harold asks what she was fighting for in her youth, she says, "Oh, big issues. Liberty. Rights. Justice. Kings died, kingdoms fell. I don't regret the [loss of] kingdoms—what sense [is there to] borders and nations and patriotism...." Such things lead to death, and/or people simply shutting down their lives. When Harold confesses as much to Maude, she advises: "A lot of people enjoy being dead. But they are not dead, really. They're just backing away from life. Reach out. Take a chance. Get hurt even. But play as well as you can...."

Jewish Maude never mentions the Holocaust, but she sometimes shares allusions to how being different can lead to evil. Most poignant is the random reflection, upon observing some seagulls in flight: "[Alfred] Dreyfus [1859–1935] once wrote from Devil's Island [a French penal colony off the coast of South America's Guiana] that he would see the most glorious birds. Many years later in [French] Brittany he realized they had only been seagulls. For me they will always be glorious birds."

Dreyfus was a French military officer of Jewish heritage wrongly accused of treason in 1894 in a secret court martial and sentenced to life imprisonment on Devil's Island. When it came out that he was innocent and that an army cover-up was keeping him in prison for no reason other than anti–Semitism, the "Dreyfus Case" became a *cause célèbre* in France. Because he was not pardoned until 1899 and it still took until 1906 before a military commission fully exonerated him, the occurrence became, and remains, an international example of injustice.

Maude's passing reference to how she, like an imprisoned Dreyfus, could reframe the most basic event into a "glorious" experience is the most movingly ephemeral of references to the concentration camp horrors she would have known. On another occasion Maude uses an additional bird motif along similar allegorical lines: "I used to break into pet shops to liberate the canaries. But I decided that was an idea way before its time. Zoos are full, prisons are overflowing ... oh my, how the world still dearly loves a cage."

So how does someone like Maude, who embraced life to the fullest, commit suicide? Granted, many concentration camp survivors later took their lives out of guilt. However, that was not Maude. Like a '60s hippie, and many of America's founding fathers, she was more of a Deist or a pantheist. Her thinking was in agreement with an observation by pantheist Albert Einstein: "My sense of God is my sense of wonder about the universe." Fittingly, Maude later tells Harold, "The earth is my body; my head is in the stars." Never one to dwell long on the serious, she coyly manages to even turn the latter comment into a joke:

MAUDE: Who said that, Harold?
HAROLD: I don't know.
MAUDE: Well, I suppose I did, then.

Though *Harold and Maude* begins with the nihilism of the boy and ends with the dark comedy lite of a geriatric love child, Maude's key message is a warning against becoming one of life's walking wounded–dead. One is reminded of a later pronouncement by former high-ranking Chinese official Bao Tong. After the Communist Party imprisoned him for intellectually challenging the status quo, he metaphorically discussed the paradox of people compelled to wear "masks": "Have you ever seen a dead person? After they have been made up they look amazing. Better than a live person."[7]

Transitioning to dark comedy's use of absurdity, one must embrace another slant upon *Harold and Maude*'s use of suicide. One is immediately struck by the illogical fact that the cheerleader for life ultimately kills herself, while the boy forever staging fake suicides ultimately chooses to live. Even more paradoxical is Mrs. Chasen's ongoing blasé responses to her son's self-murder sketches. Vivian Pickles' inspired Mrs. Chasen seems to be acting in another movie, like Margaret Dumont's proper wealthy matron in the irrational world of the Marx Brothers.[8] Cort's Method acting also contributed to Pickles' performance as an uncaring mother (so-called) figure to his Harold by consciously creating a real-life tension between them:

I used to, on her close-ups, give her the finger, and she would say things to Harold [sic; Ashby?] like, "I don't know what he's doing but it's distracting" ... [Pickles] was so into her own role that you could have a bomb drop [without rattling her....] I tormented her so much that when I finally went to London after the shoot.... I had to beg her to finally let me see her and when I finally did, we became good friends. But [during the production] we had no time to prepare. She arrived on Friday, and we started shooting on Monday. [I] took her to lunch on Sunday and terrorized her, smoked pot in front of her and did anything I could do ... and by Monday, she didn't want any part of [me].[9]

For Method actors, the end justifies the means; Cort's actions were no different than *East of Eden*'s (1955) James Dean whispering obscenities off-camera to his Bible-reading screen father (Raymond Massey, another traditional professional) in order to enhance the story-driven tension of another cinematic parent-child relationship.[10] In fairness to Cort and his extreme approach to Method and what some might consider a theater of the absurd technique, the young man reversed the process for his screen lover Gordon. He later recalled that she

took a break [during the production] and went back to New York. I don't know if it was Valentine's Day or what but I sent her a huge bouquet of flowers.... I said, "Dear Maude, I miss you. Love, Harold." And boy, when she came back, that really broke the frost. Not that there was any frost but it got us out [closer]....[11]

What's most absurd about *Harold and Maude* is that it mixes well-worn 1960s counter-culture components, from an anti-establishment norm, to the peace and love ethos of hippie basics 101, and reinvented the movement by successfully suggesting an "elderly woman could embody the most unguarded, delicate variety of Summer of Love openness and that she and a [man 60 years younger] should be able to fall in love and get married without being judged, much less stopped...."[12]

Moreover, by having an unofficial courtship begin with random encounters at equally random funerals, the narrative is ripe for a multitude of absurd situations. Conceivably the most preposterously funny yet mournful example arises before one interment, as the coffin is being taken from the church and placed in yet another hearse. Keep in mind that unlike most genres, dark comedy uses music *not* to reinforce the screen visual but rather to be at cross purposes with it. To best set up this *Harold and Maude* scene, perhaps the most mournfully poignant words ever written for a ceremony honoring a dead individual merit pondering: read W.H. Auden's haunting poem "Funeral Blues."[13]

However, just as the casket appears in this sorrowful situation, a marching band simultaneously passes the church playing a rousing John Philip Sousa composition. Whether one likes the March King's music or not, his work is patriotically happy, hardly what one wants or expects on such a sad occasion. Viewers' emotions are immediately in conflict. Plus, given that *Harold and Maude* ultimately embraces an anti-war position, the Sousa twist is even more ironic, given that he wrote military marches.

Though this Sousa scene is *Harold and Maude*'s best demonstration of dark comedy's playfully absurd clash of image with music, multiple others occur. One such example was briefly noted earlier, when Cat Stevens' buoyant "If You Want to Sing Out, Sing Out" song closes the film, following Maude's suicide and Harold's presumed last mock self-murder. Stevens' music, which one historian described as "sprightly and ephemeral," usually plays over scenes set at cemeteries, church funerals, and scrapyards.[14]

Ashby also finds ways to further tweak the genre's paradoxical use of music. For example, before Harold's film-opening sham suicide by hanging, he puts a Chopin album on the record player. The dark comedy incongruity of romantic classical music juxtaposed with self-destruction is soon mockingly topped as the sequence closes with the music briefly segueing to an instrumental rendition of the Christmas carol "What Child Is This?" Ashby has thus managed to further ratchet up the musical dark comedy with the religious blasphemy of comparing suicidal Harold to the baby Jesus.

In addition, Ashby pushes farcical use of music by trickery. For instance, when Harold's mom decides he will marry, there is an immediate sound cut (music from the next scene is heard before the visual appears) to church music. Naturally, we viewers assume we are about to witness the boy's wedding. Instead, Harold has haphazardly turned up at another funeral. Besides viewers being musically fooled, the five-times-married Ashby seems to suggest marriage is like a funeral. Fittingly, just as dark comedy's mantra is "Do not trust people," Ashby, as a filmmaker, underlined the point by saying, "You cannot even trust me." On another occasion, after Maude has affectionately chided Harold for not being musical, she engages him in song while she plays the piano. In the midst of this musical revelry, she enthusiastically gets up from the piano and begins to dance. Only then, as the music continues, does the viewer realize it is a player piano, and Maude has caught us in a modest example of teaching the absurd: Things are not always what they seem.

Harold applies the same lesson to his mother with the phony suicides. Thus, the movie has a darkly comic Lewis Carroll-on-acid aura. It is not surprising that in 1971, when Colin Higgins later turned his *Harold and Maude* screenplay, which had begun as a UCLA M.F.A. thesis project, into a novel, the dedication page contains a quote from

Carroll's *Through the Looking Glass* (1871), the sequel to *Alice's Adventures in Wonderland* (1865):

"It's very provoking," Humpty Dumpty said after a long silence, looking away from Alice as he spoke, "to be called an egg—very!"[15]

Because "Humpty Dumpty" has been referenced through time as everything from a clumsy young person to something worthless and/or flimsy (since it could not be properly put together again), Higgins' use of Humpty might be his dark comedy code for a vulnerable awkward Harold forever flirting with destruction like an egg on a wall.

Discussing absurdity in *Harold and Maude* always comes back to their love story. To illustrate, dark comedy relationships normally trade in lust (man as beast), not love. Yet, because of the age difference, the couple's love is still seen by many as perverse. Such is dark comedy. And one might compare this particular example of absurdity with a relationship in the Ashby-influenced Wes Anderson film *The Royal Tenenbaums* (2001). In this dark comedy about another wealthy dysfunctional family, the narrative's key love affair is between Richie Tenenbaum (Luke Wilson) and his adopted sister Margot Tenenbaum (Gwyneth Paltrow). Like Harold and Maude, Richie and Margot's love story is also seen as twisted because of common conventions. Hence, even when a true romantic conviction exists, this genre invariably finds a way to make it absurdly unnatural.

With this as a given, Ashby pushes the preposterous envelope further by showing Harold and Maude in bed the morning after a night of lovemaking. The director sets this sequence up with a technique which novelist-critic-Christian apologist and academic C.S. Lewis often called starting with "realism of presentation."[16] For example, in Lewis' fantasy novel for children *The Lion, the Witch and Wardrobe* (1950), the youngsters use a wardrobe in the spare room of an old English country house as a passage to another world. In fact, this "realism of presentation" might be as simple as giving Sigourney Weaver's spaceship character a cat in *Alien* (1979). Because of that, it enables viewers to relate to her as a pet owner, as well as assist the plot, such as when the cat goes missing and the spaceship essentially becomes a haunted house in outer space.

Ashby's best use of this Lewis insight occurs with the sequence preceding the aforementioned post-sex scene. Ushered in by a demented crackling, which would not be out of place for the witches' opening in *King Lear*, Harold and Maude are visiting an amusement park midway. We see the couple exiting a popular ride called the Trabant, a whirling wheel of a world, like a maverick ring from Saturn, which spins horizontally and then starts to fluctuate in a wavelike manner as it glides up and down. They then visit an otherworldly penny arcade in which we see a patron whose white, disheveled hair anticipates Christopher Lloyd in *Back to the Future* (1985), but this is Ashby in a cameo. It is one of those *Wizard of Oz* (1939) "We're not in Kansas any more" sequences. Eventually, Harold gifts Maude with an arcade-pressed penny declaration of love, which she promptly throws in the nearby sea so she will "always know where it's at!" This bizarre behavior is reminiscent of the Hitchcock line:

I aim to provide the public with beneficial shocks. Civilization has become so protective that we're no longer able to get our goose bumps instinctively. The only way to remove the numbness and revive our moral equilibrium is to use artificial [safe] means to bring about the shock.... The best way to achieve that ... is through a movie.[17]

In *Harold and Maude* Ashby embraces this "beneficial shocks" philosophy in both ways, by using amusement park abnormalities in the controlled environment of a movie.

The sequence closes with fireworks, with the white tracers in the sky dissolving into ephemeral circles. Then, in a delaying form cut (editing from one similar shape to another), we next see Harold in bed beginning to blow bubbles with a child's toy wand from a bottle of soapy fluid. Then the camera pans right to reveal Maude asleep. Lewis' "realism of presentation" kicks in here, because the viewer has been prepped by the preceding scene of absurd yet real-life sights and sounds experienced at an amusement park.

In terms of black humor's final pivotal theme (man as beast) as it applies to *Harold and Maude*, we need go no further than the concentration camp number tattooed on Maude's arm, or her brief musing about an earlier persecuted Jew, Alfred Dreyfus. In the film the phenomenon applies most basically to the three figures representing the institutions under anti-establishment black humor attack. While already acknowledged, this perspective must be drawn out in order to underline the systemic nature of the evil, and not marginalize it to just three insensitive people. Ashby has made this visually easy by placing behind these figures the sweeping symbol for each flawed institution. The priest has a portrait of the Pope behind him, General Victor has a picture of President Nixon in back of him, and the psychiatrist is shadowed by an image of Freud. To bastardize President Harry Truman's laudable signature line for dark comedy would be to say, "The buck [problem] *starts* [not stops] here."

Already, this chapter has suggested that later revelations about rampant pedophilia (and its cover-up) in the Catholic Church now makes *Harold and Maude* an even more prophetic dark comedy. The same can be said of Uncle Victor's commander-in-chief, since the film came out well before the shame that was Watergate. Moreover, even at the time the movie was released, Freud had long been relegated to psychiatry's back shelves, his decline in reputation attributed to both the rise of feminism and new developments in treating mental health. Now the helping hand credibility of a psychiatrist has shrunk to a level of essentially glorified pill pushers, with the real heavy lifting of therapy going to master degree counselors ineligible for prescription pads.

Some might say this is overstating, such as Uncle Victor "is a tight-sphinctered war veteran but he seems more comical than frightening…."[18] Yet for others, myself included, he seems like the "right hand man" of a racist Custer, *à la Little Big Man*. Screenwriter Higgins would seem to agree. What follows is a more embellished look at General Victor, in his own words, from Higgins' novel *Harold and Maude*. The excerpt is part of a military pep talk for Harold:

> There's the Army drubbing the Spicks at San Juan [Spanish-American War, 1898], clobbering the Chinks [Korean War, 1950–1953], and battling its way across the Remagen bridge [World War II battle, 1945]. Ah, it's a great life…. You'll see war—first-hand! And plenty of slant-eyed girls. Why, it'll make a man out of you, Harold.[19]

A rebuttal could state, "But it's so easy to make fun of the military and religion." To which satirist Bill Maher always quickly replies, "Yes, that's the point!"[20]

As this Higgins source material suggests, while *Harold and Maude* is this book's first film without a pre-existing novel for a foundation, between the author's original ingenious thesis, as well as working closely with Ashby as a producer on the production, the final film might just as well be credited as a major adaptation. That being said, Ashby was beyond ideal to direct the film. *Harold and Maude* might have been written by Higgins, but Ashby had lived the lives of both title characters. Here is the Harold side of Ashby: The director was from a dysfunctional family (especially with his mother); his father committed suicide when the boy was twelve; he permanently left home as the most confused of teenagers; and greatly disliked the military. In fact, he once said that the difference between his first film, *The Landlord* (1970, about another confused young rich kid with mother issues) and *Harold and Maude* was that the latter picture "deals with the military and military justice, and what a lot of shit all that is [and] it doesn't profess to give any answers...."[21]

These are additional factors on how Ashby was simpatico with Harold, but it is more important to examine the director as Maude-like. Hers was the philosophy he had morphed into by the time the picture was made. Also, for Ashby, she was what drove the film. The key is that both Ashby and Maude were hippies long before the 1960s. The following Ashby comments, made years before he made *Harold and Maude*, might just as well have been uttered by Ruth Gordon's character: "I truly enjoy the life I live. Even with its fear, frustration, and seeming madness at times, there is still the joy of just being. The joy of knowing you, of seeing—seeing, not just looking at—all the beautiful things there are in this crazy world we live in.... Life is absurd but its very absurdity makes it wonderful."[22] When asked why *Harold and Maude* had become such a dark comedy cult classic, Ashby's answer eventually comes to rest upon the significance of Maude:

> I think it's probably due to a number of things, the first being the kind of black humor that's in the film. I also think that a lot of it has to do with what Ruth Gordon says about life and love in the film. That's the impression I get from feedback. It's not that she said such profound things in the film, as it is maybe the way she said them. And the spirit of the film makes people laugh. They have a good time with it.[23]

And like Maude nurturing Harold, Ashby certainly nurtured Cort. The actor later recalled:

> I was an emotional minefield but I wanted the part, and [Ashby] took a chance on me and in so doing became not only a director but a father, a mother, a driving instructor, and a psychiatric nurse. It was a difficult part for me but Hal was so sympathetic, so understanding. And [as] I think back on it now, I must have driven him *crazy* but he never ever complained, and he was there for [me] twenty-four hours a day, six days a week.[24]

In 1997, *Harold and Maude* cinematographer John Alonzo, who later lensed *Chinatown* (1974,

If Maude's character was a geriatric hippie, here she is with a legitimate one: director Hal Ashby.

for which he was Oscar-nominated), *Norma Rae* (1979), and *Steel Magnolias* (1989), said:

> [*Harold and Maude*] turned out to be the most pleasant experience, really, of all the films I've shot.... I don't remember Hal doing an inordinate amount of takes. He seemed very gentle in his direction ... it became his bonding thing with all of us. There was no dialogue, no excessive Hollywood bull about "You look terrific, kid. I love you" and all that.[25]

As befitted a 40-plus-year-old pioneering hippie, Ashby was also very modest. His film philosophy was not unlike that of the father of the American documentary, Robert Flaherty, who directed and produced the first commercially successful feature-length non-fiction film, *Nanook of the North* (1922). The movie chronicles a year in the life of an Eskimo and his family traveling throughout northern Quebec in search of food and trade. Fittingly, "The essentials of Eskimo art are an apparent influence on Flaherty's aesthetics."[26] For example, an Eskimo does not believe he carves a figure from a walrus ivory tusk. Instead, he acts as more of conduit-conductor who merely removes the excess ivory and reveals a pre-existing form. Thus, both Flaherty and Ashby felt their films were to be found in the raw film footage they shot. The following Ashby observation on the subject, from his days as an Oscar-winning editor for director Norman Jewison, could have been uttered by Flaherty:

> Ashby had no preconceived ideas about how a film should be cut. "The film will tell you how to edit it," he said. And just as Jewison kept [producer Martin] Ransohoff at arm's length [during his productions], Ashby let Jewsion know he needed space [time and freedom] in order to edit effectively.[27]

Ashby's demand for independence also made him, like Robert Altman, receptive to collaborative improvisation. This is best demonstrated in *Harold and Maude* after the boy has sabotaged another computer date. Cort remembers briefly looking at his screen mother and then deciding as he began looking away to end the sequence that a moment of audience direct address might work:

> I knew Hal would never cut, or [cinematographer] John [Alonso], until we were finished with that—and I was still acting. So I just slowly turned toward the camera, and, I mean, Steven Spielberg said that's one of the most famous shots in the world. And that's because [the cast and crew] were all living that film moment to moment.[28]

Not surprisingly, this need for innovative freedom constantly put Ashby, as well as Altman and Arthur Penn, at creative odds with what then remained of old school Hollywood. Ironically, their theater of real-life experiences sometimes mirrored the darkly comic anti-establishment lives of their screen characters.

This brings us full circle to the chapter's opening, and how *Harold and Maude*'s release was a critical and commercial disaster. There is an irony here befitting its dark comedy status, given that the American Film Institute now ranks the movie as one of the top 100 comedies ever made—logging in at number 45, between Gregory LaCava's *My Man Godfrey*, (1936) and Woody Allen's *Manhattan* (1979).[29] (Billy Wilder's 1959 dark comedy *Some Like It Hot* topped the list.) Without belaboring the critical trouncing, positive reviews were *so* rare that a *Village Voice* ad was actually titled "Harold and Maude Thank [critic] Judith Crist," and it then simply quoted an extensive excerpt from her *New York Magazine* review:

> An enchanting excursion into the joy of living. Wonderfully perceptive satiric jabs at motherhood, the military, psychiatry and computer dating. Bud Cort is the very embodi-

ment of lost boyhood; Ruth Gordon is beautifully restrained and deeply touching—hers is a performance to cherish. Vivian Pickles is simply perfection.[30]

As suggested earlier, *Harold and Maude*'s more broad-based attack upon the establishment undoubtedly caused its initial poor reviews and low box office numbers, especially with a release during the Christmas season when patrons are likely to be more forgiving of the status quo. Yet a funny thing soon happened to the picture, which had seemed to undo the previous inroads made by dark comedy. Viewers started to embrace its all-encompassing blitzkrieg on the establishment. Moreover, this quick turnaround underscored its breadth by beginning in the American heartland. A 1974 *New York Daily News* story title phrased it best: "To Die in New York and Live in Minnesota," and satirized East Coast sophistication: "Minneapolis is an hour behind New York. But thanks to Doug Strand [a patron who thus far had seen *Harold and Maude* 138 times] and his

The original odd couple: Harold (Bud Cort) and Maude (Ruth Gordon).

ilk, we are now forced to reconsider *Harold and Maude* in light of Mary Tyler Mooreland."[31]

A *New York Times* piece from the same period further fleshed out this development by reporting, "On March 22, 1972, *Harold and Maude* opened at Westgate Theatre in suburban Minneapolis and [by] March 20, 1974, it [had] started its 105th week there [and] grossed nearly $500,000."[32] While the picture's new American ad slogans kiddingly included, "What Do They Know in New York?," "Minneapolis Is Three Years Ahead of New York," and "We've Heard of Word of Mouth But This Is Ridiculous," foreign box office number were also outstanding; it played in one Montreal theater for 112 weeks, and a single Paris playhouse two years.[33] Still, the article writer was most impressed by that then still amazing *Harold and Maude* run in Minneapolis. Yet, since when were the "fly-over states" without dark comedy angst? I am reminded of my favorite Garrison Keillor story from his 40-plus years as the host of public radio's *Prairie Home Companion*, broadcast near Minneapolis:

> On Wednesday the high school kids gathered out on the parking lot and watched Venus cross over the sun. They wore paper eye protectors and as usual when grown-ups are involved, the thrill of the moment was oversold. Kids were expecting some sort of galactic explosion and instead there was a tiny speck of shadow that some of them saw and others thought they saw and others weren't sure. It made you wonder what else has been oversold…. Maybe marriage is like this. You stand around with paper over your eyes and then it's over and she says, "Did you see it?" And you say, "I think so, I don't know."[34]

I first saw *Harold and Maude* in the early 1970s on a University of Iowa art house double bill with 1941's *The Maltese Falcon* (the Bogart cult was also in full bloom at the time). Keep in mind that Paramount pulled the plug on the Ashby-Higgins production *before* "saturation booking" (opening a film on 1,000-plus screens simultaneously across the country) was the norm. (Steven Spielberg's *Jaws*, 1975, is usually credited as the catalyst for this marketing scheme.) *Harold and Maude* was operating on the old distribution system, in which it might take weeks after opening in large markets, such as New York and Los Angeles, for a picture to reach a smaller venue. Thus, because of a skittish Paramount, *Harold and Maude* was initially never available in many areas.

Regardless, once the normally more conservative heartland embraced this dark comedy, *Harold and Maude* has enjoyed decades of a nearly unbroken distribution, and helped fuel a 1970s theatrical phenomenon: the "Midnight Movie." Playhouses suddenly found a late evening non-mainstream market for darkly comic cult movies, from neglected classics like Tod Browning's *Freaks* (1932) to *The Rocky Horror Picture Show* (1975). *Harold and Maude* soon benefitted from popularity with both conventional patrons and the midnight fringe. It demonstrated a fundamental characteristic of the midnight sensation: Patrons like Doug Strand were seeing these films dozens of times. It now seems as if dark comedy, a genre many once considered sacrilegious, à la Chaplin's *Monsieur Verdoux* (1947), was almost becoming a religion unto itself. In any event, there was no doubt the genre had firmly planted itself in the spotlight. Maybe a Higgins aside best summarized *Harold and Maude*: "We're all Harold, and we all want to be Maude."[35] She either says what she wants and we can't, or it's a matter of the previously noted L'esprit de l'escalier ("staircase wit"): thinking of the perfect comeback too late, à la on the staircase *after* the gathering.

This text has suggested that *Harold and Maude* is a "precursor to dark comedy lite." For instance, Charles O. Glenn, Paramount's vice-president in charge of marketing, later shared his 13-year-old-son's take upon the picture: "Maude replanted [and saved] Harold like she did the tree that the smog was killing."[36] However, just to play devil's advocate, could one not also call her a "nihilistic humanitarian," like poet Tadeusz Rozewicz? *What*? How could such a moniker be applied to a character that critic Pauline Kael described as representing an "advanced stage of pixiness"?[37] Here is the tipping point: For the good, a character like Maude can make one find space in oneself for something one never dreamed to understand, or, to the bad, something one never wanted to understand. Her pantheistic libertarianism seeks to maximize total autonomy from not

Ironically, after all Harold's mock suicides, one of which is depicted here with a pistol, Maude actually does it.

just all establishments but all rules in general. As she tells Harold, "It's best not to be too moral. You cheat yourself out of too much life." To embrace a godless, no guidelines world is basic dark comedy, an honest world only for the brave. Ruth Gordon herself, when asked if the age difference between Harold and Maude was credible, sent the question into topsy-turvydom by responding:

> I think, if you're an adult, it's extremely juvenile to *want* to understand anythin'. All ya can hope to do is to *feel* somethin'. Is it credible that the world's in the mess it's in and that no one knows [how] to solve anythin' or what to do about it?[38]

Maude survived Auschwitz, or a concentration camp like it. The writing of the aforementioned Rozewicz was a direct debunking of German socialist and philosopher Theodor Adorno, who famously said, "To write poetry after Auschwitz is barbaric."[39] Rozewicz, however, worked upon the premise that all literature before this Holocaust was a lie, and if any words were to follow, they must be penetratingly personal. Is that not Maude? Moreover, in combining lines from two Rozewicz poems, one has an even clearer picture of Gordon's character.

Whether or not one calls *Harold and Maude* dark comedy lite, its breadth epitomizes the searing barbarity at the hub of this genre. If Kael had rewritten her review, would she have paused over the phrase "[an] advanced stage of pixiness"?

5

Cabaret (2/14/72)

"Work comes before everything," says Sally Bowles in Christopher Isherwood's novel Goodbye to Berlin *(1939), which is the foundation for Bob Fosse's* Cabaret *(1972) line that could double as Fosse's philosophy, too. Of course, between the two productions were John Van Druten's 1951 play adaptation of the novel,* I Am a Camera, *which was filmed in 1955, and then adapted to the stage as the musical* Cabaret *(1966), which was radically changed by Fosse.[1]*

This dark comedy is nominally penciled in as a musical. Yet, as in previous sections, a director wants to be creatively subversive and fashion an anti-genre of his choice. Bob Fosse described his anti-musical *Cabaret* as "the first adult musical."[2] Plausibly, the best way to create such a scenario, short of his making a musical comedy about death (see Chapter 12's *All That Jazz*, 1979), is to place one's anti-musical in 1931 Berlin, just as the Nazis are emerging as the dominant political party.

The movie focuses upon young American singer-dancer Sally Bowles (Liza Minnelli). She performs at the seedy, depraved Kit Kat Klub, as Germany's wobbly Weimar (attempt at democracy) Republic is collapsing around her. Berlin has become Europe's new Sodom and Gomorrah, where decadence rules and those who care (old order Germany, communists, bohemian groups) must vie for power against ascending Nazism. The ambience is one of perverse escapism, as the Kit Kat's devilish master of ceremonies (Joel Grey) forever extols patrons to: "Leave your troubles outside. So life is disappointing. Forget it! In here, life is beautiful. The [performing] girls are beautiful. Even the [all-girl] orchestra is beautiful." Yet, as a *New Yorker* critic once opined about a comparable group of women from Fosse's *Sweet Charity* (1969), "You sense that anyone who spent a little time with [even] one of these women would have to go to the doctor afterward."[3]

The Kit Kat Klub is meant to be a microcosm for German society's early 1930s dry rot. Thus, since Sally utters signature lines like "divine decadence," or comparable lyrics, such as "Life is a cabaret" (from the title song "Cabaret"), she is the poster child for this indifferent descent into hell. But for all of Sally's unprofessional whoring and provocative bluntness, Minnelli's layered performance manages also to convey a certain wide-eyed naiveté, not unlike another 19-year-old—Bud Cort's Harold from *Harold and Maude* (1971).

Still, *Cabaret*'s real guileless character is the young British doctoral student Brian Roberts (Michael York), paying his way by teaching English to further his German studies. While Sally's excuse for her head-in-the-sand whoring is to become a movie star like Lya De Putti (whose filmography included the 1925 German classic *Variety*), Brian's preoccupation is academics and a growing fascination with the incendiary Sally. Naturally, the professorial Brian knows nothing about Putti, though he would have benefitted from a brief tutorial, since Sally was a most fitting Putti fan. The silent screen star's persona was that of a vamp; Sally aped the actress' short dark haircut, in the bobbed or "black helmet" style now most associated with another vampish period actress, Louise Brooks. Also, Putti died in 1931—the year in which *Cabaret* is set—after behaving irrationally Sally-like in a New York hospital for what should have been a treatable throat infection.

Sally and Brian met and live in a Berlin boarding house, a key link in Christopher Isherwood's novel, which reads more like a collection of short stories with Brian meandering through each tale, much as Yossarian in *Catch–22* (1970). Thus far, all this book's screen adaptations have had the most disjointed narratives. The boarding house, like the Kit Kat Klub, is another mini–Germany whose inhabitants (as also personified by the foreign Sally and Brian), by and large, just don't care. For instance, in Isherwood's novel there is a funeral procession for a former government dignitary from the weary Weimar democracy slowly passing in the street below the boarding house. This ceremony is undoubtedly for Herman Müller, twice chancellor of Germany during the Weimar Republic. A strong opponent of Hitler, Müller's death was one more plus for the growth of Nazism. Yet, a bored Sally is more interested in the sunset. Brian chillingly, yet prophetically, agrees:

> She was quite right. We had nothing to do with those Germans down there, marching ... or with the words on the banners. In a few days, I thought, we shall have forfeited all kinship with ninety-nine percent [of the world, like people who had] sold their souls to the devil. It was a curious, exhilarating, not unpleasant sensation; but, at the same time, I felt slightly scared. Yes, I said to myself, I've done it, now. I am lost.[4]

Though outsiders, they reflected a German apathy succinctly articulated by Brian's most famous line from Isherwood's book: "I am a camera with its shutter open, quite passive, recording, not thinking."[5] Along these lines, in Linda Mizejewski's fascinating musings on Sally Bowles in *Divine Decadence*, the scholar states:

> Considering how the cabaret has been characterized throughout the film, a historical cause-and-effect argument is suggested: The moral looseness of Weimar Berlin, in particular the sexual and bisexual play in Berlin nightlife, has made possible the tolerance of Nazism. The [cabaret's distorted] reflecting mirror wall [at the film's conclusion] further suggests that what the Nazis see on stage—the transvestites and sexually ambiguous emcee—are versions of themselves: grotesque, amoral, distorted—and homoerotic.... [Plus, the female eroticism of Sally] only reinforces the stereotypes of Weimar decadence, the richness of its temptations, the multiplicities of its sexualities—a disruption of the "natural order" which leaves the society vulnerable to Nazism.[6]

Mizejewski's excellent overview must only be qualified by the fact that Berlin cabarets initially mocked the early birthing of Nazism, though these nightclubs later pragmatically ceased such policy when Hitler's party began its ascendency—both of which are reflected in Fosse's film. The Kit Kat Klub's survival (at least for a while) by way of hypocrisy could be likened to the *Catch–22* sequence in which Marcel Dalio's old man tutors Art Garfunkel's man-child, whose knowledge of the world is no larger than that of a marble, on the history of hypocritical survival. Yet for the coming Holocaust, which serves as the backdrop for *Cabaret*, even Dalio's character would have been severely challenged. For example, in a later stage production of *Cabaret*, in which the action focuses more upon the master of ceremonies than Sally (the beauty of a hopscotching narrative), the show within the play closes, as does the play itself, by a sudden blackout on the emcee—then briefly returns to him spotlighted in a concentration camp uniform. Of course, survival need not always be by hypocrisy; Michael York's Brian eventually loses his blinders and leaves, as does the aforementioned real-life Jewish actor Marcel Dalio, whose greatest role was as a prisoner-of-war escapee in Jean Renoir's anti-war film *Grande Illusion* (1937). With the outbreak of World War II, the French actor found himself in a much more dangerous spot than Brian. With the Germans frequently using Dalio's picture to depict "the typical Jew," he quickly took his trade to Hollywood, where his films included the bittersweet romance–anti–Nazi classic *Casablanca* (1942).

Sally and Brian's ability to look the other way as history goose-stepped into Germany was greatly enhanced by *Cabaret*'s third major character, Baron Maximilian von Heune (Helmet Griem). Prior to his arrival, Sally and Brian had forged an atypical but fairly happy relationship at Fraulein Schneider's (Elizabeth Neumann-Viertel) boardinghouse, despite his bisexual past and Sally's ongoing willingness to go the proverbial casting couch route to break into the movies. Maximilian, strikingly handsome, affluent, and cultured, takes it upon himself to further corrupt his two new friends, as well as ignoring Germany's increasing Nazification. He will come to represent a major *Cabaret* constant: Things are never what they seem. Earlier examples would include the androgynous nature of Joel's emcee, who even passes for a woman in one of the nightclub sketches; the Kit Kat Klub's sometimes cross-dressing clientele and performers; and even Sally's boyishly short helmet hairdo. Regardless, after an extravagant weekend at Maximilian's country estate, Brian and Sally have a falling out over her romantic ramblings about controlling the baron. Brian caustically responds by describing her as "about as [femme] fatale as an after-dinner mint." As their argument escalates, what follows is one of cinema's greatest examples of verbal one-upmanship:

> BRIAN: Screw Maximilian!
> SALLY: I do.
> BRIAN: So do I.
> SALLY: You two bastards!
> BRIAN: Two? Two? Shouldn't that be three?

As suggested in the prologue, beyond the "divine decadence" of 1931 Berlin, this is hardly Fred Astaire and Ginger Rogers territory. This 1970s anti-genre, anti-musical blow made the period response to the term "musical" just as ambiguous as the sexuality (sometimes called "gender fuck") of *Cabaret* doubly ironic for Fosse:

> All I wanted to be [as a teenager] was Fred Astaire ... [I] would go to the neighborhood movie theater that showed quadruple features on Saturday. If they happened to show a Fred Astaire movie, I'd stay over and come home late at night dancing over fireplugs. If life had let me just dance down streets like Fred did, I don't think I would ever have gone into choreography or direction.[7]

The significance of Astaire has long been a given in dance history, or as humorist Robert Benchley observed of the performer and his dancing partner–sister Adele, long before Fred went from the stage to the screen, "When they dance, everything seems brighter and their comedy alone would be good enough to carry them through even if they were to stop dancing (which God forbid!)[8]

While Fosse was a great dancer before becoming a choreographer-director (check out his Chaplinesque "Who's Got the Pain" duet with future wife Gwen Verdon in *Damn Yankees*, 1958), he never became the next Astaire. (Of course, no one else did either. Astaire later stated that he would have loved to do a movie with Fosse.[9]) Fosse felt that film might give him the opportunity to become an Astaire *behind* the camera. Though Fosse was after the greatness of Astaire, it was not by aping his style. For example, Astaire's two basics were full-figure long takes of each dance (editing would have either taken away from the uniqueness of the movement and/or even made a viewer question the skills of the dancer), and secondly, have the musical numbers advance the storyline. Hence, there were only randomly added song-and-dance routines, regardless of how inspired the material, a rule Busby Berkeley forever entertainingly forgot.

As imaginative as Fosse's stage choreography was—and he won eight Broadway Tonys in that category—he was obsessed by the increased creative control provided by editing, what is now referenced as the "montage musical." Fosse was first drawn to dance by fragmentation of the figure after seeing John Huston's *Moulin Rouge* (1952), a film

The driven Bob Fosse.

whose influence upon Fosse is greatly expanded upon in Chapter 12's examination of 1979's *All That Jazz*. Thus, *Cabaret*'s purposely poor traditional choreography (this was supposed to be a sleazy club) was Fosse-ized when he cut to "small features of a finger motion or an eyebrow position [which] were made to carry the momentous poetic weight which would be invisible on Broadway...."[10]

Fosse's second derailing of Astaire is a more nuanced "matter of opinion" take on *Cabaret*. "It was Fosse's intention to make the songs in *Cabaret* comment on the dramatic action, even more so than in the Broadway show."[11] For example, in Leslie Taubman's *Cabaret* essay, she interprets Sally singing the relationship-splattering song "Mein Herr" during Brian's first visit to the club as a way of letting him know she is "now available."[12] However, for me, to paraphrase D.H. Lawrence's personalized art observation, "Trust the tale not the teller," "Mein Herr," is simply a softer take on Lola Lola (Marlene Dietrich) forever singing "Falling in Love Again." This was during Josef von Sternberg's 1930 film *The Blue Angel*, a picture actually shot amidst the dissipated days of the waning Weimar Republic—the period in which *Cabaret* is set. Moreover, neither Sally nor Lola has any interest in a lasting relationship. Lola is more cynical, but both are still two trains going in the same direction. When Minnelli's character sings "Maybe This Time" after allowing a fleeting romantic dalliance with Brian, it is difficult to accept the scenario's feasibility outside the domain of a conventional musical. Granted, Sally cuts her academic (York) loose before the shame which kills Lola Lola's professor (Emil Jannings), but both relationships are inevitable failures. Sally was only kidding herself; neither a man nor the fate of mankind will keep her from movie star aspirations. As Pauline Kael succinctly phrased it in her extravagantly positive *Cabaret* review, "This Sally has grown claws."[13]

Even the Kit Kat Klub's *ménage à trois* "Two Ladies" number does *not* signal a group romp between *Cabaret*'s three principal players. Yes, both Sally and Brian individually share sexual favors with Maximilian. However, as the previously noted one-upmanship dialogue between Sally and Brian which begins with "Screw Maximilian!" makes abundantly clear, neither of them has been party to a *ménage à trois*. In football, there is a name for numbers like "Mein Herr," "Maybe This Time," and "Two Ladies": "misdirection plays," which give the opposition the wrong idea what is coming next. And *Cabaret's* application of misinformation music is in perfect harmony with dark comedy's soundtrack frequently clashing with what is happening, or about to happen, visually. Again, it is a world of things not being what they seem.

Cabaret does boast some numbers with a more direct narrative link, such as Sally and Joel's emcee performing "Money Money" after she discovers the wealth of Maximilian. Sometimes even the straightforward connection can be so disturbingly fragmented that any tie to Astaire's sunny style seems superfluous. For example, in Grey's satirically sentimental "If You See Could See Her Through My Eyes" number, which foreshadows the Jewish wedding of supporting characters Fritz Wendel (Fritz Wepper) and Natalia Landauer (Marisa Berenson), the emcee performs a sham duet with someone in a gorilla suit, insinuating the Nazi propaganda of Jews as a subhuman race.

Once again, black humor's ability to crisscross inappropriate music with screen imagery is spot on. Moreover, in this wedding illustration, the dark comedy component is amazingly perverse. That is, the Jewish ceremony to follow embodies the movie's only example of love, and one naturally realizes the couple's future fate in Nazi Germany.

"Claws" and *Cabaret.*

Moreover, the weary poignancy of the situation is ratcheted up further by a final element of the ceremony: Fritz has voluntarily dropped his successful play of passing as a Christian in an increasingly Nazi state. Once more, *Cabaret* denotes that things are seldom what they seem. Plus, as with *Harold and Maude* and other black comedies, the twisted society within the film paradoxically sees the couple along unnatural lines.

One Astaire fundamental which Fosse does not bastardize, however, is generally presenting *Cabaret* along show business musical lines. That is, with one exception, the numbers are presented by professionals in a theatrical setting. Fosse's hero (Astaire) usually played a song-and-dance man, with his signature logo being a top hat and tails. In contrast, as touched on before, the other school of musicals falls under a populist banner. For instance, real people (amateur performers) spontaneously burst into song and dance as the feeling moves them, such as Gene Kelly's impromptu joyous title number from *Singin' in the Rain* (1952), when a career-saving solution comes along. Kelly, Astaire's only credible song-and-dance rival, usually played non-professionals, such as the baseball player of *Take Me Out to the Ball Game* (1949), a sailor in *On the Town* (1949), and the painter in *An American in Paris* (1951).

To Fosse's anti-genre, anti-musical credit, he also manages to debase two populist *Cabaret* numbers, despite the picture's overriding realistic (numbers performed in a cabaret) show business style. This is no small task, given that populist musicals, by their very nature, generate song and dance from wholesome settings, such as Judy Garland's euphoria over a first date on a trolley evolving into the famous "Trolley Song" of *Meet Me in St. Louis* (1944). Ironically, one of Fosse's populist numbers even qualifies as *Cabaret's* most chillingly pivotal scene. Fittingly, it is the only song performed outside the Kit Kat Klub. During a road trip, with Sally still asleep in the limousine, Brian and Maxmilian briefly stop at a Bavarian beer garden. A blonde man-child of androgynous beauty stands up and begins to angelically sing a ballad written in the style of an old German folk song, "Tomorrow Belongs to Me." Just as the viewer is moved and implicated by the complete winning ambiance of the sequence, Fosse slowly pans down from the boy's face to reveal that he is a member of the Nazi youth movement. Patrons of the beer garden are soon standing and robustly singing along with the youngster. As Brian and Maxmilian leave, the former asks the aristocrat if he still thinks the powers that be can continue to keep the Nazis in line. Maximilian says nothing. *Films and Filming* rightly stated:

> [T]he highpoint of the film [is] the beer-garden song "Tomorrow Belongs to Me" ... never before has the almost irresistible attraction of Nazism and its equally irresistible rise been more clearly, simply, and beautifully put across ... spine chillingly simple ... it is one of the great moments of cinema history.[14]

This cinematic prologue to Hitler severely taxes an axiom often attributed to populist Lincoln: "You can fool all the people some of the time, and some of the people all of the time, but you cannot fool all the people all the time."

Fosse's second polluting of the people's populist use of song returns to the Kit Kat Klub but is intercut with violence outside the nightspot. Early in *Cabaret* a Bavarian folk dance is performed on the tiny stage, and it involves a great deal of slapping of hands and feet and individual participants. Though this is a professional setting (so-called), it replicates such a basic leather shorts–attired German tradition, the routine has an "of the people" feel about it. Simultaneously, Fosse crosscuts this number with the not dissimilar beating of the club's bouncer by Nazi thugs in an alley outside. (Earlier the victim had removed from the cabaret audience a Nazi attempting to solicit funds.) With wicked effectiveness, Fosse applies this black humor shock effect to suggest that people are not inherently good (negating this key populism tenet).

This has been the anti-genre, anti-musical core which Fosse brings to *Cabaret*. One could have summarized the process by simply quoting a *New York Times* line from an article entitled "*Cabaret* May Shock Kansas": "[There is] an authentic tawdriness that one does not expect to find in a musical."[15] Regardless, as the previous scrutiny of the bouncer's beating suggests, it is time simply to start probing the picture as a dark comedy, beginning with our lead-off theme of death's significance to the genre. Yet, as the following pages demonstrate, such things continue to chronicle further anti-musical elements.

Sally (Liza Minnelli) performing in all her self-centered "divine decadence" style.

Though the presumed death of the Kit Kat Klub's bouncer is the only killing shown on the screen, the Holocaust serves as a more heightened backdrop than Maude's concentration camp number. Interestingly, this was even more the case upon the publication of Isherwood's *Goodbye to Berlin* novel. Though set in 1931, this collection of loosely connected short stories did not reach bookstores until 1939, shortly before World War II began in Europe. As the *New York Times* reviewer morbidly observes, "It describes a people who are conscious of [a] coming crisis but seem helpless [uncaring?] to do anything about it."[16] The *New York Tribune*'s praise of Isherwood's work might have doubled for Fosse's adaptation: "The best aspect of these stories is that they are not weighed down by any falsely dramatic sense of crisis [such as Hitler doing] his act in the Sports Palace … [Isherwood's] touch is so sure that something at the central quality of Berlin life is gathered … the world's most artificial capital."[17]

Ironically, the same day (March 19, 1939) that many publications reviewed *Goodbye to Berlin*, the first English-language translations of Hitler's autobiographical manifesto *Mein Kampf* (*My Struggle*) were also critiqued. In contrast to the subtitles of Isherwood's early Nazi warning and Fosse's innovatively loyal dark comedy adaptation of said work, *Mein Kampf* critiques often had a not inelegant bluntness, with shades of their own black humor:

> Let it be said that if the world is overthrown by this document and the man behind it, it is overthrown without benefit of grammar or literary style…. I do not find this unimportant…. It is perhaps fitting that a movement glorifying the instinctual and the herdlike,

and expressing contempt for the intellectual ... should, in its most apocalyptical expression, use mass words and debased language, as though to announce itself as the book to end books; the literature to end literature.[18]

Because war had yet to arrive, 1939 was soon adrift with English translations of Nazi writings which were just too inviting for satirists—material on the eve of Chaplin's seminal Hitler takedown, *The Great Dictator* (1940). One such 1939 Nazi anthology, *Lunacy Becomes Us*, "By Adolf Hitler and His Associates" (edited by Clara Leiser), elicited a witheringly dark comedy review from an exceptional but often neglected period satirist, Will Cuppy, who gifted readers with the book *How to Become Extinct* (1940) the following year. Cuppy's critique also dissected the poor writing with the loony ideology:

In one respect, Adolf Hitler and his collaborators are to be congratulated. They have probably come closer towards capturing the quintessence of lunacy than any living person. [For example,] "No other political movement has discovered that the long-haired cat is of German origin ... [and that] Hitler is a new, a greater and more powerful Jesus Christ." Yes, this book is just full of wows.[19]

Beyond this foundation upon which Fosse and others would build, Isherwood created additional 1939 anti-war tracts. He co-authored with W.H. Auden two other conflict-related works, the first a sometimes darkly comic play entitled *On The Frontier*, "about the hokum and futility of warfare."[20] The second was a book on the Sino-Japanese War, which Isherwood and Auden based upon their 1938 travels in the Far East. A variation upon *Goodbye to Berlin*, it was entitled *Journey to War*.

Such anti-war activity brings one back to *Cabaret*'s close. British Brian has finally acquired a conscience and leaves Berlin after a street altercation with leaflet-distributing Nazis. Englishman Isherwood, who later became a U.S. citizen, had named Brian's *Goodbye to Berlin* character Isherwood, too. Though he comically downplays the action in his introduction as nothing more than becoming a "convenient ventriloquist's dummy," his later writings negate this position.[21] Unfortunately, this transformation never applies to Sally, who remains in Berlin with her tunnel vision self-centered goal. People are beginning to die and she does nothing? Traditional musicals are supposed to have neither uncaring heroines nor serious politics in general. As proposed in *Divine Decadence*, moments of historical crises, like the vacuum created by the collapsing Weimar Republic, are easily connected to other periods of preoccupied, do-nothing citizenry allowing tyranny to surface, from the McCarthy era to the early birthing of the Vietnam War, which the Vietnamese call the "American War."[22] These uncaring perpetual blind spots of humanity are what drive dark comedy. In this study, however, only with *Cabaret* and *All That Jazz* (another Fosse film), does one have to confront such an ultimately unsympathetic character.

This chapter's opening quote by Sally about there essentially being no governor on her engine, with work being all important, could be likened to Europe's then greatest screen actor, Emil Jannings, Lyda De Putti's co-star in *Variety*. During *Cabaret*'s high-society dinner party at Maximilian's country estate, Sally attempts to impress a fellow dinner guest by claiming to be a friend of Jannings. Nonetheless, Sally's future potential for being like the actor merits a mini-biography of the star. After Jannings' international success with *Variety* sandwiched between celebrated F.W. Murnau's *The Last Laugh* (1925) and *Faust* (1926, with the actor fittingly playing the devil!), Hollywood called, and Jannings would win the first ever Best Actor Academy Award for his combined efforts in

The Way of all Flesh (1927) and *The Last Command* (1928). However, when sound film became the late 1920s rage, his thick German accent curtailed his American screen career, and Jannings returned to Germany. Ironically, at the same time Sally was attempting to do (and ignore) anything to become a movie star, Jannings maintained his star status by allowing Hitler's Minister of Propaganda, Joseph Goebbels, to recruit his services for films promoting Nazism. Jannings' propaganda work earned him a medal and a production company in 1938, and the title Artist of the State by 1938. Still misguided in his allegiance to work, whatever the cost, at World War II's conclusion he is said to have been carrying his Oscar when apprehended by American troops, as if that would explain and/or justify surrendering moral integrity—a "get out of jail free" card.

If blind ambition is not explanation enough for ignoring social responsibility, "divine decadence" makes for a very entertaining accompanying reason, especially if one manages to combine the two. Thus, Sally drunkenly beds everyone with a pulse to get ahead. And if Maude is obviously Hal Ashby's surrogate character in *Harold and Maude* (laid-back and anti-establishment), Sally is just as patently the drug-driven, sexaholic, workaholic Fosse's *Cabaret* substitute. For all the protests of the Vietnam era, there was also Timothy Leary's simultaneous LSD mantra of "Turn on, tune in, drop out," and the era's more generic "Sex, drugs, and rock 'n' roll." Put this in a 1960s blender of growing distrust of the government jumpstarted by President John F. Kennedy's assassination and the Warren Commission debacle, and the late Weimar looks a lot like the Kennedy Camelot crash. As Sam Wasson, Fosse's definitive biographer, has stated:

> No one knew Bob Fosse was telling his own story. A film about the bejeweling of horror, *Cabaret* coruscated with Fosse's private sequins, the flash he feared made him Fosse. From those fears emerged a nihilistic worldview of political and social double-dealing perfectly synced to the war in Vietnam, the Pentagon Papers, and the mounting sense that American virtue was little more than an act. Yet, that was a byproduct. Personally [and purposely] removed from politics and the societal unrest around him, Fosse was largely untroubled by the not-so-distant cycle of hopelessness and devastation that reached from Altamont [the 1969 bloody Rolling Stones and company concert] to Kent State, My Lai to Attica [prison riot of 1971] but [Fosse's] own gloom happened to meet the public's halfway, and he stumbled into the present.[23]

Cabaret, a darkly comic look at the provocative end days of the Weimar Republic, was a critical and commercial hit in part because it helped usher in the new brand name for the 1970s: cynicism. And the decade was just getting warmed up. The next national spectacle of disbelief after *Cabaret*'s 1972 release was Watergate, which "opened" slowly later that year, but had a big finish: bringing down the Nixon White House in 1974. "American [cynicism] had caught up to Bob Fosse."[24]

If Sally and Fosse were guilty of indifference and personal preoccupation, however, is this usually not history's way to war after war, and countless accompanying genocides? This is not an amnesty statement, just a sharing of the collective cause. Plus, Fosse was always hardest on himself (see Chapter 12). Moreover, as another of his biographers has noted:

> [T]he stage show of the cabaret was not evil; the evil lay in the audience's unresponsive, insensitive, soulless, impassive faces. The only gleeful responses that Fosse allowed the audience were in response to female mud wrestlers. It was hardly necessary to point out further the parallel between these observers and Germany of 1931, sitting still for the Nazi show.[25]

To redirect this phenomenon to a contemporary situation, as Alvin H. Rosenfeld disturbingly suggests in *Imagining Hitler*:

> Western fascination with (and anxiety about) German fascism stems partially from our "resemblance" to Germans as Westerners sharing many of the same traditions and arts; in documentary footage of the crowds cheering Hitler, we find "familiar faces in the crowd, the look of neighborly, even family, resemblance."[26]

For Fosse there was complicity in this easy manipulation of the masses. For instance, when the artist later did the original Broadway stage production of *Chicago* (1975–1977), one of its signature numbers is "Razzle-Dazzle." As Fosse biographer Martin Gottfried has noted, the song "proceeded to sum up a lifetime of Fosse—Riff being Fosse's first stage name."[27]

Selling something with the "old razzle-dazzle" is reminiscent of how German historian Gitta Sereny described her childhood response to Leni Riefenstahl's chilling display of documentary razzle-dazzle in the infamous Nazi propaganda film *Triumph of the Will* (1935), which so mesmerizingly showcased the 1934 Nazi Party Congress in Nuremberg:

> I thought it was the most beautiful thing I'd ever seen. [I'd] never seen anything as wonderful and I screamed with the best of them. "Heil, Heil" or whatever. And I don't, you know, feel guilty about that. How can I? I was eleven. What I found extraordinary was the theater.[28]

Riefenstahl's razzle-dazzle effectiveness reached well beyond children. Frank Capra, whom the U.S. government charged with making Allied documentaries to counter *Triumph of the Will*, later said of the film:

> It was at once the glorification of war, the deification of Hitler, and the canonization of his apostles ... panoplied with all the pomp and mystical trappings of a Wagnerian opera.... That film paralyzed the will of Austria, Czechoslovakia, Scandinavia and France.... That film practically paralyzed my own will....[29]

Minnelli's Sally and MC Joel Grey performing "Money Money."

Fosse biographer Wasson even makes a direct link between *Cabaret* and *Triumph*. He feels Grey's maniacal emcee could be

> the fascist of the cabaret.... When the emcee is joking, is he endorsing the Nazis or mocking them? When he sings "Money, Money," is he celebrating wealth or knocking the rich? It's so fun we can't be sure. That's the whole idea. Entertaining is seduction, *Cabaret* says, the happy face on *Triumph of the Will*. And it kills.[30]

Fosse's own career started as a teen tap dancer in sleazy burlesque houses in and around Chicago, so he was very familiar with the milieu of a Kit Kat Klub and the ease with which humanity's inherent herd mentality could be shaped by the proverbial shiny subject, the "old razzle-dazzle." Thus, his relationship with *Cabaret* was complex—one part puppeteer and one part participant—so there was even guilt mixed in with not being comfortable in his own skin. The legacy was work increasingly immersed in cynicism and disillusionment, the roots of black humor parlayed into a dance of death towards civilization in self-immolation.

He need not have been so hard on himself. One could liken it to the universal joke about how a seasoned soldier's cynicism, born of naïve patriotic gullibility, made his home country the worst place on earth ... with the possible exception of everywhere else.[31] Razzle-dazzle or not, humanity is just easily exploitable. Here is how one of the Nazi architects of World War II, Herman Göering, chillingly described it:

> Why, of course, the people don't want war. Why would some poor slob on a farm want to risk his life in a war when the best he can get out of it is to come back to his farm in one piece? Naturally, the common people don't want war, neither in Russia, nor in England, nor in America, nor in Germany. That is understood. But after all, it is the leaders of the country who determine the policy and it is always a simple matter to drag the people along, whether it is a democracy or a Fascist dictatorship or a parliament or a Communist dictatorship. The people can be brought to the bidding of the leaders. That is easy. All you have to do is to tell them they are being attacked and denounce the pacifists for lack of patriotism and exposing the country to danger. It works the same way in any country.[32]

Enough on dark comedy and death in *Cabaret*. What of absurdity and chaos? At the risk of creating a sphinx without a riddle, given *Cabaret*'s groundbreaking status as an anti-musical, the movie merits an unconventional approach to this black humor component. What follows might be called "Faust Meets 'German Expressionism'" (1919–1931), a film movement characterized by a stylized Gothic *mise-en-scène* driving a macabre, low-life narrative of chaos. And is finding reality lost in a Faustian legend so different from discovering truth in the epic yarn that is *Little Big Man* (1970)? First, Grey's ambiguous emcee was earlier referenced as a possible fascist, but that seems too modest. Though Fosse aimed for realism, with regard to when and where songs were sung, one *could* interpret his emcee as straight out of *Faust*. In this classic German legend the title character sells his soul to the devil for some earthly goal, only to eventually pay by eternal damnation. The devil's representative in these proceedings is Mephistopheles. One could posit that by story's end Sally and/or Germany has made such a Faustian arrangement, with Joel as Mephistopheles.

Throughout the movie he seems to be a hellish Greek chorus of one, with his garish makeup, fiendishly twisted grin and piercingly demonic eyes prophetically telegraphing to viewers exactly what temptation is about to succeed. The movie's opening and closing are bookended by his distorted image in the cabaret's fun house mirror. His disturbing likeness seems not to have changed, though the closing reflections, unlike the beginning, display an audience now largely composed of Nazis.

Initially, Grey's appearances are limited to the cabaret. But later Fosse uses the emcee's diabolical face in a handful of inserts at pivotal points. For example, shortly after Maximilian's excessively elaborate society party at his country chateau but before Sally, Brian, and host return to Berlin, there is a succinctly surprising insert of the emcee whispering "Money." And another disjointed intrusion occurs just following the "Tomorrow Belongs to Me" beer garden sequences, after Maximilian has no answer for Brian's question about Germany and/or its aristocracy still controlling the Nazis.

So if this is a Faustian tale, where is the big payoff for Germany and/or Sally? Well, shortly after the story's 1931 beginnings, history chronicles how, for over a decade, the Nazis bluffed and blitzkrieged themselves to amazing success before the "bill" came due. In contrast, the dividend for Sally's soul is speculative. Yet, here is where the Faust legend meets German Expressionism, via our designated emcee Mephistopheles. Late in the story, Sally has become pregnant by either Brian or Maximilian, which is not a good career move for a wannabe movie star. One night before going on stage, Grey's character comes up behind Sally and, while cupping her breasts, murmurs something to her. There is no surprise on her part, either from his sudden wraparound physical embrace, nor its intimate nature. Yet, prior to this the film has shown neither contact, nor conversations between the two. This soon results in an unseen abortion, Brian's permanent return to England, and her film ending *tour de force* performance of the title song.

One flaw in the film is that Sally has always seemed too talented for the vulgar Kit Kat Klub. But her staggering rendition of "Cabaret," the slick musical accompaniment by the hitherto mediocre house band, Sally's striking crisscross purple evening gown (the only time her performing costume has either color or class), and the unexpectedly tasteful stage lighting suggests she is about to be discovered. Moreover, Sally unexpectedly has the audience numbers to make it happen. While her earlier performances were often to practically an empty club, now it is abruptly packed? Plus, the crowd is full of Germany's new powerbrokers, the Nazis. Consequently, while one might explain this away by Fosse merely providing a big finish, the aforementioned atypical checklist (combined with Sally's self-centered "whatever it takes" philosophy), does give one Faustian pause.

Where does this intersect with German Expressionism? First, the emcee's backstage breast-cupping scene with Sally initiates a brief series of *Cabaret* events strongly reminiscent of a disturbing signature sequence in Fritz Lang's quintessential German Expressionistic film, *M* (1931). Shot at the same time and place in which *Cabaret* is set, *M* is a psychological thriller about a mentally disturbed child murderer (Peter Lorre). It opens with a young schoolgirl, Elsie Beckman (Inge Landgut), returning to her boarding house home for lunch while bouncing a ball which becomes synonymous with her, since Lang uses it to showcase plot points. For example, the ball is bounced off a wanted poster warning Berlin about the serial killer. Lang cross-cuts between Lorre stalking the child and her concerned mother forever looking down a staircase labyrinth for the daughter. Elsie's fate is ultimately revealed by her ball rolling away from some bushes.

The ball resurfaces in *Cabaret* at the time of the abortion. In quick progression the following events occur, though one eventually realizes they are not in chronological order: said ball is kicked down unidentified boarding house steps past a child; Sally and the emcee have their meeting; again the ball (which, from this shot, appears decorated with dancers) is kicked; the emcee passes Sally to go on stage; Sally, in an expensive coat (a gift from Maximilian), comes up those boarding house steps past a child and gives him the ball; the emcee is whispering to Sally; a French Can-can is performed at the club *sans* Sally; she comes in late and coatless to her own boarding house, and a waiting Brian deciphers what has occurred.

Besides the obvious link between the balls and a dead child, Fosse's disjointed narrative sequence (a dark comedy basic) also suggests the chaos and absurdity central to black humor, *M*, and German Expressionism in general. Moreover, Lang's figure of a mother hopelessly looking for comfort (a returning daughter) *down* that geometric-like maze of a stairwell anticipates the equally appalling abyss-like emotions Sally seems to be feeling upon her own staircase entanglement. In either case, there is a sense of sleep-walker helplessness, which demands a tyrant type (Sally's demonic emcee?) to restore order, *à la* the film which launched German Expressionism, *The Cabinet of Dr. Caligari* (1919). Fittingly, in both Isherwood's original text and *Cabaret*, as the Weimar Republic slides closer to collapse, a supporting character representative of the people wishes to have the (tyrant) Kaiser back."[33] So here is another reason that that black hole of a political void which was early 1930s Germany would be receptive to what seems so absurd today: embracing a Mephistopheles-Hitler. The esteemed German-American film theorist and historian Siegfried Kracauer makes a direct link between the two poles of German Expressionism (chaos vs. the tyrant) leading directly to Nazism in his 1947 book *From Caligari to Hitler: A Psychological History of the German Film*, an academic slideshow progression to hell.[34]

Finally, the previously noted bookend twisted emcee images which open and close *Cabaret* also bring to mind three concluding key and related *M* sequences. First, the viewer's initial full view of Lorre's face occurs when he peers into a mirror at his boarding house. Because he neither can believe nor refrain from his horrific crimes, he uses his fingers to misshape his face into the monster he has become. Second, when he is later on the prowl for anther victim, he stops at a shop window to look at a display of knives, his instrument of choice. Lang then reverses the camera position so that we view him from inside the store, his face framed by a reflection of blades. However, a mirror within the store display reflects the image of a child onto the window's interior plate glass. This enables the outward-looking viewer to see both the child and her effect upon Lorre. This time his almost salivating expression of bloodlust morphs naturally into something sickeningly horrific. Third, as he trails the child, she briefly pauses at a bookstore window display which features a circular, hypnotically twirling vortex sign. This spinning image summarizes both the absurd heinous act which might be about to happen, and the world in which it exists—the Nazification of 1931 Berlin. Such reflected images of ludicrous things to come seem condensed by the deformed emcee's mirrored *Cabaret* face. This is one take upon absurdity by way of Faust meets German Expressionism in *Cabaret*. One Fosse biographer has gone so far as to suggest: "That emcee was kind of Hitler, and Sally Bowles, when she crossed the Mylar curtain that separated Berlin from the cabaret, chose show business instead of life. This Fosse could relate to."[35]

There also seems to be a self-absorbed, darkly comic link between Fosse and Isherwood himself—looking for sense in life's absurdity. In the director's autobiographical opus *All That Jazz*, there are repeated morning sequences of Fosse's dying surrogate character staring into a mirror. His sardonic expression always ends with an entertainer's throwing out of his arms coupled to a weary rendition—still to the mirror—of, "It's showtime." One cannot experience this daily ritual without thinking of a sequence in Isherwood's equally autobiographical groundbreaking gay novel *A Single Man* (1964), in which his drained and dying surrogate character also stands in front of a mirror, mockingly surveying

> a face as the expression of a predicament. Here's what it has done to itself, here's the mess it has somehow managed to get itself into. Staring and staring ... it sees many faces within its face—the face of the child, the boy, the young man, the not-so-young man—all present still, preserved like fossils on superimposed layers, and, like fossils, dead. Their message to this live dying creature is: Look at us—we have died—what is there to be afraid of? It answers them: But that happened so gradually, so easily *I'm afraid of being rushed*.[36]

Each case is a volatile blend of humor and horror. And in each case their proxy person soon dies. Thus, it is no surprise that Fosse was so drawn to Isherwood's novel and strived, as this text's proceeding auteurs have done, to be true to the original work—an accomplishment universally credited to this director.

A final addendum to the absurdity strand is a topic which periodically surfaces throughout this text: the incongruity of love to dark comedy, a genre in which man as beast is the norm. Furthermore, on the rare occasion when love does occur, the response can range from the seeming perversity by age of Harold and Maude's relationship, to the tragedy inherent to the marriage of *Cabaret*'s young Jewish couple Fritz (Fritz Wendel) and Natalia Landauer (Marisa Berenson). Recent productions of *Cabaret*, such as the 2014 Broadway revival, do not have the latter duo. Instead, the play has returned to a variation of the theme in the first stage adaptation of Isherwood's stories, John Van Druten's *I Am a Camera*. In this case, the boarding house owner nearly marries a Jewish renter but calls it off for fear of Nazi reprisals. While this perspective is more realistic, because the romantic Fritz had been in the racial clear (in that he had been successfully passing as Christian), Fosse's slant is more befitting a dark comedy. This is a genre which thrives upon usurping what *should* be normal. Plus, Fritz and Natalia's relationship better highlights the impossibility of Sally and Brian as a couple. Moreover, Sally's ethics, or lack of, is the perfect segue to the next point.

What of man as beast in *Cabaret*, dark comedy's third theme in its pocket definition of the genre? Well, with a movie doubling as a prologue for the Holocaust, the chapter has already documented the thin veneer of civilized behavior. Fosse's brilliance here is to include himself as a Sally "career is everything" Bowles–like character, an inattentive accomplice to depravity. Evil is never really anonymous; that is why the preceding mirror metaphors can conjure up such powerful emotions.

Cabaret's story at first glance is less tangential to "man as beast" connections to the Vietnam War and/or the events leading up to it than the focus films of the preceding chapters. Plus, the knee-jerk response to anything having to do with the Nazis initially would seem further to let the contemporary individual off the hook—that could not happen again! Yet, the further it recedes into history's rearview mirror, a greater number of oncoming signs appear suggesting German artist George Grosz, whose savage caricatures of the late Weimar Republic Berliners have come to both define the period and serve as a model for Fosse's shot-on-location *Cabaret*, later described the situation in a manner that seems chillingly current: "The people ... had long since become inured to the strange, unusual, and repulsive.... [I] was among those who wanted to extricate themselves from absolute nothingness. We wanted something more but what the 'more' was we could not exactly say."[37]

In a newer, more complete edition of Isherwood's *Berlin Stories*, his 1954 "About This Book" states, "[I] entered a modernistic [Berlin] hotel where I was surrounded by thick-necked, cigar-smoking businessmen who might have stepped right out of the cartoons of Georg[e] Grosz. It was I, not these people who had changed...."[38]

There is a lengthy professorial passage in Isherwood's aforementioned *A Single Man* which more precisely confronts the baser subtextual danger lurking below humanity's surface for Fosse and himself. Fittingly, this clarification is triggered by a new generation's questions about Nazis and anti–Semitism. The novel's Los Angeles professor, based upon Isherwood's teaching years at Los Angeles State College (now California State University) during the 1950s and early 1960s, is asked by a student whether a passage from his Aldous

Cabaret's look was largely influenced by the caricaturist drawings of period German artist George Grosz (1893–1959).

Huxley readings means "the Nazis were right to hate the Jews? Is Huxley anti–Semitic?"[39] The professor responds with slowly growing passion:

> No—Mr. Huxley is *not* anti–Semitic. The Nazis were *not* right to hate the Jews. But their hating the Jews was *not* without a cause. No one *ever* hates without a cause.... Look—let's

Beyond the people of the Weimar Republic, George Grosz's art also effected the appearance and attitude of Sally (Art © Estate of George Grosz/Licensed by VAGA, New York, New York).

leave the Jews out of this, shall we? ... So let's think about this in terms of some other minority, any one you like but a small one ... for example, people with freckles aren't thought of as a minority by the non-freckled. They *aren't* a minority in the sense we're talking about. And why aren't they? Because a minority is only thought of as a minority when it constitutes some kind of threat to the majority, real or imaginary. And no threat is ever *quite* imaginary.... What would this particular minority [such as Isherwood being gay] do if it suddenly became the majority overnight? ... So, let's face it, minorities are people who probably look and act and think differently from us and have faults we don't have. We may dislike the way they look and act, and we may hate their faults.... If we're frank about our feelings, we have a safety valve, and if we have a safety valve, we're actually less likely to start persecuting.... [But] suppose this minority does get persecuted, never mind why.... There always *is* a reason, no matter how wrong it is—that's my point. And, of course, persecution itself *is* always wrong....[40]

In this extended quote, Isherwood is embracing "man as beast" at its most basic, absurd core. Some fundamental element of humanity invariably finds fear in something it cannot understand and only knows persecution as a response. This is dark comedy 101; humankind's only real primer has always been a variation of the aforementioned Cuppy book *How to Become Extinct*.

A final *Single Man–Cabaret* connection further enhances Isherwood and Fosse's common ground: *Cabaret*'s morality tale about not letting personal interests blind you to any approaching big picture abyss is anticipated by the single day chronicled in Isherwood's novel. It occurs during the October 1962 Cuban Missile Crisis. Exactly as in his *Berlin Stories*, a potential apocalypse had come to roost.

How had humanity again let preoccupations and/or self-centered fears occur? Well, the Cuban Missile Crisis was a pivotal point in the Cold War, precipitated by the political bullying of America's early 1950s homegrown neo-fascist politician Joseph McCarthy. This junior Senator from Wisconsin soon had America seeing communism everywhere. For example, even major league baseball's Cincinnati "Reds" had to become the "Red Stockings" for a time. And if one did not drink McCarthy's Kool-Aid, persecution soon followed, such as the blacklisting of liberal Hollywood artists. CBS's Edward R. Murrow's haunting cry, "Never confuse dissent with disloyalty," would be a better safeguard maxim than the herd instinct statement "In God we trust," but most Americans did nothing.

How does this bring one full circle to *Cabaret*'s underlying warning about how Vietnam came to occur, when Americans, like 1931 Berliners, were again playing that head-in-the-sand game? Each of the preceding dark comedy chapters has not only funneled its focus film through that conflict in some manner, the majority of works involved, especially Arthur Penn's *Little Big Man*, Joseph Heller's *Catch-22*, and Thomas Hooker's *MASH*, were created, in part, as a response to the gag order mentality of America during the preceding McCarthy era. To blow off this subtextual guilt trip as some deep-dish academic rhetoric is simply more absurdity. Period pop culture was fairly shouting, or should one say singing, the same verdict, as demonstrated by the Rolling Stones' "Sympathy for the Devil," from their very commercial album *Beggar's Banquet* (from 1968, the decade's most volatile year, implicating us in the death of the Kennedys).

Before moving on to the response Fosse's *Cabaret* received, one might summarize its meaning, and that of modern mainstream dark comedy generally, by noting both the title Isherwood had originally had in mind for a more ambitions collection of *Berlin Stories*, and just what that moniker meant to him. In a 1963 essay drawn from a lecture, he revealed the ramifications of an epic to be called

"the lost" in the sense of the entire German nation and indeed the world going astray into the paths of violence and destruction. This was the somber background.... [But] in the foreground were to be figures that were amusing ... satiric rather than tragic. These figures were also to be "the lost" in another sense, that's to say people whom established society rejects in horror ... they were to play a butterfly dance against the approaching thunderstorm of violence which was the coming of the Nazi Party into power.[41]

"The lost" *Cabaret* was anything but lost among critics and audiences, winning Academy Awards for Best Director (Fosse), Best Actress (Minnelli), Best Supporting Actor (Grey), Cinematography (Geoffrey Unsworth), Art Direction (Rolf Zehetbauer, Jurgen Kiebach, and Herbert Strabel), Sound (Robert Knudson and David Hildyard), Scoring (Ralph Burns), and Film Editing (David Bretherton)—and being one of the top-grossing movies of the year.[42] Beyond the smattering of rhapsodizing reviews already noted, a few more quotes merit inclusion. Britain's *Films and Filming* said:

> *Cabaret* is unquestionably one of the finest films to come from America within the last generation.... [T]he songs and their stagings are a perfection of horror and wit [which manages to] intercut between [a freakish nightclub, downhill characters, and Nazism] like a deformed holy trinity.[43]

According to *Variety*, "*Cabaret* is most unusual: it is literate, bawdy, sophisticated, sensual, cynical, heart-warming and disturbingly thought-provoking.... [F]or virtually everyone concerned, *Cabaret* is a career milestone."[44] *Hollywood Reporter* critic Gery Giddins wrote:

> *Cabaret* is a stunning entertainment, an exuberant marriage of talent and intelligence. Conceptually, it is a musical that will even please people who don't particularly care for musicals.... [Sally Bowles is] a gold-digging whore desperately wanting to be an actress while indulging in decadence as though it were a religion.[45]

Fittingly, given both the praise garnered by the film and the significance of Bowles' character, some critical kudos, like the following from the *New York Times*, focused upon Liza Minnelli's performance:

> [When she is] working in a space defined only by her gestures and a few colored lights, it becomes by the simplest means an excavation of both the power and fragility of [a] movie performance so beautiful that I can think of nothing to do but give thanks.[46]

So why did this camouflaged anti-genre dark comedy meet with more universal praise and less criticism of its black humor than any film thus far scrutinized in this text? Stanley Kubrick even pronounced it "the best movie I think I have ever seen."[47] Part of the answer might be found in this random reference to Kubrick. Just two months before, in December 1971, the American expatiate had released his disturbing dark comedy adaptation of Anthony Burgess' novel *A Clockwork Orange*, which *The New York Times* praised by way of calling it "essentially [a] British nightmare [about] the value of free will, even if the choice exercised [results] in robbing, raping and battering the citizens until they lie helpless [in a near future hell]."[48] In marked contrast, in Fosse's lull before the storm, viewers know what is coming, but as one critic described it, one might hope that "civilization may still persevere, if only at the next train station [as Brian leaves Germany by rail]."[49] Thus, one is essentially spared seeing what the central character of *A Clockwork Orange* likes to describe as "the real red vino [blood]." Moreover, by *Cabaret* vacating American history, be it unnecessary mid–20th century wars, or Western Frontier genocide, one is spared discomfort via the guilt by association with human complacency. In fact, if Kubrick had adapted *Cabaret*, he might very well have goosed up audience self-reproach, not to mention bloodletting, by drawing upon actual rebellious German nightclub performers who had not gone along with Hitler's program. For example, after the Nazis came to power,

> cabarets were all but obliterated, and its best artists were killed. Still, there were some shining moments, as when Werner Finck, who was eventually sent to a concentration camp,

asked groups of Nazis attending his early 1930s shows if he needed to speak slower so their poor small brains could comprehend his jokes.[50]

While Fosse's *Cabaret* received almost universal acclaim, the much-praised but polarizing *A Clockwork Orange* was eventually banned outright in Britain, and a disturbed-by-its-response Kubrick soon took it out of general distribution in other markets, despite consistently decent box office returns. Ironically, however, both films were pitching the same safeguard message. For instance, after Burgess had seen Kubrick's adaptation of his novel he observed, "[If it] takes its place as one of the salutary literary warnings—or cinematic warnings—against flabbiness [of ethics], sloppy thinking, and overmuch trust in the state, then it will have done something of value."[51]

Fosse will better understand the response to a controversial anti-genre dark comedy classic when he makes *All That Jazz*, a musical about death and oh so much more. Until Chapter 12's focus on that film, suffice it to say that multi-faceted 1970 black comedy cinema continued to find ways to remain mainstream.

6

Slaughterhouse-Five (3/23/72)

> When [director George Roy] Hill was having trouble casting the role of Billy
> Pilgrim, [*Slaughterhouse-Five* author] Kurt Vonnegut suggested, "I think
> you're looking for a Paul McCartney, someone with a childlike, open face."
> The result was Michael Sacks, a perfect pilgrim.
> —critic Louise Sweeney[1]

Slaughterhouse-Five returns the text to the realm of the opening chapters on *MASH* and *Catch–22* (both 1970), in which the dark comedy ludicrousness of the Vietnam War is subtextually attacked through other conflicts. In this case, the poorly trained American soldier Billy Pilgrim (Michael Sacks), an anti-heroic chaplain's assistant, is captured (as was Vonnegut) during Germany's desperate final offensive of World War II—the Battle of the Bulge (in late 1944). However, what immediately separates *Slaughterhouse-Five* from the other two works avoids a service comedy façade by way of science fiction–fantasy. Former Second World War pilot–director George Roy Hill does a masterful job of adapting Vonnegut's novel about a coming-of-age man-child who becomes "unstuck in time."[2] Pilgrim's Sad Sack pinballs through random moments in his life, including the war, different points in his post-war optometrist existence, and being part of a zoo-like exhibit on the planet Tralfamadore (a token Earthling along with porn star Montana Wildhack, played by Valerie Perrine). Along with *All That Jazz* (1979), *Slaughterhouse-Five* is the dark comedy most densely populated with other genres. All these veils add complexity to the genre by increasing the absurdity factor. Some of these genre masks are straight-up renditions of specific film types; others play at being anti-genre misdirections. An example of both would be calling it an anti-war film and a war film, with Pilgrim chronicling his experiences as a prisoner of war in Dresden—a German city unnecessarily firebombed near the conflict's conclusion. Ironically, because Allied prisoners of war (Vonnegut is writing from experience) are held in underground slaughterhouses (thus the title), they escape the horrific incineration of civilian life caused by what the later Vietnam War would know as napalm (jellied gasoline).

The time-tripping component represents the most anti-genre distraction to *Slaughterhouse-Five*'s dark comedy base. Vonnegut has moved the viewer to the realm of science fiction and/or fantasy—a pigeonholing of his writing, which he abhorred. Yet, in this case, the novelist and the filmmaker realize something no other work herein accomplished: Vonnegut's genre-crossing work has managed to take the horror out of death— hardly good form for dark comedy. As Pilgrim explains it in the novel:

> The most important thing I learned on Tralfamadore was that when a person dies he only
> *appears* to die. He is still very much alive in the past, so it is very silly for people to cry at

his funeral. All moments, past, present and future, always have existed, always will exist. The Tralfamadorians can look at all the different moments just the way we can look at a stretch of the Rocky Mountains…. [When one sees a corpse], all he thinks is that the dead person is in bad condition in that particular moment but that the same person is just fine in plenty of other moments.[3]

One need not be concerned by this sci-fi defusing of death lessening the full strength of *Slaughterhouse-Five*'s dark comedy base, because Tralfamadore's quasi–time-tripping religion merely maximizes another key component of black humor: absurdity. The silliness of one religion's invisible people being more important than another's has always been a target of dark comedy. Thus, how is Pilgrim's goofy sci-fi quasi-religion any different than *New York Times* critic and author Benjamin Moser's description of *The Book of Mormon* as a "turgid sci-fi novel," whose "followers believe that the earth was created somewhere in the neighborhood of the planet Kolob, and that the Garden of Eden was created somewhere in the neighborhood of Kansas City…."[4] Of course, why stop at that? An actual sci-fi author, L. Ron Hubbard, concocted Scientology upon the belief that 75 million years ago the evil tyrant Xemu brought billions of aliens to Earth, and through the detonation of many hydrogen bombs their evil souls ("thetans") attached themselves to earthlings. Now Scientologists work "religiously" to isolate and neutralize these thetans for the good of mankind.

In fairness to such bizarro religions, which immensely contribute to the ease with which dark comedy can play its anti-establishment absurdity card, one cannot stop there. To return to the *Times* critic Moser, while it is easy to mock Mormonism and Scientology theology,

it is surely no more absurd to believe [the Mormon claim] that the resurrected Christ visited America in A.D. 34 than it is to believe that Moses parted the Red Sea, or that Muhammad ascended to heaven on a winged horse, or that Jesus was born of a virgin. To see [religion] in this broader context is to be constantly confronted with questions of belief, of how much nonsense humans will suffer for the sake of making sense of their lives.[5]

On a more individual sideswiping basis, *Slaughterhouse-Five*'s use of sci-fi as a distraction from another of its black humor core themes merits comparison to Stanley Kubrick's 1971 adaptation of British novelist Anthony Burgess' *A Clockwork Orange*. Set in the near future, Kubrick's picture also qualifies as sci-fi. Yet the Vonnegut-Hill work guts the very theme which drives *A Clockwork Orange*: that any sort of aversion therapy to correct anti-

Time-tripping Billy Pilgrim (Michael Sacks) during one of his visits to World War II in *Slaughterhouse-Five*.

social behavior, however vicious, is wrong because it deprives the individual of free will. Burgess states: "I don't know how much free will man really possesses ... but I do know that what little he seems to have is too precious to encroach on, however good the intentions of the encroacher may be."[6] In contrast, Vonnegut's novel notes a position underlined in Hill's adaptation:

> If I hadn't spent so much time studying Earthlings, said the Tralfamadorian, I wouldn't have any idea what was meant by "free will." I've visited thirty-one inhabited planets in the universe, and I have studied reports on one hundred more. Only on Earth is there any talk of free will.[7]

This declawing of a key dark comedy component does not eliminate Kubrick's film from the genre. As with the previous sweeping example addressing death, another of the genre's pivotal themes is suddenly augmented: man as beast becomes the irreversible norm in *A Clockwork Orange*.

Another anti-genre veneer initially deflecting one's thoughts about the innate dark comedy nature of *Slaughterhouse-Five* involves Francois Truffault's previously noted "profile films." These are not exactly biographies or memoirs, yet they are galvanized by real lives. More than any other adapted text in this study, including the previous chapter's explanation of Christopher Isherwood's direct links to *Goodbye to Berlin* (1939) and *Cabaret* (1972), *Slaughterhouse-Five* has the most high-profile autobiographical tie. This is best explained by Hill biographer Andrew Horton:

> There were two major difficulties to overcome in adapting Vonnegut's extremely popular novel: what to do with the opening chapter in which Vonnegut appears as himself giving the personal and historical background to Dresden and thus his story; and how to capture a cinematic equivalent of Vonnegut's catchphrase, "And so it goes." ... The opening chapter accomplishes at least four important tasks! (1) it fuses Vonnegut's role as witness and writer; (2) it provides background on Dresden; (3) it explains the subtitle of the book, *The Children's Crusade*, as his effort to write not just another "war book" but rather a book that reflects the stupidity of all wars; (4) it sets the tone for the rest of the book.[8]

Not surprisingly, adapting the novel without actually using Vonnegut himself to open the movie was no easy task. Yet, between Stephen Geller's script and director Hill, an artist with a propensity for adapting brilliantly complex novels, such as his 1982 cinematic reworking of John Irving's 1978 dark comedy *The World According to Garp*, *Slaughterhouse-Five* the film works splendidly. Vonnegut later wildly praised the adaptation in the preface to his *Between Time and Timbuktu* (1975): "I love George Hill and Universal Pictures, who made a flawless translation of my novel *Slaughterhouse-Five* to the silver screen ... because it is so harmonious with what I felt when I wrote the book."[9] Shortly after the film's release, Vonnegut told *The Christian Science Monitor*, "That's exactly what it looked like; it's an extraordinary recreation."[10]

How did Hill and Geller manage to make such a successful adaptation? They began by cutting what might be called the novelist's prologue, and beginning with Billy Pilgrim typing in what passes as the story's "present," some time in the 1960s. What he has recorded on the page is a pocket summary of the tale: "I have come unstuck in time." *Slaughterhouse-Five* has immediately gone from Vonnegut's omniscient opening narrator to Billy's first person helter-skelter storyline.

This switch works on several levels. First, it technically applies an anti-genre whammy to the profile approach, since Vonnegut is literally scissored out. This enhances dark comedy's sense of the absurd, since a living, all-knowing anchor of an author is jettisoned and the viewer is now dependent upon a single, limited-in-perspective character relating a sort of a "Tumbling Time Machine to Hell" misadventure, except for occasional porn star R and R trips to Tralfamadore. Like time-tripping Billy, the viewer is equally unstuck with someone who has no control over what is about to happen. Welcome to dark comedy, via the cover of an initially profile approach.

A second manner in which this Vonnegut-to-Pilgrim switch works could be compared to *Little Big Man*. Like 121-year-old Jack Crabb's tall tale–like revelations about the true ugly side of our celebrated cowboy mythology, Billy Pilgrim's sci-fi twist on tall tales easily tops Crabb's longevity, because Billy experiences a Sisyphus-like existence of constant repetition. Moreover, what each of those seemingly infinite lives suggests is that, as sickening as the genocide of Dresden and the American Indian, the incidents were more norms than aberrations in mankind's history. Old Testament Christianity embraces a God who dispensed genocide against His own children as quickly and easily as *Catch–22*'s Yossarian (Alan Arkin) realizes life can become so much garbage.

Like the *Waiting for Godot* duo waiting endlessly for a God who will never come, Billy and Jack are playing their own variation of waiting on metaphorical treadmills. In either case, to paraphrase a line from Stanley Kubrick's dark comedy *Eyes Wide Shut* (1999), "Life will go on ... until it doesn't." And if Jack was slow in revealing anti-genre Western truths about the good old All-American West versus the original Americans, the not-so-bright Billy took countless gerrymandering trips through time before finally leaking his "no free will" bombshell. But did it matter if we had no free will with which to respond? Plus, the Tralfamadorians were a literal bombshell unto themselves—accidentally destroying the universe one day, and yet managing to have eternal do-overs prior to this "oops" apocalypse. This gaffe to end *all* gaffes is explained thus in the film:

> TRALFAMADORIAN: We know how the world ends and it has nothing to do with Earth, except that it gets wiped out, too.
> BILLY PILGRIM: Really? How does it end?
> TRALFAMADORIAN: While we're experimenting with new fuels, a Tralfamadorian test pilot panics, presses the wrong button, and the whole universe disappears.
> BILLY PILGRIM: But you have to stop him. If you know this, can't you keep the pilot from pressing...?
> TRALFAMADORIAN: He has always pressed it, and he always will. We have let him, and we always will let him. The moment is structured that way.

Another way in which this Vonnegut-to-Pilgrim switch works is a full circle ricochet back to the novelist himself. That is, even by dropping Vonnegut from the adaptation equation, the viewer cannot help but still retain, paradoxically, a strong sense of the author's profile status. Moreover, to paraphrase biographer Leslie Jamison, "Whether one is writing fiction or nonfiction, one is still constructing characters sometimes drawn upon re-configurations of self."[11] In this particular case, a Vonnegut-Billy bond is difficult to break. This added degree of profile absurdity is because Vonnegut and *Slaughterhouse-Five* are so emblematic of that era, especially among baby boomers. As author-critic Kurt Anderson summarized it:

> Along with his friend Joseph Heller, Vonnegut helped transform irony—appalled but not unamused by injustice, absurdity and the grotesque—into mass market American reflex. And by dawdling for two decades on what he called his "war book" [*Slaughterhouse-Five*] he (ironically) hit the perfect critical and commercial sweet spot. The book's catch phrase, "So it goes," repeated dozens of times whenever death is mentioned ... schooled millions of young readers in the existential shrug, world-weary before their time.[12]

Consequently, present or not in the movie, Vonnegut's aura persists. Youth of that period (myself included) so frequently had a Vonnegut paperback in a back pocket or book bag, that we often communicated in a sort of "Vonnegut-speak," from that signature line "So it goes," to references to the ephemeral character Kilgore Trout, a figure who continually surfaces in the novelist's work. This fictional character, though loosely inspired by a minor writer, Vonnegut's friend Theodore Sturgeon, is a mediocre sci-fi writer who serves many purposes. For example, an ongoing objective, regardless of the specific situation, is to spoof the very genre (sci-fi) into which Vonnegut hated to be categorized.

In fact, my only fault with Hill's adaptation is that neither "So it goes" nor "Trout"—both highly visible in the text—can be found in the movie. Arguably, Trout is less essential to *Slaughterhouse-Five*, though he serves amusing in-joke purposes. For instance, at one point in the novel he underlines Billy's vacuousness, a boy who will never graduate to being a grown-up William, in part because he is a fan of this little-known hack:

> Billy had not only read dozens of books by Trout—he had become Trout's friend, to the extent that anyone can become a friend of Trout, who is a bitter man. [Here Vonnegut affectionately spoofs all those underappreciated novelists out there, an army which once included himself.][13]

In fairness to what Hill has cut, both Vonnegut and Trout can be entertainingly didactic, even to the point of the relentlessly satirical self-flagellation of the beloved "So it goes." Hill's version gets the same points across with what in American humor is often referenced as the "soft sell," whether viewers are aware of the Vonnegut aura or not.

How so? Hill's cutting (with editor Dede Allen) is reminiscent of Oscar-winning editor-turned-director Hal Ashby's *Harold and Maude* (1971). *Slaughterhouse-Five* frequently uses a more jarringly formalistic (self-conscious filmmaking) editing technique for added irony—the sole purpose of the "So it goes" mantra. As previously stated, Hollywood was once famous for "invisible editing," cutting together a film in such a subliminally logical manner that the casual viewer was essentially oblivious to such scissoring. Yet, this is hardly standard sequence-changing procedure in *Slaughterhouse-Five*. A viewer, especially a male viewer, is much more likely to be voyeuristically blindsided as he gazes upon the sexy Valerie Perrine—described by *Cue*'s critic as being "attractive on any planet"—when one suddenly experiences the slap-in-the-face early "sound cut" from the next scene: "Who the fuck are you?"[14] The question is addressed to Billy, who has now time-traveled back to World War II and his first encounter with his constant nemesis and future assassin, Paul Lazzaro (Ron Leibman). And "so it goes" throughout Hill's film *Slaughterhouse-Five*.

Another anti-genre lamentation to *Slaughterhouse-Five*, that sometimes briefly distracts from its dark comedy center, is to appraise it along strictly war movie lines. And yes, since it has already been briefly discussed as an anti-war film, there is a certain bipolar tendency (how fitting for black humor) going on here, just as there was in the duality of analyzing it as a profile film. Nevertheless, even Edward Shores' book on director Hill notes how the film is filled with "war movies clichés, such as baseball players, dog tags, love of guns, and fanatical [fighting, with Billy being that standard soldier yet] to solidify his character, and is therefore manipulable."[15] Thus, several fundamental war movie components exist. First is the normal group hero configuration, which habitually includes a child-like figure (Billy), an older fatherly character who attempts to help everyone adjust

Ironically, Billy's (Michael Sacks, left) real war enemy was fellow GI Paul Lazzaro (Ron Leibman, right).

to hellish conditions (Eugene Roche's Edgar Derby), and a hotheaded kid who needs maturity (Leibman's Lazzaro). Though there is initial tension among these and other characters, fans of war films are initially not surprised, because this is a standard adjusting period for men at war. And when they are soon captured by the Germans, the film's calm and collected peripheral fellow British prisoners would not be out of place in an assortment of war pictures, from Jean Renoir's *Grand Illusion* (1937), to John Sturges' *The Great Escape* (1963).

Second, war films often demonstrate a certain respect for an honorable and/or wily enemy. For instance, one Hill study describes *Slaughterhouse-Five*'s German prison officer (Friedrich Ledebur) as having a "dignity to his role that is not unlike [Erich] von Stroheim's [prisoner of war camp commander] in Renoir's *Grand Illusion* [that] appears to have influenced Vonnegut."[16] Though one might first associate this tendency with antiwar pictures, *à la* Renoir's film, the trait is common in standard war pictures, too. For instance, the only World War II German soldier openly admired by Allied audiences is General Erwin "The Desert Fox" Rommel. He has been much acclaimed in several war films, from Henry Hathaway's *The Desert Fox: The Story of Rommel* (1951), to Franklin J. Schaffner's lionized *Patton* (1970). Indeed, Rommel was portrayed with such kudos in Hathaway's critical and commercial hit, that Robert Wise's *The Desert Rats* (1953, about Rommel's British opposition in North Africa) was made, in part, to downplay the daring and innate dignity of Hathaway's portrayal of Rommel.[17] More recently, Clint Eastwood directed the exceptional *Letters form Iwo Jima* (2006), which again pivots upon an admirable adversary, Japan's General Kuribayashi. His correspondence poignantly depicts the battle of Iwo Jima from the enemy's perspective.

World War II is commonly considered the 20th century's only "good war," or at least necessary conflict, since Hitler and Hirohito seemed to leave the free world no other choice.[18] Thus, Allied viewers of the Second World War films are allowed and expected to enjoy a conventional victory, and see at least some of their movie soldiers, such as Pilgrim, return home. A signature scene for Billy, even before the war is over, occurs when he gets caught up with fellow soldiers "liberating" (looting) enemy buildings as the German army has fallen back. When the danger of getting caught is expressed, two justifications are expressed: "We ain't gonna get caught. The Krauts [Germans] have all left. If we don't steal it, the Russians [advancing from the east] will." Thus, Billy is cajoled into helping fellow soldiers "liberate" a grandfather clock. Yet, when Russians suddenly approach, the Americans flee, allowing the giant clock to fall on Billy. Abruptly, one has a visual summary of Pilgrim's story, being briefly pinned down by "time," before attempting to use it as a hiding place, *à la* Tralfamadore.

However, all three of these traditional war film components embrace an anti-genre route, just as *Little Big Man* jumps its Western convention tracks. For example, the natural camaraderie which would normally be produced by the father figure, such as Harry Carey's Master Sergeant in Howard Hawks' *Air Force* (1948), never comes to pass. Not only is Roche's Derby character unsuccessful in this task, he is casually executed on a German work patrol, after he has found a porcelain figure in the Dresden ruins, a figure which had innocently reminded him of a similar one back home. (In the novel, the object is a teapot.) For Billy, whose less than sympathetic father had died before Billy was drafted, this is the most personally traumatic event of the war. A reeling-from-pain Pilgrim might be compared with Vonnegut's torment over not only being at Dresden but also losing a parent—a troubled, often insensitive mother—who committed suicide on Mother's Day when the novelist was overseas. Regardless, Billy's devastation over Derby's death, even in light of Dresden's devastation, might best be explained by a passage from a study of famed World War II photographer Robert Capa:

> The horrific tendency of modern warfare is to dehumanize. Soldiers are able to use their weapons of mass destruction only because they have been trained to conceptualize their victims not as individuals but as a category—the enemy. Capa's strategy was to repersonalize war, to emphasize that those who suffer its effects are individuals with whom the viewer of the photographs [or movies] cannot help but identify. [Derby was such an individual.][19]

Derby's inability to help Leibman's Lazzaro become level-headed, as Harry Carey did for a young, troubled John Garfield in *Air Force*, meant Billy would eventually be murdered by the revenge-happy Lazzaro. An elderly Billy fleshes out the situation in a speech, shortly before being shot:

> You see in Tralfamadore, where I presently dwell, life has no beginning, no middle, and no end. For example, many years ago a certain man promised to have me killed. He's an old man now, living not far from here. He's read all of the publicity associated with my appearance. He's insane. And tonight he'll keep his promise…. You see, it's time for you to go home—to your lives and your children. It's time for me to be dead for a little while. And then live again. I give you the Tralfamadorian greeting: Hello. Farewell. Eternally connected, eternally embracing. Hello. Farewell.

After this Groucho Marx–like exit line—in *Animal Crackers* (1930) the mustached one sings "Hello, I Must Be Going"—Billy is shot and killed by Lazzaro from a balcony in the auditorium.[20]

The second fundamental war film element in *Slaughterhouse-Five* also deteriorates. The von Stroheim–like sympathetic prison officer played by Friedrich Ledebur cannot keep the sweet-hearted Derby from being shot for a porcelain figurine deemed so insignificant by his executioners that they immediately discard it. Of course, in this film's murky perspective on free will, once Derby shared the following thoughts upon first meeting Billy, his demise was only a matter of time: "I used to tell my students there's a monster loose in the world. I got tired of telling them and joined up ... America's about self-determination and free enterprise. Backing itself all the way. That's why we're in Europe stopping Hitler."

To his credit, he is not like the teacher in the novel *All Quiet on the Western Front* (1929), whose blindly nationalistic lecturing keeps sending grade after grade of students off to war while he stays safely behind. Yet a uniformed Derby is still preaching the same pap.

The final war film basic to go anti-genre is getting Billy home. But being "unstuck in time" means World War II never ends for Billy. Plus, given that most of his military time was spent as a prisoner of war, with a fellow American (Leibman's Lazzaro) who ultimately proves more lethal than any German enemy, there is nothing positive about any of his time-tripping back to the army. Even when the psychopathic Lazzaro was not threatening him, Billy would be distressed by Leibman's character menacing everyone in sight ... on our side, no less. For example:

> That [American] corporal. He'll get back home after the war. He'll be a big [war] hero. Dames'll be climbin' all over him. Couple of years go by, and one day there's gonna be a knock on the door and there'll be this stranger. "Paul Lazzaro sent me," the stranger will say and then he'll pull out a gun and shoot his pecker off. [The] Stranger will give him a couple of seconds to think about who Paul Lazzaro is and what life's gonna be like without a pecker. Then he'll shoot him once in the guts and walk away. Yes.

Moreover, if the time-tripping Tralfamadore-like religion was not confusing enough, Billy's war position as an assistant chaplain would have been even more disorientating, since he was neither good at it, nor did it make any difference in morale. Though his activities along these lines were minimal, like the experiences of *Catch–22*'s Chaplain Tappman (Anthony Perkins) and *MASH*'s Father "Dago Red" John (René Auberjonois), religion was of no help in a war zone.

Death is one of the three dark comedy themes in *Slaughterhouse-Five*. Initially, one might apply a metaphorical Post-Traumatic Stress Syndrome to the 20-plus years in which Vonnegut struggled to write *Slaughterhouse-Five*. Yes, the Dresden firebombing deaths of 130,000 civilians in a city which posed no threat to the Allies was horrific. But what about the Nazis' Final Solution, in which they methodically killed six million Jews, not to mention Germany targeting civilians throughout the war? Was this not an Allied application of the Biblical axiom, "an eye for an eye" (Matthew 5:38), or for the more secularly minded, "quid pro quo" or "something for something"?

The official word on the subject was that it was necessary in order to help end the war early. This is the perspective suggested late in the film when a 1960s Billy finds himself in the hospital following a domestic plane crash. In the next bed is a professor writing an official Army Air Corps history text which includes a positive take on the Dresden firebombing. When Billy attempts to share the real story, the professor brushes him off with a paraphrasing of a line President Theodore Roosevelt once used on Supreme Court Justice Oliver Wendell Holmes, Jr.: "I could carve a better man out of a banana." In short, victors write the "history," and as a Tralfamadorian might say, "Nothing changes."

During the writing of this text, an absorbing documentary upon another endless war and the quid pro quo factor appeared: the Oscar-nominated Israeli film by Dror Moreh entitled *The Gatekeepers* (2012). One cannot help thinking that Vonnegut and Hill would have been fascinatedly bemused by Moreh's documentary. It involves six separate in-depth interviews with former heads of the Shin Bet, Israel's Security Service (ISA), whose motto is "the Defender that shall not be seen." Going back to the Six-Day War of 1967, these former leaders of a counterterrorist agency whose clandestine activities often involved direct reprisals and/or pre-emptive strikes against Palestinians, reflect upon the ethical and strategic impact of the ISA upon Israel. These hardline, essentially underground commanders (seen as terrorists themselves by the Palestinians) had never before spoken on-camera about their activities. Surprisingly, to a man, they stated that ISA's pursuits had not helped Israel; in fact, they often had made situations more inflammatory. Amazingly, or maybe not so amazingly, as of this writing, no one in a position of power in Israel's present government has even consented to view the film. Can we get another "And so it goes"?

While one cannot negate the millions of needless deaths symbolized by Dresden and showcased in Vonnegut's novel and Hill's film, major credit for *Slaughterhouse-Five* not becoming yet another swashbuckling heroic yarn about war and glorified death must go to Mary O'Hare, the wife of Vonnegut's old friend and fellow POW Bernard V. O'Hare. The novelist had met with his buddy to rehash memories about their shared war experiences in order to help jump-start his book. After Mary had eavesdropped on one too many anecdotes, she angrily broke up their pow-wow by saying *Slaughterhouse-Five* was just going to be one more brainwashing romanticized war tale about dashing heroes dodging death: "You'll pretend you were men instead of babies, and you'll be played in the movies by Frank Sinatra and John Wayne or some of those other glamorous, war-loving, dirty old men."[21] One is reminded of an extended quote from Dalton Trumbo's inventively macabre anti-war novel *Johnny Got His Gun* (1939), a savage slash of a title at the lyric "Johnny Get Your Gun" from George M. Cohan's patriotic propaganda show "Over There" (1917), which led to many young Americans enlisting in both world wars:

> When armies begin to move and flags wave and slogans pop up, watch out little guy because it's someone else's chestnuts in the fire not yours.... You can always hear the people who are willing to sacrifice somebody else's life. They're plenty loud and they talk all the time.... They sound wonderful. Death before dishonor. This ground sanctified by blood. These men who died so gloriously. They shall not have died in vain. Our noble dead. Hmmmm. But what do the dead say? ... [Only] the dead know whether all these things people talk about are worth dying for or not. And the dead can't talk. So the words about noble deaths and sacred blood and honor and such are all put into dead lips by grave robbers and fakes who have no right to speak for the dead.[22]

Regardless, Mary O'Hare, more than her husband Bernard, had helped push Vonnegut towards writing a story about innocence betrayed by dirty, pretty lies about war.

Consequently, the now all but neglected subtitle of *Slaughterhouse-Five* is *The Children's Crusade: A Duty-Dance With Death*. This references a tale falling somewhere between fact and hyperbole, alleged to have occurred early in 13th century Europe, when a boy believed Jesus had told him to lead a crusade to the Middle East. He was to gather a band of children to peacefully convert Muslims to Christianity. The journey was to be assisted by the Mediterranean parting once they reached Italy. When this did not occur, seafaring merchants are said to have promised them passage to their destination. Instead, the children are alleged to have been either sold into slavery and/or drowned by capsizing ships. Consequently, when a captured Billy (Sacks) is marched into the pre-bombed Dresden wearing boots from a POW production of *Cinderella*, describing the majestic old university city as "a land of Oz," one gets a sense of him as "a pied piper, a child among children, oblivious to the concerns of war"[23]—a regular updated "children's crusade: a duty dance with death." At the very least, one might call him an existential problem in Cinderella boots. That is the foundation of sand upon which Vonnegut and Hill placed an anti-hero with the name of both a child (Billy) and a traveler to foreign lands (Pilgrim). This was an act of central casting fit for neither a Frank Sinatra nor a John Wayne.

Ironically for a story about both documented death (Dresden) and a relief from death, by way of the Tralfamadorian quasi-religion of unstuck in time parallel lives, each of Billy's abrupt time-tripping transitions is predicated upon a fear of death. The first example of this Billy phenomenon occurs when his agitation over the possibility of dying in the Battle of the Bulge sends him careening back in time to a similar terrorizing event. His father has thrown young Billy into a pool for that cruel sink-or-swim approach to forcing a child to improvise some sort of dog paddle for life survival. Fittingly, just as Billy needs to be taken care of by fellow soldiers during the war, when he is not being threatened by them, young Billy must be rescued from the bottom of the pool during his father's exercise in fear-based learning.

Moreover, there is an ugly paradox in the Tralfamadorians' alleged relief from death, not unlike Ricky Gervais' clever *The Invention of Lying* (2009). In the world of this film, everyone tells the absolute truth, until a desperately compassionate Gervais tells a lie (there is a heaven) to alleviate the pain of someone facing imminent death. This "good news," as hip New Age Christianity of my youth once put it, quickly caught on. And while this is an entertaining yet essentially one-joke movie, aren't all religious people, at their most sympathetic best, anchored to an attempt to mitigate the pain of dying and/or losing a loved one?

So how is the Tralfamadorians' promise of a sort of sci-fi eternal life pinned to a cruel conundrum? Well, to be Dresden specific, while all those thousands of citizens who burned to death are soon alive and well at some other time in their existence, it still does not negate the fact that they will eternally be periodic victims of the most horrific death. And if these revolving door casualties follow a pattern anything like Billy's, that means a daily flaming extinction. One is reminded of the Stephen Sondheim song "Every Day a Little Death," yet shorn of any softening added music which might lessen the sting. The best Dresden-related presentation of the song was given by that once frequent interpreter of Sondheim, Elaine Stritch. Her raspy rendition in Broadway's *A Little Night Music* (2009/ 2010 revival) transformed it into a grimly honest poem befitting those Vonnegut victims.

As with the Gervais movie, another modest but diverting picture which also puts the Dresden situation in a more personalized perspective would be Robert Wise's 1977 adaptation of Frank DeFelitta's reincarnation thriller *Audrey Rose*. The story focuses upon a little girl who graphically dies trapped in a burning car. Her persistent father (Anthony Hopkins), like an apprentice Tralfamadorian, somehow manages to trace her through several reincarnations … yet each time this harmless 12-year-old girl must again be consumed by flames. Maybe *Slaughterhouse-Five*'s "So it goes" dark comedy is derived not from twisted sci-fi but rather horror's warning "Be careful what you wish for," *à la* eternal life.

Before leaving the subject of somehow staying alive through time by unique means, one cannot help but think of Hill's conclusion to his signature film *Butch Cassidy and the Sundance Kid* (1969). Though there have remained a few doubters through the years, the general consensus is that these real-life beloved bandits died in a shower of Bolivian army bullets early in the 20th century, after fleeing America.[24] Yet Hill wanted an instant legend conclusion, versus the macabre massacre which ends Arthur Penn's *Bonnie and Clyde* (1967). Hill's solution was to deny the characters' dash to death by way of a French New Wave–influenced freeze frame ending. Though overwhelmingly outnumbered, as they came out shooting, the two never fall. Then, as this freeze frame is quickly drained of color, the viewer soon has an invincible sepia-toned image of the now forever young duo in cinema amber. Moreover, Hill has remained true to their American Frontier ambience by having this final portrait resemble an old Western poster.

An ironic semantic reference to death transitions one to dark comedy's second pivotal theme, absurdity. How paradoxical that Billy Pilgrim and his fellow POWs are saved from death while housed in an underground (catacombs come to mind) facility known as Slaughterhouse-Five. Nevertheless, by having the narrative foundation of both the novel and adaptation be that of time travel, one is immediately enfolded in dark comedy's inevitable disjointedness, something *One Flew Over the Cuckoo's Nest* (1962) novelist Ken Kesey succinctly suggests as "a collaboration of Kafka and Mark Twain and [a] Martini."[25] I prefer Dalton Trumbo's more specific capsule statement, topped off with a literary spoofing:

> If you can keep track of time you can get ahold of yourself and keep yourself in the world, but if you lose it why then you are lost too…. He remembered how Robinson Crusoe was very careful to keep track of time even though he never had any appointments.[26]

Billy's time travel *sans* a joystick makes him eternally lost, even with a periodic porn star on another planet. This fate is not unlike a paraphrasing of Maude's (Ruth Gordon) explanation and defense of stealing to Harold (Bud Cort) in *Harold and Maude* (1971): "It reminds people that everything is transitory, including themselves."

Sentencing Billy to absurdity squared might be said to start with one of Shakespeare's most famous monologues, *As You Like It*'s "All the world's a stage / And all the men and women merely players. / They have their exits and their entrances / And one man in his time plays many parts…" (Act II, Scene VII). Challenging as it may be to play "many parts," Billy must perform the task on two planets and in many time periods—*simultaneously*. Moreover, Billy never has any cues for his exits and entrance." Thus, if, as Woody Allen once observed, "The overwhelming amount of logic and evidence is that we're all victims of a bad deal," then Billy's bad deal is the template of all templates for an absurd situation.[27]

This does, however, allow Vonnegut and Hill to expose the absurdity inherent to many American institutions beyond the military. Previous chapters, especially those dealing with *Catch–22* and *MASH*, have implicitly yet quietly satirized an American society self-muzzled by McCarthyism. And equally inherent to all the chapters has been a subtextual attack upon how the upper echelon of 1960s society insulated itself in a bubble world analogous, in some ways, to the self-centered indifference of *Cabaret*'s Weimar Republic.

Vonnegut's novel, in the sections devoted to the 1960s "present," zeroes in on the shallowness of suburbia, where America has lost its reason for living. Hill's adaptation better highlights this casual banality, not unlike Christopher Isherwood's *A Single Man*'s

(1964) study of lethargy with a potential Cuban Missile crisis Armageddon for a backdrop. Billy Pilgrim has gone to the "burbs" for a Norman Rockwell security he thought he had found in the brief fatherly protection of the sweet yet clueless Americanism of Edgar Derby. Still, the absurd execution of Derby has a profoundly tragic impact upon Billy, when he realizes the painful worthlessness of the older man's Babbittry.

In contrast, Derby's counterpart in the "present" is a dull, safe marriage to Valencia, whose sole purpose for living might be reduced to materialism, status and pound cake. Fittingly, while Derby's death is devastating, Valencia's demise is pure farce. Hill's show-casing of her exit is arguably the movie's funniest scene, a perfect mix of dark comedy's sudden juxtapositioning of broad humor with death. The catalyst is Billy's near passing in a commercial plane crash, with Valencia's Keystone Cop–like crash-ridden drive to the hospital played to the slapstick hilt. Only after she somehow manages to reach her destination is it revealed that she has suffered an off-screen death from carbon monoxide poisoning. The quick transition of moods is not unlike the *Bonnie and Clyde* (1967) sequence in which a cartoonish comic bank robbery exit suddenly turns deadly when Bonnie shoots a pursuer point blank in the face. Appropriately, however, Valencia's death is not seen, in order that viewers can still revel in the "thank God she is gone" humor of a character who literally and figuratively represented "dead weight" to Billy. It was also most suitable that Valencia's death was a result of her driving incompetency (the optimum word for the woman), that it occurred in an oversized symbol of her materialism, and that it represented the hysterical behavior enacted by only those people who have never contemplated anything beyond "the small end of nothing whittled to a fine point...."[28] The plane crash then allows Billy to be whisked to (the real or imagined) Tralfamadore and "given an opportunity to create the mythic American world that [he had hoped, with a boost from Derby or Valencia] could have guaranteed happiness."[29]

When discussing absurdity in *Slaughterhouse-Five*, one might also mention Billy's profession in the "present": optometry. How ironic. Here is a man-child whose profession involves helping people see, yet for much of the story he is blind to the most basic truths around him, such as the fact that life is a jerry-rigged system which makes as much sense as a paraphrased George Carlin crack from Billy Pilgrim's 1960s "present": "When one dies your soul goes to a garage in upstate New York."[30] Of course, one could reverse the argument and say Pilgrim was Carlin hip, and his ephemeral upstate New York garage was the planet Tralfamadore.

Yet that is hardly the case. Carlin was cognizant of the disconnect; Billy is not. A more realistic take on Billy is that like Yossarian's "escape" at the conclusion of *Catch-22*, it is all in his mind. As in so many dark comedies, if the ending is unbelievably happy, such as Billy starting a new family on another planet with his favorite Earthling porn star, it is not to be believed. Moreover, Hill's ending might even be an improvement upon Vonnegut's still excellent close to the novel. Whereas Vonnegut's text ends with Billy back in World War II Dredsen and a bird (is that a "cuckoo" bird?) saying to him "Poo-tee-weet?," Hill provides our anti-hero with a do-over (at least until getting unstuck in time again) on another planet.[31] After all, if one is to furnish a fantasy close to too good to be true, why not pull out all the stops? Plus, it provides the student of dark comedy with a wickedly wonderful insight about happiness: It is not possible in this world. And for Alice (Audrey Meadows), of classic television's *The Honeymooners*, being married to the comically threatening "To the moon, Alice, to the moon!" Ralph Kramden (Jackie Glea-son), just forget about happiness anywhere.

To play devil's advocate, however, and give Billy a time-tripping pass on his sci-fi tall tale, as was suggested earlier in a comparison with *Little Big Man*'s Jack Crabb and his Western whoppers, is to connect the men in another way. Though they were slow to act upon sharing their special messages (the true nature of the Old West, and the quasi–time-tripping Tralfamadore religion), both eventually teach, after a fashion, about their alleged experiences. This was no small task for Billy, who is *the* milquetoast man-child of the movie, sort of a space age Wally Cox, who played the definitive mild-mannered title character in the pioneering television series *Mr. Peepers*. Billy's evolution to a more strong-willed figure on Tralfamadore, especially regarding the respect he demands for his sexy companion, qualifies as its own form of absurdity, since earlier, the aforementioned military historian told him he "could carve a better man out of a banana."

In fact, Billy is such an indifferent non-presence in his marriage to Valencia that once he realizes the Capraesque world Derby described is either forever gone, or never existed, he somehow allows his troubled son to morph into a Vietnam-bound Green Beret. How does a war-scarred survivor of fire-bombed Dresden manage to let this happen? Moreover, the boy even thinks it will make his father proud. Now *that* is absurd. Is it Billy just embracing Tralfamadore's study of a universe in which only Earth believes in free will? And if so, why is Billy eventually lecturing (the setting in which he is forever assassinated) on not fearing death, since one's life goes on in another time and place? One is again reminded of Dustin Hoffman's title character in *Little Big Man*. Like so many of these 1970s dark comedy anti-heroic youths, he also is a rudderless, vapid youngster slow to act, ultimately fated to be misunderstood. Hoffman's Crabb has only an audience of one (the academic recording his oral history), but like the audience with which Billy is sharing his Tralfamadore insights, one questions his comprehension.

Finally, what about dark comedy's man-as-beast theme as applied to *Slaughterhouse-Five*? As has occurred in each of the preceding chapters, by this point in the scrutinizing of each focus film, numerous examples of man as beast have already unavoidably came forward. To state the obvious here, one runs the gamut from Dresden's fate to the Holocaust itself: Man's cruelty to man does not get any more horrific. To Vonnegut, however, the most devastating example of this phenomenon for Billy, and the world in general, was the random execution of Pilgrim's surrogate father, Edgar Derby.[32] Vonnegut biographer Gregory D. Sumner traces this trauma directly back to how the novelist's values were equally sideswiped by the war:

> Derby is the part of Kurt Vonnegut who never unlearned his junior civics lessons from PS 43 in Indianapolis, the expansive democratic dream he absorbed so innocently as a child during the Great Depression. And yet it is all undercut by the tone of the narrative [in both the novel and the adaptation]. Are good intentions and humane values *enough* in an absurd world? Vonnegut is doubtful. *Characters* get steamrollered all the time—Derby was shot, Dresden was destroyed.[33]

Consequently, between this travesty and Billy's sad realization that the kindly yet guileless Derby did not know how the real world worked, the youngster's faith in all things American began to dissolve.

For me, Leibman's psychopathic Lazzaro runs a close second in the man-as-beast category. If Derby represents what we once were, or the myth of what we thought we were, Lazzaro is what we have become. Indeed, he is more typical with each passing year, from spousal murders and suicides and school shootings, to road rage. Post Traumatic Stress Disorder is not just about returning soldiers any more. Regardless, returning to the ironically named Lazzaro (in the Bible, Jesus restores Lazarus to life four days after his death), Billy's Lazzaro is more likely to kill someone every four days. During war, one expects atrocities from the enemy ... not one's comrades. Yet, when one of your own becomes a lifelong threatening presence which ultimately culminates in your murder *ad nauseam* ... as Billy forever ricochets about in time, this Vonnegut-Hill anti-hero begins to know what it feels like to be a man with neither a country nor even a planet.

If one is allowed some speculative dot-connecting, Lazzaro is not unlike the character Pooh (Brenda Currin) in Hill's 1982 adaptation of another celebrated dark comedy, John Irvings' 1978 novel *The World According to Garp*. Though a murderous threat is never officially made by Pooh to the sympathetic title character Garp (Robin Williams), as was the case with Lazzaro to Billy, it is obvious that she will eventually do him mortal harm. As was also the case with Hill's *Butch Cassidy and the Sundance Kid*, the director seems drawn to empathetic characters fated to die in dark comedies, which is what this Western has become by its conclusion. For instance, as the badly wounded duo reload their pistols, obviously aware that their deaths are imminent, Butch and Sundance affectionately banter and bicker about where they will go next. In fact, in a documentary about the making of *Butch Cassidy and the Sundance Kid*, Hill makes an observation, without actually using the phrase "dark comedy," which helps reveal why he was so attracted to the black humor of quintessential literary examples of the genre like *Garp* and *Slaughterhouse-Five*:

> I don't think there's any difference between directing for comedy or directing for tragedy. I think the director and actor have to go for the truth, the reality of the situation and make it believable. If Paul Newman [Butch] is in a funny situation and we believe him, we laugh. And if he's in a tragic situation, we cry. You don't play funny; you play real.[34]

To make a final connection between *Slaughterhouse-Five* and Hill's other work, one must quote a passage from the novel *Garp* which both reiterates Hill's dark comedy philosophy and returns this text to the man-as-beast theme. To set the scene, Robin Williams' Garp is a writer whose black humor novels are critically well-received but produce minimal sales. He frequently gets hate mail from people who are similar to Lazzaro, like one letter whose salutation starts "Dear Shithead." Garp's response, in part, to this "man as beast" type, summarizes dark comedy and suggests there is an ever-growing number of Lazzaros whose fear and/or ignorance of what they do not understand make many of them potentially lethal:

> [I]n regards to what's comic and what's tragic ... the world is all mixed up. For this reason I have never understood why "serious" and "funny" are thought to be opposites. It is simply a truthful contradiction to me that people's problems are often funny and that the people are often and nonetheless sad. I am ashamed, however, that you think I am laughing at people, or making fun of them. I take people very seriously.... Therefore, I have nothing but sympathy for how people behave—and nothing but laughter to console them with. Laughter is my religion.... In the manner of most religions, I admit that my laughter is pretty desperate.[35]

In some ways the Lazzaro-Pooh personalities, like simply saying "Hitler," are more disturbing than the numbing mass killing numbers of a Dresden because it gives human evil a face. I am reminded of a comment in British comedian Eddie Izzard's concert film *Dress to Kill* (1999). This surrealistically dark comedy–based comedian often satirizes history and/or Americans along the lines of satirist Will Cuppy, like this typical Izzard *Dress to Kill* crack: "I grew up in Europe, where the history comes from."[36] But the lengthy,

Slaughterhouse-Five–related Izzard observation to which I make reference can be briefly paraphrased, "People have great difficulty comprehending death in numbers much beyond that shooting down the street." For example, how does one process the Nazis' slaughter of six million Jews? Narratives of the truly horrific attempt to take "something messy and devastating [and make it into] something contained and meaningful...."[37] Vonnegut and Hill disagree; it is unfathomable—and people should be ever-conscious of the fact.

Ironically, since we now live in a country in which the Supreme Court has granted corporations the status of individuals, the unfathomable experience, big and small, has just taken a quantum leap forward. The modest example might be comedian-father Louis C.K. describing his daughter's "new math" to David Letterman, as, "It's like, Bill has three goldfish. He buys two more. How many dogs live in London?"[38] On the opposite Armageddon end of the situation, one can again return to Vonnegut, in yet another time-tripping novel, *Timequake* (1997). It comes in his description of a short story by the aforementioned and sometime alter ego of the novelist, Kilgore Trout. Called "Bunker Bingo Party," it is set in

> Adolf Hitler's commodious bomb-proof bunker underneath the ruins of Berlin, Germany, at the end of World War II in Europe. In that story, Trout calls his war, and my war, also, *Western Civilization's* [my italics] "second unsuccessful attempt to commit suicide." He did that in conversations, too, one time adding in my presence, "If at first you don't succeed, try, try, please try again."[39]

Based upon Vonnegut's letters, maybe he was merely recycling a thought first planted in his mind by a book written in World War II by a fellow Hoosier writer he admired, Will Cuppy's *How to Become Extinct* (1941).[40] Ironically, yet maybe fittingly, Vonnegut remembered the Cuppy title as *The Night the Old Nostalgia Burned Down*.[41] Thus it should come as no surprise that Cuppy committed suicide (1949) and Vonnegut attempted the same act in 1984.

As a final musing upon man as beast, there often remain situations which are thought to qualify but are actually the mirror opposite. Man's obsession with sex in dark comedies is another basic way to depict his animalistic nature. For example, Peter Sellers' former Nazi scientist title character is obsessed with the subject, even as the world comes to a mushroom cloud conclusion in *Dr. Strangelove or: How I Learned to Stop Worrying and Love the Bomb* (1964). In contrast, Billy's relationship with his Tralfamadore porn star companion might sound lustful, especially when the aliens (whom we never see) ask if the couple are preparing to mate, but our time-traveler has finally found love. Billy invariably requests that a sort of curtain be activated in their prize exhibit in this planetary zoo. Of course, one could pile on the added irony that true love has now become so rare it only exists on a distant planet, and even then, it is in the rarified confines of a *zoo*. Regardless, like the age difference between Harold and Maude, which made society see their love as perverse, as so often happens in dark comedy, even real love is construed as another variation upon man as beast.

So how did the movie adaptation of *Slaughterhouse-Five* fare? The novel had been such a critical and commercial success that Vonnegut's first tinges of suicide thoughts appeared. Even though he had worked twenty-plus years to write a cathartic book about his Dresden experience, he felt great guilt over its triumph. Critic Anna Holmes would later write about this experience as it pertained to other artists attempting to find their own purging when it came to "9/11" (September 11, 2001): "The possibility that an individual might profit—creativity, commercially, or both—from the pain of others is, I think, where some of the concern over fictionalizing, marketing and selling our most deeply felt [experiences] stems from...."[42] This is noted only to say that the reception accorded *Slaughterhouse-Five*'s film adaptation would not put director Hill through similar self-condemnation. Though the picture's reviews were mixed to good, it is the only work in this text which did not even create a commercial ripple.

Cue magazine wrote: "One of the year's major movie events, *Slaughterhouse-Five* is a unique achievement."[43] Esteemed critic John Simon, in a *New Leader* review entitled "In Praise of the Well-Made Film," called the movie "a true space-age Candide."[44] This is no small praise, since Voltaire's 1759 novella is considered one of civilization's most influential books, and often reads like a blueprint for the life of Billy Pilgrim. Candide is also a young pilgrim who gradually becomes disillusioned with the world. His pica-resque tale has fantasy elements, yet in its anti-genre spoofing of action stories, *à la Slaughterhouse-Five*, it references actual historical events. Most fittingly, with regard to Billy Pilgrim's war, *Candide* has ties to the Seven Year War (1755–1764), which even involved America, where it was known as the "French and Indian War." Moreover, both Voltaire and Vonnegut were considered controversial writers, with the former artist avoiding the use of his real name, Francois-Maria Arouet. Both of their works were ini-tially often banned for religious blasphemy. Thus, Billy was indeed a "space-age Candide." However, *The Hollywood Reporter*, with a review by noted film historian Arthur Knight, was the film's greatest champion:

> [I]n *Slaughterhouse-Five* everything works, and beautifully.... [The] interaction of past, present, and future ... gives the film its tremendous lift and sense of originality.... "Live for those [positive] moments," it seems to say, "when you are most alive." With those moments, life can transcend itself. It can lift us to immortality.[45]

These reviews ran into a proverbial buzzsaw from the entertainment publication most driven by potential box office numbers: *Variety*. And its recriminations were a two-pronged attack, starting with its description of Michael Sack's Billy Pilgrim as being so "still, unsympathetic and skin-deep" it justified calling him the "boob Everyman" and the "dumb draftee."[46] Not surprisingly, the comments came from the *Variety* reviewer Murf, the pseudonym for the self-described curmudgeon Art Murphy, who pioneered mixing number-crunching audience prospects with criticism. This crass moneyman con-fused quasi-stiffness with the chastity of Vonnegut and Hill's Children's Crusade. By con-trast, another critic noted, "Michael Sacks makes an absolutely perfect Billy, in both his [minimalist] acting and open-faced, innocent appearance."[47] At this late date, Murf even had issues with using this subject matter for comedy: "The Dresden fire-bombing is too serious an occurrence to serve as spray-on sociology, but it's there."[48] Yet Murf's tone here is not so much moral indignation as simply negative piling-on.

Vincent Canby's *New York Times* review was more indicative of the critiques which essentially praised the movie but with certain qualifications. Thus, after calling it a "wild, noisy, sometimes very funny film," he addressed the narrow acting line required of its lead:

> Billy Pilgrim, very nicely played by a new young actor ... who looks like a cartoon fall-guy copied in flesh, is Everyman and, like most Everymen, he becomes a bit tiresome, since ... Billy simply endures, a passive figure set against a background in which the author inven-tories man's idiocies to man, from the little deceptions of childhood to the legalized luna-cies of war.[49]

In a manner of speaking, Canby simply wants more outrageousness in the film. But that misses the story's point. If a comic strip Beetle Bailey (the antiheroic private created by Mort Walker in 1950) can survive Dresden, there really must be no free will. At least Canby appreciates much of what Hill was able to bring to the film. The worst misreading of the picture came in Jay Cocks' "Lost in Space" *Time* magazine critique. Once he stated that Vonnegut's novel was "an attempt to impose comic order onto moral chaos," it was time to fold up the tents and go home.[50] Vonnegut wanted art to remind its audience of life's inherent chaos—there is no order.

Maybe the best review of the film merely recycles an insight from a critique of the novel itself. Starting with a quote from Vonnegut's text, it flows into an absorbing overview:

> "Like so many Americans, [Billy's wife] was trying to construct a life that made sense from things she found in gift shops." The pathos of human beings enmeshed in the relentless triviality of contemporary American culture has never been more adequately expressed.... Only Billy's time-warped perspective could do justice to the cosmic absurdity of his life.[51]

Granted, Billy's leaf-in-the-wind existence would make *Clockwork Orange*'s Anthony "anything for free will" Burgess gnash his teeth. Regardless, some of Vonnegut's critics seem to lambaste his big picture perspective rather than his inspired expression of that view. As my friend and colleague Robert Mugge has often observed, "It's amusing how uncomfortable critics can be made by art with an unfamiliar point of view." "So it goes."

7

Chinatown (6/21/74)

"Forget it, Jake, it's Chinatown."
—Operative Duffy (Bruce Glover) to his private eye boss,
J. J. "Jake" Gittes (Jack Nicholson), at *Chinatown*'s close

Despite going from this text's most passive lead character (last chapter's *Slaughter-house-Five*) Billy Pilgrim, to the study's most formative figure, Jake Gittes, one is still living in a world of unchangeable fatalism. The opening quote is an attempt at comforting a shattered character who has unintentionally helped facilitate the death of client and lover Evelyn Mulwray (Faye Dunaway) after, paradoxically, trying to help her. Jake broke his own rule of not getting involved, because he has been the victim of a similar (yet never fleshed out) incident earlier in his career. Moreover, Jake has fragmented the unwritten rule of the Los Angeles Police Department, for which he once walked a beat. In all things concerning Chinatown, "[Do as] little as possible." In fact, a shocked Jake mumbles those equally fatalistic words prior to Duffy's effort to console him. That is, fewer people get hurt if one just does not get involved.

Paradoxically, another parallel between Bill and Jake is that this fictionalized fatalism is based in fact, the lie that tells the truth. Just as *Slaughterhouse-Five* was founded on the real horrific firebombing of Dresdon, *Chinatown* scriptwriter Robert Towne's research found:

> The title [*Chinatown*] had come from a Hungarian vice cop. He said that he worked vice. And I asked him what he did and he said, "As little as possible."
> And I asked, "What kind of law enforcement is that?"
> And he said, "Hey, man, when you're down there with the Tongs and the different dialects, you can't tell who's doing what to who. And you can't tell whether you're being asked to help prevent a crime, or inadvertently leading the color of the law to help commit a crime. So we've decided the best thing to do when you're in Chinatown is to do as little as possible."[1]

Speaking of Towne, each of the text's proceeding focus films, with the exception of *Harold and Maude* (1971), was founded upon a quality novel. And even with *Harold and Maude*, the script was drawn from a Colin Higgins graduate school thesis, which he turned into a novel the same year the film appeared, followed by hit stage productions in London and Paris.[2] Working from an original Towne script, however, does not take away from the strong literary base which has been a pivotal part of this book. In 2006 the Writers Guild of America rated Towne's screenplay the third greatest script ever written, ranking behind *Casablanca* (1942) at number one and *The Godfather* (1972) at two, and ahead of *Citizen Kane* (1941) at four. Not surprisingly, Towne's Academy Award–winning Best Original Screenplay is also often used as a guide in scriptwriting texts.[3]

Chinatown is unlike *Little Big Man* (1970), which turned the conventional Western on its ear; the anti-genre tendencies of *Chinatown*, with regard to film noir, are not as obvious. Nevertheless, Towne and director Roman Polanski were attempting to break several basic conventions of the genre in a film which is ultimately a black comedy. For example, Towne observed: "Most [noir] detective movies had been about exotic falcons [such as *The Maltese Falcon*, 1941], about heists, jewels, and weird crimes of one kind or another [but] water and power [the crux of *Chinatown*], that was unusual [for the genre]."[4]

In the same interview, Towne emphasized even more the breaking of another fundamental noir convention:

> The classic female in a noir film is a black widow [femme fatale]. The Faye Dunaway character who gives you those expectations as being potentially that. But in fact, she's the heroine of the movie. In fact, she's the one person in the film who's operating out of decent and selfless motives.[5]

Thus, she was *not* a noir template temptress, like Mary Astor's Brigid O'Shaughnessy of the aforementioned *Maltese Falcon*, who had no compulsions about lying and killing for personal gain. Dunaway's character was interested in both getting at the truth in a murder case, and ultimately she died trying to protect someone from a man, Noah Cross (John Huston), who, in his own chilling admission observed, "Most people never have to face the fact that at the right time and the right place, they're capable of *anything.*"

Moreover, while Jake was meant to be more in the noir detective tradition, there were some major lapses here, too. Before addressing them, I need to flesh out how the noir private eye was a new breed of investigator in the realm of murder mysteries.[6] Prior to his arrival, the gold standard in the detectives business was Britain's Sir Arthur Conan Doyle's Sherlock Holmes, though America's own Edgar Allan Poe had provided a blueprint, of sorts, many years before. Regardless, Holmes is a being so superior, one half-expects he could ascertain from a footprint how much change the suspect had in his pocket. The key to a Holmes story is the final page (or movie scene), in which he dazzles the reader (or viewer) with so much deductive reasoning, the poor audience member feels no smarter than a cabbage. Needless to say, all story questions are answered.

In contrast, the noir detective is a tough seasoned individual well-versed in murder cases. And while intelligent and fast-thinking, his I.Q. level falls far below Holmes. Indeed, Raymond Chandler, a seminal artist in the creation of the new genre, by way of his signature character Philip Marlowe, even has the character observe in the writer's greatest novel, *The Big Sleep* (1939), "I'm no Sherlock Holmes…."[7] In Chandler's pivotal essay on the subject, "The Simple Art of Murder" (1950), he goes so far as to describe this new character as "a common man or he could not go among common people."[8] Yet, the accent on "common man" is more about what my grandmother, a woman of Chandler's generation, would describe as "lack of ego" (whereas Holmes radiates self-worth like a movie premiere beacon). Nevertheless, there is nothing common about Marlowe's intelligence.

Despite his shrewd moxie, however, the noir detective does not, *cannot* wrap everything up in a cute little rational world conclusion. Neither the genre, nor life in general, is like that. In this world of noir *à la* dark comedy, one brushes against hard reality. In a godless world, there can be no God-like Holmeses. Though this existentialist state comes, in part, from the full post–World War II revelations about the nature of man, this noir philosophical linchpin might just as well have been inspired by a French veteran's musing about World War I:

> As soon as you start to use your reason, to look for a rainbow, you always run up against the great excuse, mystery.... God? Come off it, the heavens are empty, as empty as a corpse. There's nothing in the sky but shells and all the other murderous devices made by men.... This war has killed God [and reason]....[9]

In contrast to some idyllic Holmes, Chandler was fond of saying that he wanted to write stories in which, if the last page was missing, it would not make any difference. What he meant was that the process was all about the fascinating character-driven journey towards an ending which would never be entirely fathomable. Even among the living, Chandler could describe Marlowe "as empty of life as a scarecrow's pockets."[10]

Chandler was also fond of calling his noir detective a "tarnished knight." Marlowe was not perfect, but he had a code, and "to use a rather weathered phrase, [he was] a man of honor."[11] Fittingly, this was coupled with being "a relatively poor man, or he would not be a detective at all."[12] Not surprisingly, in Howard Hawks' adaptation of *The Big Sleep* (1946), Lauren Bacall's character affectionately mocks the sparseness of Marlowe's (Humphrey Bogart) office. But Chandler has Marlowe describe his poorness hauntingly in the actual text of the novel:

> [T]his was the room I had to live in. It was all I had in the way of a home. In it was everything that was mine, that had any association for me, any past, anything that took the place of family. Not much; a few books, pictures, radio, chessmen, old letters, stuff like that. Nothing.[13]

Another fundamental basic of noir is sexually driven crimes of passion earmarked for money, such as Billy Wilder's *Double Indemnity* (1944), in which an insurance agent (Fred MacMurray) and his lover (Barbara Stanwyck) conspire to murder her husband (Tom Powers) for the extra money attached to the film's insurance policy–related title. However, during the heyday of the Breen Office, which encompassed the period in which Wilder's film was made, stories were forced to focus more on the actual crime than the blatant sexuality of the situation—since violence has always been more acceptable than sex to bluenose Americans. Nevertheless, sex was invariably part of the formula, and was often underlined in noir titles, such as *Murder, My Sweet* (1944), *Scarlet Street* (1945), *Kiss of Death* (1947), and the later neo-noir *Body Heat* (1981, essentially a variation upon *Double Indemnity*).

The Chandler noir detective, while no prude, had a code which minimized sexual dalliances with sultry clients. No doubt Marlowe's greatest temptation was the nymphomaniac Carman Sherwood in *The Big Sleep*, a part played in the 1946 film adaptation by the most provocatively alluring Martha Vickers. In the text she bluffed her way into Marlowe's apartment bed. When he arrived home, after some brief banter, she played her sex card:

> "You're cute." She rolled her head a little, kittenishly. Then she took her left hand from under her head and took hold of the covers, pausing dramatically, and swept them aside. She was undressed all right. She lay there on the bed in the lamplight, as naked and glistening as a pearl.[14]

Marlowe, the man with the code, somehow manages to turn Carman down. In asking her to leave, he offers an almost fatherly explanation, which includes the fact he is working for her family. In the movie, while censorship restrictions toned it down, Bogart's Marlowe does the same thing. Moreover, even in a Marlowe moment of weakness, such as pilfering an unwelcome kiss in Chandler's text for *The Long Goodbye* (1953), he is posthaste apologetic: "Very wrong. But I've been such a nice faithful well-behaved gun dog all day long...."[15]

This sexual honor code does not always apply to another iconic noir figure, Dashiell Hammett's Sam Spade, whom the novelist described in his short story "A Man Called Spade" as having a "likeness to a blond Satan."[16] In point of fact, Spade (Bogart) had been sleeping with his partner's wife in Huston's adaptation of *The Maltese Falcon*. However, sometimes these two seminal noir detectives, Marlowe and Spade, seem cinematically indistinguishable because Bogart played the conclusive examples of both in *Big Sleep* and *Maltese Falcon*. Yet there are differences, excepting their intellect and toughness, not to mention Chandler being much more prolific, making a career out of turning out one classic Marlowe novel after another. Plus, Chandler spent more nonfiction time musing on the subject. Thus, despite noir fans often meshing the two figures, Marlowe is essentially the standard, and was uppermost in Towne's mind as he composed *Chinatown*.

Jack Nicholson's Jake Gittes has none of the divine tendencies of Holmes. But beyond that, Towne's Jake is in over his head, with his agency specializing in matrimonial disputes, not murder. One Nicholson biographer bluntly addresses his comprehension deficiencies: "[H]e's no Sam Spade, merely, in Towne's description, 'persistent and insatiably curious ... capable within certain limits.'"[17] In point of fact, by the time Towne wrote the much later sequel *The Two Jakes* (1990), "Gittes has become a solid citizen. He's a war hero with a country club membership, a lovely fiancée and a healed nose."[18] This hardly sounds like the philosophical loner—past, present or future—of a Marlowe or a Spade.

The *New York Times* review of the original *Chinatown* probably best delineated Nicholson's character: "[He] wears an air of comic, lazy, very vulnerable sophistication...."[19] Polanski even observed, "The comic side to the story ... was important to me, so occasionally I made the hero [Jake] a little laughable, like when he complains about his [expensive] lost shoe."[20] However one wants to play it, Jake is made to look foolish early in the story. An actress (Diane Lane) posing as the Los Angeles water commissioner's wife, Evelyn Mulwray, hires Jake's firm to see if her husband is cheating on her. The commissioner soon is caught by the detective's team in what seems to be a love triangle. And once the newspapers get involved, it is front-page "love scandal" stuff, and Jake is briefly seen as a savvy detective. But when Faye Dunaway's real Mrs. Mulwray appears and threatens to sue, Gittes realizes he has been played to discredit the water commissioner. Someone saw just how easy it would be to bait him and his one-dimensional operation. This flatfoot had literally been caught "flat-footed." Jake's fear of a damaged reputation and a ruined detective business directly leads into another anti-genre element.

Instead of the financially poor detective mapped out by Chandler, Gittes has a prosperous agency, with a receptionist, several operatives, and even a full-time photographer, who probably doubles as a publicity agent. (However, in this case someone else made sure the phony Mrs. Mulwray's story hit the newspapers.) Indeed, this unknown party was well aware of—even banked on—Jake having a sort of movie star PR mentality—a perfect situation for discrediting someone prominent, like the water commissioner. In fact, shortly after the story breaks, Jake's barber actually tells him he is getting to be like a film star.

Gittes certainly dresses the part, with tailored suits and monogrammed shirts. Even if the lettering was not easily discernible to the audience, Polanski wanted Nicholson to feel this stylishly debonair role. For the actor's part, he based the look on that of his grandfather:

[B]efore he had his problems in life, he used to win the Ashbury Park [New Jersey] Easter Parade [competition] a lot, as one of the best dressed men. So he was a blade, and [of] Gittes' style [era] which is the Thirties ... who was very natty. I've used him a lot actually....[21]

Polanski's immediate response to the *Chinatown* script was that Towne wanted "no pale, down-at-the-heel imitation of Marlowe ... [Towne] had conceived him as a glamorous ... operator."[22] Fittingly, therefore, Gittes' office walls are covered with autographed pictures of movie stars. Yet, the attention to detail, with regard to the term "glamourous," is impeccable. The actor whose portrait is most prominently displaced is Adolphe Menjou, a well-known Hollywood fashion plate who titled his memoir *It Took Nine Tailors* (1948).

In terms of *Chinatown*'s anti-genre (noir) take on sex and crime, Polanski was enthusiastic about most of Towne's script, including his comment that "Gittes was overwhelmed by the intricate and almost incomprehensible plot."[23]

But it is hard to overestimate the radical anti-genre position this sex-crime-noir component takes in *Chinatown*. Earlier Towne had stated part of this by revealing his narrative was driven by the control of "water and power," instead of an "exotic" theft. Yet it goes much deeper than that. For example, the attempted theft of something like the historically venerable bejeweled Maltese Falcon is a singular act of wrongdoing. It involves no more than a handful of players. In contrast, *Chinatown*'s unlawful act—Los Angeles' water reservoir being secretly tapped by the city's powerbrokers unscrupulously securing water rights (in the northwest San Fernando Valley)—represents widespread establishment corruption. The number of greased palms would be unlimited, and any murder was just business.

Consequently, *Chinatown* constitutes a sense of crime, a political crime, better described as a societal dry rot of epic proportions. (How appropriate that another broad political scandal, with a name which might have doubled as *Chinatown*'s title—Watergate—would force the resignation of President Richard Nixon just a few months after the film's release.) Hence, this Towne-Polanski film of all-encompassing depravity goes well beyond the dissipation of noir's golden age. And as if to underscore the noxious nature of the groundbreaking *Chinatown*, the kingpin of the operation, John Huston's Noah Cross, had committed incest with his daughter Evelyn (Faye Dunaway). Moreover, with Evelyn's movie-numbing death at the picture's close, attempting to save the child of that union, Cross now has custody of another beautiful potential teenage victim, his daughter-granddaughter Katherine (Belinda Palmer). Sexuality has again been part of a noir film but in the most perverse manner possible, with no sense of the genre's provocative sensuality for a voyeur audience. But most importantly, though crime and sex are again mixed in a noir picture, the illegal act is not contingent upon this deviant sexuality of over a decade earlier.

This was no gratuitously provocative addition. It accentuated the monstrous nature of Huston's ironically named Noah Cross. An earlier, comparably charismatic noir villain, such as *The Maltese Falcon*'s Sydney Greenstreet, was casually capable of letting a young protégé take the blame for a murder rap but this pales in comparison to someone who is "capable of *anything*." The richness of Towne's script adds such nuances to the simplest scenes. For example, when Jake and Evelyn investigate the Mar Vista Inn retirement home, they find proof that many of the patients, past and present, have been used by name only as a cover-up for Cross' secret buyout of acreage in the "northwest valley" just outside of what will soon be part of Los Angeles. Huston's character needed Water Commissioner Mulwray dead to divert city reservoir water from this land to drive down prices and enable him to control a potential real estate bonanza ... once water was again made available. Thus, while viewers are already well aware of the breadth of the corruption involved, and equally aware of the non-populist nature of noir people in general, a small part of Jake and Evelyn's ruse to get into the nursing home further embellishes the world's ugliness.

The couple has bluffed their way into Mar Vista by claiming they wanted to place Evelyn's father in the establishment. They even used Jake's bandaged nose, cut by Polanski in a thug cameo scene, as evidence of the volatile relationship between him and Evelyn's parent as the reason for the visit. But during their small talk with the establishment administrator Mr. Palmer (John Rogers), the following exchange occurs:

JAKE: Do you accept people of the Jewish persuasion?
PALMER: I'm sorry, we do not.
JAKE: Don't apologize. Neither does Dad.

This is merely an aside, with no direct bearing on the case. Yet, the home's anti–Semitic policy further augments the negative nature of not just the noir world but the planet in general. Polanski's slow, methodical playing out of Towne's rich script gives both the scene and the movie a more realistically casual sense of just how nefariousness passes for normal in noir and dark comedy.

Polanski grasps another anti-genre element when he takes this film noir—a genre of the night normally defined by an impactful black-and-white imagery which shrouds twilight people—and shoots it in picturesque Panavision colors of sun-drenched California. In contrast, Chandler said, "The [noir] streets were dark with something more than night."[24] Yet, the genre's murderous German Expressionistic nights seldom come to *Chinatown* until its disturbingly murky finale, when the viewer is exposed to something best chronicled by a line from Edgar G. Ulmer's *Detour* (1945): "Whichever way you turn, fate sticks out its foot to trip you."[25]

Of all the genre facades for dark comedy, no cover is more appropriate than noir's up-close look at the underbelly of American life. Starting with black humor's theme of all-pervasive death, what could be a more appropriate character study than the domain of a detective? Singularly, it brings an added casually macabre note, because the gumshoe is accustomed to a sphere of human eradication. This is best exemplified by the *Chinatown* scene in which the police anonymously entice Jake to the apartment of Ida Sessions (Diane Ladd), the woman who had impersonated Dunaway's Evelyn Mulwray. Sessions is dead on her kitchen floor, murdered by someone connected to the death of Evelyn's husband, Hollis, and they (in hiding) want to see how he responds to Ida's demise.

Sessions' home is open, with a broken pane of door glass near the lock. Jake slowly and carefully enters the small apartment, surveying first the living room, then glancing into the bedroom. As he advances towards the kitchen, a wayward head of lettuce lies on the floor just inside. As the camera slowly pans right, one first sees other items from her torn brown grocery sack—canned goods, an elongated container of Cut-Rite wax paper, a box of Cream of Wheat, a case of Brillo pads, and melted ice cream from a now lid-less container signifying the drop from a sudden death blow (these groceries now frame her body).

Nicholson's Jake smoothly navigates around the kitchen corpse like a bored cleaning lady saving the biggest mess for last. Recognizing that this is the woman who has set him up, he nonchalantly picks up her purse with the indifference of passing the salt. The detail Polanski has brought to the sequence is topped by his meticulous attention to the billfold, with the contents providing a possible mini-résumé to someone who helped hoodwink Jake. In quickly rifling through the billfold, the corpse's identity is quickly established by her Social Security card, a Screen Actors Guild card and a worker's ID from an indiscernible company. There is also a driver's license and a $2 bill. Gittes now knows he was fooled by a professional performer, albeit seemingly not a very successful one, given her back-up job and a mere $2 bill to her name. The currency is an inspired touch, since it immediately establishes three things: Sessions' deed; a time period (the film's late 1930s setting was the heyday of the $2 bill), and the currency was considered jinxed, especially in that decade.

So why the bad luck? This merits pertinent elaboration. In the 1930s, a $2 bill bought someone a five-minute, keep-your-shoes-on interlude with a low-end prostitute. In the same period, a $2 bill was the standard price for both buying a vote and betting on a horse race—winners were paid in $2 bills. The first two activities were illegal, and since gambling was then frequently prohibited in much of the country, many respectable persons wanted no part of a $2 bill. But this story of bad luck only gets better ... or worse. Another unsavory connections comes from its nickname, a "Deuce," a slang term for the devil. For example, "What the deuce!" Is there any protection from this superstition? If one or more corners of the $2 bills is torn off, the bad luck was said to leave the currency.

One might even connect this $2 bill saga with Western folk hero "Wild Bill" Hickok's famous "dead man's hand." Ever since he was shot in the back during a poker game, his hand of "aces and eights" has been considered a dead man's hand. "Aces and eights" was a two-pair poker hand of black aces and black eights and an unknown hole card. Based upon such superstition, Sessions hardly seemed to have a chance. And given her apparent poor financial situation, this Noah Cross victim might have dabbled in prostitution and/or gambling, if one considers the $2 bill's 1930s history.

So how does this tabloid of death play as dark comedy? First, the genre has given a new shock element to the old comedy theory of surprise, such as Jake's indifferent response to a scene which would radically disturb most people. A normal reaction to a similar situation would be Jacqueline Bisset's repulsion in a sequence in Peter Yates' nourish *Bullitt* (1968). Going in search of her detective lover Steve McQueen, she stumbles upon a murder scene where he and several associates are acting in the same unbothered manner as Jake. Moreover, one need not make this about tough guy detectives and skittish women. In Robert Wise's *Born to Kill* (1947), true noir femme fatale Claire Trevor also happens upon the body of a murdered friend, no less. But she leaves without a trace of emotion and goes directly to a phone. A natural assumption would be she is calling the cops. Instead, Trevor is checking the train depot's next departure out of town.

Second, beyond a darkly comic non-response to the *Chinatown* murder scene is the fact that this most grisly of settings does not even inhibit added humor, such as the picture's biggest laugh line. That is, the police hiding at Sessions' apartment—to gauge Jake's response—are led by the detective's former friend on the force, Lieutenant Escobar (Perry Lopez) and associate "Loach" (Richard Bakalyan). The latter character is forever baiting Nicholson, especially about the multiple stitches in his nose:

> LOACH: What happened to your nose, Gittes? Somebody slam a bedroom window on it?
> JAKE: Nope. Your wife got excited. She crossed her legs too quick. You understand what I
>   mean, pal?

Sessions' death scene also provides dark comedy from the humor theory of incongruity. There she lies with wide open eyes that seem to register the incompatibility of a dead body, surrounded by assorted groceries. Only the container labeled "Cut-Rite" provides an aptly bad pun. Regardless, this merely represents a macabre initial postmodernism response to seeing Andy Warhol's Campbell Soup Cans exhibit first displayed at New York's Museum of Modern Art. To play at being a Warhol devil's advocate, he might have contested this sense of comic incongruity. Seeing as the artist had long been obsessed by eating this product, he was fond of describing and/or justifying his soup can art as a way of showcasing how "life has dominated me." But since it was *Sessions* who died among the canned goods, this writer is sticking with incongruity. Moreover, as George Carlin riffed in more than one routine, the closest thing to "death with dignity is not drooling."

Another darkly comic, surreal element to Sessions' death scene did not make it to the screen. In Towne's third draft of his *Chinatown* script he says of the victim, "Her eyes are open, a stream of ants is moving across the ice cream end into her mouth."[26] One cannot read this without thinking of Salvador Dali and Luis Buñuel's *Andalusian Dog* (1929), the black humor takeoff of both commercial and art house films whose imagery included the slitting of an eye and decay suggested by ants crawling out of a man's hand. This birthing of surrealism was replicated two years later in Dali's cartoonishly unearthly painted dream *The Persistence of Memory* (1931), in which death and decay is exemplified by melting watches and swarming ants. And for Dali, the ants could possibly have described Sessions *prior* to the personification of death, too. Besides decay, Dali scholar Robert Goff states the artist felt ants epitomized anxiety and apprehension.[27]

Beyond the Sessions sequence, probably *Chinatown*'s most blatantly dark comedy sequence related to death involves Jake's visit to the morgue. Again there is the casualness of death, with Charles Knapp's Morty the mortician even more immersed in the subject than a detective. Both men essentially trade black humor lines:

MORTY: Jake, what're you doing here?

GITTES: Nothin', Morty, it's my lunch hour [compounding black humor by mixing eating with a grisly subject]. I thought I'd drop by and see who died lately.

[Gittes picks up the sheet covering the toe-tagged Mulwray]

MORTY: Yeah, ain't that something? Middle of drought, the water commissioner drowns—only in L.A.

[After some small talk:]

GITTES: So how are you, Morty?

[The overweight, smoking Morty is wheeling in another dead body.]

MORTY: Never better. You know me, Jake.

[This is soon followed by a spasm of coughing. Gittes asks about the other body.]

MORTY: Leroy Shuhardt. Local drunk ... [Brushing sand from Leroy's face, Morty laughs] Quite a character. Lately he'd been living in one of the downtown storm drains—had a bureau dresser down there and everything.

GITTES: Yeah.

MORTY: Drowned, too.

GITTES: Come again?

The conversation continues with Jake comically questioning the report: "Yeah, well, he ain't gonna drown in a damp riverbed.... I don't care how soused he was...." But Morty is not persuaded. A confused Jake is gifted with a clue from a morgue body other than Mulwray's, but the detective has yet to realize and/or understand it.

Another dark comedy puzzle piece soon follows when Jake nearly drowns, too. While investigating Mulwray's mysterious fascination with the reservoir, Jake is swept away by yet another systematic dumping of water. This dangerous sequence, in which the need for the actor to appear on screen negated using a stunt man, was not shot until the end of production, in case of injury. A water-propelled Jake is only saved by grasping a wire mesh fence as he is almost swept to death on a sudden man-made wave.

Beyond darkening up the old Mack Sennett adage that anything is funny if you add speed and a sudden dunking, is the fact that Jake's immediate reaction is not one of joyful survival but petty comic anger over losing a shoe. Additionally, to take this in a more macabrely merry direction, the viewer has just seen how, at this point he or she thinks Mulwray died—including his corpse also having lost an expensive shoe. Even this twist is legitimate black humor, given the nothing-is-off-limits axiom of pioneering dark comedy icon Lenny Bruce: "You're right [about the artist's provocative material]! They're [a potentially disturbed audience] wrong."[28] This immediately segues to unchallenged black humor with the abrupt appearance of Polanski (billed as "Man with Knife") and a sarcastically soggy Jake calling him a midget:

> You're a very nosy fellow, kitty cat. Huh? You know what happens to nosy fellows? Huh? No? Wanna guess? Huh? No? Okay. They lose their noses [a flick of his knife cuts open Jake's nostril]. Next time you lose the whole thing. [I'll] cut it off and feed it to my goldfish.

The logical close to contemplating death in *Chinatown* is to notice how Polanski and Towne argued about the movie's conclusion. The director later recalled:

> [Towne] in those days wanted a happy ending. He wanted [Dunaway's character] to survive and Cross to die. I was absolutely adamant that she has to die at the end if the film is to have any kind of meaning. So we fought and we parted before finishing the script. So there was no end to the script. And I wrote that [end] scene literally like a couple of nights before we shot it. And I walked into [Nicholson] trailer with the scene and said, "Rearrange the dialogue into your style." Jack took my dialogue and he started changing wording and [editing] and that was the words you have in the film.[29]

By their very nature, dark comedy and film noir are predisposed for just such an ending. And no one knew this better than the controversially world-weary Polanski, whose pregnant wife, the beautiful blonde Sharon Tate, had been brutally murdered in Los Angeles by the Manson Family five years before *Chinatown*. Even with Towne's inspired script, notwithstanding the ending, he had been reluc-

Director Roman Polanski in his "Man with Knife" cameo.

Jake (Jack Nicholson) had broken his code of caring and involvement, only to make things worse, with Evelyn Mulwray (Faye Dunaway).

tant to return from his European residence to the site of a bloodbath city with a name which so ironically translates to City of Angels. Is it any wonder that, like so many other artists addressed in this text, he has long acknowledged the influence of writers such as Samuel Beckett and Franz Kafka?

Nonetheless, the shooting death of Dunaway's Evelyn Mulwray, after she attempted to escape incestuous father Noah Cross, in order to save her daughter, had two added black humor sardonic links from Towne's tightly woven script. Both examples drew upon earlier sequences in the movie. The first involves Jake noting a flaw in one of her eyes, which she describes "as sort of a birth mark." Evelyn's imperfection, like Achilles' heel, proves equally vulnerable, when this is the eye through which her fatal exit wound will occur.

The second pertinent previous scene involves what might initially be called a "surprise tittering sequence." Jake and Evelyn are heatedly talking in a parked car when she leans forward and accidentally honks the horn. It seems like nothing more than a quick laugh in an intense discussion. Plus, it is incidentally realistic, since many an individual has inadvertently done the same thing. Yet, as writer Michael Eaton reminds us, "Tales, unlike life, are not permeated by meaningless noise; like dreams there is nothing in them which cannot be interpreted, even if erroneously. As Chekhov put in print, if we see a gun on the wall in the first act then we know it will be fired in the third."[30]

Consequently, Dunaway's character seems to have almost escaped by car when the distant vehicle inexplicably slows. Simultaneously, viewers hear the sudden ongoing blare of a car horn. One has been coached to realize Evelyn must be slumped over the steering wheel, the victim of a random police bullet. Soon the screams of her teenage daughter are neither unexpected nor necessary, since Towne's tightly written script has foreshadowed all.

Moving from everpresent death, in all its ramifications, dark comedy's use of *Chinatown* absurdity might begin in many places. Jake is meeting and sharing with a balding client named Curly (the naturally comic character actor Burt Young) a series of photographs showing his wife committing various sexual acts with a stranger in a park. An anguished Curly starts to wreak havoc on Jake's office. However, when Young's cuckold husband starts in on the Venetian blinds, Nicholson's detective verbally intervenes, saying, in part, "You can't eat the Venetian blinds, Curly. I just had 'em installed on Wednesday." Jake provides the still stunned client with a shot of whiskey as Curly mumbles, "She's just no good." With dry humor Jake concurs: "What can I tell you, kid? You're right. When you're right, you're right." After some other small talk, he patiently and paternally escorts Curly out.

The opening should be categorized as the misdirection sidestep. Things are about to become not what they seem. Most importantly, this starts with the pictures. Curly's case is the last time photographs are "read" correctly. Let the absurdity begin. When Jake is later set up by the fake Mrs. Mulwray, it is based upon two sets of pictures he takes of Evelyn's husband Hollis and her daughter—who they have in hiding from the incestuous Noah. But Jake, the media and eventually the police interpret the photographs as the soon-to-be-dead water commissioner caught in an affair. And the police and the media will never know otherwise. Indeed, based upon the stills, Lieutenant Escobar eventually thinks Jake might even have taken pictures of who murdered Hollis Mulwray.

Later Jake will berate his staff photographer Walsh (Joe Mantell) about pictures he has taken of a nasty argument between Hollis and a yet to be identified Cross in front of a restaurant. Nicholson's private eye is so incensed about this alleged waste of time, he starts a lecture, "Let me explain something to you, Walsh. This business requires a little finesse." Yet these photographs are eventually major clues. Nicholson's detective can be forgiven for not immediately realizing their importance, since Hollis has yet to turn up dead. However, it takes Jake until nearly the film's conclusion to recognize the significance of Walsh's work. As suggested earlier, Gittes is no Philip Marlowe. Even when Jake sees water commissioner Mulwray's outer office photographs with Cross and learns they were once co-owners of Los Angeles' water supply, his epiphany takes forever. Here, pictures are *not* worth a thousand words, yet, like numbers, they can be used to mean or misunderstand anything. Even the 8x10 movie star glossies in Jake's office are suggestions of something he is not: a princely player in a world that sounds unworldly, Hollywoodland. This kingdom depends upon things not being what they seem, too. Consequently, *Chinatown* photographs might best be defined by trailblazing dark comedy writer Ambrose Bierce: "A picture painted by the sun without instructions in art. It is a little better than the work of [a primitive]."[31]

The second divertingly absurd element of *Chinatown*'s beginning is creating what passes for an amusingly effective detective norm (soon forever to vanish). Imagine if at the outset of Samuel Beckett's *Waiting for Godot* (1953) his Laurel and Hardy–like tramps Vladimir and Estragon had played a detective-client scenario before the play's existentialistic mantle also weighed them down. Jake would be the know-it-all Hardy, and Curly the Laurel sidekick. Keep in mind, *Chinatown* scholar Eaton said of Gittes' later apparent smooth operator, after Jake has told a bawdy story, with the real Mrs. Mulwray unknowingly behind him: "[Screenwriter] Towne wanted to show that Gittes is exposed as a cheap [comic] 'pimp in a suit, when a woman of class and substance appears.'"[32] But in the opening, Nicholson's character is all sophisticatedly slick drollness, and he even helps calm the discombobulated Curly by telling him not to worry about his bill. Thus, just as the evidence of Curly's unfaithful wife will be the story's only example of truthful photographs, this sequence showcases a last look at a confident, self-assured Jake.

Chinatown's third opening deflection to establish a forthcoming anti-genre absurdity involves Curly's adulterous deceitful wife. This is what one expects in a noir, especially if it is also a genre-crossing dark comedy. Nevertheless, just as the text's other examples have played the same crafty card, so does *Chinatown.* Dunaway's Mrs. Mulwray has enough of these traits to keep viewers briefly guessing, especially if one expected any carryover from her *Little Big Man* (1970) whore. However, as previously explored, she is the ultimate victim here. Moreover, even the film's fake Mrs. Mulwray, Ida Sessions, whose first appearance could easily dovetail into femme fatale land, turns out to be a relative straight arrow, too. Yes, she successfully helps kick off the derailing of Jake and most of Los Angeles. But it turns out she was just a struggling actress hired to play a perfunctory part in a "play" with an unknown but lethal ending ... rather like life itself. Sessions even anonymously calls Jake up to offer an apology of sorts over the murder of Hollis. Did that contribute to her own murder? Quite possibly. There is no question, nonetheless, that noir and/or dark comedy seldom offer rewards for doing the right thing. Instead, one is more likely to turn up dead on a kitchen floor, paradoxically surrounded by products which normally sustain life.

This apparently standard noir starting set-up, which almost straightaway goes into topsy-turvydom, is a fitting euphemism for the absurd dark comedy developments soon to follow in its la-la land setting. But catching the down-ride on the Ferris wheel which follows might best be consolidated around the subject of water. While Los Angeles' water commissioner drowning during a drought at the hands of a water-obsessed murderer named Noah first qualified *Chinatown* for dark comedy consideration, this is only the beginning. Jake and associates track Hollis to various reservoir dumping sites on the sea coast. And the first misleading pictures of Hollis and his alleged lover are shot on Echo Park Lake, a region of central Los Angeles flanked, in part, by Chinatown and Elysian Park, a fitting name for this story, since "elysian" is a term associated with the afterlife. Aptly, at this point, the soon-to-be-murdered Hollis is described as "having water on the brain." In short order, the viewer will see his drowned body being unceremoniously dragged by rope up a cement causeway from the reservoir. Again, involvement meant death.

Jake nearly meets the same watery fate on another reservoir causeway. This sequence introduces Polanski's nose-cutting appearance and the threat to Jake that, if he does not stop his investigation, his nose will be given a comical watery grave—food for his goldfish bowl. Plus, this thug is merely taking orders from Cross and his nefariously rich partners whose private abominable club is ironically named after the Albacore—a ten dollar word for the type of tuna sold as Chicken of the Sea. Finally, it turns out that an already dead Hollis had been dumped in the reservoir, with the real drowning having taken place in his estate's tidal pool—a paradoxical death setting for an entity from which primitive life on earth first began.

If piling all these darkly comic water factors were not absurdity enough, it only gets better ... or worse. Towne's Oscar-winning Best Original Screenplay was inspired by true events known as the California Water Wars. This represented a series of conflicts between

Los Angeles and Owen Valley Farmers in Eastern California early in the 20th century. Los Angeles Mayor Fred Eaton orchestrated the building of a 1913 aqueduct from Owens Valley in a manner not inconsistent with much of the chicanery and subterfuge associated with Noah Cross and company. Ultimately, the city prevailed; by the mid–1920s Owens Valley Lake was completely dry and the agricultural situation was all but ruined. Towne creatively embellished this history, and moved it into a late 1930s noir setting.

Finally, while Towne put together this absurdly waterlogged-squared screenplay, Polanski's watery input on the subject is often missed. But first some background on Polanski. Producer Robert Evans had wanted him to direct, given that noir's bleak take on the world had European origins, from the genre's fatalism and look of German Expression, to displaced Jewish-German film artists like Fritz Lang and Billy Wilder, who helped pioneer the subject in 1940s America. All this is well and good, especially given Polanski's noirish real life, from being a Polish child used as target practice by the Nazis, to the brutal 1960s Los Angeles murder of his pregnant wife by the Manson Family. And then there is the still-standing 1978 United States statutory rape charge against the director, which continues to make him a fugitive from American justice. This means he can no longer work in countries where he might face arrest or extradition. The man who had always defined himself as a historical "fugitive" has become one.

What, however, of Polanski's ironic water-related connection to *Chinatown*? One might start with a statement made by Roger Gunson, the prosecutor assigned to the rape charge when it appeared to be re-opened early in the 21st century. In a brief prepared for a trial which was never to take place, based upon a retrospective of the director's films, Gunson observed, "Every Roman Polanski movie has a theme: corruption meeting innocence over water."[33] While the Marina Zenovich documentary from which this statement is drawn, *Roman Polanski: Wanted and Desired* (2008), makes a strong case for a miscarriage of justice in the original 1978 criminal proceedings brought against Polanski, Gunson does make an intriguing observation. The catalyst, of course, had been that the seduction occurred in a Jacuzzi.

Gunson's statement is a broad over-generalization of Polanski's screen work. However, when water is used in the director's milieu, it is always at absurd odds with the general Christian ideology of it representing a spiritual cleansing that comes with an acceptance of Biblical salvation. For example, in Polanski's first feature *Knife in the Water* (1962, nominated for an Academy Award for Best Foreign Language Film), water is associated with one of cinema's most erotic scenes—a young Jolanta Umecka's morning musing on a sailboat shrouded with fog. This serves as a prelude to a provocative sex scene and potential violence, *à la* the title. In Polanski's horror classic *Rosemary's Baby* (1968), in which Mia Farrow is given over to a sexual scene with Satan, there is a pivotal nightmare sequence scene set on a drifting boat. Yet another key example is Polanski's *Ghost Writer* (2010), about an author hired to write the memoir of a controversial former British Prime Minister after the mysterious drowning of the original ghostwriter—a fact which haunts his replacement, played by Ewan McGregor. Violence and sexuality will then permeate the isolated watery settings.

A 1969 *Positif* interview with Polanski found the themes of his films similar to those of Alfred Hitchcock, which brings to mind the latter director's signature scene in his signature movie: the shower sequence in 1960s *Psycho*.[34] Again Christianity's use of cleansing water is made "deadly" absurd. That is, the film's central character has stolen a large sum of money, only to decide she must return it. Thus, the shower which follows her decision begins with a sense of rebirth and baptismal forgiveness—only to be destroyed by her fatal stabbing. Keep in mind, this is a basic application of dark comedy: Lull the viewer into a strong traditional expectation and then—*bang*—utilize an anti-genre shock effect. Is it any wonder that Hitchcock always called *Psycho* a dark comedy? Regardless, there are other, lesser Polanski implementations of atypical instances of water imagery miles away from, say, Ingmar Bergman's miraculous *Virgin Spring* (1960, which even here is the result of brutal violence). Nevertheless, the previous Polanski examples should suffice. A concluding linked addendum to the subject at hand brings one full circle back to *Knife in the Water* and Polanski's cameo billing in *Chinatown*: "Man with Knife."

Casual racism permeates this late 1930s period piece and delays solving the mystery. On the verge of meeting the real Mrs. Mulwray, who is unknowingly standing just behind Jake, the detective launches into telling a fresh-from-his-barber joke to his business associates:

> So here's this guy Walsh [other agency operatives soon gather], you understand? He's tired of screwin' his wife.... So his friend says to him, "Hey, why don't you do like the Chinese do?" So he says, "How do the Chinese do it?" And the guy says, "Well, the Chinese, first they screw a little bit, then they stop, then they go and read a little Confucius, come back, screw a little more, then they stop again, and then they go and contemplate the moon or something like that. Makes it more exciting." So now, the guy goes home and starts screwin' his own wife, see. So he screws her for a little bit and then he stops, and he goes out of the room and reads *Life* magazine. Then he goes back in, he starts screwin' again. He says, "Excuse me for a minute honey." He goes out and he smokes a cigarette. Now his wife is gettin' sore as hell. He comes back in the room, he starts screwin' again. He gets up to leave again to go look at the moon. She looks at him and says, "Hey, what's the matter with ya? You're screwin' just like a Chinaman!" [Jake laughs hysterically.]

Before targeting the story's pertinent racism, one must again note the multi-faceted nuances of Towne's script. The punchline reinforces the noir–dark comedy tenet that people cannot be trusted—the implication being the wife's knowledge of the subject comes from her already having had sex with a Chinaman. While her husband has attempted to experiment within the marriage to correct a dissatisfying sexual scenario, his wife has perhaps cheated. As with Towne having Jake ask the nursing home manager whether Jewish clients were welcome, though it is not necessary for plot advancement, it also enhances the story's nefarious ambience. Also, the joke further underscores the less-than-Philip-Marlowe crassness of Jake. Chandler's detective was the proverbial "tarnished knight," or as a character described him in the novelist's *The High Window* (1942), "The shop-soiled Galahad."[35] At the close of *Farewell, My Lovely* (1940), a character even calls him "sentimental," with the print Marlowe casually deflecting it by observing, "Sure it sounded like that when I said it. Probably all a mistake anyway. So long...."[36] Yet, the best summation for Marlowe's take on relationships fittingly comes in a late Chandler novel about his iconic character, *The Long Goodbye* (1953): "I stood up and walked around the desk and faced him. 'I'm a romantic, Bernie. I hear voices crying in the night and I go see what's the matter. You don't....'"[37]

Returning to bigotry contributing to a man as beast agenda:

> Towne had said he used the naked racism of the joke as a way of characterizing Gittes' attitude to ethnic differences as being emblematic of the time as an efficient way of encoding a whole nexus of Jake's [chauvinistic] attitude towards women.... [Jake asked his receptionist to leave the room before telling the joke.][38]

Part of the reason the movie's Chinatown area is a mystery is no mystery at all. For the same reason Noah Cross never attempts to pronounce Jake's last name correctly throughout the picture, Los Angeles shows neither respect, nor even interest, in the Chinese. This ethnic group is an invisible lesser race who merely launder clothing, such as the movies' comic slurs involving spitting in the wash, working in a multitude of domestic servant positions, and serving as the butt of jokes. Indeed, Jake's mocking of their broken English has him missing a key plot point early in the movie. While waiting for Mrs. Mulwray, Gittes spots a shiny object in her backyard saltwater tidal pool. Before her sudden appearance prevents him from fishing it out, Jake engages in a brief, condescending exchange with Evelyn's tidal pool-cleaning Chinese gardener, whose accent makes him seem to say, "Bad for glass [grass]," a phrase Nicholson's haughty character flippantly parrots back. Only later, during another visit to the same location, when the gardener further fleshes out his original statement, "Saltwater ... bad for glass," does Jake begin to connect the dots: The drowned Hollis had saltwater in his lungs, despite being removed from a freshwater reservoir.

Nevertheless, Nicholson's character is moving in the right direction, especially when the absence of Evelyn provides time for him to have the gardener pull the bright item from the tidal pool. (And even this epitomizes another example of racial superiority, since the depth of the gleaming-in-the sun article results in the water going over the top of the Chinese laborer's hip boots.) The retrieved shiny clue turns out to be a pair of broken glasses, which Jake still manages to misinterpret. He correctly assumes the spectacles-wearing Hollis was killed in this tidal pool, but he stumbles over what this means. When chauvinistic Jake confronts Evelyn about the hypothesis, a woman once again bests a man, be it Evelyn's post-joke first meeting in Jake's office, or even the wife in the joke which began this analysis. Evelyn tells Jake those could *not* be her husband's glasses because he did not wear bifocals. Only then does Jake realize they belong to Cross—the murderer.

Racism or sexism is an important component of man as beast in *Chinatown*. However, they embody a mere microcosm of the depraved superiority of the Noah Crosses of the world. In the American Film Institute's List of the 100 Greatest Villains, Huston's Cross ranks 16th, sandwiched between *Schindler's List*'s (1993) Nazi Amon Goeth (Ralph Fiennes) at 15 and *Misery*'s (1990) psychotic literary fan Annie Wilkes (Kathy Bates) at 17. (The AFI list was topped by Hannibal Lector [Anthony Hopkins] in *The Silence of the Lambs*, 1991.)

Cross' aforementioned admission and embrace of the statement, "Most people never have to face the fact that at the right time, the right place, they're capable of *anything*," would seem, however, to place Cross clearly in Hannibal Lector Land. In any event, his incestuous relationship with his daughter, and the orchestration of various murders, including that of his former friend and son-in-law, seem to be only a warm-up act to a future he relishes controlling in an ever more malevolent manner. Consequently, the shattering of Nicholson's character at the film's fatalistic "Forget it, Jake, it's Chinatown" conclusion really has two chilling interpretations. This chapter opened with the most basic "reading": Jake's attempt to help someone for whom he cared not only leads to her death, but it unleashed an establishment monster to victimize and control both an ever-expanding Los Angeles and the custody of his granddaughter-daughter. Worse yet, though the viewer is never privy to just what occurred in Jake's past prior to *Chinatown*'s opening, it is clear something like this had happened before ... and now he feels doubly shredded for letting down his survivor code of minimalism: getting involved only makes things worse.

All this is more than enough to explain his failed final mumbling mantra of resignation, "[Do] as little as possible." Yet, one could posit a much more monstrous take on the film's conclusion. That is, in Jake's last conversation with Cross, Huston's character confessed that every demonic thing he had done was about the future. Thus, I would suggest Jake's ultimate foundering disintegration went far beyond the immediate localized evil which was then unwinding. Instead, it would seem Jake suddenly realized for the first time the totality of modern man's fatalistic futility. He might just as well have been the equally terrified Kurtz at the close of Joseph Conrad's 1902 novella *Heart of Darkness* crying, "The horror! The horror!"[39] Jake, like so many Conrad anti-heroes, finds himself in crisis mode forced to face the fact that life has no meaning or truth. Maybe this is dark comedy's ultimate anti-genre trick upon the film noir detective's personal code in a codeless world. Today it is nonsensical to think any code workable.

So how did this deep dish dark comedy commercial hit fare with reviewers? *Cineaste* provides the perfect overview:

> *Chinatown* has been praised to the heavens by almost all the critics and it's not difficult to see why.... It presents politics on strictly an Evil Man's field of action [and it inspires literary-intellectuals] who can cite [William] Blake, [Samuel] Beckett and others in confirming that ... there is nothing that one can do, the world is evil....[40]

Variety's opening line was a direct "*Chinatown* is an outstanding picture. Robert Towne's complex but literate and orderly screenplay takes gumshoe Jack Nicholson on a murder manhunt all over Los Angeles...."[41] *Newsday* said:

The courtly but evil Noah Cross (John Huston), with Jake (Jack Nicholson) sporting the work of Polanski's knife.

Paranoia is in the air. We absorb it into our lungs and hearts and minds every [Watergate] day now. If we're not reading about plots, conspiracies and dirty tricks in the papers or hearing about then from television, we get it at the theatre. The two outstanding movies of the past week [*Chinatown* and *The Parallax View*] ... paranoia movies about powerbrokers and the politicians who work them [while today the Nixon White House is in a state of collapse].... Polanski uses the fact that we like Nicholson so much to hurt and threaten him constantly and thereby to worry and scare us for his sake. That's a device that Polanski learned from Hitchcock.... The film is funny, sardonic.... It's a treat. I look forward to Polanski movies now the way I used to wait impatiently for Hitchcock pictures....[42]

Films and Filming added:

Shrewdly written by Robert Towne ... *Chinatown* is primarily a rich affirmation of Roman Polanski's caliber as director.... [And] for the explicit 1970s it offers a blunter frankness, an uglier yet fascinating grope at the vulnerable underbelly of humanity and a sidelong sneer at dirty politics.[43]

Roger Ebert's *Star Ledger* review declared:

[Polanski] achieved a tour de force.... Relationships with Watergate quickly suggest themselves [where] villains have actually convinced themselves they're doing the right thing ... [It is] more about "evil itself," a favorite subject of Polanski's.... He seems particularly interested in the kinds of men who are capable of inhuman deeds [such as a wannabe star becoming involved with Satanists in *Rosemary's Baby*, 1968].[44]

Ebert's revisionist critique on *Chinatown* almost three decades later was both poetic and now pointed towards dark comedy: "[A noir detective is] a kind of man who occupies human tragedy for a living.... From Gittes forward, Nicholson created the persona of a man who had seen it all and was still capable of being wickedly amused...."[45] In Peter Biskind's later reassessment of *Chinatown*, he described it in terms which further validate its inclusion here: "[An exercise] in genre demolition."[46]

Ultimately, dark comedy, whatever its genre-crossing tendencies, has become as pervasive as Jake's response to whether his recently sliced nose still hurt: "Only when I breathe."

8

Love and Death (6/11/75)

How I got into this predicament I'll never know. Absolutely incredible. To be executed for a crime I never committed. Of course, isn't all mankind in the same boat? Isn't all mankind ultimately executed for a crime it never committed? The difference is that all men go eventually, but I go six o'clock tomorrow morning. I was supposed to go at five o'clock but I have a smart lawyer. Got leniency.

—Boris (Woody Allen) in *Love and Death*

This is Woody Allen's dark comedy credo in a nutshell: derail one's existential angst with divertingly entertaining ludicrous comments which ironically give as much legitimate clarification to life's unexplainable questions as anything. Nonsense seems a natural response to a nonsensical world. The dark comedy genre-crossing thrust of this chapter, however, embraces a category camouflage thus far new to the text: using the personality comedian.

Love and Death is essentially Bob Hope caught in Ingmar Bergman land—two of Allen's greatest influences. Allen was first mesmerized by Hope. As a child when he watched Hope and Bing Crosby's *Road to Morocco* (1942) opening song "We're Morocco-bound," while navigating on camels, "[I] knew from that moment on exactly what I wanted to do with my life."[1] Hope's breezy wit even had Allen recalling that "as a teenager I used to pretend I was Bob Hope before I went on a date."[2] Yet, the Hope effect upon Allen went beyond help in dating or wanting to be just a comic:

There are moments in his older movies when I think he's the best thing I have ever seen. It's everything I can do at times not to imitate him. It's hard to tell when I do, because I'm so unlike him physically and in tone of voice, but once you know I do, it's absolutely unmistakable.[3]

Not surprisingly, when the Film Society of Lincoln Center planned a 1979 salute to Hope, the organization called upon Allen:

Because Woody repeatedly claimed that Hope had been his major influence, the Society asked him to compile and narrate a sixty-minute film tribute to the comedian, an anthology that he entitled "My Favorite Comedian."[4]

Beyond Hope's persona of a cowardly yet egotistical, womanizing anti-hero, which is also a given for Allen's screen character, Woody's voice-over narrative tribute is also applicable to the younger comedian's persona:

Hope's bantering style—the fantastic ad-lib, the verbal interplay—reached a point of graceful spontaneity rarely equaled in films…. [T]he lightness is everything. The puns, the

139

asides, the fast one-liners, the great quips that appear throughout his work are quick, bright, and delivered lightly.[5]

Though Allen's *Love and Death* character morphs into Hope's personality comedian style, by placing him in the angst-ridden art house world of Bergman landscape the incongruity already has one well on the way to the absurdity of dark comedy. This same odd coupling is true of the film's title, which might double as the name for all Allen films.

So what of Bergman's influence upon Allen? No artist better tackles such unanswerable questions as "Why am I here?" "Is there a God?" "What about the death which awaits us?" than Bergman. And of these unsolvable subjects, nothing weighs more heavily upon Allen's mind than death:

> There are some laughs you have in life, provided by fortuitous moments with your family or friends or something. But most of life is tragic. You're born, you don't know why. You're here, you don't know why. You go, you die. Your family dies. Your friends die. People suffer. People live in constant terror. The world is full of poverty and corruption and war and Nazis and tsunamis. The net result, the final count is, you lose—you don't beat the house.[6]

Given that Allen feels that Bergman was the greatest filmmaker who ever lived, it is only natural that the comedian would gravitate toward the Swedish artist's take on death.[7] Allen has stated, "Bergman made the definitive work on the subject [of death] with *The Seventh Seal* [1957]. And I've always wished that I could come up with the correct [serious film] metaphor that would be able to express my observations and feelings on it."[8] While Allen feels he has yet to accomplish this goal, *Love and Death* is a most successful loose parody of *The Seventh Seal*.

Besides the analogy of randomly dropping Hope into a Bergman movie, one could also reframe the absurdity by stating the time tripping–like obvious: A contemporary (circa 1975) Allen suddenly finds himself in Russia during the Napoleonic Wars, around the time of the French invasion of 1812. Beyond period clothing, the Allen personae remains intact: the Hope–like, witty yet cowardly anti-hero periodically peppered with false bravado. There is the same Allen disheveled hair and the anachronistic large glasses. And when he is forced into the 1812 Russian army, the then current (1970s) anti-war spirit is brilliantly bolstered by having a tough black drill sergeant on the order of Louis Gossett, Jr.'s later Oscar-winning performance as Gunnery Sergeant Emil Foley in *An Officer and a Gentleman* (1982).

The latter scenario also anticipates Allen's later *New Yorker* story "The Kugelmass Episode" (1977), which won the O. Henry Award for Best Short Story the same year his *Annie Hall* (1977) won multiple Oscars for the artist, including Best Director and Best Original Screenplay. "The Kugelmass Episode" is an inspired tale about a standard disgruntled Allen intellectual, an unhappily married New York professor named Kugelmass, looking for a unique affair. His answer comes from an odd little Brooklyn inventor named Persky, who has constructed a literary magic cabinet of sorts. One enters said device with a favorite novel and is suddenly transported into that book as a character. Pesky tells the professor:

> You can meet any of the women created by the world's best writers. Whoever you dreamed of. You can carry on all you like with a real winner. Then when you've had enough, you give a yell, and I'll see you're back in a split second.[9]

Initially everything is fine. Kugelmass is soon Madame Bovary's lover—not bad, the professor thinks, for someone who failed freshman English. But soon there is trouble.

Boris (Woody Allen) being taken by death *à la* Ingmar Bergman.

On an attempted sexual romp through *Portnoy's Complaint*, the machine shorts out, Persky dies of a heart attack, and Kugelmass is somehow "projected into an old textbook, *Remedial Spanish*, and was running for his life over a barren, rocky terrain as the *tener* ("to have")—a large and hairy irregular verb—raced after him on its spindly legs."[10]

Because one expects a bad conclusion for Kugelmass, there is no doubt about Boris' end of the road. As with *The Seventh Seal*'s knight, death comes for Allen's character, too. Consistent with the artist's real world interview about life, though his work is often artfully distractive with its dark comedy, "the net result, the final count is, you lose—you don't beat the house."

The preceding comments about awards, from Oscars to the O. Henry Award, document the unique quality and diversity of Allen's work. This is only noted to suggest, as was the case with Robert Towne's much celebrated screenplay for *Chinatown* (1974), that while this text's focus films are usually adapted from memorable print texts, the original Towne and Allen screenplays merit the same esteemed literary status. To underline that point, with regard to Allen, a rare admission was later made by the Pulitzer Prize selection committee. The year Allen made *Hannah and Her Sisters* (1986), for which the writer would eventually win another Best Original Screenplay Oscar, newspapers across the country were suggesting that Allen and his screenplay are Pulitzer Prize quality—but movie scripts have never been awarded Pulitzer drama prizes.[11] Key critics selected to decide the prize winner that year sent the Pulitzer board an unprecedented letter stating:

> The only narrative script they agreed upon was Allen's screenplay for *Hannah and Her Sisters*. Since movies [are ineligible, the board] didn't give a drama award Thursday, for the 13th time. Allen "is America's Ingmar Berman; both write plays that happen to appear in films under their own direction," said the letter sent by Mel Gussow, *The New York Times*; Edwin Wilson, *The Wall Street Journal*; and Bernard Weiner, *San Francisco Chronicle*.

[Other board members, such as] Eugene Roberts, executive editor of the *Philadelphia Inquirer*, said, "I happen to agree with their assessment of the Woody Allen movie."[12]

Regardless, Allen's *Love and Death* anti-genre assault upon personality comedy adroitly trips up all the basic components of the clown category.[13] The genre's first characteristic is a specific comedy shtick. Allen sabotages this element by essentially hijacking, by his own admission, Hope's persona and using it as a hilarious incongruity mouthpiece for comments the older comedian could never have made:

> [I]f it turns out that there *is* a God, I don't think that He's evil. I think that the worst you can say about Him is that, basically, He's an underachiever. After all, you know, there are worse things in life than death. I mean, if you've ever spent an evening with an insurance salesman, you know exactly what I mean. The key here, I think, is to ... not think of death as an end but think of it more as a very effective way of cutting down on your expenses....

A second clown genre element is to place a high premium on physical-visual comedy. Traditionally, visual humor represents an end in itself, such as Bob Hope's discombobulated response to a shot of whiskey in *My Favorite Brunette* (1947), the spirit of which might best be described by an essay passage from Hope friend Robert Benchley's humor book *The Treasurer's Report and Other Aspects of Community Singing* (1930):

> In about eight second the top of the inhaler's head rises slowly ... until it reaches the ceiling where it floats, bumping gently up and down. The teeth then drop out and arrange themselves on the floor to spell "Portage High School, 1930," the eyes roll upward and backward, and a strange odor of burning rubber fills the room....[14]

All this is not to say *Love and Death* does not have superb moments of throwaway slapstick, like a sequence of prolonged bowing among Boris, Sonia (Diana Keaton) and two of Napoleon's envoys, which was no doubt inspired by a similar sequence in another of Allen's favorite influences, the Marx Brothers' *Duck Soup* (1933). Yet *Love and Death*'s most sparkling gags resonate beyond each sequence. For instance, after a sex scene with the beautifully erotic Countess Alexandrovna (Olga Georges-Picot), Boris' almost immediate post-coital exhaustion (despite a bedroom so disheveled it appears to have been an all-night match) is symbolized as a shot of the most comically fatigued stone lion statue. Allen is spoofing one of world cinema's signature scenes. In Sergei Eisenstein's *Battleship Potemkin* (1925), the Soviet director symbolizes the appalling Czarist troop massacre of civilians by creating a montage which includes a stone lion at rest rising in protest. Pioneering Allen scholar Maurice Yacowar called this targeting of Eisenstein *Love and Death*'s "funniest film allusion."[15] The sequence is hysterical whether or not you have ever heard of Eisenstein, but knowledge of the *Potemkin* connection pushes this beyond a mere passing gag.

Another way in which Allen's *Love and Death* awards the—to borrow the football phase—"one and out" visual gag, is to create the most surreal of sequences. For instance, early in the film a young Boris shares a dream which makes him think he will *not* grow up to be like other men. Suddenly, the viewer sees a v-shaped series of coffins standing upright. Immediately, a waiter carrying a tray exits from each coffin, which is followed just as swiftly with each waiter finding a partner with whom to dance. This sight gag tends to linger with the viewer, as does his brief visit from death. In fact, the latter gag is tied directly to the film's finale, where Boris, like the characters from *The Seventh Seal*, are led away in a dance of death by the Grim Reaper.

Another essential personality clown component is an underdog status. Obviously this applies to the Hope-like Allen in *Love and Death*. Yet there are none of Hope's periodic shaking-with-fear bouts. Indeed, Boris is granted several powers which are far from antiheroic, such as breezy direct address commentaries to the audience, including a long post-death elucidation, ranging from a comic denigration of God (who must exist if Boris is still addressing us), to a rambling discourse on the nature of love. In the latter case, in an alleged state of death, there is a comic incongruity to offering tips on romance: "Regarding love, hey, you know, what can you say? It's not the quantity of your sexual relations that count. It's the quality. On the other hand, if the quantity drops below once every eight months, I would definitely look into it...."

Even before his presumed earthly exit with a Reaper so casual he prefers a summer white shroud, Boris has the ability to speak with the recently deceased. For instance, one such victimized comrade even asks him to run an errand regarding the retrieval of an engagement ring, a conversation which soon comically descends into an argument over how Boris could have gotten him a better price on the ring.

The clown genre often involves a nomadic existence, thus allowing a given personality to comically interact with an ever-changing assortment of characters set against atypical backgrounds, such as Chaplin's Tramp shuffling around icebergs and prospectors in the Klondike of *The Gold Rush* (1925). Boris experiences this picaresque existence in *Love and Death*, too. Nevertheless, as with his status as an atypical anti-hero, there are unusual circumstances. Unlike the standard comic "road picture" in which these misadventures lead to personal growth (such as with Steve Martin and John Candy in *Trains, Planes and Automobiles*, 1987), for Boris all roads lead to potential death. This is the most blatantly anti-genre personality comedy situation yet encountered. Allen, the reluctant soldier, is marched off to a war which ultimately results in his demise, followed by a postmodern extinction exit dance with Mr. Reaper. This is hardly the happy time that Hope had with Crosby when they were off on their fun "Roads" to Bali, Singapore, Morocco, Rio, Utopia, and so on.

Paradoxically, Boris' ultimate passing is not in battle but by execution, after he and Keaton's Sonia have undertaken a final deadly jaunt to attempt to assassinate Napoleon. Yet, like Boris' family forcing their pacifist son into battle, Sonia presses him to make his fatal trip. In contrast, the normal comic wants and/or needs to make a journey, like Pee-wee Herman (Paul Reubens) in *Pee-wee's Big Adventure* (1985) going on a nationwide search (including the Alamo) for a stolen bike. Even Boris' earlier, seemingly safe furlough trips to St. Petersburg are not without potential death. For example, after his dalliance with the provocatively sensual countess, one of her jealous lovers forces Boris into a duel in which he is wounded.

A final common character of the clown genre is the often unnoted importance of a team interaction. Even solo clowns frequently need someone off whom to bounce their humor. Their comic interpretations with others are what begin to differentiate pure shtick (the concert film) from a personality comedy picture. Obviously, little needs to be said about the acknowledged comedy teams, like Laurel and Hardy and the Marx Brothers. Unofficial ones merit attention, too—clowns only periodically teamed, such as the pioneering Hope and Crosby. And with their many couplings, much the same could be said of Allen and Keaton. Yet, even here, Woody also goes anti-genre on the audience. Allen best teams with himself and/or the audience as he shares his thoughts in voice-over, or breaks the fourth wall and directly addresses the viewer. Call it either Allen being a team unto himself, or credit him with the largest comedy troupe possible—everyone viewing the film. He uses both techniques so frequently in *Love and Death*, it is a captivating example of a new age of personality comedians, as if the concert comic has merged with the traditional narrative. Moreover, since narrative proves no match for characterization in any sort of comedy, Allen as a densely populated "team" sets new precedents.

Another *Love and Death* anti-genre subterfuge involves parody. Allen goes to great lengths to loosely spoof Bergman's *The Seventh Seal* and the art house film in general; he also burlesques scores of literary and cinematic allusions, usually with a Russian connection. Though his parody is broad, given the very intellectual nature of the non-mainstream art house picture, there is often a tendency for *Love and Death* to seem more like the genre being affectionately undercut. For example, near the film's close, Keaton's Sonja observes:

> To love is to suffer. To avoid suffering, one must not love. But then one suffers for not loving. Therefore, to love is to suffer; not to love is to suffer; to suffer is to suffer. To be happy is to love. To be happy, then, is to suffer, but suffering makes one unhappy. Therefore, to be unhappy one must love or love to suffer or suffer from too much happiness. I hope you're getting this down.

As the *Marble* critic noted, a *Love and Death* conversation like this often turns into "an illogical philosophical squabble that ends in tautologies that only a Kierkegaard or perhaps a schizophrenic could understand."[16]

The *Marble* reviewer, however, would seem most taken with the sequence in which Boris plans to murder Napoleon:

While Sonia (Diane Keaton) has no problem with killing Napoleon (James Tolkan), Boris (Woody Allen) struggles with the concept.

Murder, the most foul of all crimes. And not just abstract murder like shooting an unknown enemy on the battlefield but standing in a closed room with a live human being and pulling the trigger, face to face. And a famous human being, a successful one, one who earns more than I do…. My God, you figure Napoleon has got to be good for 10,000 francs a week….

Thus, the *Marble* critique suggests: "However zany an Allen film may be, there is always a morality that surfaces, and here he is concerned with the right to murder; specifically, killing in war, and killing for the good of society. He is a coward but brave enough to admit his fear of death."[17]

Nevertheless, the last two *Love and Death* quotes have ended on an obvious comic tone, from Sonja asking, "I hope you're getting this [intellectual conjecture] down," to Boris trying to guess Napoleon's weekly salary. Yet, other passages are straight reaffirmation parody, with the only humorous payoffs limited strictly to intellectuals. For instance, there is the conversation in which Boris and his father speak completely in Fyodor Dostoyevsky references:

FATHER: Remember that nice boy next door, Raskolnikov? [He is the central character in Dostoyevsky's novel *Crime and Punishment*, 1872. This figure plans and executes a murder along Leopold and Loeb lines—some people are superior, and he compares himself to Napoleon.]
BORIS: Yeah.
FATHER: He killed two ladies [Raskolnikov's plan was to kill a nasty woman pawnbroker and put the money to better use. In the process, he also kills her sister, who accidentally stumbles onto the murder.]
BORIS: What a nasty story.
FATHER: Bobak told it to me. [Bobak is the name of a frustrated writer title character in a 1873 Dostoyevsky short story. While attending a funeral, Bobak can hear the voices of the recently deceased entertaining themselves by relating evil facts about their lives.]
BORIS: He must have been possessed. [The 1872 Dostoyevsky novel *The Possessed*, now generally known as *The Devils* or *Demons*, is about ideologies colliding, and society collapsing into a horrific chaos of demons.]
FATHER: Well, he was a raw youth. [*Raw Youth* is an 1875 Dostoyevsky novel about an intellectual teenager who rebels against Russian society.]
BORIS: Raw youth, he was an idiot! [*The Idiot* is Dostoyevsky's 1869 novel in which a young man, Myshkin, is romantically torn between a kept woman and an innocent young girl.]
FATHER: He acted assaulted and injured. [Myshkin is attacked and ultimately goes mad.]
BORIS: I heard he was a gambler. [Dostoyevsky's 1867 novel *The Gambler* is a tale of a young man's gambling addiction and how it is created and driven by a merry love affair. Yet, he is often successful at gambling.]
FATHER: You know, he could be your double. [In the Dostoyevsky novella *The Double*, the central character is an antiheroic government clerk who keeps meeting "twins"—but they are his opposite in their confidence and success.]
BORIS: Really, how novel.

Unless you're a literature major, many of these references will fly over a viewer's head, and that is precisely the point of reaffirmation parody, or what is sometimes called mockumentary. That is, this Dostoyevsky-peppered dialogue could be accepted as a serious exchange between two characters in an earnestly philosophical novel, *à la* a work by this Russian writer. In other words, reaffirmation parody, with scheming slyness, toys with being received as the genre being spoofingly sabotaged, which for *Love and Death* is the art house film. This creates a fascinating tension between what one expects of the genre, and how many recognized it as a burlesque. For an acclaimed early historical example of the process, one could turn to Buster Keaton's reaffirmation parody of the action film in his greatest movie *The General* (1926). Unfortunately, his comic chicanery was so successful that the film was initially a box office failure—always a risk for this more sophisticated take upon parody.

Ironically, this burlesque approach is sometimes criticized for being a one-joke, trivial piling on of joke, such as *Newsday*'s otherwise positive review of *Love and Death*: "It's interesting that in his new movie ... Allen spends so much time sneering at official culture in the form of a parody.... It's as if Allen felt the need to write 'Woody was here in 1975' on Grant's tomb."[18] Far from sneering, Allen is kiddingly but fondly taking one to a higher appreciation of the subject under comic attack. That is the whole point.

Reaffirmation parody creates another comic wrinkle: It is ambitiously self-referential in nature. Instead of leaving it to the audience to anticipate each art house cliché, Allen's characters directly talk about the story in coded "Dostoyevsky Speak." If one retreats, and compares the saga of Boris and Sonia to the annotated conversation just dissected with his father, a blueprint for *Love and Death* unfolds. Not everything dovetails together, but there are enough parallels to make it engaging. Thus, Boris is a rebellious "raw youth" who, like Bobak, is a frustrated writer capable of hearing negative things said by the dead (his *Love and Death* conversation with the fallen comrade over the price of an engagement ring reveals the deceased had another woman on the side). Also like the "raw youth," Boris is torn between a woman of title and a girl, though Sonia is less than innocent. In addition, like Raskolnikov, Boris sees the world divided between superior beings and the worm-like, though in a twist, he includes himself among the latter. Still, like Raskolnikov, he also plans a murder and compares himself to Napoleon. After Boris references the often lucky "gambler," his father tells him he could be his "double" which, in the reverse logic of the latter novel, means the father has just called his son an anti-hero—always an apt description of an Allen character. At the film's close, Boris is executed, despite an alleged angel of God telling him he will be saved ... which sounds more like the work of "devils" and "demons," either of which is the now preferred title for *The Possessed*. Plus, the nihilistic conclusion of this novel comes about because the Russian church has been weakened by arguments with the liberal left, and Boris is forever questioning whether God exists. Finally, these Dostoyevsky titles all smack of death and insanity, subjects at home in *Love and Death*.

Such dwelling upon Dostoyevsky furthermore encourages one to look for additional personal insights about *Love and Death* tied to the novelist himself. For example, like Boris, Dostoyevsky was accused of questioning the czarist government and was also sentenced to be executed. He was pardoned at the last moment, an expectation the Mother Russia–questioning Boris had been given by, in hindsight, the demon-like false angel. Dostoyevsky literature and life were packed with flawed and/or failing relationships, another ongoing component of the filmmaker's work. The novelist was forced to be a soldier, as was Boris, and both were not up to the task. The philosophical questions Dostoyevsky constantly poses in his work anticipate much of Allen's oeuvre, such as the novelist's challenging of religion and politics. As one historian observed, "What makes Dostoyevsky writing so compelling [as with Allen] is that he asks the big questions but never finally decides between faith and politics."[19] (Allen's best comic mix of the faith-politics non-answer is a line from 1980s *Stardust Memories*: "To you I'm an atheist; to

God, I'm the loyal opposition.") Nevertheless, such doubts would identify Dostoyevsky as a pioneering existentialist. Indeed, Franz Kafka often called the novelist his "blood relative," a connection seemingly most obvious in the younger writer's *The Trial* (1935), which brings one full circle back to Allen's chapter-opening quote, which notes, in part, "Isn't all mankind ultimately executed for a crime it never committed?"

An even more engrossing link between Dostoyevsky and Allen is that the novelist was nearly executed for reading material by the Russian author Nikolai Gogol, a writer whose work influenced Dostoyevsky, Kafka ... and, arguably, Allen. For instance, in Gogol's inspired short story "The Nose" (1836), a major awakens to find his schnozzle missing, with only smooth skin covering its place. Gogol's figure soon spots his clothed proboscis escaping down the street. Eventually the police apprehend the nose, but it cannot be re-attached to the major's face. Weeks later the officer awakens to find his beak back in place. Thus, in an otherwise realistic story, Gogol pricks the pompous and/or self-important by a touch of absurdity, only to end with normalcy. In Allen's world this is called "magic realism," and one immediately thinks of Allen's short film "Are the Findings of Doctors and Clinics Who Do Sexual Research Accurate," in his 1972 *Everything You Always Wanted To Know About Sex (But Were Afraid to Ask)*. In one episode, Allen plays a sexuality researcher planning to interview a prominent scientist (John Carradine), only to find himself at risk with this unstable doctor. During Allen's escape he and a reporter companion (Heather Macrae) are threatened by a forty-foot–high breast which has escaped Carradine's lab. But all returns to normal when the horrifying hooter is lured into a giant brassiere. Regardless, like Gogol, in *Love and Death* Allen seeks to "convey a serious message about the human condition, while poking fun not only at the message itself but also at some of the artistic vehicles [herein Russian literature and film] traditionally used to convey it."[20]

These, then, have been some of the anti-genre diversions, utilizing personality comedy and reaffirmation parody, which semi-camouflage *Love and Death*'s inherent dark comedy base. But to address its black humor core, one must start again with the omnipresence of death. For starters, as with most of the films addressed in this volume, *Love and Death*'s war focus is a logical setting for death. Granted, by going back to the time of Napoleon it only plays subtextually with the Vietnam War. Yet, the latter conflict was suddenly topical again, since the fall of Saigon (April 30, 1975) occurred only weeks before Allen's film was released. Fittingly, the catalyst for one of the picture's best sardonic jabs at death is a battlefield covered with corpses. Boris' unit comes upon the carnage and the following exchange occurs:

SOLDIER: Oh, God is testing us.
BORIS: If He's gonna test us, why doesn't He give us a written [exam]?

Death appears in multiple ways from the film's opening minutes, ranging from Old Nehamkin being reduced to ashes when struck by lightning, to young Boris' dream about coffins and a brief breaking-the-ice visit from the Grim Reaper himself. Later Sonia promises to marry him only because she thinks he will be killed in battle:

BORIS: If, by some mistake, I'm not killed tomorrow, would you marry me?
SONIA: What do you think the odds are?

Moreover, as demonstrated in earlier chapters, on the rare occasion when love is expressed in a dark comedy, it occurs and/or is perceived to occur in a perverse situation. In *Love and Death*, that contrariness involves death:

Sonia: You were my one great love.
Boris: Oh, thank you very much. I appreciate that. Now, if you'll excuse me, I'm dead.
Sonia: What's it like?
Boris: What's it like? You know the chicken at Tresky's Restaurant? It's worse.

Of course, Sonia waiting to express alleged love with death lurking about is her modus operandi. For example, this is Sonia "comforting" her first husband on his deathbed:

Sonia: I know I could have been a better wife to you ... kinder [she has bedded every other man in the area]. I could have made love with you more often ... or once, even.
Vorkovec: Once would have been nice.

Death is also an excellent foundation for Allen to go into his near cloning of the cowardly Bob Hope persona. For instance, when a dual with the countess' primary love is about to unfold:

Inbedkov: We'll do it now ... and to the death.
Boris: Oh no, I can't do anything to the death. Doctor's orders. You see, I have this ulcer condition, and death is the worst thing for it.

The subject of death even provides a segue to a superb *Love and Death* example of dark comedy's second key theme: absurdity. As Boris gets his last chance to kill Napoleon, he begins another philosophical monologue which naturally succeeds in being arguably the film's supreme sampling of satirical silliness:

Boris: If I don't kill him, he'll make war all through Europe. But murder ... the most foul of crimes. What would Socrates say? All those Greeks were homosexuals. Boy, they must have had some wild parties. I bet they took a house together in Crete for the summer. A: Socrates is a man. B: All men are mortal. C: All men are Socrates. That means all men are homosexuals. Heh ... I'm not a homosexual. Once, some Cossacks whistled at me. I happen to have the kind of body that excites both persuasions. You know, some men are heterosexual and some men are bisexual and some men don't think about sex at all, you know ... they become lawyers.

The ancient Greeks seem to incite jocularity among many satirists, such as Will Cuppy, a popular practitioner during Allen's youth. For instance, Cuppy wrote in *How to Become Extinct* (1941), "Is it my fault if anything one [now] quotes from Aristotle sounds as if he was a little touched in the head? And [how] does that necessarily make him the greatest thinker of all time?"[21] Allen, like Cuppy, believed in neither superhumans (especially not Greek philosophers) nor the supernatural.[22]

Alluding to the super-anything feeds Allen's ability to blitz various *Love and Death* examples of institutional absurdity, a black humor norm. Religion proves to be the film's favorite establishment target. This is most advantageously showcased in a quote noted earlier in this chapter (if God exists, He's an underachiever). This strategy also includes riffling on the Bible, or the religious handbook of your choice:

And so I walk through the valley of the shadow of death. Actually, make that "I run through the valley of the shadow of death"—in order to get *out* of the valley of the shadow of death more quickly, you see.

Allen also provides pocket examples of scriptures being strafed—a righteous man will "dwell in the house of the Lord for six months with an option to buy." Thus, as in the world of his hero Ingmar Bergman, "[T]he voice of God cannot be heard; but [thankfully] Allen fills the silence with one-liners."[23]

Another societal foundation Allen distrusts is any government, especially its proclivity to wage war. For instance, his *Love and Death* sergeant tells the soldiers, "If they kill more Russians, they win. If we kill more Frenchmen, we win." Boris is then quick to reply, "What do we win?" And in another parody homage to Eisensteinian editing ("intellectual montage"), foot solder Boris suggests during warfare that distant leaders see the battlefield differently, at which point Allen cuts to a herd of terrified sheep.

Connecting "What do we win?" to Napoleon's 1812 French invasion of Russia had an especially timely "war is absurd" connection to a film released in 1975. The Russian army's scorched-earth policy in 1812, as it continually retreated before the advancing French, eventually gave Napoleon the most pyrrhic of "victories." He took Moscow, but essentially lost most of his army to Russia's battle plan (actually, non-battle plan) and the country's bitterly cold winter. Almost simultaneous to Allen's film, the aforementioned fall of Saigon occurred a scant two years after the 1973 Paris Peace Accords had provided the Napoleonic superpower of the day (the United States) the most pyrrhically brief "victory" to maintain two Vietnams, after a war in which the North also chose to avoid conventional battles. Governments being inherently absurd is uniquely depicted by war, since these conflicts chronicle the most easily discernable historical markers through time ... a time never seemingly remembered by future regimes, buried under the eternal malaise of paper pushers. One could liken this bureaucratic amnesia to the absurdity of F. Scott Fitzgerald's short story "The Curious Case of Benjamin Button" (1922): The title character is born old, proceeds to age backwards, and fittingly cites another unnecessary war:

> The past—the wild charge at the head of these men up San Juan Hill [during the Spanish-American War, 1898]; the first years of his marriage when he worked late into the summer dusk down in the busy city for young Hildegarde whom he loved; the days before that when he sat smoking far into the night in the gloomy old Button House on Monroe Street with his grandfather—all these had failed like unsubstantial dreams from his mind as though they had never been. He did not remember....[24]

Even Fitzgerald's description of Benjamin's "grows down" fate metaphorically captures one's disappointment with institutional absurdity.

A further establishment bastion bombarded by Allen is the academic world. Though Boris and Sonia are constantly parrying precepts not unlike the chapter-opening quote which could be whittled down to, "Isn't all mankind ultimately executed for a crime it never committed?" the philosophers' musings either seem to be of no assistance in a world inherently absurd, or they morph into an obtuse diatribe not that far removed from Allen's specific spoofing of the occurrence:

> SONIA: Judgment of any system, or a prior relationship or phenomenon exists in an irrational, or metaphysical, or at least epistemological contradiction to an abstract empirical concept such as being, or to be, or to occur in the thing itself.
> BORIS: Yes, I've said that many times.

Sonia's observation is close enough to comments by some real academics to encourage a slight tweaking of the earlier Boris crack, "There are worse things in life than death. Have you ever spent an evening with a semiotician?" (Allen had used "insurance salesman.")

Moving from school to home, dark comedy loves to satirically savage dysfunctional families—the most basic of institutions, and the core of society itself. Thus, Boris has little in common with his two older brothers, who are oversized Russian folk dancing jingoists anxious for war. In contrast, by his admission, Boris is a "militant coward" so small ("twenty-eight dwarf") it is questionable whether he can own land. He also pulls a muscle when he attempts to join his siblings in dance and prefers to collect butterflies. He is such an embarrassment to his family that the following exchange occurs between Mother and her child-man son:

> MOTHER: He'll go and he'll fight, and I hope they will put him in the front lines.
> BORIS: Thanks a lot, Mom. [In direct address to the camera-viewer, *à la* Bob Hope he observes:] My mother, folks.

Given that life is so absurd, one could just push Allen's dark comedy battering of the establishment to include all of society en masse—"modern times"—as the ultimate institution, and justify it by his frequent excursions into fantasy, *à la* a variation of James Thurber's Walter Mitty on steroids. Allen is the first to admit:

> [A] big theme in my movies [has] got to do with the difference between reality and fantasy. It comes up very frequently in my films. I think what it boils down to, really, is that I hate reality ... it comes from my [Depression era] childhood, where I constantly escaped into the cinema.... You would leave your poor house behind and all your problems....[25]

Certainly, whether one is speaking of Gogol's "The Nose," Thurber's "The Unicorn in the Garden" (1939), or Allen's *oeuvre* in general, they are all attempts to soften the

If movies were Woody Allen's escape from reality, his sequences with Countess Alexandrovna (Olga Georges-Picot) would have helped.

absurdity of reality through laughter. How else, as Boris observes, could "Young Greggor's son ... [be] older than Old Greggor? Nobody could figure out how that happened." Liken it to a dark comedy defense of fighting absurdity with absurdity, just as medical serums often contain strains of the very diseases they are fighting.

Beyond absurdity looms the final dark comedy theme: man as beast, which must start with Napoleon, as best explained through this short exchange with Allen's character:

> BORIS: You're a tyrant, and a dictator, and you start wars!
> NAPOLEON: Why is he reciting my credits?

As a postscript, during the Napoleonic Wars, English newspapers were so frightened of him, and the possibility of an invasion by the French, that Napoleon was given the disrespectful Grim Reaper–like nickname "Boney." This expression, in turn, was sometimes bastardized to bogey and bogeyman. Thus, for a time, the cross-cultural mythological bogeyman, or boogie man (which long predated the dictator), used to keep mischievous children in line, had a British connection to Napoleon.

Boogie man or not, *Love and Death*'s Napoleon had no corner on man as beast. For instance, Keaton's beautiful Sonia was a cross between Madame Bovary and Lady Macbeth. That is, like Gustave Flaubert's bored Bovary, she has countless adulterous affairs. Sonia is also characteristic of Shakespeare's Lady Macbeth, who goaded her husband into killing a king, just as Keaton's character hounds Boris into an attempted murder of an emperor (Napoleon). And as Macbeth was desolate with guilt over what he does, Boris' pangs of conscience keep him from even acting. Moreover, *Love and Death* ends with comic variations of *Macbeth*'s eventually swirling into madness and death. Boris is executed, and while Sonia is not exactly certifiable at the end, the fact she is sharing love letters (not correspondence but the actual vowels and consonants) with her cousin Natasha (Jessica Harper) of someone for whom they both cared, does not place her high on the stability chart. Plus, Allen then seems to second this perspective by juxtaposing the women's two heads in the exact iconic manner of two disturbed women in Bergman's *Persona* (1966).

Love and Death's man as beast is also a government universal, beyond the famous-infamous Napoleon. High-profile members of his administration are even plotting to overthrow him, right down to having found a manipulatable twin-like double whom they can use as a cover for their coup. No one or no thing is to be trusted, not even an alleged angel of the Lord, who has falsely promised Boris that the czar will commute his execution at the last moment. Again, however, the conversation comes back to war. One is reminded of an early passage from Béla Zombory-Moldován's posthumous memoir of World War I's 1915 Eastern Front—*The Burning of the World*, about a young man, from the precarious multinational realm known as Austria-Hungary (1867–1918), in a total daze about being drafted. Despite this jolt, however, over the coming "war as an absurdity ... an anachronism," he says that he's noticed

> that the more narrow-minded a person is, the more easily he finds a way through this [ludicrous] maze. He'll declare confidently.... "We'll soon teach the Serbs their lesson, and that'll be that." Afterwards, a victorious Hungary will win because it has to: it's obvious.... It doesn't matter to them if events prove them wrong, because they immediately find another, equally certain, solution.[26]

In fact, there would be no solution; the Empire (which in some ways was an indirect product of the much earlier Napoleon Wars) would collapse upon its World War I defeat (as part of the Central Powers).

Disguised as personality comedy meets reaffirmation parody, this dark comedy was a box office success and a hit with the critics. *Love and Death*'s most succinct summation came from Penelope Gilliatt, a critic who once shared *New Yorker* reviewing duties with Pauline Kael:

> [It's] imperially funny ... we turn out to be not really so much in Russia as in Russian liter-ature. It is a literature seen through Woody Allen's unique prism ... as if it were being read by a student racked by anxieties about both the afterlife and the common cold.[27]

Variety called it "another mile-a-minute visual-verbal whirl by these two mighty comedy talents [Allen and Diane Keaton].... Writer-director Allen will delight his lat-terday broadened audience base in this handsome ... production."[28] The *New York Times* called *Love and Death* "a side-splitting spectacle, a tormented, hilarious love story, and film comedy that is about as personal a work as any American star-writer-director has made since the days of Keaton, Chaplin and Jerry Lewis."[29]

While most of the reviews minimized and/or missed *Love and Death*'s dark comedy core, one exception was the *Chicago Sun-Times*' Roger Ebert's critique. He led with the aforementioned Allen quote which begins, "All men live under a sentence of death...." Ebert went on to say:

> The quotation serves as illustration of the film's strategy, which is to juxtapose serious mat-ters with a cheerful anarchy.... [It] is his most ambitious experiment with the comic possi-bilities of film.... [His screen persona is] sweet, he wants to do the right thing, he represents the possibility that simplicity still can prevail in the world....[30]

Interestingly, the irritatingly entertaining Kael's take on *Love and Death* ultimately strikes a serious tone anchored to the Vietnam War era. Also, in her potentially provoca-tive style, she both covers a lot of ground and manages to contradict herself:

> I do not particularly like *Love and Death* and I don't particularly like the Bob Hope movies it resembles [in which] Hope played those coward-heroes [who] were always running from danger and always being menaced.... When Woody does it ... he stands for the whole gen-eration that was anti–Vietnam.... [suddenly a panned movie has purpose?][31]

Arguably Allen's funniest film was a disappointment to him because other than a handful of fleeting review references of anything serious going on, critics and the public alike were not tuned into the filmmaker's dark comedy goal. Allen wanted the people to say: "[Yes] this was a very funny movie but there is a kind of, the futility of life and the ... transience of love and the inconstancy of love and the difficulty of love and the pathos and tragedy of death and, and how it haunts all our affairs."[32]

In another interview, Allen described his frustrations as being an "imbalance between the ideas and the crazy comedy.... [P]eople don't connect with the seriousness tone."[33] Yet, he was happy with some of *Love and Death*'s thoughts, especially on the ran-domness and lack of significance given to any death, such as: "When Keaton's husband dies, and she says, 'Life is really terrible—so where do you want to eat?' To me that said more about death and how we deal with it than I could have if I were being genuinely serious."[34]

Something also needs to be said about how a gourmet journal with dark comedy tendencies could have reviewed this film. Throughout the movie, Allen forever links food with death and/or sex (with the latter often linked to black humor and dying any-way). For example, besides the aforementioned comments by Sonia after her first husband dies, when she later asks Boris what death is like, he compares it to the bad chicken at the restaurant they often visited. Napoleon is more concerned with inspiring a famous dish to be named after him (*à la* his arch rival's Beef Wellington), than all the death and chaos he has caused. When Boris receives an invitation to one bedroom escapade, he joyfully responds that he will bring the soy sauce. When Sonia tells him she feels like she is half saint, half whore, Allen hopes he gets "the half that eats." Since Boris is being held in a French jail awaiting execution, his last meal resembles those dessert carts at the priciest of restaurants. At one point Allen actually considered calling the film *Love, Food and Death* or *Love, Death and Food*.[35] Like so many of his comedy heroes, Allen simply finds the subject of food funny. Indeed, some of the most celebrated examples are also straight dark comedy, such as *The Gold Rush*'s (1925) Chaplin cooking a shoe for Thanksgiving, or being subjected to the automatic feeding machine in *Modern Times* (1936)—two of cinema's most iconic moments. And in that all-important-to-Allen *Road to Morocco*, one of the funniest scenes involves Hope's character's pretense of being touched in the head for some free food—an alleged custom in that part of the world.

Yet, on another level, just as a ludicrous crack following a long existential monologue makes for comic surprise, so does a food reference after some angst-ridden art house question about death, or the existence of God. However, what makes the Russian-based *Love and Death* examples especially important is that the Allen-like Gogol did the very same thing. Moreover, while allusions to Dostoyevsky and even Tolstoy are connected to this film, Allen literally *sounds* like Gogol. For instance, the following line from another seminal Gogol short story, "The Diary of a Madman," might just as well be Boris: "I believe that all troubles stem from the misconception that human brains are located in the head. They are not: human brains are blown in by the winds from somewhere around the Caspian Sea."[36] Consequently, is it any surprise that Gogol's application of food comments anticipates Allen? For instance, early in Gogol's "The Nose" his central character smells freshly baked bread, a sensation soon to be in danger when his nose comes up missing. Plus, again foreshadowing Allen, food is also the subject of comic Gogol relationship issues. To illustrate, initially in "The Nose" the lead figure's wife bitingly muses, "It's fine with me if the fool wants bread. That'll leave me another cup of coffee."[37]

Finally, with fitting dark comedy irony, *Love and Death*, with the most ongoingly direct suggestions of this genre, seems to have been, among this text's focus films, the least likely to be recognized as such. The personality comedian-reaffirmation parody distractions, with a healthy dose of fantasy, apparently derailed the connection. Allen assumes the blame: "[T]he film was too light and silly [for] anyone [to] respond to that [dark comedy] aspect of it. It was my fault."[38] Be that as it may, it still demonstrates at this late date that some viewers were still not fully cognizant of the genre.

All passionate artists are fully vested in their work. But in dark comedy, some strains are more self-consciously visible, such as the genre's fascination with suicide, a subject also explored in *Love and Death*. And as previously noted, such varied pioneering architects of the genre as Cuppy and Vonnegut either took their own lives, or attempted suicide. And that says nothing of artists like Bob Fosse, who chose lives which essentially made them their own executioners. Thus, I was struck with a 2011 Roger Ebert thought piece on Allen, what *The New Yorker* would call a "casual" essay. Ebert shared the following comments by a filmmaker who, over time, became a friend:

Allen the serious director on the Napoleon set, with James Tolkan.

The first time I spoke with him, in 1971, he told me there wasn't a day when he didn't give serious thought to suicide. I asked him again every time I saw him, until 2000, if that was still true. It always was.[39]

Most of the dark comedy artists explored herein take their work close to a precipice they know only too well, regardless of any cross-over genres they might use as decoys.

9

One Flew Over the
Cuckoo's Nest (11/20/75)

... one flew east, one flew west,
One flew over the cuckoo's nest.
                                        —Children's folk rhyme

What do you think you are [addressing patients in a mental institution], for
Christ's sake, crazy or something? Well, you're not! You're not! You're no crazier
than the average-age asshole out walking around on the streets and that's it!
                                        —Randle McMurphy (Jack Nicholson)
                                        in *One Flew Over the Cuckoo's Nest*

Cuckoo's Nest is unlike the previous chapter's examination of *Love and Death* (1975), in which the strength of Woody Allen's masking of dark comedy, via anti-genre use of parody and personality comedy, initially minimized serious consideration of the movie's inherent nihilistic black humor. Instead, *Cuckoo's Nest*'s institutional setting lends itself more readily to dark comedy. Nevertheless, if a genre-bending camouflage is in place, one can easily fall back on the traditional Western and the non-traditional social problem film. Plus, the movie boasts a Nicholson performance with enough anti-establishment broad comedy to match the classic cult status of the 1962 Ken Kesey novel from which the film is adapted. Again this text explores a 1970s dark comedy with a celebrated literary source, which also once more draws upon autobiographical "research": Kesey worked as an orderly at a mental health facility in Menlo Park, California. By taking a graveyard shift, the novelist had more freedom to prowl the premises, talking to patients and generally studying the institution's sordid other-side-of-the-moon secrets. Plus, he voluntarily "tested" many of the patients' prescribed medicines—a "fact-finding" mission which was hardly a chore given his established recreational drug use.

Cuckoo's Nest is especially reminiscent, beyond this text's expected norm, of this study's first three focus films: *MASH*, *Catch–22*, and *Little Big Man* (all 1970). For example, like *MASH*'s Hawkeye (Donald Sutherland), McMurphy served in Korea and is also an iconoclastic individual who finds himself "sentenced," after a fashion, to a regimented military-like setting—a state mental health facility. One first needs to establish the story arc. Nicholson's character has opted out of a short prison term for what he believes will be an "R & R"–like short mental ward stay, simply to avoid correctional work details. But McMurphy does not realize he has stumbled into a mission to martyrdom.

The catalyst for McMurphy's undertaking is the ward's dictatorial Nurse Ratched's (Louise Fletcher) delight in being repressive, and ultimately holding more control over his fate than he first realizes. Yet, to viewers, especially anti-establishment baby boomers, when seemingly thwarted, McMurphy's responses are a rousing validation. Thus, when Ratched does not allow the patients to watch the televised World Series, McMurphy is livid and concocts a series of events best described by Oscar-winning director Ron Howard, who credits what follows as being *the* signature scene of his film-viewing life:

> [McMurphy] suddenly ignites all the patients by simply willing the World Series into existence through the power of his imagination. I remember everybody slowly gathering around him and catching on to what he is doing: creating this very eccentric play-by-play [commentary to a blank screen]. He describes Sandy Koufax striking out Mickey Mantle, saying, "Koufax's curveball is breaking like a fucking firecracker" and all sorts of stuff like that. Everybody cheers. The scene was a turning point in the movie, alerting Nurse Ratched to the galvanizing power of this amazing character. He asked his fellow inmates to use their imaginations to escape within themselves, and yet also to really share something. He created the mental environment that made this possible. It's a great moment for me.[1]

Such praise comes from an auteur (Howard) whose career has largely been anchored to populist pictures (the mirror opposite of dark comedy), like *Cocoon* (1985), *Parenthood* (1989), *Apollo 13* (1995), and his multiple Oscar-winning Best Picture *A Beautiful Mind* (2001).

Unfortunately, however, unlike Hawkeye, McMurphy is unstable ... yet maybe he

Another example of McMurphy's (Jack Nicholson, right) ability to revitalize patients, with Charley Cheswick (Sydney Lassick).

is Hawkeye in ten or fifteen years, trying to cope with the war. Indeed, in the later TV series *M*A*S*H* (1972–1983), Hawkeye does briefly crack up at the end. In any case, one could also call McMurphy the most stubbornly appealing psychopath since Paul Newman's sometimes similar title character in *Cool Hand Luke* (1967). In fact, the latter figure's self-destructive martyrdom also foreshadows that of McMurphy's, as does Luke's ability to (drawing from Howard's quote) inspire his fellow chain gang members "to use their imaginations to escape within themselves, and yet to really share something." And Luke had his own Nurse Ratched nemesis in the form of Strother Martin's warden, with his memorably macabre cinema history understatement, "What we have here is a failure to communicate." If time permitted, one could elaborate further on the troubling conditions of *Luke* and the equally disturbing circumstances in *Cuckoo's Nest*'s penitentiary-like mental institution. Thus, a genre-crossing problem film status can be applied to both dark comedies.

Similar to *Catch–22*'s Yossarian (Alan Arkin), possibly the horrors of war have given McMurphy his truthfully twisted world perspective. Though not fleshed out in the film, Kesey's novel provides ample explanation for why McMurphy has yet to settle into civilian life, a prospect Hawkeye has yet to attempt. This potential for becoming unhinged is there in McMurphy's advice to the equally doomed Billy (Brad Dourif):

> [You have] to be cagey … you should know that as well as anyone. What could I do? I can't fix your stuttering. I can't wipe the razor-blade scars off your wrists or the cigarette burns off the back of your hands…. And as far as the nurse riding you … rubbing your nose in your weakness till what little dignity you got left in gone … I can't do anything about that either…. [In the war] I saw a buddy of mine tied to a tree fifty yards from me, screaming…. [The enemy] wanted me to try to go out and help. They'd have cut me in half [with machine gun fire].[2]

But McMurphy ends up not being "cagey" when he responds non-rationally to another, ultimately fatal baiting of Billy. Along similar lines, unique circumstances end up pushing the last vestiges of sanity from Yossarian's mind as *Catch–22*'s "happy ending" is all in his mind, as he believe he will be able to row to Scandinavia from Sicily in a rubber dinghy.

While *Little Big Man*'s title character (Dustin Hoffman) fluctuates between playing Native American and Caucasian, *Cuckoo's Nest* provides a significant character to embody both ethnic groups, McMurphy and Chief Bromden (Will Sampson), who ultimately work in tandem. As suggested earlier, in American pop culture, such allegiances are not without important symbolic meaning. Giving a loner iconoclastic anti-hero (by choice) a minority sidekick deemed an outsider by a prejudicial society underlines the anti-hero's quest for change. Examples would include Huckleberry Finn and the slave Jim, *Moby-Dick*'s Ishmael and Polynesian native Queequeg (a Melville-Kesey connection will also be dissected), and the Lone Ranger and Tonto.

The novels *Little Big Man* and *Cuckoo's Nest* are also linked by first person narration, which is sometimes suspect, unlike in *Huckleberry Finn* or *Catcher in the Rye*. That is, *Little Big Man* is narrated by a 121-year-old man with tall tale tendencies, while Chief Bromden is often a highly medicated hallucinating chronicler of a mental institution. Granted, Milos Forman's adaptation shifts the emphasis to Nicholson's McMurphy and downplays the novel's sometimes surrealistic haze, but there is still a folklore feel to parts of the picture. Illustrations range from the mythic Paul Bunyan–like film-closing exit by Chief Bromden, to Kesey scholar John C. Pratt's describing Nurse Ratched as "unbelievable in the same fashion as many characters in Joseph Heller's *Catch-22*...."[3] Still, the commonality of *Cuckoo's Nest*, *MASH*, *Catch-22*, *Little Big Man* and *all* creative endeavors herein examined is that each belongs, to borrow a phrase from critic James Parker, to "a select band of survivor [artists] whose work is [sometimes] adequate to the destructive reality we inhabit."[4]

Returning to the text's standard formula of recognizing anti-genre decoys from *Cuckoo's Nest*'s inherent dark comedy nature, one must start with the aforementioned social problem film as a smokescreen.[5] Keep in mind the problem film's unconventional nature. It is not purely entertainment-driven. For years Hollywood even denigrated it with a comment credited to enough people to fill Yankee Stadium: "If you want to send a message, use Western Union."

So what gives *Cuckoo's Nest* problem film status, despite the anti-genre masking of Nicholson's bravado performance? The formula components are all in place. First, the problem—in this case, poor mental health care—must impact a large number of people. Second, is this issue recognized as such by a preponderance of the population? Third, is there a power base strong enough to take on the problem? Fourth, and a possible *coup de grace* to one's quandary qualifying as a problem film, does that same large group of citizens feel something can actually be done about said situation? One might call this "the Vonnegut question." As was noted previously in the text, some criticized the novelist's writing of the anti-war *Slaughterhouse-Five* (1969) as having all the validity of writing an anti-glacier book. The implication was that mankind has always had war, and always will. Whether anti-war literature makes any more sense than anti-glacier material remains to be seen. Yet, at a time when a bumbling (or is that a blind?) mankind is still making those once seemingly everlasting glaciers disappear, maybe it is time to get serious about an anti-war world, and also anything else which might pose a threat to planet Earth.

Naturally, one can sometimes apply to problem films the same grizzled axiom synonymous with satire and dark comedy: "It doesn't play well on Saturday night." That is, mainstream moviegoers usually want mind candy, an escape from reality. Why pay to see something which might be depressing, like a problem picture? However, there are always exceptions. For example, the Michael Douglas–produced *The China Syndrome* (1979, about an attempted cover-up of an accident at a nuclear power plant) scored a critical and commercial home run when it opened shortly before the March 28, 1979, Three Mile Island accident in which a nuclear reactor had a partial meltdown in Pennsylvania. Paradoxically, just as Nicholson's Oscar-winning performance, which could ricochet from poignancy and pep talks to broad outrageous comedy, not only helps this anti-genre problem film obscure *Cuckoo's Nest*'s black humor base, McMurphy's *tour de force* performance arguably makes the black humor more palatable for those who see through the cover-up.

Anti-genre Western elements can also be applied as a veil to *Cuckoo's Nest*'s fundamental black humor. If one comes to the film without having read the novel, this Western slant might seem tangential. But the carryover from Bromden narrating the book, such as educating McMurphy in the racist ways of the West both in print *and* on the screen, keeps the chief at the story's center. What's more, even if he was only the symbolic sidekick, the tale would warrant scrutiny along anti-genre Western lines. Regardless, in a pioneering dissection of the sagebrush saga, such as John G. Cawelti's *The Six-Gun Mystique* (1971), there are multiple categories of Westerns to which an anti-genre twist might be applied. The most fertile would be the sub-category often termed the "cavalry and the

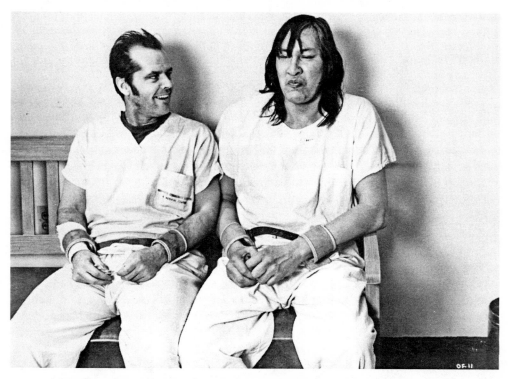

McMurphy (Jack Nicholson) and the surprising Chief Bromden (Will Sampson).

Indians."[6] As was demonstrated in the *Little Big Man* chapter, this type of Western is the most ongoingly timely, since this picture was instrumental in encouraging viewers to switch allegiances—rooting for the Native Americans over the bluecoats.

Consequently, Chief Bromden, like *Little Big Man*'s title character, survives as the solo anti-genre Western figure—the only institutional escapees in body and soul. Furthermore, he guarantees that the mythic spirit of insurrectionist McMurphy lives on in the ward after Nurse Ratched has had his friend lobotomized. (Nicholson's character had lost his ability to be "cagey" and attempted to kill Ratched after her mind games with Billy Bibbit led to his suicide.) Thus, Browden protects McMurphy's legend through euthanasia, which also represents a metaphorical victory for a friend who had planned the escape. In addition, McMurphy's near strangulation of Fletcher's Ratched had forever destroyed her mystic power and allowed Chief, in Huckleberry Finn's words, "to light out for the territory."[7]

Along more conventional Western sidekick lines, Chief Bromden's years of playing deaf and mute had reduced him to the institution's ignored "invisible" minority figure. This allowed him to be privy to conversations and situations to which Ratched and the rest of the staff thought he was oblivious. (One is reminded of Ralph Ellison's 1953 novel *The Invisible Man*, about being black in Jim Crow America.) Regardless, the chief's unusual status, which he only revealed to McMurphy, proved helpful to Nicholson's character.

Like the anti-genre mentoring of Dustin Hoffman's figure by Chief Dan George in *Little Big Man*, Will Sampson's Chief Bromden is also allowed to be a crackerbarrel-like sage, a role normally given to a veteran white western figure. For example, Bromden shared with Nicholson's McMurphy:

My pop was real big. He did like he pleased [like you]. That's why everyone [the powers that be] worked on [or hassled] him. The last time I seen my father, he was blind in the cedars [trees] from drinking. And every time he put the bottle to his mouth, he don't suck out of it, it sucks out of him until he shrunk so wrinkled and yellow even the dogs didn't know him.

Bromden also shares Chief Dan George's gift for seeing into the future. For instance, this story of his father's death-like fate anticipates McMurphy's lobotomy. As an ironic addendum, Chief Bromden's gargantuan size, like that of his father (a combination of NBA-NFL physical dimensions), gives the "invisibility" element a darkly comic spin. To reference the last chapter, the huge, occasionally hallucinating chief would not be out of place in the sometimes surreal world of Gogol's "The Nose."

After considering these anti-genre diversions, how is *Cuckoo's Nest* more directly and appropriately labeled a dark comedy? Since death is the genre's first primary theme, war has often been a logical backdrop for that component in previous chapters. And why not, as *New York Times* critic A.O. Scott has noted: "[War] presents a tangle of moral ambiguity and a fog of confusion."[8] Technically, *Cuckoo's Nest* is not a war film but it feels like a prisoner of war picture, be it Nurse Ratched as the proverbially sadistic camp commander, to an escape finale, after a bungled earlier attempt. One could also double up on Ratched as a modern-day Josef Mengele, the Nazi physician at Auschwitz concentration camp during World War II, who performed deadly human experiments on prisoners. In comparison, when Ratched's patients become troublesomely disruptive, she orchestrates her own "scientific" experiments on them with shock treatments and lobotomies.

Ironically, however, her first victim for viewers, Billy Bibbit, is essentially bullied into

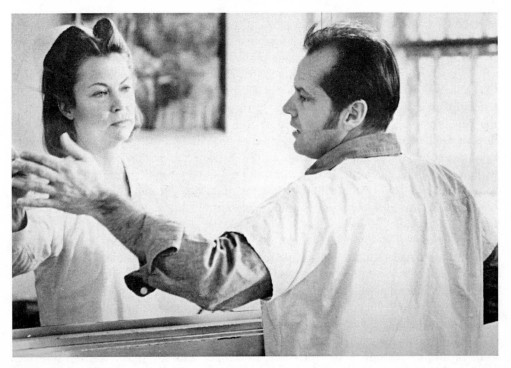

Like an Edward Hopper painting of people caught under glass, glass often separates *Cuckoo's Nest*'s two adversaries, McMurphy (Jack Nicholson) and Nurse Ratched (Louise Fletcher).

dark comedy's seminal "exit" procedure: suicide. Since his death is the catalyst for McMurphy's attempt of revenge and subsequent lobotomy, Bibbit is the best place to start evaluating this dark comedy theme. A popular ploy in a narrative study such as this is to play the Christianity card, with Billy's death eventually resulting in the martyrdom of McMurphy for the good of the other ward patients. Minimize the temptation. It is the most hoary and overworked of analytical answers. Granted, viewing elevator eyebrow Nicholson on the cross is darkly comic. Woody Allen applies that very principle to *Love and Death* (1975), when the comedian's young glasses-attired character imagines himself on a cross as a sight gag—though one must acknowledge the anti–Semitic nature of czarist Russia.

Nevertheless, if one wants to utilize classic fiction for a better understanding of *Cuckoo's Nest*, the novella to examine is Herman Melville's posthumously published *Billy Budd* (1924), as well as several of the author's other works. For instance, both Melville's title character Billy Budd and Kesey's Billy Bibbit are young, naïve, androgynous boys-men whose stuttering only worsens when accused of mutiny. The younger novelist underlines the coupling by kiddingly gifting his Billy with a stuttering-like last name. Moreover, both young figures are fated to die through the actions of heinous authority figures largely because each is child-like in his compliance to those around him. For all their potential, their weaknesses make them figures in essentially golden handcuffs. Moreover, despite the long delay in *Billy Budd*'s publication, it still took additional 20th century decades for the intelligentsia to recognize its groundbreaking elements.

For example, early in the novella is the following passage: "I am not certain whether to know the world and to know human nature be not two distinct branches of knowledge, which while they may co-exist in the same heart, yet either may exist with little or nothing of the other."[9] Such an insight explains the downfall of many besides the two Billys. These are deaths of an absurd world. Albert Camus, a seminal writer in the rise of the philosophy known as absurdism, counted Melville and Franz Kafka as major influences.[10]

As with *Cuckoo's Nest*, *Billy Budd* also deals with two deaths. In the latter case, the title character is a sailor unfairly accused of mutiny by the ship's master-at-arms John Claggert, with both men brought to their captain's quarters to discuss the charge. Billy's severe emotional state so intensifies his stuttering inability to speak that he inadvertently strikes Claggert, accidentally killing him. Though the captain and other officers know Budd is neither an insurrectionist nor guilty of a premeditated murder, wartime maritime law states that even in accidently killing a lying officer the boy must die—a victim of how man's arbitrary rules fuel the absurdities of life. Melville accents this by having Billy's last ship be named the *Rights-of-Man*.

These Billys are also reminiscent of Kurt Vonnegut's *Billy* Pilgrim and the full title of the novelist's signature work *Slaughterhouse-Five, or The Children's Crusade: A Duty-Dance with Death* (1969). War and war-like settings are most likely to have old men send young men to die and/or cause the frightened to suddenly act with the irrationality of a child. Such is Nicholson's McMurphy's instantaneous attempt, after Bibbit's suicide, to kill nurse Ratched ... which essentially leads to his own death. Most of the tales in this text play upon some sort of misguided "children's crusade," whether it is a lead character or a supporting player. Both can be exemplified by Bud Cort figures. In *Harold and Maude* (1971) his co-starring boy-man treats suicide merely as a game until he comes face to face with Maude's real suicide. And in *MASH* his peripheral juvenile orderly is almost reduced to suicide by mean-spirited surgeon Frank Burns (Robert Duvall), who falsely blames him for the death of a patient. Then a toned-down McMurphy, Elliott Gould as a comically vengeful McIntyre, lays Duvall out with a haymaker. Of course, *Harold and Maude* and *MASH* are both "dark comedy lite" movies, while *Cuckoo's Nest* ends upon a darker tone, despite Chief Bromden escaping and the civil disobedient spirit of McMurphy living on in the ward.

And if Billy Bibbit is straight from Melville's *Billy Budd*, McMurphy's figure owes a great deal to Melville's title character in *The Confidence-Man* (1857). This is still arguably the most ambitious novel ever dedicated to the huckster character, which perfectly describes McMurphy. Melville's Confidence-Man is capable of transforming himself into multiple figures, a talent McMurphy does metaphorically, whether as a dissident antagonizing Nurse Ratched, or as an inmate advocate–cheerleader–modern-day pirate "borrowing" a commercial fishing ship for an unsanctioned outing with the most motley of "crews." Just as this text's focus films use a collage of genres to misdirect viewers from a dark comedy core, Confidence-Man McMurphy keeps things distractingly off-kilter for survival and/or sanity's sake. Besides this moniker, Nicholson's figure could also be labeled con artist, grifter, huckster, diddler … whatever the name, a type present since there have been people.[11] Sometimes this devilish character literally has been associated with the devil. Yet, as in the world of Milton's *Paradise Lost*, if this be a Satan, he is more understandably benevolent than God.

However, as previously noted, Biblical conjecture is better kept from *Cuckoo's Nest* analysis. A more productive insight to McMurphy would come from Melville scholar Hennig Cohen's reading of *The Confidence-Man*: "[A figure scrambling] how to live in a world in which nothing is what it appears to be, in which the only thing knowable is that nothing can be known, and the only thing believable is that nothing can be believed."[12]

The Confidence-Man at his darkest is sometimes associated with traits of the author himself, as another expert on the novel has suggested: "[O]ne must suppose that Melville was well enough aware of similarities to himself in the picture [of this character]."[13] This hypothesis for Melville (which actually parallels the thinking of Kesey) can be strongly anchored by a passage from a letter the older novelist wrote years before penning *The Confidence-Man*:

> It is—or seems to be—a wise sort of thing, to realize that all that happens to a man in this life is only by way of a joke, especially his misfortunes, if he have them. And it is also worth bearing in mind, that the joke is passed around pretty liberally and impartially, so that not very many are entitled to fancy that they in particular are getting the worst of it.[14]

The Melville–*Cuckoo's Nest* connection hardly stops there. *Moby-Dick* offers another link. McMurphy and Chief Bromden are in a state of siege with Nurse Ratched, just as Ishmael and Queequeg are overwhelmed by Captain Ahab. If one were forced to engage in religious assessment, one might apply the *Moby-Dick* description of Ahab to Ratched— "ungodly, [yet] godlike"—though it is doubtless more likely she would be delineated as the antichrist.[15] Regardless, as in many battles of good versus evil, the playing field is often reduced to a small contained space, a microcosm of the world. McMurphy and Chief Bromden are caught in the amber of a mental ward, while Ishmael and Queequeg are sentenced to Ahab's ship, the *Pequod*. And with the appropriate twist of dark comedy, one member of each anti-hero team survives because of the other. McMurphy has both destroyed Ratched's spell and inspired Chief Bromden to escape. Queequeg's premonition of death, and his elaborate coffin surfacing after Ahab's suicide attack on the whale, sparks the *Pequod*'s sinking, resulting in Ishmael having the most ironically macabre of "lifeboats."

Melville scholar Clifton Fadiman has called suicide "the true end of *Moby-Dick*."[16] That is, Fadiman suggests that Ahab is a painfully divided person, with the whale and himself being one and the same:

> [C]ertain men are artists in suicide, who carve out for themselves over many years, careers which have as their goal self-destruction. Ahab is such a man, and all his adventures, rages, conversations, soliloquies are but the joists and floorings of an immense structure of self-ruin.[17]

Thus, when Ahab and the whale turn upon each other (one and the same), the captain is really attempting to end his own troubled existence. Fittingly, suicide is also the true end of *Cuckoo's Nest*. Billy literally takes his own life, while McMurphy's actions, even after he learns his continued disruptive behavior will result in a permanent "home" on the psych floor, are clearly the actions of a man whose "goal is self-destruction." And his attack on Ratched, in her starched white uniform, is just another variation of Ahab's assault on the great white whale. While initially there is no confusing Ratched's outward behavior with McMurphy, they are still both self-destructively obsessive over their attempts to control the tenor of the mental ward. This is also a configuration of the theme most central to a Milos Forman film:

> [The direction] always emphasizes that freedom and responsibility are inseparable and that those who do not understand their world, for whatever reason, must pay a price.... [An individual] has the opportunity to accomplish more than he actually does if he can learn to work within his limitations rather than continually oppose them.[18]

A concluding *Cuckoo's Nest*–Melville bond provides the quintessential transition to dark comedy's use of absurdity, the genre's second central theme. Melville's consummate short story is "Bartleby the Scrivener" (1853), now deemed a forerunner of absurdist literature. The tale, narrated by an aged New York lawyer, chronicles the story of the most puzzling individual he has ever met, a scrivener (notary or clerk) in his employ named Bartleby. In the beginning the sorrowful-looking staffer is the lawyer's best worker. But before long, when assigned a task, Bartleby responds with what will become his constant mantra, "I would prefer not to." In no time this scrivener is doing no work at all. And when the narrator attempts to draw Bartleby out on what is happening, the exchange never goes beyond, "I would prefer not to." Yet paradoxically, in time the lawyer finds that Bartleby has literally moved into the office.

Though the situation naturally produces edginess at the workplace, the narrator is surprisingly patient; he even avoids a confrontation by actually leaving the business. Moreover, when the new owners cannot budge Bartleby, the lawyer returns at their request for another round of reasoning with this quirky character. Shockingly, the narrator unexpectedly finds himself inviting Bartleby to come live with him. But as always this extraordinary eccentric responds, "I would prefer not to." Eventually the new owners have this odd clerk forcibly removed and he is incarcerated. After visiting Bartleby, the narrator is more concerned and makes special arrangements that his former clerk be properly fed. On the old lawyer's next visit, less than a week later, he discovers Bartleby has died of starvation. Obviously, when food was offered, he had said once again, "I would prefer not to."

So how does one connect this Melville story to *Cuckoo's Nest*? First, most of the patients in the mental institution had voluntarily admitted themselves, essentially saying, "I would prefer not to" participate in life. They had embraced a variation of Bartleby's slow suicide. Second, though Chief Bromden finally chose to live, this psych ward veteran had even embraced Bartleby's "I would prefer not to" more literally—choosing not to talk for twelve years. Thus, before McMurphy's arrival, the chief was nearing Bartleby's fate. Moreover, in the novel, Nurse Ratched even recruited similar walking dead orderlies—people who had literally shut down because of life's horrors:

> [One of her staff was a] twisted sinewy dwarf the color of cold asphalt. His mother was raped [and] the boy [had] watched from a closet, five years old and squinting his eye to peep out the crack between the door and the jamb, and he never never grew an inch after.[19]

One is also reminded of a similar situation in Güther Grass' award-winning and darkly comic novel *The Tin Drum* (1959, also adapted to the screen in the 1970s). The story finds three-year-old Oscar Matzerath receiving the title toy drum and refusing to grow after he realizes the complicity of German adults in the atrocities of World War II.

Instead of applying Bartleby's absurdist axiom to more obviously damaged goods like the chief and the other ward patients, one could direct it at *Cuckoo's Nest* power players Ratched and McMurphy. Ironically, while they represent more moxie, the two seem less initially aware that their embracing of a variation of Bartleby's dictum, "I would prefer not to [change]" is a more direct path to self-destruction—versus the slow death waiting on the sideline situation of the institution's inmates. Are the latter souls that much different from Samuel Beckett's *Waiting for Godot* duo of Estragon and Vladimir (see earlier chapters), waiting for a God who will never come? Regardless, while McMurphy scores a moral victory, he is still dead, and Ratched is reduced to a shattered psycho not unlike Nicholson's detective at the end of *Chinatown* (1974).

Melville's catchphrase has a magnitude which resonates well beyond its application to *Cuckoo's Nest*. Just as this author's once long-neglected work now personifies a seminal point in the history of absurdist theory, one could legitimately credit "I would prefer not to" as a precursor to Kurt Vonnegut's now universal dark comedy mantra "And so it goes" as a deflecting device from a harsh modern world. Both phrases are couched in a world-weary cynicism that flippantly envelops the inherent irrevocable state of life's absurdity.

In fact, the seemingly Melville-channeling Kesey-Forman overview seems to out Vonnegut's fatalistically dark comedy position: "And so it goes" implies a tacit acceptance of mankind's absurdist conditions, not unlike Jean Renoir's perspective that in life one's plight, one's lack of power is not unlike a cork floating randomly downstream. In contrast, Bartleby's "I would prefer not to" seems more like prepping for death and/or a more lobotomy-like state, and forgoing a long shot hope for whatever might float by. For consistency's sake, however, Bartleby's short anthem does circle back to Forman's basic theme: Those who do not accept responsibility must pay the consequences.

"I'd prefer not to" also nicely applies to Czech-born Forman's breakout dark comedy film from his censorship-minded homeland, *The Fireman's Ball* (1967). For example, no one in the picture takes responsibility for the simplest tasks in orchestrating a small town celebration to honor the local fire department, be it putting together a gift table, to planning a modest beauty contest. What is worse, the citizens are less than trustworthy in what, ironically, initially suggests a Czech version of a Capraesque town. People keep stealing presents from the aforementioned awards stand, and brazenly lie that they didn't. The thefts even involve the central endowment, a present which paradoxically could be said indirectly to foreshadow *Cuckoo's Nest*'s Chief Bromden: an elaborate fireman's ax—which instead resembles an Indian tomahawk—which has been sealed away, *à la* Bromden, for years.

The phrase "I'd prefer not to" clearly taps into the intrinsic lack of compassion for the individual which is ingrained in the establishment institution of one's choice. In fact, these organizations are better described as anti-individual. One need only watch the news and/or read a newspaper to be bombarded with a litany of ways global institutions have failed and/or endangered the individual. In fact, as I write this chapter, today's *New York Times* (October 27, 2014) has a front-page story entitled "In Cold War, U.S. Spy Agencies Used 1,000 Nazis."[20] The tale only becomes more depressingly typical ... or darkly comic ... as the essay chronicles a C.I.A.-F.B.I alliance-collaboration-cover-up which would play well in *Dr. Strangelove or: How I Learned to Stop Worrying and Love the Bomb* (1964). That film's title character (Peter Sellers) was inspired by former Nazi aerospace engineer Wernher von Braun, an integral part of the American NASA program which put a man on the moon in 1969. Instead of being tried at the post–World War II Nuremberg military tribunals for his part in the V-2 rocket attacks on London, he ends up in America and receives the prestigious National Medal of Science in 1975.

Forman was no stranger to controversy surrounding institutions and absurdity. *The Fireman's Ball* was acclaimed as a notable example of the Czechoslovak New Wave, then "banned forever" after the 1968 Soviet invasion of the country. However, even prior to this suppression, the Czech Communist party pushed for censorship, claiming the film could be interpreted as a sardonic allegory assailing the party. Forman went into exile. Seen today, the picture remains an offbeat dark comedy lite picture about the catastrophically comic events which often follow any institution's attempt, big or small, to either make sense of its own organization or the world around it. Forman repeatedly stated there was no specific allegorical target; he was equally surprised that many Czech firehouses simply saw the film as a blow against their ethics.[21]

Given Forman's reason for exiting his country after it essentially became a police state, is it any wonder he would be attracted to the anti-establishment, anti-institution perspective of *Cuckoo's Nest*? Ironically, some reviews, like Roger Ebert's ultimately positive *Chicago Sun-Times* critique,[22] still felt Forman overemphasized this big picture society hamstringing of the individual versus a simple tale of lost souls, especially in the time of Watergate. But how does one separate these two perspectives? In due course, however, Ebert also embraced the former standpoint. He upgrading his *Cuckoo's Nest* critique from "a film so good in so many of its parts," to simply a great movie.[23]

The added paradox, of course, to this scenario is that Forman's *Fireman's Ball* had actually taken Ebert's little people dark comedy stance, and it had still gotten the director blackballed out of Czechoslovakia. Thus, why not swing for the fences with a genre (dark comedy) in which one's chances of being misunderstood and/or attacked are appreciably higher? *Los Angeles Times* critic Charles Champlin understood this stance immediately, and essentially reviewed *Cuckoo's Nest* the novel and the film with the same gusto received by a companion work of 1960s protest, *MASH*:

> [Kesey's novel] spoke to the angers and anxieties of a generation that was shortly to start ripping the campuses apart in frustration ... *Cuckoo's Nest* used an unquiet ward of a mental hospital as a symbolic battleground for the life-celebrating loner versus the suffocating system [and] has now become one of the year's strongest, best-made and most engrossing movies.[24]

Film historian and *Hollywood Reporter* critic Arthur Knight also strongly praised the anti-establishment base of *Cuckoo's Nest*, and closely intertwined the novel and the adaptation in his critique:

Nicholson illuminates the dark recesses of…. Kesey's trenchant metaphor … for the state hospital [in which] one can readily substitute the state, with its laws maddeningly devised to protect the individual. Let the individual test or protest these laws, however, and they can be turned into an instrument to crush him.[25]

History bore out this perspective. Not only did *Cuckoo's Nest* turn into 1976's top-grossing film, it became only the second movie in history, after *It Happened One Night* (1934), to win all five major Academy Awards: Best Picture, Director, Actor, Actress, and Screenwriter.[26] (In 1992, *The Silence of the Lambs* joined this singular group.)

Ebert's faulty complaint with *Cuckoo's Nest*'s dark comedy perspective centering too much on the medical institution as villain also might have been laid on *MASH*. One even has a budding Nurse Ratched in Hot Lips. This flawed take would have been even more of a travesty if it was applied to the Altman film, because now the catalyst for chaos would be the twin evil rigidities of both the military and military medical protocol. As suggested earlier, stateside surgical procedures upset the eternal emergency necessities of "meatball" operations so near the battlefield.

Institutional absurdity is merely a lockstep away from black humor's final primary theme—man as beast. As the Great Man theory of history now resides in the dustbin, prey to people being products of their social environment, modern culture is more encouraging to a monster theory of history, with unsound states themselves being incubators for the world's Ratcheds. These man-made monsters seem to attract and/or train satellite figures of depravity. This would include Chaplin's pioneering dark comedy demonic title character in *The Great Dictator* (1940) inspiring Herring's (Billy Gilbert) discovering many new ways to liquidate people to Nurse Ratched's army of staff thugs.

If things get really sinister in these dark comedies, even the nominal hero–anti-hero can be driven to barbaric acts. For instance, when Ratched's perversely twisted "Momism" leads to Billy's suicide, Nicholson's McMurphy (normally a person of amusing smirks, quirks and the most diverting eyebrows since Groucho Marx) compulsively attempts to strangle Ratched. To paraphrase Alfred Hitchcock, a man who judged most of his films as some form of dark comedy, "Anyone is capable of killing another individual."

Maybe the best Rosetta Stone for unscrambling all things *Cuckoo's Nest* comes in the form of a book with the most outlandish of titles, *The Electric Kool-Aid Acid Test* (1968). This decoder biography of Ken Kesey, as unorthodox as the novel, fluctuates between author Tom Wolfe being bluntly informative and metaphorically insightful. With regard to the former position, he states:

> The whole [psychiatric] system—if they set out to invent the perfect Anti-cure for what ailed the men on this ward, they couldn't have done it better. Keep them cowed and docile. Play on the weakness that drove them nuts in the first place. Stupefy the bastards with tranquilizers and if they still get out of line, haul them up to the "shock shop" and punish them. Beautiful—[27]

And to reiterate, Kesey worked in such a facility, and witnessed this sort of medical care. The Wolfe metaphorical message is wrapped in a road trip tale fanned by freedom and a mobile pharmaceutical store:

> [I]n July of 1964 not even the hip world in New York was quite ready for the phenomenon of a bunch of people roaring across the continental U.S.A. in a bus covered with swirling Day-Glo mandalas [artistic patterns] aiming movie cameras and microphones at every freaking thing in this whole freaking country….[28]

Kesey represented the conduit between Jack Kerouac's beat generation uncovering America, especially via his signature nonconformist novel *On the Road* (1957), and a hippie generation quickly seeing the country through blood-covered radical glasses. And the latter movement was jump-started with that acid-fueled "bus covered with swirling Day-Glo mandalas." If the Kerouac beats were about rediscovering America, Kesey and company were about shaking up or "freaking" out traditional America.

Along related perplexing lines, Ebert's aforementioned review was paradoxically most bothered when "McMurphy escapes, commandeers a school bus, and takes all the inmates on a fishing trip in a stolen boat…. [B]y now, we've met the characters, we know them in the context of hospital politics, when they're set down on the boat deck, they just don't belong there. The ward is the arena."[29]

But this is media modification 101. As *New Yorker* critic Emily Nussbaum said of another dark comedy, "the creators honor the law's adaptation [when one] 'opens it up' and 'raises the stakes.'"[30] Ebert notwithstanding, when those patients are "set down on the boat deck," it miraculously gives them a pulse again. This positive outing, however brief, shows them that someday they just might be able to re-enter the real world on a permanent basis. Sometimes breaking out of the doldrums, like an unbelievable circus catch in a tight football game, or *Cuckoo's Nest's* sport of hooky in a water world circus, can make all the difference. It was the perfect thing for Oscar-winning Forman to have done. Moreover, the director was merely giving sight and sound to a sequence from Kesey's novel. Forman's boating sequence also fleshes out another key aspect of their ocean getaway: male bonding in tough times. The novel describes their survivors' group laugh:

> It started slow and pumped itself full, swelling the men bigger and bigger. I [Chief] watched … laughing with them…. [I see] the boat rocking there in the middle of those diving birds, see McMurphy surrounded by his dozen people [patients], and watch them, us, swinging a laughter that rang out on the water in ever-widening circles….[31]

Though this laughing scene of empowerment is quoted from Kesey's novel, it had precedence in earlier films, like the close of *The Treasure of the Sierra Madre* (1948), and early in *The Wild Bunch* (1969), when other desperate men also use it as a brief safety valve reprieve from an uncaring world with a less-than-ideal ending. Indeed, Robert Redford best articulates the momentousness of *Cuckoo's Nest's* laughter sequence when he states that the comparable *Sierra Madre* scene was the signature episode in his movie viewing life: "[It] had a great effect on me, laughing in the face of adversity … I remember sitting in the movie theater [as a ten-year-old] thinking, 'Oh, I see. This is what a film can really be….' It awakened me to the potential of film."[32]

The fact that *Cuckoo's Nest's* pivotal laughter sequence should occur on a ship is so appropriate, given that Nicholson's character is a former sailor, and the novelist seems to have a Melville-driven, water-on-the brain fixation (see the aforementioned links to *Moby-Dick* and *Billy Budd*). Plus, one could certainly argue that the symbolic taste of freedom and the in-your-face act expressing that fact by the McMurphy-orchestrated bus trip to the sea was a possible catalyst from Kesey's later not-to-be-missed, Day-Glo–covered bus trip of America expounding the same principles.

Regardless, both *Cuckoo's Nest* the novel and the film resonated with the critics and the public. *The New York Times*' Vincent Canby added some dark comedy comments of his own:

There is always ... a certain sentimentality attached to this conflict [of the establishment versus the individual] ... Americans feel terrifically ... envious of nonconformists [like McMurphy] while knocking themselves out to look, sound, talk and think like everyone else. The only good nonconformist is the fictional nonconformist, or one who is safely dead. We [deify *Catch–22*'s] Yossarian while electing presidents whose public images have been created in advertising agencies.... [T]he film betrays nothing except the director's concern for people who struggle to bring some order out of chaos. It's a struggle [Forman] finds supremely funny and sometimes noble, even when the odds are most bleak.... [Another positive] is the extraordinary way Forman has been able to create important identifiable characters of psychotics, people who are most often represented in films as misfit exotics, creatures as remote from our experience as members of a Stone Age tribe in the Amazon.[33]

Variety called the film "brilliant cinema theatre," and posed a question often answered in other reviews.[34] That is, given McMurphy's erratic behavior and the fact he could easily have escaped at the close, was the man seemingly feigning being a sociopath actually one? Like most explanations, might it not fall somewhere in between? The *Daily Show*'s Jon Stewart, who sees himself as much a political provocateur as a satirist, might provide an alternative answer: "When you feel like you want to express yourself, you need an impetus, a catalyst. And part of the catalyst is to get yourself in trouble."[35] That sounds a lot like Nicholson's McMurphy.

Not a little shockingly, even at this late date (1975) a genre-crosser like *Cuckoo's Nest* can still disguise and/or embrace subject matter not deemed dark comedy. For example, the normally edgy leftist *Newsday* stated: "[It] ultimately fails as black humor because it is too real for anyone who wants to think about it not to realize what is causing the laughter. Sick persons are not funny. And McMurphy may be the sickest of them all."[36]

With an overemotional *Newsweek* review title of "Laughter at Their Expense," one might assume it was a period critique of Chaplin's *The Great Dictator* (1940), in a time in which few could mix comedy and Nazis. Thus, for the *Newsweek* critic, *Cuckoo's Nest* is a problem film which avoids the anti-genre element (Nicholson's broad comedy notwithstanding).

As noted earlier in the text, the viewer must "trust the tale not the teller." The meaning is what the observer takes from it. This text merely belabors the scenario to underline that dark comedy remains a controversial genre which is still unacknowledged by many.

10

Annie Hall (4/21/77)

> I feel that life is divided into the horrible and miserable. That's the two categories. The horrible and miserable. The horrible are like, I don't know how they get through life. It's amazing to me. And the miserable is everyone else. So you should be thankful that you're miserable, because that's very lucky, to be miserable.
>
> —Alvy Singer (Woody Allen) in *Annie Hall*

To many viewers *Annie Hall* might represent this text's most surprising application, thus far, of a dark comedy designation given a film not seemingly close to this genre. After all, Woody Allen's most honored picture was a veritable blueprint for two of the seminal romantic comedies of the last quarter of the 20th century, Rob Reiner's *When Harry Met Sally...* (1989) and Stephen Frears' *High Fidelity* (2000). (The male lead in the Reiner picture was originally offered to Steve Martin, whose talents and persona often had him being called "The West Coast Woody Allen." Martin reluctantly turned down the role, partly to avoid reinforcing that label.) Just as Reiner's picture celebrated New York City *à la* Allen's film, *High Fidelity* star and co-writer John Cusack (from Nick Homby's British novel) also utilized his hometown of Chicago in an idealized romantic manner. Plus, as with Allen's *Annie Hall*, Cusack frequently engaged the audience in direct address by talking to the camera.

So how does the anti-genre classification apply to *Annie Hall* as a romantic comedy? Well, as the title character Diane Keaton says in her memoir: "Love was the glue that held those witty vignettes together. However bittersweet, the message was clear. Love fades. Woody took a risk; he let the audience feel the sadness of goodbye in a funny movie."[1]

While neither *When Harry Met Sally...* nor *High Fidelity* is without bittersweet components, each picture finally reaches a soulmate scenario in which the phrase "love fades" does not—cannot—exist. Gifted critic-biographer Richard Schickel observed in his text on the comic artist:

> With some notable exceptions, Woody continues to set his movies in the milieu he began exploring with the widely beloved *Annie Hall*.... Yes, these films are still often about romantic misalliances, in which the principals are discovered in a state of restlessness, or open rebellion with their relationships, embark on new ones, and end up not much better off. But even when Woody maintains the conventions of what we might call the *anti-romantic comedy* [my italics], as he more or less single-handedly developed them many years ago, he has, within that form, greatly expanded his subtext and refined his style.[2]

Besides the most basic anti-genre element to defuse *Annie Hall*'s romantic comedy moniker—the couple do not end up together—several other things are at odds with the fundamental ingredients of this film category.[3] First, while there are a great deal of varied humorous pieces inherent to romantic comedy, the genre is generally dead serious about love. This characteristic is frequently showered in sentimentally idealized ways. For instance, James Stewart's character in *The Philadelphia Story* (1940) poetically observes:

> There's a magnificence in you, Tracy [Katharine Hepburn], a magnificence that comes out of your eyes, that's in your voice, in the way you stand there, in the way you walk. You're lit from within, bright, bright, bright. There are fires banked down to you, hearth fires....

In each of the three film versions of *Love Affair* (1939, 1957, 1994), a charming older person represents not only a testimonial to the movie's romantic male lead but also a corroborative witness for a sentimental celebration of her own past love. The most entertaining inspired update on the latter perspective occurs in *When Harry Met Sally....* Peppered throughout the movie are a series of interviews with elderly couples briefly but warmly chronicling their love story. In each instance, they are fittingly placed on a love seat looking straight at the camera. The first such instance has an older man observing:

> I was sitting with my friend Arthur Kornblum, in a restaurant ... and this beautiful girl walked in [he points to the woman beside him], and I turned to Arthur and I said, "Arthur, you see that girl? I'm going to marry her." And two weeks later we were married. And it's over fifty years later and we're still married.

When Harry Met Sally... further underlines the importance of these segments by opening and closing the picture with them. Moreover, by making the finale duo Harry and Sally a few years into their union, it further suggests the permanence of their relationship. That is, the viewer identifies them with all the proceeding golden-aged testimonials to love. Nora Ephron, the credited screenwriter for the film (with much tweaking by Reiner and Billy Crystal), observed, "I just love that you can ask a married couple how they met and it's their favorite story. You know—the little circumstances that brought them together. Even the most miserable married couples get all warm and cuddly when they tell you that story."[4]

In contrast, *Annie Hall* is a testament to the aforementioned perspective that "love fades." Allen's Alvy Singer is a serial lover. There is no one special someone, the proverbial soulmate: "You know, even as a kid, I always went for the wrong women. I think that's my problem. When my mother took me to see *Snow White*, everyone fell in love with Snow White. I immediately fell for the wicked queen." And in contrast to those random *When Harry Met Sally* testimonials to love, when Allen-Alvy introduces the seemingly indiscriminate couple, cynical beats sentimental every time:

> ALVY SINGER [flagging down an attractive duo on the street]: Hey, you look like a very happy couple, um, are you?
> THE COUPLE: Yeah.
> ALVY SINGER: Yeah? So, so, how do you account for it?
> ONE PARTNER: Uh, I'm very shallow and empty and I have no ideas and nothing interesting to say.
> THE OTHER: And I'm exactly the same way.
> ALVY: I see. Wow. That's very interesting. So you've managed to work out something.

Fittingly, most of Alvy's street witnesses to relationships are single people. One such elderly woman succinctly states the movie's optimum phrase, "love fades." And even early in Alvy and Annie's (Diane Keaton) relationship, when things seem most promising, he is quite capable of mocking love—something verboten in true romantic comedy. Thus, when Annie asks him about the "L" word, he spoofingly replies, "Love is too weak a word. I lurve you. I loave you. I luff you."

The classic romantic comedy builds on some early trauma. *Sleepless in Seattle* (1993) starts at the funeral of Tom Hanks' wife. Early in *Sabrina* (1954), Audrey Hepburn's character, a chauffeur's daughter, attempts suicide because she fears never being part of some fairy tale–like high society love story. In *An Affair to Remember* (1957, the most high-profile of the three *Love Affair* versions), Deborah Kerr is seriously injured when hit by a car as she anxiously hurries to meet Cary Grant at the top of the Empire State Building. Bonnie Hunt's underrated *Return to Me* (2000) has David Duchovny lose his lovely wife (Joely Richardson) in the picture's opening moments. In each case, romantic comedy then refines populism's key component—getting a second chance—and applies it to love. The trajectory is about moving towards a happy ending, just the opposite path of a tragic love story. And if in a populist film everyone is inherently good, in a romantic comedy that universal goodness is *all* focused in helping someone find the right person … whether he or she wants it or not.

There is no tragic catalyst, early or late, to the love affair of Alvy and Annie. No one dies, commits suicide, or fails to look both ways before crossing the street. *Annie Hall* begins at the end, with Alvy doing a comically analytical postmortem on why their relationship died … which then segues into the couple's story. Again, there is nothing close to any real anguish. There are merely spoofs of torment, like the "rescue" cause of their brief reunion ("Honey, there's a spider in your bathroom the size of a Buick") which Alvy kills with slapstick tennis racket enthusiasm.

Instead their break-up is merely a comically mundane litany of why most relationships fail. For instance, Alvy is jealous of Annie's casually familiar connection with her college instructor. "His name is David, right? Isn't that religious? What does he call you, Bathsheba?" She likes marijuana, he doesn't: "I took a puff five years ago and I tried to take off my pants over my head!" She wants to move to sunny California; New Yorker Alvy hates everything about the West Coast:

> ALVY: I don't want to move to a city where the only cultural advantage is being able to make a right turn on a red light….
> ANNIE: It's so clean out here [California].
> ALVY SINGER: In Beverly Hills they don't throw their garbage away—they turn it into television shows.

She wants to socialize more and live a less intellectually centered private life. However, being culturally driven is what defines Alvy, and like Shaw's *Pygmalion* professor, Henry Higgins, Allen's character can be a tutorially taxing person to people around him. For instance, while shopping, Alvy tells Annie, "I—I—I'm gonna buy you these [philosophical] books, I think, because I—I think you should read them. You know, instead of that cat book." One might best summarize Alvy's inability to be anything but cerebral by his comment, "I don't respond well to mellow. If I get too mellow, I ripen and then rot." In contrast, Alvy's attempt to reconnect one final time with Keaton's character, after her move to California, elicits Annie's own encapsulation of why they do not work as a couple: "I [now] meet people and I go to parties and—and we play tennis. I mean, that's … that's a big step for me, you know. I mean…. I'm able to enjoy people more…. Alvy, you're incapable of enjoying life, you know that?"

There was a softer, funnier Annie take on the stress of living with Alvy during their first breakup, when they are sorting through an array of items and deciding what belongs to whom:

ALVY SINGER [looking at a book]: This *Denial of Death*. You remember this?
ANNIE HALL: Oh—
ALVY SINGER: This is the first book that I got you.

    [Annie comes over and they both look at the book.]

ANNIE HALL: God.
ALVY SINGER: Remember that day?
ANNIE HALL: Right. Jeez, I feel like there's a great weight off my back. M'mmm.
ALVY SINGER: Thanks, honey.
ANNIE HALL [patting his shoulder]: Oh, no, no, no, no, no. You know, no, no, no, I mean…. [Now I won't feel guilty about never having read it.]

While *Annie Hall* does follow the traditional romantic comedy dating ritual of the male initiating the relationship, there is none of the genre's normally accompanying romantic small talk. For instance, in *Return to Me*, widower Duchovny, after years away from dating, poignantly asks Minnie Driver if he can hold her hand, since his late wife (Richardson) had been his high school sweetheart, implying he needed to take it slowly. And director/co-writer/co-star Bonnie Hunt effectively stages this potentially schmaltzy sequence without either a breakout of diabetes, or making viewers' eyes glaze over.

Allen's Alvy is at such a variance from this affectionate small talk that he is capable of being condescending from day one. For example, when it becomes apparent that Annie is fond of Sylvia Plath's poetry, Alvy responds, "Interesting poetess whose tragic suicide was misinterpreted as romantic, by the college girl mentality." And when a surprised Annie can only manage a modest defense that some of her poems "seem neat," Alvy cannot resist jumping on the term "neat," "Uh, I hate to tell ya, this is 1975, you know that 'neat' went out, I would say, at the turn of the century."

Romantic comedy pacing slows towards the conclusion, allowing audiences to squirm and wonder whether the couple will overcome whatever detail hinders the hoped-for validation of love. To illustrate, in *An Affair to Remember*, will Cary Grant discover why Deborah Kerr did not make their appointed romantic rendezvous, despite both parties agreeing to ask no questions if either one did not appear? But while *Affair* and a host of other romantic comedies ultimately provide the viewer with the desired happy results, *Annie Hall*'s slower stride dispenses an anti-genre mournful close. That is, later, a chance meeting and pleasant lunch back in New York result in a montage of all Alvy and Annie's good times together … yet they then still go their separate ways. The montage also ups the ante on the mournful meter, since one immediately thinks of all those brief testimonial moments to love, *à la When Harry Met Sally…*, in the traditional romantic comedy.

Beyond these romantic comedy basics, the greatest precept of romantic comedy is that you *change* for someone, or as it is more lyrically phrased in *As Good as It Gets* (1997), "You make me want to be a better person." In *Annie Hall* Alvy is inflexible in his views. And Annie's changes are ones of personal growth, not couple-directed. Consequently, while Alvy's Professor Higgins position has been important to her, she has outgrown him. If ever a word described their amicable split, it would be bittersweet.

Ironically, sometimes even a unique work of art can be lost in the passage of time. For instance, Allen created his groundbreaking example of anti-genre romantic comedy, *Annie Hall*, in 1975. Yet, in a 2014 *New York Times* article one finds the puzzling statement that *500 Days of Summer* was hailed as "an innovative anti-romantic comedy" in 2009.[5]

There is no denying that *Summer* is an entertaining example of "anti-romcom," yet most of its "innovative" storytelling was anchored in Allen's picture. Where is the historical perspective? One might tag this as yet another dark comedy variation of "And so it goes," sort of a cultural version of Alzheimer's disease.

While romantic comedy has been the obvious anti-genre camouflage to black humor-crossing *Annie Hall*, other cinematic masking elements are also at work. By Allen's own admission, despite his constant focus on art house and/or darkly comic issues, brilliant witticisms emanating from that goofy appearance often make one instinctively label anything he does "personality comedy." That was certainly my first inclination back in the 1970s. But just as Allen so effectively used this anti-genre moniker (as applied to personality comedy ploy in *Love and Death*, 1975), by dropping his Bob Hope–like persona into Ingmar Bergman land, a variation of this occurs in *Annie Hall*. With Allen's disheveled, clown-like appearance, planting him in the land of romance is almost as strange as him popping up in Bergman-ville. Plus, as with romantic comedy, our ludicrously quirky comedians were supposed to get the beautiful love interest. There are now even some revisionists who suggest Chaplin's Tramp won the girl at the end of *City Lights* (1931), a verdict unheard of at the time.[6] Regardless, there is no ambiguity at the close of *Annie Hall*; Alvy and Annie are amicably over.

Another anti-genre cloaking element in *Annie Hall* involves inquiries about its profile nature. Allen has always had to parry questions that his screen character was merely a variation of the real man. What made the issue high-profile was Diane Keaton's involvement. As in the movie, she and Allen had once been lovers and still remained close friends. Moreover, Keaton's maiden name is Hall, and her nickname is Annie. Also paralleling the film, Keaton began her career wanting to be a singer, was chronically insecure (and often struggled for words), had the mismatched *Annie Hall* look well before the picture, and still remains somewhat uncomfortable in the fast track world of a Woody Allen. In her 2011 autobiography, Keaton confessed, "I miss Woody.... I still love him. I'll always be his ... simple-is-as-simple-does...."[7]

Naturally, the obvious autobiographical links to his *Annie Hall* character merely add to the stereotype of the person and persona as interchangeable—a comedian with a New Yorker's belief in the city's intrinsic eminence. Moreover, he is also an affluent entertainer, sought after by television, frequently recognized in public, and even in demand on the college comedy tour circuit. With all these givens, especially the added direct links to Keaton, it is easy to see how a profile picture designation would prove a distraction to recognizing both *Annie Hall*'s dark comedy base, not to mention its most frequent classification as a romantic comedy.

Anti-genre elements of *Annie Hall* as a profile film are not, however, as significant as those applied to the picture if designated as a romantic comedy. One can, however, note two anti-genre profile film fundamentals. First, famed biographer Paul Mariani has defined the goal of his profession with the tongue-in-cheek phrase "reassembling the dust"—bringing the dead back to life with what another profiler (Paul Murray Kendal) has called the "best truth possible."[8] But in the case of Allen's construction of *Annie Hall*, he has done his best to do what might be called "blow the dust into no discernible pattern." That is, he included just enough real facts with which to draw in the viewer, and then disengaged ... allowing himself to create his own comic make-believe elements. For instance, he neither grew up under a Brooklyn amusement park roller coaster (his *Annie Hall* childhood home is forever shaking), nor did his father operate a bumper car ride—

which allowed Allen to amusingly depict a young Alvy's antiheroic baptism by having his miniature car be constantly crashed into.

The phenomenon is not unlike what Luis Buñuel and Salvador Dali did in the pioneering surrealistic film *Andalusian Dog* (1928). This dream-like dark comedy, with no intended meaning, was an abstract, avant-garde collection of imagery with just enough of a disjointed narrative that the filmmakers correctly assumed audiences would attempt to make a story from the strands of an anti-story.

The other anti-genre technique Allen applied to a quintessential profile core involves what biographer Frank E. Vandiver calls "history made personal."[9] For example, one might have no interest in World War II. But a biography of a major participant in said conflict, such as General George Patton, might draw a reader or viewer into an active interest in this event. Unlike *Love and Death* with its scattergun use of the Napoleonic Wars as a backdrop, *Annie Hall* plays no "history made personal" games with the viewer. Beyond the time capsule component attached to any period in which any artistic item is created, *Annie Hall* is not a window into a major historical schism. Dark comedy (or for that matter, romantic comedy) is a genre for indeterminate time and space. These entertainment formulas are infinitely adaptable.

Now that certain anti-genre masks have been removed from *Annie Hall*, how is the film most advantageously showcased as a dark comedy? First, Allen assails every aspect of the film with the genre standard—death. And as one explores this theme in *Annie Hall*, remember how dark comedy often plays upon a disjointed narrative. This bit of artistic chaos, like life, keeps one off-balance. Thus, Allen's deployment of death references in

Though the fence separates Rob (Tony Roberts, middle) and Annie (Diane Keaton) from Alvy's (Woody Allen) old schoolyard, the comedian is constantly revisiting the past via fantasy.

Annie Hall, like everything else about the picture, involves a sometimes fantasy-like telescopic journey, a back and forth through Alvy and Annie's past. Moreover, like many dark comedy noirs, one can double down on the disjointed narrative by remembering that the movie starts at the end. And then the storyline caroms around enough in time to remind one of *Slaughterhouse-Five*'s time-tripping Billy Pilgrim. Of course, in Alvy and Annie's case, they are well aware of their touchdown areas. And the duo sometimes even simultaneously wander through these past tense excursions, with their previous selves oblivious to the fact. Aware or not, *Slaughterhouse-Five* again comes to mind, with regard to its precept that all time exists concurrently. Maybe if that projection is applied to *Annie Hall*, some of the plaintive pain is deleted from the film's closing montage of once happy moments.

Annie Hall's death-related thesis is there from film frame one, with Allen-Alvy's direct address stand-up comic patter about aging and his split from Annie. As *New York Times* critic James Parker has said of comedians, "[In a] spotlight framed by vacancy, [he is] existentially alone. By what right does he or she hold this space? By no right at all, unless it be the right of sheer presence."[10] This is like a description of survey class on *Waiting for Godot*–God.

Though called *Annie Hall*, the picture is equal parts of Alvy, who was originally to be the focus. Regardless, death is forever looking over his comic shoulder. Though he does not actually meet the Grim Reaper as a youngster, which occurred in *Love and Death*, in flashback the audience is privy to this precocious child suddenly refusing to do his homework because, "well, the universe is everything, and if it's expanding, someday it will break apart and that would be the ending of everything ... what's the point?" Flash forward to adulthood and Alvy waits for a delayed Annie at Manhattan's Upper East Side Beckman Art Theatre. Everything about the extended sequence is permeated with death or a death-like framework. For instance, the movie they plan to see is Ingmar Bergman's *Face to Face* (1976), which chronicles the mental illness of a psychiatrist (Liv Ullmann) so haunted by images from her past that she ultimately will be unable to function—an art house version of the living dead.

As Alvy waits, he is bothered by thug-like fans, an experience he later describes as like "standing with the cast of *The Godfather* ... guys named Cheech!" Because Annie is tardy, and the Bergman film has started, he drags her to Marcel Ophüls' *The Sorrow and the Pity* (1969), a four-hour documentary about the Nazi occupation of France and the collaborating Vichy government established by Germany. While they wait in line for tickets, a pontificating professor ahead of them expounds upon a host of existential subjects, from references to Theatre of Absurd author Samuel Beckett, to Frederico Fellini's Chaplinesque tragedy *La Strada* (1954, which turns upon the tragic death of Giulietta Masina's waif). After watching the Ophüls film, it become a topic of discussion:

ALVY: Boy, those guys in the French Resistance were really brave, you know? Got to listen to Maurice Chevalier sing so much.
ANNIE: Mmmm, I don't know, sometimes I ask myself how I'd stand up under torture.
ALVY: You? You kiddin'? If the Gestapo would take away your Bloomingdale's charge card, you'd tell 'em everything.
ANNIE: That makes me feel guilty.
ALVY: Yeah, 'cause it's supposed to.

When Alvy attempts to pivot on this subject to sex, Annie is not in the mood. As Allen's character becomes upset, she reminds him how he shut down a former wife, Allison (Carol

Kane), sexually, with a new twist on how dark comedy sometimes links death and intercourse—except here the chaotic loss of control means no sex. For example, eventually during his relationship with Allison, often when they were in an amorous situation, he would avoid sex by seguing into one of their common discussions—a debate over whether John F. Kennedy's assassination was a conspiracy, showcased via flashback:

> ALLISON: The FBI, and the CIA, and J. Edgar Hoover and oil companies and the Pentagon and the men's room attendant at the White House [were in on it]?
> ALVY: I—I—I—I would leave out the men's room attendant.

Soon the story returns to an early point in Alvy and Annie's relationship. As the couple discuss her naiveté, there is a new flashback of a pre–Alvy Annie at a party with a budding actor. Again, death is front and center as Keaton's character and Allen look on:

> JERRY: Acting is like an exploration of the soul. I—it's very religious. [Obviously hitting on her.] Uh, like, uh, a kind of liberating consciousness. It's like visual poem....
> YOUNGER ANNIE [laughing]: Oh, right. Right, yeah, I—I think I know exactly what you mean, when you say "religious."
> JERRY: It's like when I think of dying. You know how I would like to die?
> YOUNGER ANNIE: No, how?
> JERRY: I'd like to get torn apart by wild animals [again the sex-death scenario].
> ALVY'S VOICE: Heavy! Eaten by some squirrels....

The transition back to the contemporary setting has him telling Annie how lucky she is to now have him. But she defends her former immaturity with men by contrasting it to Alvy's interest in complicated New York women. This triggers a flashback scene from an Alvy marriage to a woman named Robin (Janet Margolin). Another sex scene is negated by a footnote to death: In bed, Robin complains that a sudden blaring siren has kept her from getting an orgasm:

> ROBIN: I'm too tense. I need a Valium. My analyst says I should live in the country and not in New York.
> ALVY: Well, I can't.... We can't have this discussion all the time. The country makes me nervous ... there's the [window] screens with the dead moths behind them, and ... ya got the—the Manson family probably....

After a few Valiums and the city quiets down, Alvy again attempts to have sex with Robin. But she now has a headache so severe she compares it to Lee Harvey Oswald and ghosts. One now wonders who first used the Kennedy assassination as a death-related tool, to now block sex.

The next sequence is yet another period in time—when Annie and Alvy first talk, following a mixed doubles tennis match arranged by friends. As they prepare to have a drink in Annie's small apartment, death and/or the horrific is casual material for comedy. For example, when Annie describes a giving grandmother seemingly out of a Norman Rockwell painting, Alvy says, "Jesus, my—my granny ... n-never gave gifts, you know. She—she was too busy getting raped by Cossacks." When the conversation moves to culture, the first in a litany of Alvy intellectual putdowns of her involves dark comedy's favorite exit: suicide. For example, the previously noted crack by Allen's character when he spots a collection of Sylvia Plath poetry among Annie's books.

The most intriguing mix of death and comedy is a short monologue Allen has written for Annie. Moreover, it is certainly the most disconnectedly startling, which fits dark comedy's random (like life) discharge of death. Nevertheless, the pair's small talk before some wine has warm-heartedly made it apparent that Annie is either a delightfully "la-de-da" dolt, or the most guileless of child-women. So it is difficult to decipher whether the following homily she shares with Alvy is a feeble attempt at a joke, an offbeat anecdote, or just a bizarre attempt to keep the conversation going:

> [My uncle] George was real sweet, you know, he had that thing. What is that thing where you, uh, where you, uh, fall asleep in the middle of a sentence, you know—what is it? Uh … [*Alvy says "narcolepsy"*] Narcolepsy, right, right. Right. So, anyway, so … [*laughing nervously*] George, uh, went to the union, see, to get his free turkey at Christmastime because he was … [*Annie's hand gestures suggest that George was crazy*] shell-shocked, you know what I mean, in the first World War. [*Annie laughs almost uncontrollably as she gets a bottle of wine*] Anyway, so, so … [*more laughter*] George is standing in line, oh, just a sec … uh, getting his free turkey but the thing is, he falls asleep and he never wakes up. So, so [*laughing*], so, he's dead…. [*More laughter*] he's dead. Yeah. Oh, dear. Well, terrible, huh, wouldn't you say? I mean that's pretty unfortunate.

A stunned Alvy says, "Yeah, it's a great story, though, I mean, I … I … it really made my day…."

Why this Kafkaesque Keaton rambling—contemporary shorthand for bizarre—especially resonates here is that it is not coming from some angst-ridden New York intellectual, such as the even greater malaise of Allen's figure (again very much like himself) in *Stardust Memories* (1980). An in-film psychiatrist describes this figure:

> He saw reality too clearly. [With a] family denial mechanism, he failed to block out the terrible truth of existence. In the end his inability to push away the awful fact, of being in the world, rendered his life meaningless, or as one great Hollywood producer said, "Too much reality is not what the people want." Sandy Bates [Allen] suffered a depression common to many artists in middle age….

One expects this perspective from a cerebral analytical type like Allen's *Annie Hall* or *Stardust Memories* characters. But a corn-fed, unsophisticated, transplanted Midwesterner like Annie spouts this dark comedy diatribe, though she's almost less than lucid. The anti-genre factor related to romantic comedy is alive and well. Plus, there is a death-related postscript to the more twisted bittersweet romance of *Stardust Memories*, which was initially often criticized for being narcissistically defensive about the bipolar-like nature of film fans, *à la The Day of the Locust*. Allen's point was tragically proven correct a few months later. That is, *Stardust* Memories takes place at a weekend Sandy Bates film festival, which seemingly results in his character being assassinated by a onetime devotee. A few months later this scenario played out in reality with the shooting death of John Lennon. In fact, this whole phenomenon of fan worship and/or confusion about the distinctions between the performer and his persona could also be another anti-genre element of the profile film.

Returning to *Annie Hall*'s ongoing intertwining references to death, this love story gone south has Alvy's college-of-one education for Annie staying on the dark side. During their first breakup, Keaton's character complains, "You only gave me books with the word 'death' in the titles." The catalyst for the charge is Thomas Mann's novella *Death in Venice* (1912, about the life of a writer ruined by love, dying of cholera). Later Annie signals that her Alvy-directed education is over during his last attempt at reconciliation when she justifies the split by referencing Mann's book.

Yet, even without this dark literary "graduation" by Annie, the viewer's first lengthy introduction to Keaton's sweet rube produces her long-winded narcolepsy death story. Later, when Alvy travels to Annie's heartland home, he experiences an equally weird death-related confession from her high school–aged brother Duane (Christopher Walken):

> I tell you this because, as an artist, you'll understand. Sometimes when I'm driving ... on the road at night ... I see two headlights coming toward me. Fast. I have this sudden impulse to turn the wheel quickly, head-on into the oncoming car. I can anticipate the explosion. The sound of shattered glass. The ... flames rising out of the flowing gasoline.

Alvy retires from this situation with an aplomb which could double as an affectionate spoofing of Vonnegut's Billy Pilgrim's travel to another planet, "Right. Tsk. Well, I have to—I have to go now ... because I—I'm due back on the planet Earth."

Death-related references prompted by others occur in other Alvy encounters. In one example, a more traditional dark comedy linkage between sex and death occurs. After his first split with Annie, Alvy briefly dates Pam (Shelley Duvall), a *Rolling Stone* reporter. After a bedroom tryst, she apologizes for taking so long to have an orgasm. But fittingly, for dark comedy, abnormal seems the new normal, with Pam praising Alvy: "Oh, sex with you is really a Kafkaesque experience.... I meant that as a compliment." Leave it to Allen's character, however, to put this praise in Grim Reaper perspective:

> I think—I think there's too much burden placed on the orgasm, you know, to make up for empty areas in life.... I don't know [who said it]. It might have been Leopold and Loeb [the teenage thrill killer intellectuals who believed themselves Nietzschean Übermensch supermen neither governed by mankind's normal laws, nor subject to guilt by mankind's normal laws].[11]

Along related lines, as one dissects the profusion of death allusions in the genre-crossing dark comedy *Annie Hall*, as with *Love and Death*, the references usually collate around linking two subjects to sex and violence: significant cultural elements (such as Bergman movies and/or a Mann novella) and historical markers (like the Kennedy assassination and Leopold and Loeb). Two additional *Annie Hall* examples along these lines are driven by violent jealousy. Both are related to Alvy's failed Los Angeles mission to retrieve Annie from an unlikely musical career while living with rock star Tony Lacey (Paul Simon). The first example occurs before Alvy even leaves New York and involves another random street conversation:

> STRANGER: Don't tell me you're jealous [of Lacey]?
> ALVY: Yeah, jealous. A little like Medea.
>
> [In Greek mythology, Medea used her magic to assist her lover Jason, not unlike Alvy helping Annie to sing. But when Jason sought someone else, Medea's revenge included killing her own children with him.]

The second example occurs after Alvy's Los Angeles arrival, culminating with his anger over her concern for Lacey's nerves shortly before the Grammys. Alvy leaves yelling, "Awards! They do nothing but give out awards [in California]! I can't believe it. Greatest fascist dictator, Adolf Hitler!"

While the death-related exploration of Annie and Allie's failed relationship could go on *ad nauseam*—a most apt word for love in Woody Allen-land—two final diverse illustrations merit inclusion. The first is broadly comic and arguably the picture's funniest line: "A relationship, I think, is—is like a shark, you know? It has to constantly move forward or it dies. And I think what we got on our hands ... is a dead shark."

The second example is somewhere between poignancy and pity turned to narcissism:

"I can't enjoy anything unless ... everybody is. I—you know, if one guy is starving some-place, that's ... you know, I—I ... it puts a crimp in my evening...."

There is virtuosity behind Allen's hiding black humor behind an anti-genre shield of romantic comedy. Despite a machine-gun raking of ephemerally fleeting love with death, he still manages to bring an affectingly "maybe next time" hope to relationships ... despite his underlying sense that lasting love is absurd. In other words, Allen's masterful mix of this maddening subject never approaches the title of Charles Bukowski's dark comedy collection of poetry on the same subject, *Love Is a Dog from Hell* (1977, the same year *Annie Hall* was released).[12]

Bukowski's dark comedy is not, however, without crude parallels to Allen, as well as making an excellent transition to the genre's theme of *Annie Hall* absurdity. Ironically, a signature line from Bukowski's novel *Factatum* (1975, the year *Love and Death* opened) might just as well have been uttered by an Allen character pondering the absurdity of existence: "For each Joan of Arc there is a Hitler perched at the other end of the teeter-totter."[13] Nevertheless, the quintessential absurdity quote from *Annie Hall* is the film's closing joke about the preposterousness of love. And since Allen saw fit to dip into Greek mythology with his earlier Medea citation, it seems fair game to liken Alvy's joke to Sisyphus attempting a chicken-or-the-egg witticism. After all, the subject is absurdity:

> I—I thought of that old joke, you know, this ... guy goes to a psychiatrist and says, "Doc, uh, my brother's crazy. He thinks he's a chicken." And, uh, the doctor says, "Well, why don't you turn him in?" And the guy says, "I would, but we need the eggs." Well, I guess that's pretty much how I feel about relationships. You know, they're totally irrational and crazy and absurd and ... but, uh, I guess we keep goin' through it because, uh, most of us need the eggs.

This is definitely the fiction-lie that tells the truth. From a personal standpoint, this story was part of my affectionately rambling toast at my eldest daughter's first wedding, which of course, preceded my third separation. Above all, this is the chapter's absurdity section.

This circumstance is reminiscent of a Tennessee Williams story which certainly applies to Allen, as well as representing the subtext to *Stardust Memories*. That is, above all, Williams was often told he was drawn to neurotic people, and the playwright replied, "When you penetrate into almost anybody, you either find madness or dullness."[14] This text has extensively explored the inherent absurdity to be found in war and all of the major established institutions. But Allen's *Annie Hall* entertainingly suggests it is right in bed with us. Still, he never counsels Bukowski's much repeated description of yet another marriage, "I'd rather drive a car backwards from California to New York."

Besides Alvy's *pièce de résistance* "most of us need the eggs" story, *Annie Hall* is also richly laced with other examples of absurdity. However, the best one is bolstered by a variation of "staircase wit"—the problem of thinking of the perfect retort too late. The sequence occurs while Annie and Alvy are in line for a movie and a college instructor in front of them is pontificating like he is Aristotle's second cousin:

> INSTRUCTOR: It's like Samuel Beckett, you know—I admire the technique but he doesn't ... he doesn't hit me at a gut level.
> ALVY TO ANNIE: I'd like to hit this guy on a gut level....
> INSTRUCTOR: It's the influence of television. Yeah, now Marshall McLuhan deals with it in terms of it being a—a high, uh, high intensity, you understand? A hot medium ... as opposed to a ...

Alvy: What I wouldn't give for a large sock o'horse manure…. [Eventually this leads to a confrontation.]

Instructor: Wait a minute! Really? Really? I happen to teach a class at Columbia…. So I think my insights into Mr. McLuhan … have a great deal of validity. [Alvy and the professor go through another verbal exchange before Allen's character essentially unloads a variation of "staircase wit" on steroids.]

Alvy [in response to the "validity" comment]: That's funny, I happen to have Mr. McLuhan right here [Alvy brings out the real McLuhan from behind a one sheet stand-up film poster and unleashes him on the instructor.]

McLuhan: I heard what you were saying. You—you know nothing of my work. You mean my whole fallacy is wrong. How you ever got to teach a course in anything is totally amazing.

Alvy [in direct address to the viewer]: Boy, if life were only like this!

In Alvy and Annie's sphere, absurdity might not directly address the life-and-death impact it has in other film worlds, such as *Catch–22*'s (1970) World War II bombardier Yossarian (Alan Arkin). But modern humor, dark or not, sometimes hides behind the mundane day-to-day absurdities and frustrations—yet another relationship derailment, for instance. This is to distract one from the really dicey difficulties of existence: The question of why we are here: religious hate and/or wars over someone's invisible people being superior to others; lack of a God, or to paraphrase Vonnegut, "If God were alive, today, He'd be an atheist." And so on—or should that be another "And so it goes"?

The presence of man as beast in *Annie Hall* is more one step removed from the pictures. Instead of Yossarian fighting Nazis and his own side, Annie and Alvy discuss Nazis and torture after seeing a documentary. And there are ethical issues in *Annie Hall*. Having a friend (Tony Roberts) cheat on quality by adding a laugh track to his television show does not reverberate like struggling for a rationale to assassinate Napoleon (*Love and Death*). On a modest level, one could even call Alvy a man as beast, though it is a difficult task to do, especially when one briefly sees him as a cartoon character. But in his relationship with Annie, Alvy is an enigmatic ally of decency, selfishness, love, and indifference. In other words, he is a one-size-fits-all type of beast … like most of us, which even more quickly contributes to the film's ultimate dark comedy message, "love fades." Or maybe it's as depressingly simple as the Chris Rock mantra on relationships, "bored or lonely": one is always eventually bored with someone, or lonely with no one. The numbers certainly suggest this position. Someone is forever quoting the fact that fifty percent of marriages fail. But as observational comedian David Brenner reminds us in his 2000 HBO Special, when people further break down those numbers: Of the fifty percent success rate, only about half of the couples are together for love.[15] These other folks are sticking it out for the kids, or for financial reasons, or are just being too lazy to go through the paperwork. Yet, here is where one comes back full circle to Allen's "most of us need the eggs" absurdity. In the closing minutes of Brenner's HBO Special he hurriedly marries for the second time … a union which barely lasted a year.

Whether or not *Annie Hall* was, to paraphrase critic-historian Timothy W. Johnson, "a navigation through Alvy's mind," it was a major critical and commercial success. If Allen had won an Oscar for Best Actor (he lost to *The Goodbye Girl*'s Richard Dreyfuss), *Annie Hall* would have been only the third film (at that time) to have won the five major Academy Awards; it did win for Best Picture, Best Director (Allen), Best Screenplay–Original (Allen and Marshall Brickman), and Best Actress (Diane Keaton). Not surprisingly, there is a host of additional critical honors. For example, *Annie Hall* also swept

This split-screen separation of Annie (Diane Keaton) and Alvy (Woody Allen) at their shrinks perfectly chronicles why "love fades."

these categories of the BAFTA (British Academy of Film and Television) ceremony, their equivalent of the Oscars.

Arguably the greatest critical praise for *Annie Hall* came from a mock interview *New York Times* critic Vincent Canby conducted with himself, a sort of Woody Allen homage. But before this occurs, Canby posits a brilliant insight to 1970s cutting edge art and Allen's *Annie Hall*: "If art is life recorded, as now seems to be the instant replay [a time for modern life contemplation is increasingly stolen from our lives]."[16] This problem is even more relevant in today's helter skelter world, with a growing number of people being diagnosed with "Conversion Disorder," in which stress in their recent past causes them suddenly to suffer a multitude of ailments, ranging from random epileptic-like seizures, to an abrupt exhaustion which can cause total collapse. It would seem to represent a sort of second tier Post Traumatic Stress Disorder.

In either case, modern life—of our choosing—allows us less and less time for a healing "instant replay" contemplation. Without using the medical jargon, Allen addressed the subject in his *Hollywood Ending* (2002): After a prolonged period of declining career stress, Allen's central character, filmmaker Val Waxman, finally gets an A-picture to direct and promptly goes temporarily blind—also a sometime condition of Conversion Disorder. (He directs it anyway, and naturally it is awful. But because Allen satirically has the French hailing it as a masterpiece, a suddenly seeing Waxman has a major comeback!) Regardless, what follows is Canby's synthetic interview:

QUESTION: Is [Allen] some kind of reflection of America's collective unconscious?
ANSWER: I'm not sure what the collective unconscious is. Or whether that has anything to do with … [my belief that he is America's Ingmar Berman]. What I mean is that it's about time that we recognize Woody Allen as one of the most original, most personal, most passionate, most introspective filmmakers.[17]

One might simply retitle Canby's think piece "Woody Allen *Is* the American Bergman."

In a second Canby *Annie Hall* review, he suggests the film's dark comedy base, often echoing Allen: "[His central character feels life's] not great—in fact, it's pretty evenly divided between the horrible and the miserable—but as long as it's there he wants more."[18] Again, the essay's title states it succinctly: "Somber Comedy."

Without actually saying dark comedy, Penelope Gilliatt's *New Yorker* review amusingly also gets at the film's black humor core:

Alvy was brought up in Brooklyn: a small, skinny boy in spectacles whose growth seems to have been impeded by his bearing the millstone of the world on his head [again, vestiges of Gunter Grass' *Tin Drum* child, who decides not to grow physically during the Nazis' rise to power]…. This is a love story told with piercing sweetness and grief, for all its funniness…. [H]is feeling about hypocrisy was never so ringing, his sobriety never so witty.[19]

Even more indirectly, but no less importantly, Gilliatt has made a most astute observation: "Like Buster Keaton, Woody Allen has made one of the rare comedies in existence about a well-heeled hero [who] is intelligent."[20] Unlike Keaton's only artistic silent film rival, Charlie Chaplin, his work invited a cerebral questioning of existence itself. As pioneering Keaton scholar Rudi Blesh stated, "His comedies were perhaps the first examples of the Theatre of the Absurd."[21] This perspective has only been more documented in the years since. For instance, Keaton biographer Tom Dardis wrote:

[There was a] darker, enigmatic side of Keaton, the side that keeps showing up in so many of his films and that Samuel Beckett found so intriguing that he had Keaton in mind when he wrote *Waiting for Godot* [1953]. This is the Keaton none of his friends ever reached, the private Keaton that remained cut off from the world….[22]

In 1964 Keaton starred in Beckett's short subject *Film*, in which a camera follows Buster through New York streets from behind, so that viewers do not see his face until cornered by the camera at the close. The comedian's take on the picture was pure modern world absurdity: "What I think it means is that man can keep away from everybody but he can't get away from himself."[23]

Still, for the absurdity of life, Keaton had topped even Beckett decades before with a sequence from his *Daydreams* (1922). In this metaphor for the treadmill nature of life, Keaton is caught in a whirling boat paddle wheel and climbs ever faster to avoid becoming a victim. It is life in an eternal holding pattern, like the two clowns forever waiting in *Godot*, or Lewis Carroll's Alice running faster and faster just to stay in one place.[24] Besides this Keaton-Allen connection on absurdity, the older comedian's decidedly anti-genre perspective on romantic comedy certainly plays through in *Annie Hall*.

Variety's review mixed its high praise with an appreciation of a darker Allen perspective, noting that *Annie Hall* is not so different from Ingmar Bergman's probingly painful but honest *Scenes from a Marriage* (1973, about a disintegrating civil union):

[Allen's] film could be called *Scenes from a Relationship*. Allen and Keaton go through just about all the emotional changes one could expect from an intelligent contemporary couple, only in this case the anguish is masked by the surface bravery of Allen's wisecracking and Keaton's deft retorts.[25]

Woody Allen's "whatever works" philosophy while he plays the *Godot* waiting game is caught here as he types in bed, which is also his normal work zone.

Nation critic Robert Hatch's positive critique was also driven by recognition of Allen's innovatively growing dark perspective.[26] The reviewer perceptively notes that Allen's last role, as an actor only, was in Martin Ritt's 1976 political dark comedy *The Front*—about Congress' House Un-American Activities Committee. The movie played at being fiction/nonfiction, since it realistically chronicled this 1950s blacklisting fueled by communist paranoia. Many of the cast and crew suffered through this absurdity, including director Ritt, screenwriter Walter Bernstein, and co-star Zero Mostel. Allen felt strongly about this injustice, and his star status involvement enabled the film to be made—a rare example of Allen appearing in someone else's picture. Thus Allen, like many of the other anti-genre artists already cited in this text, including Arthur Penn, Joseph Heller, and Richard Hooker, were repulsed by what had become known as the McCarthy Era (after the junior senator from Wisconsin, Joseph McCarthy, 1908–1957). While *Annie Hall* was not as directly influenced by the damaging ludicrousness of this blacklisting as *MASH*, *Catch–22*, and *Little Big Man* (all 1970), Allen's commitment to *The Front* just prior to his *oeuvre* becoming darker hardly seems coincidental.

As Allen scholar Foster Hirsch has detailed, *Annie Hall* is the first time Allen "expresses a genuine unhappiness with himself ... [underlined by the picture's working title, *Anhedonia*, the] non-contagious psychological condition that prevents its victims from enjoying themselves."[27] Ultimately, one might best liken Allen's art to "Kafkaesque vaudeville," since nothing escapes his anti-genre skepticism, be it faith or the questionable panacea promise of your choice.[28]

11

Being There (12/20/79)

Look here: I raised that boy [Chance the Gardner, a.k.a. Chauncey Gardiner] since he was the size of a piss-ant. And I'll say right now, he never learned to read and write. No, sir, had no brains at all. Was stuffed with rice pudding between th' ears … dumb as a jackass.
—Louise the maid (Ruth Attaway) in *Being There*

Peter Sellers [observed] that he saw Gardiner [whom he portrayed] as the key figure of contemporary life, the blank, disembodied observer, God perhaps…. Himself, if you like.
—[London] *Sunday Telegraph* (July 27, 1980)[1]

Hal Ashby's *Being There* is the 1979 adaptation of Polish-born American Jerry Kosinski's 1970 novel, with a screenplay adapted by the novelist. The book chronicles a series of fortuitous acts which happen to a special needs gardener when he is released from his place of employment upon the death of a wealthy benefactor called the Old Man. The novelist implies early in the text this was probably his father: "[Chance] had no family. Although his mother had been very pretty, her mind had been as damaged as his…."[2] With neither a name nor any sense of identity, Chance's whole life had been in virtual isolation, save for tending the Old Man's garden. Chance's only real companion is his obsession with television, inspiring his simple-minded mantra, "I like to watch"—which is sometimes interpreted in multiple ways, including an innocent sexual innuendo.

With the Old Man's death, Chance is quite literally sent packing, like a brainless Adam banished from the garden. His life will take another drastic turn when he is befriended by a quickly smitten Eve (Shirley MacLaine as the wife of elderly Melvyn Douglas' wealthy political powerbroker Ben Rand). All Chance has going for him is an expensive, conservatively tailored vintage suit and a suitcase of similarly tastefully cut hand-me-down clothing from the Old Man's wardrobe. However, to borrow a description of Gogol's writing (a literary land where *Being There* divertingly fits), Kosinski and Ashby "make the most unlikely of event[s] … seem not only plausible but convincing…."[3] *Being There*, as with many of the works addressed herein, demonstrates the gauze-thin veil which separates stability from humanity's herd mentality.

Before exploring the inherent black humor of *Being There*, which Ashby's film really ratchets up with an ending not in the novel, one must first concentrate upon its intrinsic anti-genre distractions from dark comedy. Most obviously, if a film, any film, stars Peter Sellers, one's opening thoughts should be "personality comedian genre." At the time of *Being There*, no less a talent than actor-composer-comedian-humor historian Steve Allen called Sellers "our most gifted and versatile motion picture comedian."[4] Allen goes on to

Chance (Peter Sellers) and Louise (Ruth Attaway), the only one who knows the gardener's real story in *Being There.*

write in his book *Funny People* (1981), a text as groundbreakingly perceptive about comedians as his *The Funny Men* (1956):

> Before his Inspector Clouseau-Pink Panther period it ... was the very breadth of [Sellers'] ability [which made it difficult] for the public to get him into focus.... Almost all actors and comedians play a variety of characters. But if Bob Hope plays an astronaut, a knight in armor, a gangster [and so on], he always looks exactly like Bob Hope wearing funny clothes.... But Sellers seemed to be physically transformed in each of his characterizations. And this ... was due, in part to his essential personal invisibility.[5]

Sellers' "invisibility" factor might also be compared to dramatic performers like Dustin Hoffman and Meryl Streep, who can also disappear into a part. This camouflaging flair beyond mere mimicry was something which Sellers poignantly clutched as if he were a mere empty vessel until filled by a particular role, an analogy frequently used in biographer Peter Evans' pioneering study *Peter Sellers: The Mask Behind the Mask.*[6] Evans fleshes this out with an excerpt from a 1964 Sellers interview:

> When a role is finished, I experience a sudden loss of identity. It's a funny thing but when I'm doing a role I kind of feel it's the role doing the role, if you know what I mean. When someone says, "You were great as so-and-so" I feel they should be telling so-and-so and not me.[7]

Sellers' sometimes indiscernible component is at the heart of an anti-genre personality comedian situation, given that an otherwise all-important 20th century screen clown was not always readily recognizable.[8] Paradoxically, maybe there is a certain appropriateness that Sellers' often-hidden-in-outlandish-character-humor first came to fruition as a member of Britain's surreal BBC radio program *The Goon Show* (1951–1960). The broadcasts were an ongoing collection of bizarre sketches and an equally bizarre use of language and sound, with chief credit going to its main writer and creator Spike Milligan and Sellers' talent for mimicry. This program was Sellers' launching pad to fame.

The show's zany brand of humor also had a major influence on such later celebrated comedy troupes as Monty Python, America's Firesign Theatre, and even the Beatles. John Lennon was particularly fascinated by *The Goon Show,* with his definitive biographer, Philip Norman, stating, "For [young teenage] John, between 1953 and 1955, [the *Goon* cast members] were the brightest spot in his whole existence."[9] The eccentric, often dark comedy influence is apparent in Lennon's essay collection *In His Own Write & A Spaniard in the Works*, especially the short story "No Flies on Frank," in which Frank takes his head off in order to club his wife."[10] The effect is also there in the Beatles' music. For example, another chronicler of the group, Steve Turner, said of their song "You Know My Name," when Lennon and Paul McCartney put the final touches on the number, it "sounded like a karaoke night in Hell, organized by the Goons...."[11]

Sellers, the Beatles, and theater of the absurd comedy had several other links. While living in London, the American performer-director Richard Lester, whose similar sense of humor quickly made him a fan and friend of the *Goon* players, began working with the troupe. In 1958 he managed to get a special *Goon Show* production on the BBC, and later directed a surrealistically slapstick short film produced by Sellers, *The Running, Jumping, and Standing Still Film* (1960). The Beatles loved the fragmented, sight gag–laden movie, and Lester ended up directing the musical group's inventively comic films *A Hard Day's Night* (1964) and *Help* (1965), as well as casting a solo Lennon in *How I Won the War* (1967). The Beatles pictures were so commercially successful, especially the critically acclaimed first one, that many reviewers felt the naturally witty group could easily have continued as a modern-day variation on the Marx Brothers. But whereas Groucho and company act crazy in a sane world, the Beatles were merely trying to be normal in Mad Hatter–ville. Unfortunately, the musical team's increasingly varied interests did not allow that to happen. However, as a provocative closer to the Sellers-Beatles connection, the group also managed to influence the comedian. Thus, coming full circle, the aforementioned chronicler Turner observed:

> Peter Sellers, once a member of John's favorite radio comedy group the Goons, recorded "A Hard Day's Night" by speaking the lyrics as if he was Laurence Olivier delivering a Shakespeare monologue. It made the British Top 20 in December 1965.[12]

Beyond Sellers' anti-genre lack of a specific personal comedian shtick, other than his periodic forays into Clouseau-land, his screen characters also placed less of a premium on physical and visual comedy (again excepting Clouseau) than is the screen clown norm. For radio-born Sellers, his characters started with the voice, and on *Being There* he worked for days with a tape recorder and his fourth wife Lynne to perfect the child-like minimalism of Chance's vocalization. This soft, slowly modulated speech pattern was pivotal to both the figure and the film itself. Otherwise, everything risked slipping into campiness—a one-joke movie. Paradoxically, when the thin American (Chance) voice, with a touch of English accent, finally came to Sellers, he later discerned it sounded like Stan Laurel speaking.[13] Thus, even here, Sellers felt he was not being original. Ironically, he had befriended Laurel late in the older comedian's life. And both men firmly believed in reincarnation.

Another anti-genre *Being There* blow to Sellers matching the personality comedian formula is his nominal use of a nomadic existence. For instance, when Laurel and Hardy turn up *Way Out West* (1937), or Chaplin's Tramp is skidding around a glacier in *The Gold Rush*'s (1925) frozen north, the incongruity of each situation is hilarious.[14] *Being There* is not without such instances, such as Chance being expelled from the Old Man's garden into the real world, or Sellers' simpleton appearing on a late night TV talk show. Yet his almost immediate quasi-adoption by Eve to live in another rich "old man's" mansion results in little physical change for Chance. People and events are more likely to come to him, including even a visit from the United States president (Jack Warden), via the chief executive's ties to Douglas' politically powerful character. Given that Chance takes his every cue from the nearest television, Sellers' figure is never in comically alien territory, as long as a proverbial "idiot box" is nearby.

The film parodies the feel-good populism associated with a Frank Capra movie, and/or pictures made from that mold.[15] Populism celebrates the belief that the superior and majority will of the common person is forever threatened by the usurping, sophisticated, evil few. The genre represents the classic underdog story, be it Capra's own *Mr. Smith Goes to Washington* (1939) or Julia Roberts' title turn as grassroots muckraker *Erin Brockovich* (2000). Populism suggests that one can just about pluck anyone from the democratic populace, and common sense egalitarianism will save the day. For instance, in Ivan Reitman's *Dave* (1993), Kevin Kline's everyman title character merely looks like the incapacitated crooked president, but in an entertainingly farfetched premise, he briefly and anonymously (rather like a Sellers character) steps into the White House and saves the country. When one gets past the sainted Abraham Lincoln, there are so many men and women "of the people" who are nothing more than homegrown demigods ready to lead naïve folks to a fascist fate. For every Lincoln, there are a dozen potential Huey Longs and Joseph McCarthys, and/or apprentice Sarah Palins. And when Sinclair Lewis warned of just such a danger in his prophetic 1935 book *It Can't Happen Here* (or, to bastardize Capra, *Mr. Totalitarianism Goes to Washington*), the novelist correctly warned in various ways that these false prophets would come wrapped in faultless Old Glory patriotism.[16]

Undoubtedly, Great Depression era Lewis was inspired by both the early 1930s rise of Adolf Hitler and populist Louisiana Senator Huey "The Kingfish" Long. Despite Long's assassination in 1935, real fascist fears continued in this country. Capra directed his own alarm bell version of a *It Can't Happen Here* when he did *Meet John Doe* (1941), in which a good but naïve Gary Cooper almost helps totalitarianism get a foothold in America.

An even more provocative Jekyll and Hyde anti-genre populism poser comes in Elia Kazan's *A Face in the Crowd* (1957, adapted by Budd Schulberg from his short story "The Arkansas Traveler"). The picture is a precautionary tale about both McCarthyism and the 1950s media market dangers inherent in the rise of television. The protagonist, Rhodes, coaches a potential presidential candidate on being more natural on television, like actor-director Robert Montgomery doing the same thing for candidate Dwight D. Eisenhower prior to his 1952 presidential run. The added good-evil duality of the Kazan film was a few years in the making, since *Crowd* was the film debut of Andy Griffith, three years prior to his hit homespun TV series *The Andy Griffith Show* (1960–1968).

In Kazan's picture the actor plays a charismatic singing hobo nicknamed "Lonesome Rhodes," who is discovered by Patricia Neal's small town Arkansas radio personality. Between her initial mentoring and Walter Matthau's radio staff writer, Rhodes' ad libbing earthiness soon makes him a national sensation. He quickly becomes an updated Huey Long equivalent packaged like a television Will Rogers, with Matthau's character writing an exposé entitled "Demagogue in Denim." However, "Lonesome" had already self-destructed on air by ranting about the stupidity of the people when he thought the audio of his television program had been cut during the closing credits.

Griffith's underrated *tour de force* performance as a monster populist radically clashes with the American Solomon–like Sheriff Andy Taylor the actor played on television throughout the 1960s. His marshal, who also doubled as the judge in Mayberry, North Carolina, was the model of crackerbarrel philosopher wisdom. A widower thoughtfully raising his son Opie (Ron Howard) in a household run by Aunt Bee (Frances Bavier), he kept things safe and sane in a sleepy small town whose greatest danger was probably his bumbling deputy Barney Fife (Don Knotts). So which Griffith is right—since American humor was initially anchored in a folksy common sense comedy stretching from Benjamin Franklin to Will Rogers? They are both correct, which is why one must be ever-vigilant, as well as explaining why some question the complete authenticity of Will Rogers (see Richard Schickel's *Elia Kazan: A Biography*, 2005) or label potential populist loose cannons "Lonesome Rhodes," as was once done with political commentator Glenn Beck.

An athletic analogy would be pertinent here, since sports (especially baseball) is often associated with populism.[17] Whether it is *Field of Dreams* (1989) or football's *Rudy* (1993) and *Remember the Titans* (2000), sports often makes true populism components like sacrifice and teamwork more palatable to an increasingly cynical audience. There is an old football axiom which, in the spirit of populist colloquialism, might best describe the genre's parameters: "Smash mouth" running game–focused football coaches tend to say, "When you pass the ball, only three things can happen, and two of them are bad—the hoped-for catch versus an interception or a dropped ball." In populism a similar triad applies. One could get Mayberry's angelic Andy Taylor, but there is a greater risk of getting either a Lonesome Rhodes or a sweetly gullible front for corruption like Capra's baseball-playing John Doe.

However, Sellers' *Chance* suddenly adds another negative mathematical option to the populism equation: What if the potential populist leader, which Chance has become by the end of the picture, is none of the previous types mentioned but rather, to recycle a portion of this chapter's opening description of him, a boob "stuffed with rice pudding between th' ears [and] dumb as a jackass"? And the learned (so-called) American overlords, such as Warden's president and his chief advisor (Douglas' Ben Rand), actually think chowderhead Chance is best for America's future?

To have a complete cipher as a populist president sets a new low—or is that a final dumbing down of America leadership? Of course, history has forever charted decline of earlier empires along related trajectories, be it the proverbial gene pool–scraping conclusions of past royal dynasties or societies so steeped in decadence (*à la* the hyperbolic tale of emperor Nero fiddling while Rome burned), that no one really cares. Whatever one's take about this dancing on the precipice, it leads to some provocative metaphorical "readings" of *Being There*, starting with the everpresent dark comedy death component.

The story is framed by the demise of powerful wealthy old men—Chance's likely father, and the movie's closing Ben Rand funeral, another even more powerful and wealthy ("rand" being a basic monetary unit of several countries) old man and Chance benefactor. Rand and company have been overly impressed with everything about Sellers' character, beginning with the modest minimalism of his verbiage seemingly peppered with Biblical, prophet-like parables. For instance, upon first meeting Warden's president, Chance randomly observes, "As long as the roots are not severed, all is well—and all *will* be well—in the garden." The chief executive, whose administration is suffering through a downturn in the economy, is startled by this comment, with Chance continuing, "In a garden, growth has its seasons. First comes spring and summer. But then we have fall and winter. And then we get spring and summer again." A still befuddled president attempts to make sense of Chance's comments, with Rand coming to the metaphorical rescue by stating, "I think what our young friend is saying is that we welcome the inevitable seasons of nature but we're upset by the seasons of our economy."

Both the book and the film manage to weave wisdom into Chance saying nothing at all. For instance, the Fourth Estate credits the illiterate character with a confident circumspection when he admits to having neither read the president's latest speech (which put Chance on the political map), nor even the positive reviews of this simpleton's appearance on television. Thus, the demise of two old men has unleashed a brainless childlike messiah on the earth and suggests a near future which embraces the subtitle of Vonnegut's *Slaughterhouse-Five: The Children's Crusade: A Duty Dance with Death*.

Being There pushes the proposition of a brainless, childlike torchbearer leading us all over the cliff like so many lemmings. And the latter term is not used lightly. More and more the general populace seems to be neither vetting and/or even voting during elections. Ironically, from time immemorial old men with seemingly some sense of intelligence have sent young men off to die for nebulous causes. Now, Kosinski and Ashby have cut out any sense of leadership comprehension. (In the novel, this Armageddon scenario is further accented by having the witless one actually be the age of an older child.)

A Chance-driven march to oblivion is anchored in a dark comedy absurdity beyond the norm—that the powers that be, the media, and the electorate should accept this idiot-

A most unlikely couple, Peter Sellers' Chance and Shirley MacLaine's Mrs. Rand.

squared person as the future—by a simple wild card change to the ending by Ashby. The novel closes with Chance meandering off into another garden after Rand's funeral. Kosinski doubles down on the character's cipher-like state by describing him as if he were just part of the vegetation: "Now and then, boughs rustled and gently shook off their drops of water. A breeze fell upon the foliage and nestled under the cover of its moist leaves. Not a thought lifted itself from Chance's brain. Peace filled his heart."[18]

Ashby essentially shot this close but added MacLaine's Eve finding him there. After the sequence was filmed, the director's screenwriter friend Rudy Wurlitzer asked him how the shoot was going. Ashby replied, "Peter Sellers and Melvyn Douglas are achieving such clarity, such simplicity, it looks like they're walking on water." It was a moment of inspiration. Ashby shot a new ending.[19]

The film now concludes with Chance walking out onto the garden's lake. Sellers' character slowly realizes that something is amiss. He then, without hurrying, places his umbrella well into the water, determining that he has not simply wandered onto some glorified puddle, and the picture concludes. One of Ashby's crew told him, " 'You can't have him walking on water.' I said, 'Why?' 'Well, you know the only person that walks on water.' 'I said, Jesus, or maybe some other godlike figure?' He said, 'Yes.' And I said, 'Well, what is wrong with childlike innocence being godlike?' You could break it down that way if you wanted to. Or, whatever [way you wanted]."[20]

With that one stroke, Ashby had taken an excellent dark comedy and ratcheted it into the stratosphere. I was reminded of how John Lennon and Paul McCartney co-signed all their Beatles songs; the tracks were written separately but then they got together and the non-composer frequently tweaked the song into something greater. This was precisely what had happened with *Being There*'s conclusion. Dark comedy absurdity is all about man's irrational institutions, especially religion. And all of Chance's Biblical-sounding blarney made him the perfect idiot foil for the genre's standard attack on the church. However, Ashby took Kosinski's lead and cemented the religious connection with Chance as an imbecilic Christ, or his code name in the novel—a double "Blank Page, Blank Page."[21] No genre handles absurdity as deftly as dark comedy, but this was a masterstroke. Jesus and God had rarely, if ever, been so negated in a movie, with the possible exception of God as a comatose homeless man by *Harold and Maude*'s Bud Cort in Kevin Smith's dark comedy *Dogma* (1999). By making Chance—even the name now makes more ironic sense—an idiot messiah, it suggests that God feels we are all foolish pawns in some celestial game that He will arbitrarily end.

Ashby has truly returned the viewer to this question of what is almost unspeakable. Like Samuel Beckett, the director has stumbled onto the concept of silence, as Chance quietly ignores and/or immediately forgets his umbrella experiment. That is, "No one has understood better than Beckett that silence is not an absence of sound but also [an absence of] a physical presence [like an absent or uncaring God]."[22] In previous pages, this silence is at the heart of most artists addressed herein—especially Woody Allen's *oeuvre*, by way of Ingmar Bergman.

If God is silent, or M.I.A., what of a more loquacious Satan? The close of *Being There* makes one think of Mark Twain's late fragmented novel, the posthumously published *The Mysterious Stranger* (1916). The time is 1590 and the title character visits the Austrian town of Eseldorf—which is roughly translated from the German as Stupidville, *à la* the world which believes in Chance. The setting is also essentially a stand-in for Twain's childhood home of Hannibal, Missouri, but could also double as Anywhere, Anytime Idiotville.

The title character, Satan, systematically dazzles and frightens some boys during periodic visits to their medieval town—an acknowledged age of ignorance and superstitious Christianity, a period Twain effectively attacked in his dark comedy *A Connecticut Yankee in King Arthur's Court* (1887). In *Stranger* the boys can be seen as variations upon Tom Sawyer, Huckleberry Finn and a young Twain (Samuel Clemens), or even a gullible humanity (symbolized by youngsters) in general, with Eseldorf as the world. Twain scholar Maxwell Geismar suggests the humorist is

> denigrating human beings to the point of not being worthy of Satan's or God's interest—of indeed having really created a monstrous God, an amiable but disinterested.... Satan. And quite like the Shakespeare of *The Tempest* ... Clemens was dismissing not only life itself but the life of his own artistic Kingdom! Even while [they] stood apart from their work as the Master Magicians who created and could just as easily obliterate it.[23]

The Mysterious Stranger is often told in the first person voice of a boy, as is *Huckleberry Finn* (1884), in which the title character also deals with his creator (Twain) and truth. For example, *Finn* opens:

> You don't know about me, without you have read a book by the name of *The Adventures of Tom Sawyer* [1876] but that ain't no matter. The book was made by Mr. Mark Twain, and he told the truth, mainly....[24]

The Mysterious Stranger concludes first with his revelations:

> It is true, that which I have revealed to you; there is no God, no universe, no human race, no earthly life, no heaven, no hell. It is all a dream—a grotesque and foolish dream. Nothing exists but you. And you are but a *thought*—a vagrant thought, a useless thought, a homeless thought wandering forlorn among the empty eternities! [The Stranger] left ... me appalled; for I knew, realized, that all he had said was true.[25]

This is Melville's "Bartleby, the Scrivener" (1856, see last chapter), or Beckett's *Waiting for Godot* (1952), with all of Kafka thrown in between. The Stranger's description of nothingness acutely suggests the close of *Being There*. Because Chance, whether divinity or doofus, seems to be fading into plant life, which is also reflected in the film's poster art. Interestingly, though Maude (Ruth Gordon) of Ashby's *Harold and Maude* is no doofus, her pantheistic philosophy of essentially cosmic recycling with no God does draw some parallels with the Stranger's nothingness. *Being There* pushes the envelope further by saying that nothing matters because there is nothing—the Stranger's definition of a non-life as a "foolish dream." The last words of the film are, "Life is a state of mind," which was also *Being There*'s marketing mantra.

One could apply the "it was all a dream" proposal to Chance's absurd TV perception of the world. He cannot tell the difference between the small screen and what passes for *Being There* reality. This is ingeniously demonstrated in the sequence just after Chance has been evicted from the Old Man's mansion. Once a fashionable part of Washington, D.C., the stately home is now in a ghetto. When Chance engages a street gang in some simple-minded conversation, they think he is giving them attitude, and a young thug draws a knife. It is all for effect; Chance is never in danger. Yet, since this Stan Laurel–like character also matches the older comedian's definition of Stan and Ollie's mentality, "Two minds without a single thought," Chance is frightened.[26] To protect himself, he produces a TV remote control and points it at the gang and presses the channel control. For Sellers' character, he has come across a scary small screen program, and now he will escape by changing channels. Such is the dream-like world of Chance ... and the satirical suggestion that this is the fate which awaits everyone after prolonged exposure to the proverbial "idiot box."

Absurdity abounds in *Being There*, starting with the simple fact that society's best and brightest (and one should use the phrase loosely) could be so easily fooled by a minimalist, babble-talking zero. But perhaps that is life, or the dream-nightmare—an unexamined life adds up to nothing. One might call it the "Sarah Palin Fate." Did a major modern political party really push for a Chance-like character potentially to lead the nation, or was that a mere fleeting hallucination? Oops, I just described the plot of *Being There*. Nonetheless, Twain's late work, such as *The Mysterious Stranger*, made his egalitarianism increasingly contemptuous of mankind's gross stupidity concerning racism, nationalism, and invisible deities. Twain could comically semi-lighten the savaging of what his Stranger would call the "nothing" and/or netherworld, too. For example, when robber baron industrialist Andrew Carnegie told Twain, "America was a Christian nation," the humorist replied, "Why, Carnegie, so is hell."[27]

Since dark comedy hits the jackpot by pulling back the veil of absurdity via institutions, *Being There*'s continuing shish-kebabbing of religion merits further trolling. Biblical allusions abound in the film, whether it is being cast out of the garden and parable-like expressions, or walking on water. Another significant but less obvious link is Chance's frequent statement, "I like to watch." Though a dark comedy reference to Chance's constant TV viewing, Ashby has also managed to pull sexual innuendo jokes from it, involving both Shirley MacLaine's Eve, and a gay diplomatic guest at a Soviet Union reception.

"I like to watch," however, is decodeable. If one factors in Chance's water-walking escapade, God is neither capable nor concerned with earth. Also, given that Eve successfully masturbates because Chance has simply stated "I like to watch" is further proof of how easily people attribute significant acts to a belief in "drinking the Kool-Aid" quasi-religious comments. Moreover, even if God is quiet because He either does not care, or exist, the brief nothingness of man has had no reservations jabbering gobbledygook explanation for Him throughout time. Fear drives everything, and the false security blanket comfort of religion and other institutions calms the apprehensions of the masses. That is the secret behind the swift embrace of Chance by all who meet him in *Being There*—people want a quick fix for innumerable fears.

Dark comedy's "man as beast" component in *Being There* might not seem as obvious, but look again. The president's eulogy for Ben Rand validates what discerning viewers have long suspected: Douglas' character is an Ayn Rand disciple, even sharing the same name. The earlier "rand" association with money was a not unimportant shorthand for his wealth. But the link to novelist Rand and such works as *The Fountainhead* (1943) and *Atlas Shrugged* (1957) is, from a humanist's perspective, abominable. Ayn Rand's jump-starting of the Libertarian movement and reactionary conservatism (but of a 1940s strain even more vitriolic than today) is a philosophy of "radical capitalism" and "rational selfishness."[28] That is, it expounds that if an individual cannot pull oneself up by the bootstraps, he or she be damned. No account is made for those who were never gifted with any metaphorical bootstraps. Thus, Ben Rand is the most monstrous of villains, made all the more chilling by his courtly, well-mannered, grandfather-like demeanor. And this is yet one more way that old man Rand is like the unnamed Old Man who opens the story— the apparent father of Chance, who never made any contingency plans for his special needs child-man. Such Rand–like characters (think of Jon Voight's Milo in *Catch-22*, 1970) are both right at home in dark comedies and deserve partial credit and/or blame for being architects of the genre. While the Old Man deprived Chance of love and early developmental needs, Rand (whom the film acknowledges as a kingmaker) has created the more dangerous situation: the opening of a Pandora's box of potential abhorrent populist possibilities.

Douglas' nuanced performance as Rand won him an Oscar as Best Supporting Actor, and represents an unbeatable transition to *Being There*'s backstory. Sellers and Douglas had struck up a friendship during World War II: Both were stationed in Burma when the older actor was already a long established Hollywood star, and the young Brit was a wannabe performer. Other actors were briefly considered for the part including Laurence Olivier—but he preferred not to play a part which involved Shirley MacLaine masturbating for his benefit. Sellers pushed hard for Douglas' casting, a fitting reward for yet another artist blacklisted by the McCarthyism 1950s.

Ironically, the bigger casting long shot was Sellers getting to play Chance. He had essentially auditioned for the part throughout the 1970s:

> Sellers was obsessed with a nobody [Chance] who became a somebody nobody could really know. As his secretary Sue Evans once said, "You have to understand that *Being There* was a daily conversation." [The novelist's author] Jerzy Kosinski concurred, "For seven and a half years [1973–1979], Peter Sellers become Chauncey Gardiner. He printed calling cards as Chauncey Gardiner. He signed letters Chauncey Gardiner.[29]

The novel constantly describes Chance's handsomeness: "Manly; well-groomed; beautiful voice; sort of a cross between Ted Kennedy and Cary Grant."[30] But by the time the movie was made, Sellers was nearing his mid–50s. However, he had an ace in the hole for getting the part. The actor later shared, "When I read *Being There*, I was crazy about it. I had just seen *Harold and Maude* [1971], which I thought was sensational, so I rushed a copy of the book to Ashby."[31] Unfortunately, neither artist was then in a position to adapt the novel, which Ashby immediately enjoyed, too. Thus, as Sellers recalled:

> [Ashby and I] made a promise to each other that if we ever got a break with it, he would come to me, or I would come to him. And suddenly [1978] Hal phoned me one day in Vienna, and said, "I hesitate to say this but I think we've got it off the ground. It's really going to go."[32]

This is consistent with Ashby's memory of the project. Because Sellers had first made him aware of Kosinski's wonderful novel, the director was loyal to the actor. Later when a producer, unaware of the project's history asked, "Would you be interested in doing this thing called *Being There*?" Ashby said, "Absolutely. But I wouldn't do it with anybody but Peter Sellers."[33]

Shirley MacLaine took a supporting role in *Being There* "just to see a genius [Sellers] at work."[34] Both performers believed in reincarnation, and how that had sometimes assisted them in playing parts they had once lived. But while always pleasant to the actress, Sellers forever turned down her invitations to lunch together. The explanation was that Sellers, not one normally to take Method acting to such extremes, attempted to stay in character throughout the shoot. Ashby provides an entertaining tribute during the closing credits by some outtakes in which Sellers breaks up trying to maintain that fine line between the slow, measured voice of a believable simpleton and something which could easily slip into unintended campiness.

Possibly an explanation for Sellers' extreme focus can be found in a remark he repeatedly made in his last years which can be paraphrased as, "I think I have one more great role in me." If that seems overly melodramatic, keep in mind the actor had had more than one serious heart attack, was fitted with a pacemaker, and made no attempt to change a self-destructive lifestyle.

Sellers' obsession with playing Chance still bordered upon the dark comedy absurdity of many fictionalized incidents examined in the text. For example, despite Ashby's demand for Sellers, Kosinski was not initially convinced. He preferred casting young pretty boy Ryan O'Neal, who more closely resembled the novel's Chance. Sellers was unrelenting in his attempts to win over the writer. Kosinski confessed that shortly after the novel was published, he received the following cable: "Available my garden or outside it. C. Gardiner."[35] The telephone number attached to the correspondence turned out to be Sellers.' What follows is Kosinski's description of how he was finally won over:

> Every time I met Peter Sellers over the years he would devote half of our meeting to portray Chauncey Gardiner. Once we were in a hotel room suite with a lot of guests, and he physically moved to one side so he could turn on the television. Once he sat in front of a set that wasn't turned on and chided a waiter who interfered with his view. "Can't you see I'm watching?" he said. The waiter apologized. Nobody even caught on to what he was doing, just as nobody in the novel ever realized that Gardiner had no substance.[36]

Acclaim came Sellers' way for playing Chance, but had the actor's casting helped or hindered the movie? First, given the minimalist control and focus which the actor brought to the part, it is hard to believe such a nuanced performance could have been drawn from anyone else, let alone young Ryan O'Neal. Plus, the quick acceptance of Chance, with his Biblical-style all-knowing dialogue, is more easily believable by an in-film cultured, establishment, inherently conservative audience. Moreover, as the actor frequently noted in interviews, if Chance had lived a largely sedimentary life for a number of years, he would be an older, overweight figure. (Sellers gained weight for the role.) In addition, he was more age appropriate for the romantic relationship orchestrated by a dying Rand. The only potential downside to Sellers as Chance is that O'Neal would have approximated Jesus' age during his early ministry. Thus, the darkly comic walk-on-the water sequence would have had even more bite.

Being There made Ashby one of *the* 1970s directors. Kosinski himself had been attracted to Ashby as a socially responsible American director: "I think [Ashby] brings the social concern of his movies *Coming Home* and *The Last Detail*. He is also the ultimately American director.... I think this is a very American story, and I wanted someone whose every fiber is American as it can be, to direct."[37]

Ashby ran a communal set, with anyone free to make suggestions, and he had an actor-friendly style. He was an auteur despite not making films which had the distinctive look of a John Ford Western or a cultish Tim Burton picture. Unfortunately, this often resulted in the left-handed labeling of Ashby as a "craftsman" ... but *not* an auteur.[38] All this is not to say his work was without flair, such as an editing style which often featured form and advanced sound cuts (best showcased in *Harold and Maude*). He won a Best Editor Oscar for the Norman Jewison–directed *In the Heat of the Night* (1967).

But the true measure of an auteur is consistent themes and characters—something seen again and again in the *reel* world of Ashby. His movies invariably have a central child-adult character whose youth and/or circumstances have resulted in a very sheltered existence. This text has demonstrated the phenomenon with both Bud Cort's Harold and Sellers' Chance. But it is equally true of Randy Quaid's foolishly simple sailor in Ashby's *The Last Detail* (1973) and Jane Fonda's naïve Marine wife in *Coming Home* (1978), a film for which Ashby received a Best Director Academy Award nomination. These rudderless types are all in need of a mentoring figure to rectify their situations—unless each one is truly "the homeless thought" of Twain's *Mysterious Stranger*. Ashby's auteur tendencies befit a director whose forte is dark comedy. Despite the open-ended promise of *Harold and Maude*, the other film noir pictures, like *Chinatown* (1974), often suggest that good-intentioned kindness only makes things worse. Even *Coming Home*'s positive makeover of Fonda contributes to the film's closing suicide of her husband (Bruce Dern).

In the Ashby dark comedies, *Harold and Maude* and *Being There*, a warped supernatural game seems to be in play. With Chance as a cypher Christ-God, the fate of humanity is best defined with Twain's favored axiom "that damned human race." But the figure of Maude (Ruth Gordon) is a puzzle. Thirty-five–plus years of speculation by my college students, not to mention some critics, have lobbied that Maude has a non-divine immortality about herself on several counts. First, her basic mindset is a curious notion of civil disobedience, including grand theft auto, smoking dope, and casual anarchy. Second, she definitely does not believe in a future of harps and angels, or, as Mark Twain observed, "One of the proofs of the immortality of the soul is that myriads have believed in it. They have also believed the world was flat."[39] Maude's comments and insinuations about returning to the physical cosmos could be interpreted as a New Age pantheist nothingness. Most importantly, the viewer never actually sees her die, and she seems as lively as ever at the end. While Harold is definitely convinced that Maude has expired, one might liken her to Milton's mischievous Satan in *Paradise Lost* (1667), a figure more entertainingly reasonable than the poet's distant God.

Being There was a major critical hit, though a muddled ad campaign only made it a modest commercial success. Its dark comedy cult status has grown and generated further revenue since its initial release. Sellers almost joined Douglas in the Oscar circle, only to lose in a major Best Actor category upset to Dustin Hoffman in *Kramer vs. Kramer* (1979). To paraphrase later comments by Hoffman, "I just assumed Sellers had it won," though in his acceptance speech Hoffman had diplomatically added, "I refuse to believe that I beat Jack Lemmon [*The China Syndrome*] and Al Pacino [*... And Justice for All*]..."[40]

Academy Awards have so many intangibles beyond the performance itself, including an actor's age, having been passed over many times before, some sentimental twist, how well the picture did at the box office, and additional factors *ad nauseam*. In *Being There*'s case, as much as Sellers had always wanted to win a statuette, like many Brits of his generation, in the past he had not always been positive about Hollywood. Moreover, despite being most accommodating during the production, a regular Chance, Sellers had often been the proverbial diva in past years; so many potentially helpful bridges had been burned. Still, what remains is that he had given that one last great performance he had hoped to leave before dying the following year (1980). However, unlike his two other greatest performances, both with the Beckett ilk (in Stanley Kubrick's *Lolita*, 1962, and *Dr. Strangelove*, 1964), Chance in *Being There* did *not* have that inner scream. Like Billie Whitelow's part in Beckett's *Rockaby*, Chance had somehow "banished life from ... expression [leaving] a death mask so devoid of blood it could be a faded, crumbling photograph."[41] Ironically, he saw Chance as the "ultimate Peter Sellers ... [the aforementioned] figure of contemporary life, a blank disembodied observer ... [so much like the uncaring Twain God]."[42] As critic Paul Hyman noted, cypher Chance always said, "'I understand'—but he [was] nowhere close."[43] Beckett has seldom been better capsulized.

An air of Beckett and Twain also surfaces in the *London Observer*'s matchless summarization of *Being There*: "The simple-minded message is that you don't need to bother about fooling all the people all the time, because they'll do it for you."[44] Thus, one has an inspired derailment of Lincoln's alleged populist (dark comedy's mirror opposite genre) credo, "You can fool some of the people all of the time but you cannot fool all the people all of the time."[45] Of course, if one were determined to have a period mantra close to the suspect Lincolnesque quota, get colored with black humor reality, one need go no further than the hyperbolic line credited to huckster P.T. Barnum, "You can fool some of the people all of the time, and all of the people some of the time.... [But] you can fool too many of the people too much of the time."

Regardless, *Being There* generated the same positive reviews as the novel. As with the film, the novel critiques recognized the ugly inclinations of the story. *The London Times* stated of the novel, "It takes intrusive outsiders like [Polish-born] Jerzy Kosinski to show insiders what they are really like. Kosinski's wryly horrified little parable—hits where it hurts, right on the bottom, again and again."[46] Like the novel, the adaptation "modestly [also] parodies the myth of the Natural Man."[47] The *New York Times* said of the film:

> *Being There* is a stately, beautifully acted satire ... Ashby directs ... at an unruffled, elegant pace, the better to let Mr. Sellers' double-edged mannerisms make their full impression upon the audience. Mr. Sellers never makes a false note, as he exhibits the kind of naïveté that the film's other characters mistake for [wise] eccentricity.[48]

The Nation's praise flirts with the inherent dark comedy horrific warnings of the picture:

> *Being There* is as spooky a film as I've seen in some time. It is also a socio-political satire and a tour de force by Peter Sellers. It is quite absurd, utterly fantastic, more than a little uncomfortable—a very nettle of foolishness.[49]

The sagacity of *Being There* wants the reader-viewer to believe Kosinski-Ashby could join "the select band of survivor poets whose work is adequate to the destructive reality we inhabit."[50] A less than optimistic-for-humanity Kosinski said of the film, "Sellers gives a medically correct portrayal of what your children are going to be like—restrictive, non-verbal, passive."[51]

Ashby made a more hopeful observation about the possible box office of *Being There* even before the shooting began. Since *New York Times* critic Aljean Harmetz rightfully saw Kosinski's book as similar to the anti-genre dark comedy novels *Catch–22* and *Slaughterhouse-Five*, she asked the director if he had commercial concerns about *Being There*. Ashby responded, "I think we have a better chance because *Being There* is not on as large a scale. [The other two] took on the whole war."[52] His prediction proved true though, sad to say, more patrons does not guarantee more thinking. Additionally, Ashby might have noted *Being There*'s auxiliary dark comedy jab at the idiot box called TV. Chance represents an extreme example of how obsessive TV viewing continues to dumb down society, a gloomy state of affairs indeed. Yet some period critics still did not fully appreciate this message—a lack of shock which makes it more shocking. For example, the *New York Sunday News* reviewer glibly observed: "I love this film. I love the story. It's about people hearing what they want to hear, seeing what they want to see. And a perfectly adorable, charming idiot who walks through life just being himself."[53]

Unlike an eleventh hour rescue conclusion from a world of robotic pod people duplications in the original *Invasion of the Body Snatchers* (1956), there is now *no* stopping all the new Chances growing among us. In fact, early in Kosinski's novel, when he described Chance as going "through phases, as garden plants went through stages," I was reminded of how the *Body Snatchers* pods often grew in garden settings.[54] Ironically, while the original pod sci-fi story was driven by 1950s McCarthy-era paranoia about external communism, the current sorry development is all of our own making. The even more blank slate of modern society might be described in the opening line of Poet Laureate Mark Strand's "Remains": "I empty myself of the names of others. I [even] empty my pockets" (from a poetry collection also of the 1970s and fittingly called *Darker*).[55] But such is the absurdity of black humor, where death is the essential human story.

One cannot close the chapter, however, without an addendum concerning Werner Herzog's *The Enigma of Kaspar* (1974, also more fittingly known as *Every Man for Himself and God Against All*). Loosely based upon a true story of a young man (Kaspar) mysteriously kept in confinement from birth, only to be left in the streets of 1820s Nuremberg (Germany) by a wealthy father (God?) in black. Lack of human contact had made him seem like Chance—to be intellectually impaired. Yet his state of "absolute [mental] confusion" did not fool the public, as in *Being There*. Yet, again like Chance, this puzzling figure both finds a rich benefactor and fascinates the public. And as Kaspar receives some education, his metaphorical observations receive attention, as did Chance's. One such Kaspar story involves a caravan of people climbing a mountain with Death looking on. Soon after, Kaspar is found stabbed, after having been told to watch the garden. Though this attack, and a second fatal assault, occur without witnesses, Kaspar will claim it is the father in black.

Depiste the parallels with Chance, this darker conclusion is more reminiscent of Twain's *Mysterious Stranger*, who is a devilish harbinger of nihilism, like Kaspar's vision of death on the mountain. Either way, one has Chance as a halfwit Jesus incapable of helping humanity, or Kaspar as the son of Twain's literary Beelzebub—the demonic Fly (a.k.a. "Lord of the Flies"), who torments humanity for humor. So much for any comforting thoughts on life and death as we know it.

12

All That Jazz (12/20/79)

> [*All That Jazz*] is an uproarious display of brilliance, nerve, dance ... and ego. It's a little bit as if Mr. Fosse had invited us to attend his funeral—the wildest show-business send-up a fellow ever designed for himself—and then appeared at the door to sell tickets and count the house; after all, funerals are wasted on the dead.
> —Vincent Canby, *New York Times* (December 20, 1979)[1]

How apt that chronologically the film that best represents this study's genre-bending, genre-crossing 1970s dark comedies should surface at the eleventh hour of the decade. *All That Jazz* is both the most densely populated dark comedy considered between these covers, as well as the one that sends up the most camouflaging other genres. But in all this postmodern fragmentation, each of the directors of this book's twelve focus films, going back to Robert Altman's comments in Chapter 1 on *MASH* (1970), speak about anti-genre filmmaking coming to a dark comedy fruition during that decade. For instance, here is Fosse's take on the experience:

> [He] feels that some moviegoers are confused by [*All That Jazz*] because it doesn't fit into a familiar category. "It is off-beat. Some people are locked into certain channels of thinking. They're rigid. They think you shouldn't show an operation in a musical.... I accomplished what I set out to do, to move people out of the ordinary movie experience."[2]

Before diving into *Jazz*'s abundant illustrations of nuanced dark comedy, there is the always engaging task of scrutinizing the profusion of anti-genre distractions leading to its black humor core. One naturally starts with the musical, or in this case, the anti-musical. To avoid rehashing a terrain already mined in Fosse's *Cabaret* (1972, see Chapter 5), this will be brief. Technically, among all the musical sub-genres, *Jazz* is a backstage story, probably most synonymous for modern audiences with *A Chorus Line* (1985, adapted from the long-running Broadway production first staged in 1975). Nevertheless, just as *Cabaret* was a backstage story which focused on a most atypical subject for traditional musicals (politics and Nazis), *Jazz*'s unorthodox lynchpin is death, or as *Playboy* critic Bruce Williamson engagingly put it, "When was the last time anyone made a big musical about a coronary seizure, especially one that proved fatal?"[3]

At this point in the text one might complain, "Sure there's singing and dancing, but we all know this is a dark comedy. All these alleged anti-genre smokescreens and cover-ups for black humor aren't fooling anyone." You would be wrong. For example, Janet Maslin, one of the country's most esteemed critics and a pioneering defender of early dark comedy, failed to recognize the genre in *All That Jazz*. Her *New York Times* "Sifting Flaws" essay complained, "Once Mr. Fosse shows his audience close-up footage of actual open-heart surgery, he might as well pack up his tents and go home.... People don't go to the movies to watch open-heart surgery—it's as simple as that. A miscalculation this violent becomes unforgivable."[4]

One would have thought dark comedy's seemingly breakthrough surgery sequences in *MASH* would have more than set the (operating) table for Fosse's use of such subject matter. Yet, all genres are gradually morphing into new configurations, like Alfred Hitchcock's *Psycho* and Michael Powell's *Peeping Tom* (both 1960) helping nudge horror films towards more contemporary settings, notwithstanding the 1940s B-producer Val Lewton.[5] Dark comedy even manages to out-shock shocking horror in its sudden transformations to something darker. Ironically, *MASH* is a much more surgically bloody movie than *All That Jazz*, but the latter picture includes a single sequence which pushes the medical template too close to reality for some viewers, despite almost an absence of plasma.

Jazz's second anti-genre distraction from dark comedy comes from its "profile" nature—it's a movie which could almost double as a biography. Yet, unlike Orson Welles playing this game in *Citizen Kane*, the 1941 movie that tells a tale very similar to the epic life of newspaper publisher William Randolph Hearst, Fosse twists the twist of a profile picture being a biography by making *Jazz* about himself. This diversion from dark comedy is not unlike what Woody Allen does in *Love and Death* (1975) and *Annie Hall* (1977). Fosse biographer Kevin Boyd Grubb briefly notes parallels between *Jazz* and *Love and Death*, especially the "obvious connections between falling in love and dying."[6] All three movies are by directors synonymous with New York, all of whom play distractingly closely on their own lives. They underline these autobiographical flourishes with fantasy flashbacks often close to reality, which also embraces a dark comedy basic, a disjointed narrative. Each artist's philosophy could be reduced to three options: bad, worse and terrible. Fosse and Allen egotistically contemplate their own deaths, but these Chaplin fans always do it with an iconoclastic sense of humor, such as a dying Joe Gideon (Roy Scheider as Fosse) looking towards the heavens and saying, "What's the matter, don't you like musical comedy?" Plus, each cinematic surrogate is frequently wracked with guilt ... but he does *not* let it disrupt his work. Paradoxically, instead it often becomes part of the art, such as Allen's play within the film at the close of *Annie Hall*, or Gideon's girlfriend in the movie and life (Ann Reinking) telling him during an argument, "Oh, you give all right, presents, clothes. I just wish you weren't so generous with your cock." The latter comment does not remotely generate anger in Gideon-Fosse. Instead, he immediately goes into a contemplative mode and says, "That's good. I can use that." Finally, though both Fosse and Allen are uniquely successful in their work, they frequently pummel show business, from Allen's *Annie Hall* disgust over laugh tracks and pointless award shows, to Fosse's devastatingly cold close to *Jazz*: Gideon being zipped into a body bag while Ethel Merman belts out her theme song "There's No Business Like Show Business" on the soundtrack.

After *Jazz* was released, Fosse persistently denied that the film was autobiographical. However, he soon confessed:

> I'm afraid of saying [it *is* autobiographical] because people have used the word "self-indulgent" about the film. But critics are constantly saying that an artist should draw more from himself and less from others. This is what I've done. So why do I get this reaction? It frightens me. That is why I keep disclaiming.[7]

Shirley MacLaine, a Fosse friend who had starred in the director's underrated *Sweet Charity* (1969), had insightfully turned down the pivotal role of Gideon's ex-wife because she felt her star quality would distract from *Jazz*'s overall story—though she goaded the director with her "star quality" phrasing, since he had once used the same reason for not casting her in another project. Concerning the film's autobiographical start, she added, "He had been attracted to his own death for many years. In fact, his greatest film [*Jazz*] was a depiction of just that. The erotica of his demise, *All That Jazz*."[8] Playing upon MacLaine's "erotica of his demise" statement, what follows is Fosse addressing that very subject:

> Casting Jessica Lange [a former Fosse lover] as the Angel of Death comes from a personal fantasy. For me, many times, Death has been a beautiful woman. When you think something's about to happen to you in a car or an airplane, coming close to The End, this is the flash I'll get—a woman dressed [sexually as death].[9]

Shirley MacLaine and Bob Fosse on the set of *Sweet Charity* (1969).

Gideon (Roy Scheider) and *his* Angel of Death, Angelique (Jessica Lange).

The idea of *Jazz* as a Fosse profile–autobiographical film is best demonstrated by a short dual focus backstory on both his life and the pre-production research done for the picture. *Jazz* is based upon Fosse's 1975 manic attempt to edit his biography film of pioneering black comedy comedian Lenny Bruce *Lenny*, while simultaneously staging the dark comedy musical *Chicago* on Broadway. The workaholic had two heart attacks and nearly died. In *Jazz* his character attempts to edit the death-driven movie *The Stand-Up* (starring Cliff Gorman, who played Lenny on Broadway) while mounting a satirically sexy stage musical on the Great White Way. Gideon, his film alter ego, also has two heart attacks, and then he dies.

Though the Fosse-Gideon parallels could be referenced indefinitely, they are best summarized by the second part of the backstory—the pre-production Fosse process:

> [A]s research for *All That Jazz*, he and [producer] Bob Aurthur were going to interview everyone who knew him or had been working or dealing with him at the time of his heart attack[s]. As [Aurthur's wife] Jane said, "The two Bobs were just nutty, going around with tape recorders asking everyone, 'What were you doing while Bobby [Fosse] was in the hospital?' 'What did you think?'"[10]

One must add that when Richard Dreyfuss broke his contract to play Gideon, Fosse briefly proposed playing the part himself. But he was never taken seriously by the moneymen for a variety of reasons, from the director's age (he was in his 50s) and health (heart-related), to critics crucifying the picture as too much of a vanity piece. However, one might ask, with good reason, why in the world sign the short, stocky non-dancer Dreyfuss (born 1947) to play the lean, nearly Fred Astaire–talented Fosse? As Fosse biographer Sam Watson noted:

Released only two weeks apart, [the Dreyfuss-starring] *Goodbye Girl* and *Close Encounters of the Third Kind* [both 1977] showed his mastery of the manic yet likable intensity that Gideon needed. A dancing Dreyfuss wouldn't be a problem—Fosse could cheat that if the performance was strong enough....[11]

Dreyfuss put it bluntly and honestly when he confessed, "I can't get up there with my big Jewish ass and try to be a dancer.... I don't like Fosse and he doesn't like me. I just don't feel mentally prepared to do this thing."[12]

A paradoxical irony thus occurs. In the recasting of *Jazz*'s Gideon with Roy Scheider, the film actually further reinforces the correlation between the director and his screen persona. Scheider, while more handsome, bears an actual (tall, lean) resemblance to Fosse. Moreover, he better understood the most basic of profile and/or autobiographical rules. Scheider was eagerly and earnestly agreeable to whatever Fosse suggested, whether it was about the part or his working methods.[13] Scheider, then best known as an action hero in such films as *The French Connection* (1971), *Jaws* (1975, with Dreyfuss), and *Marathon Man* (1976), was "mentally prepared" to stretch his acting résumé. While not a dancer, he had been an outstanding multi-talented athlete (including an exceptional Golden Gloves career), which was a major factor in Fosse casting him. Scheider quickly became Fosse's shadow. The film's rehearsal pianist, Don Rebic, chronicled both the actor's dedication and his growing friendship with the director:

> Roy was so committed, if he was there during one of Fosse's coughing fits, he'd follow Bob out into the bathroom. Then Bob would return with a cigarette. Roy too. Fosse worked on Scheider's cough like it was a monologue, bringing him down to a deeper, gutsier hack—his own. They laughed while they did it, rehearsing dying to perfection.[14]

Roy Scheider *is* Gideon-Fosse.

Even when *Jazz* had a brief bleep away from the real Fosse, with the initial Dreyfuss casting, something like kismet brought it back in line. The production accomplished with Scheider what Virginia Woolf understand to be the artist's hardest task: "Few capture the phantom [of a character]."[15] Scheider's performance would garner him a Best Actor Oscar nomination, though Dustin Hoffman would take the statuette for *Kramer vs. Kramer* (1979).

If ever a movie involved raised issues, it was this one: Why are we here? What comes next? Are you your own executioner? How does one stay sane knowing that life never gets beyond the rehearsal stage? Since death is the brass ring for the genre *à la* Ingmar Bergman's *The Seventh Seal* (1957), still arguably the template for art house films, Fosse's first anti-genre gesture towards this cinema type is breaking the stereotypical image of death. Instead of the hoary likeness of a Grim Reaper shrouded in black, Fosse's figure is a sexy woman in white, Angelique (Lange).

Fosse's second anti-genre approach to the art house film embellishes his Angelique touch by often initially giving serious themes a seemingly superficial façade. For example, while *Jazz* offers a soft touch opening to the most somber of situations, Peter Weir's classic example of the genre, *Dead Poets Society* (1989), has Robin Williams' prep school instructor immediately challenging his conservatively sheltered students with a *carpe diem* (seize the day) teaching style. He wants his young charges to "make their lives extraordinary." And keep in mind, Bergman promptly put his *Seventh Seal* knight in a game with death for answers to questions forever fated to be enigmas. Fosse's approach, however, is more sadly typical: The unexamined life is less wrought with pain for most people. Or as the complete title of Alejandro G. Iñárritu's ingenious 2014 dark comedy put it, *Birdman or (The Unexpected Virtue of Ignorance)*. One could go back a decade for a variation on this position with Charlie Kaufman's equally brilliant script to *Eternal Sunshine of the Spotless Mind* (2004), a dark comedy hiding behind a science fiction-romantic comedy base. Except here, the telling subtitle is about the ability to erase bad, often relationship-related memories. Consequently, when *Jazz*'s veiled anti-genre art house moment finally arrives (with Fosse still cloaking it in his "old razzle-dazzle as long as possible"), and Gideon must face his self-centered life and death, it packs more power. Ironically, just as this genre has helped to disguise *Jazz*'s dark comedy core, Fosse even camouflages this camouflage for much of the picture.

Fosse's final anti-genre utilization of the art house film involves humanism, a frequent ingredient of this sort of picture—for example, Julian Schnabel's poignant adaptation of Jean Dominique Bauby's haunting memoir *The Diving Bell and the Butterfly* (2007). Yet again, the catalyst for the depiction of the genre opens the picture. The time is late 1995, just as French fashion editor Bauby is awakening from a stroke so severe that he was left permanently paralyzed and speechless—a prisoner of what medical science call the "locked-in syndrome." With his mental facilities remaining intact, Bauby's only means of communicating was by blinking his left eye. Staggeringly, he managed to dictate his memoir by blinking when the correct letter was spoken by an assistant slowly going through an abbreviated alphabet (most frequently used letters) over and over again. Bauby's feat of "writing" this uplifting (butterfly-like) text, despite the almost "diving bell" death sentence of a stroke, is miles away from Fosse's questioning dark comedy. Yet the "locked-in syndrome" describes both artists' final days—"It was all about the work"— which was also essentially Gideon's mantra. Fosse has managed yet again to apply his anti-genre talents to an art house picture by draining it of the humanistic compassion one feels for the central character.

Fosse felt so strongly about underlining the negative perspective of his *Jazz* alter ego that the director piled on unsympathetic characteristics. And since Fosse revered John Huston and credited his own montage musical style to the older director's *Moulin Rouge* (1952), it is conceivable that Huston also contributed to Fosse's self-deprecating depiction of Gideon. The possible parallel comes from novelist Peter Viertel's *White Hunter Black Heart* (1953), based upon the making of Huston's *The African Queen* (1951, on which Viertel played script doctor).[16] The writer later confessed

> how he nervously approached John Huston to discuss the barely disguised description of him in the filming of *The African Queen* for *White Hunter*. He had portrayed the fictionalized director as obsessed with hunting elephants [which Huston was] at the expense of the movie, not to mention common sense. Not only did Mr. Huston not object, he offered to sign a release without even reading the unpublished book. After reading it, Mr. Huston proposed an ending that made the director appear even crueler than in Mr. Viertel's original ending. Mr. Viertel used it.[17]

If this Fosse-Huston influence seems tenuous, again, keep in mind Fosse's feeling for Huston's work. And beyond the aforementioned *Moulin Rouge* influencing Fosse's later montage musical, the picture was one of the younger man's favorite screen musicals. However, the topper to all this is that Fosse scholars have somehow failed actually to view Huston's *Moulin Rouge*, the colorful story of 19th century Parisian painter Henri de Toulouse-Lautrec. Yes, the inspiration for Fosse's montage musical style is there. But of equal yet unacknowledged importance is that Huston portrays Toulouse-Lautrec's death as a hallucination of the big razzle-dazzle shows that so influenced his art—a smaller scale of what Fosse precisely did to end *Jazz*! This represents a major omission from earlier Fosse studies, and suggests that a closer Huston reading of the former artist's work merits consideration.

Regardless of any lingering Huston influence, a final *Jazz* postscript is necessary in discussing Fosse-Gideon the terrible. There are moments in the movie, especially involving his screen daughter Michelle (Eisébet Földi), in which a softer man momentarily slips through. As *Nation* critic Nora Sayre observed, "As far as this Fosse doppelgänger, I've rarely seen a film that so closely absolved a character who claims to be culpable."[18]

Now comes the fun of moving beyond Fosse's often flamboyant anti-genre distractions to *Jazz*'s dark comedy nucleus. In starting with the genre's close link to death, one must first step back briefly for some additional pre-production *Jazz* information. Otherwise, one risks today's ever-growing problem of "words [which] cannot wait for thoughts."[19] Regardless, the film is generally seen as Fosse's *8½* (1963, Federico Fellini's intensely personal movie about a director struggling with a new undertaking). Scheider shared:

> When I first read the script I thought: "This is Bob Fosse's *8½*." We never discussed the Fellini film, yet Fosse has the same wonderful [Fellini] confusion about women in his movie. Joe Gideon's got his wife, mistress, child ... and the desire to be worshipped and adored by all at the same time.[20]

Moreover, Fosse was a Fellini fan, and his first movie as a director, *Sweet Charity*, was a musical adaptation of the Italian filmmaker's *Nights of Cabiria* (1957, the Oscar-winning Best Foreign Film about a waifish prostitute with dreams). Fellini's frequent cinematographer Giuseppe Rotunna even handled the same position on *Jazz*. But Fellini's director does not die. Thus, part of the preamble simply exists to provide an additional factor on why Gideon dies. That is, so far the death explanation has been tied to a worka-holic frantically attempting to simultaneously edit a major movie while staging a Broad-way play. Yet in *8½*, the director's alter ego (Marcello Mastroianni) demonstrates the huge stress level attached to even one major creative project. And *Jazz* constantly show-cases Gideon struggling with his choreography (to the point of throwing up) before show-ing it to his philistine money men—more stress, and more opportunity for dark comedy. Consequently, even without the Fosse-Gideon–driven, unhealthy lifestyle, *Jazz*'s black humor is perfectly happy to rest on the ever-increasing anxiety of anyone attempting a creative work. (Fosse was once asked to name the key difference between dancing and being a choreographer. Fosse said before he performed he threw up. But he threw up *twice* prior to one of his choreographed numbers being performed.)

A second backward slide to further set up Fosse's use of dark comedy death is the director's fascination with yet another favored maverick director, the aforementioned Chaplin. But beyond Fosse borrowing the Tramp's bowler hat and cane and that sidewise movement for his dancers, what poet Carl Sandburg described as Charlie's "east-west feet," the director simply had an obsession with the comedian. This ranged from Fosse naming his German shepherd Charlie, to having an extensive collection of books on Chaplin.[21] If one looks closely during *Jazz*'s surprise dance tribute "Everything Old Is New Again," performed by his girlfriend and daughter, just behind a seated Gideon is a framed picture of Chaplin directing. Keep in mind that this is a facsimile of Fosse's real apartment, right down to his famous wall poster proclaiming "OH WOW."

Given these factors, is it not possible that *Jazz* was influenced by Chaplin's last great film *Limelight* (1952)? Both movies are about self-destructive, self-indulgent artists closing a film by dying at their own tributes, despite having a love-hate relationship with show business, and feature a lovely young dancer as a quasi-love interest. Moreover, Chaplin's picture appeared at the same time Fosse was about to come into his own as a choreog-rapher, not to mention iconic dancer Gene Kelly's almost simultaneous fleeting salute to Charlie in the Oscar-winning picture from the year before, *An American in Paris* (1951).

Jazz's use of dark comedy death is best demonstrated, beyond Lange's deadly Angelique, by the film within the film, *The Stand-up*. Starring a Lenny Bruce–like come-dian named Davis Newman (Cliff Gorman), this concert movie which Gideon is editing throughout *Jazz* gives viewers, via Gorman, a repetitive take on the five stages of death. Drawing from psychiatrist Elizabeth Kübler-Ross, Davis adds, "without the benefit of dying herself," chronicles the process in her book *On Death and Dying* (1969): denial, anger, bargaining, depression, and acceptance. Thus, between Fosse's constant interjection of Newman's death routine, and the more subtle recurrent fantasy images of Angelique and Gideon increasingly closer together (*à la* the director ever closer to death), the observer gradually comes to realize that death permeates *Jazz* at an ever escalating pace.

Jazz's death-related film-within-a-film tactic is also reminiscent of Jean Renoir's dark comedy *The Rules of the Game* (1939, another Fosse favorite), in which a play within the picture foreshadows another death. Both victims (Renoir's naïve romantic flyer and Fosse's jaded yet driven Gideon) could be described by *Jazz*'s tribute show death host (Ben Vereen): "He didn't know where the games ended and reality began. Like for this cat, the only reality is death...." Angelique notwithstanding, the clips from Gorman's *The Stand-Up* sequences interspersed throughout *Jazz* set the picture's death theme for several reasons. First, it emphasizes that for art to ask hard questions, artists often must make single-mindedly sacrificial choices, what Christopher Hitchens called "taunting the

Reaper."[22] Second, the repetitiveness of the sequences, however numbing to some film and audience members, is of utmost importance. People constantly need to be reminded that life is short. As a disconcerting excerpt from *Rosencrantz and Guildenstern Are Dead* (1967) reminds us, "It must have been shattering [first discovering one dies]. And yet I can't remember it…. What does one make of that?"[23] (Evoking life's brevity was also a central mission of Ruth Gordon's Maude with young friend Harold.) Third, while Gideon is more aware of death then most, be it his creative projects or the innumerable times he checks his pulse, he does not fully comprehend the death process until he is taken to the hospital with chest pains. (It is also absurdly ironic to keep checking his pulse, since he refuses to change anything about his life.)

One more significance of Gorman's riff on Kübler-Ross is another variation on deathly repetition. The first phase is seemingly random. When Gideon goes to a specialist he is in total denial, claiming all he really needs is a rewrite of the show. When told that his treatment would involve several weeks of rest, he morphs into anger, which brings on more chest pain. This results in immediate hospitalization. His condition eventually stabilizes and his specialist (Michael Tolan) suggests moving him to a private room if he will maintain strict hospital rules. Gideon immediately accepts, bargaining, and then he proceeds to party himself (by way of smuggled-in booze, multiple carousing guests, sex with a nurse) back to his original critical condition. When his new picture receives a bad television review, he has a heart attack. An examination reveals he has total blockage in two of his arteries. Prior to surgery, Gideon and his girlfriend watch yet another installment of the O'Connor Flood-Ben Vereen hypocritical television tribute show, which will be incorporated into his big fantasy finale.

At this point it comes out that the girlfriend has been cheating on Gideon. The depression he immediately feels is beyond betrayal; it suggests she is simply moving on because of his impending death. But as he is later wheeled into surgery, he exhibits acceptance tinged, as always, with dark comedy—telling his former wife (Leland Palmer), "If I die, I'm sorry for all the bad things I did to you." Then, without breaking a beat, he turns to his girlfriend and says, "And if I live, I'm sorry for all the bad things I'm going to do to you." What follows, cued by a clapper board entitled "Hospital Hallucinations," are several brilliant musical numbers, three of which each highlight the women in Gideon's life—the loyal ex-wife, his daughter, and the girlfriend.

The surgery seems to be a success. But he has another heart attack. Gideon is next restrained to his bed awaiting some new procedure, despite the director having noted he feels something breaking up. During a hospital emergency unrelated to him, when the staff is distracted, Gideon manages to escape and randomly wanders around the facility. This brings another round of the five stages of death which are more direct and, at times, literally involve voice-over on the subject from the *Stand-Up* Kübler-Ross routine of Gorman's title character. One such Gideon-directed line: "I'm dying." The lengthy sequence also dramatically manifests his anger early when he pounds his head against a partition and smears blood along the wall as he drags himself down the hall.

Moving through the rest of this arc of life sequence is largely a study in acceptance showcased in actions ranging from broad humor and poignancy to hospital black humor. At one point, while splashing through a semi-flooded hospital basement almost reminiscent of *Singin' in the Rain*'s signature scene, he looks up and asks the aforementioned heaven-directed question, "What's the matter, don't you like musical comedy?" At another junction he enters the hospital room of an elderly yet still lovely woman in a great deal of pain. He kisses her and briefly provides a moment of relief by praising her beauty. But the black humor *pièce de resistance* for deathly acceptance is his detour through the Department of Pathology: Autopsy Suite. After some comic banter towards the jars of assorted organs, his exit line is, "I'll be back."

Eventually he ends up in the bowels of the hospital smoking his cigarettes while hanging out with an older janitor (actor–jazz musician George "Tiger" Haynes, 1914–1994) and repeatedly joining him in singing, "Pack Up Your Troubles in Your Old Kit Bag and Smile, Smile, Smile." Both men are really enjoying themselves until two orderlies break up the party and steer Gideon back to his hospital bed. Once again tied to the bed, the director looks over at his heart monitor, which morphs into a television screen showing Ben Vereen's tribute show. And the film is ready for one more Hospital Hallucination. Not surprisingly, Gideon is the subject of Vereen's atypically less-than-positive introduction to his guest. Yet, with the director soon joining him in this most unusual of quasi-salutes, things immediately take on an upbeat perspective. Fittingly, for a dark comedy, the crucial song is juxtaposed to the cheery visuals of an approaching death, even with a reworking of its lyrics: Fosse has taken the Everly Brothers' 1957 hit "Bye, Bye Love" and rechristened it "Bye, Bye Life," and substituted the word "die" for "cry" in the line "I think I'm going to…." To compound this contrast, the normally mournful song about a lost teen love is performed by Vereen and Gideon with an upbeat tempo (despite lyric changes) through a buoyant "going away show." The audience for this extravaganza of a light show musical with medical-related dancers (such as wearing tights with vein outlines) are pivotal people from Gideon's life—people the audience has gotten to know during the course of the movie.

This rousing "Bye, Bye Life" close is entertainingly drawn-out. One of my college students once suggested, "Wasn't it a little long," and even before I could respond, several other students immediately defended its length with essentially the same explanation: "If you were staging an end-of-your-life show, wouldn't you probably want it to be drawn-out?!" (It has since become a popular paper topic in my genre class: How would you put on your show-stopper finale … and who would you invite from that life?)

In addition to the Bruce-like comic's repeated riff and Angelique, *Jazz* is bombarded with death allusions. When Fosse goes for his insurance physical, his doctor nearly coughs up a lung in his nonstop hacking, as both men have cigarettes dangling from their lips. The hospital hallucinations scene closes with the three principal women sitting on a hearse reminiscent of a seminal *Harold and Maude* icon. The backers of the play-within-the-film meet with their insurance people after Gideon's first heart attack without any sense of compassion, despite death being the subject on the table. One of many darkly comic questions posed by *Jazz* might be "What does success really mean in any field of life?" Gideon likens his work and life to being a tightrope walker; and when he is not putting it all on the line, life is just waiting. In one of his scenes with Lange's angel of death we see him literally fall off a high wire. While the death references seem countless, one might best close with a throwaway line from Gorman's comic: "You know what death with dignity is, man? You don't drool."

Moving on to dark comedy's absurdity theme, the script is equally rich. Though previously noted, one has to reiterate that *Jazz* is a musical comedy about death. And it never gets produced, except as a hallucination in a dying man's head. Moreover, death comes by way of a kiss from a beautiful messenger of death. Gideon's demise will make his play the first show to turn a profit ($500,000 plus) without opening on Broadway. *Jazz*'s "Airotica" number, Fosse's sexy revamping of the dance routine for the aviation-related song "Take Off with Us," ends with the most Brechtian of axioms, "We take you everywhere but get you nowhere." It is evocative of this book's frontispiece, the still of Richard Dupoint's sculpture "Going Around By Passing Through." And that is essentially the absurdist pocket definition of the text: a Brecht-like theme of passing through life by going in circles.

There is also a gripping absurdity in the clash of the three women in Gideon's life. They all care for him in distinctively different ways. There is the young daughter who loves him unconditionally and simply wants a full-time dad. His girlfriend almost parallels his daughter's scenario in love and time but is already starting to drift away from neglect even before his death. The most complicated relationship is with his ex-wife. They have a child together, have seemingly grown up together in the theater, and she appreciates his genius more than anyone. But there is bitterness about her wanting to be more than just a friend and advisor with whom he works. Moreover, there is possible opportunism here, too. She is an aging dancer, while the life of a brilliant choreographer has no expiration date. Thus, as she desperately wants to hold on to her theater career, there is a need to accept life on his terms. Dark comedy always seems a given when it comes to human interaction, especially when love is involved. One might paraphrase Woody Allen's analogy between the difficulties in relationships and the Middle East: There is no solution.

Gideon also flirts with an absurdity of fear. Is he losing his passion for what has always driven him, the theater? One is reminded of early portions of Philip Roth's novel *The Humbling* (2009, adapted to the screen by Al Pacino and Barry Levinson in 2015). Roth's book is about an aging stage actor seemingly losing his gift; his empty life is often sex-driven. While sex-obsessed Gideon still seems to have the talent, it is progressively harder for him to get motivated. Each morning he performs the same darkly comic mantra: He plays his wake-up music CD "Toulousa Chamber Music," puts in eye drops, drinks a glass of Alka Seltzer, showers (at some point unseen during this morning procedure he has lit up his first cigarette, which he sleepily forgets to remove while showering), takes the stimulant Dexedrine (Gideon's prescriptive bottle's address is Fosse's real address, 61 West 58th Street, New York), and uses more eye drops. Then viewers see him dressed before a mirror saying variations of "It's Showtime." As the movie progresses, this regimen is progressively harder to perform.

This practice is reminiscent of the last years of the underrated humorist-actor Robert Benchley, whose increasingly alcoholic partying lifestyle eventually necessitated pills to sleep, pills to wake up, and retiring from writing his inspired comic essays by the 1940s. According to daughter-in-law Marjorie, when she told her husband of his father's death (the son was returning to New York on a troop train and initially no one had been able to contact Lt. Commander Nathaniel—also a future writer), the young man "didn't seem at all surprised; distressed but not surprised, so I think [Nathaniel] felt he [Benchley] was rather giving up."[24] If death had not taken Gideon, this could have been his eventual fate, too.

Moving to "man as beast," the final seminal dark comedy theme, one must start with Gideon. After standing up his daughter early in the film, the director berates himself as "some fuckin' father." And there are similar verdicts to himself about his inability to be a faithful husband. Yet, when Lange's character asks him if he believes in love, he self-servingly replies, "I believe in saying 'I love you.'" Along similar lines, when his daughter asks why he doesn't get married again, Gideon affectionately tells her, "I don't get married again because I can't find anyone I dislike enough to inflict that kind of torture on." There is also a short confession to Angelique:

> GIDEON: I always look for the worst in other people.
> ANGELIQUE: A little of yourself in them?
> GIDEON: A little of myself. And I generally find it.

It has already been noted that Fosse attempts to make his alter ego harsher than the norm. But while viewers do get to see the occasional positive Gideon, this is not true of others—particularly Broadway financial backers. In the cattle call tryouts which begin *Jazz*, with Gideon sweating proverbial bullets over whom to cut, the money men are the theater's bored philistine onlookers. When Gideon has his first heart attack and the key producer promises cast and crew help while they sort things out, he calls them "family," which immediately elicits a "bullshit!" aside from one of his alleged "clan." The producer is also slick and quick to act on Gideon's health issues by briskly approaching an equally slimy replacement director (John Lithgow). This rival substitute feigns the same false "family" attitude.

There is also the aforementioned insurance meeting in which the backers display a lack of concern for both Gideon *and* culture, since their key motivation is profit. This money mentality reaches its most tellingly insensitive moment, however, during Gideon's big "Bye, Bye Life" finale. One of these "suits," as they are derisively called within the business, is in the audience as the director periodically wades into the crowd for farewells. One would finally expect a compassionate goodbye. But no, the "suit" enthusiastically observes this death production number "must have cost a fortune." Granted, this is Gideon's final hallucination, but the audience has already seen enough slights by the well-heeled to make it ring true. Of course, his presence at the exit might be Fosse saying, "Evil is both banal and unavoidably arbitrary."

The catalyst for the final deadly heart attack and thus the ultimate contender for the "beast" category is the TV critic who pans Gideon's *The Stand-Up*. The critique is reminiscent of the entertainingly, vicious diatribes which sometimes passed for reviews by *The New Yorker*'s Pauline Kael. She was an award-winning writer who on occasion used self-serving, savage attacks in place of constructive criticism during her adventures in egotism. This is one such example. The audience has seen Gideon tweak *The Stand-Up* over a period of months while watching *Jazz*, yet this critique suggests the director simply hung his title character out to dry, with no artistic input. Ironically, this might seem like one of those cinema sequences which is conveniently contrived. However, it actually happened. In the *New York Times* article "Ann Reinking Plays Herself in *All That Jazz*," the dancer-actress reveals she was with the hospitalized director when a major TV critic brutally reviewed his friend Stanley Donen's adaptation of Antoine de Saint–Exupéry beloved 1943 novella *The Little Prince* (1974, in which Fosse had a small part). Just as played in *Jazz*, Fosse was so upset he had a heart attack "and there really *was* a nurse who wouldn't believe he was in agony because he had just had a shot [for his heart condition]."[25]

As a dark comedy attachment to *The Little Prince*, both the story and Fosse's brief dance appearance anticipates much of *Jazz*. First, it is a musical fantasy about an inquisitive alien child discovering that adults are phonies, lacking imagination, and struggling with relationships, all potential reasons for why boy-man Gideon is so cynical. Fosse reinforces this mindset in the film by playing a snake in human form, though the child allows the snake to bite him so he can leave barren earth. Fittingly, Fosse's most important *Little Prince* line could double as a fundamental truism for most of his work: "All you can learn here [on Earth] is sorrow." Interestingly, Fosse's slender, darkly clad *Little Prince* garb and slithering dance movements are often cited as having influenced the young Michael Jackson, a great fan of the classic children's story *The Little Prince*. (When viewing Fosse's scene, it is difficult to deny the possibility of a connection.)

Just as *All That Jazz* closed the decade as this book's best example of a genre-bending, genre-crossing 1970s dark comedy, *Jazz* also generated the most provocative reviews, as suggested by an excerpt from the chapter-opening *New York Times* critique: "[It] is an uproarious display of brilliance, nerve, dance ... and ego."[26] Though well over budget, it was a commercial success which garnered nine Oscar nominations: Best Picture (losing to *Kramer vs. Kramer*), Best Actor (Roy Scheider lost to Dustin Hoffman in *Kramer*), Best Director (Fosse lost to *Kramer*'s Robert Benton), Best Original Screenplay (Fosse and Robert Alan Aurthur lost to *Breaking Away*'s Steven Tesich), and Best Cinematography (Giuseppe Rotunno lost to *Apocalypse Now*'s Vittorio Storaro). But *Jazz* won for Best Editing (Alan Heim), Best Art Direction (Philip Rosenberg, Tony Walton, Edward Stewart, and Gary J. Brink), Best Costume Design (Albert Wolsky), and Best Original Song Score and Its Adaptation (Ralph Burns).

Like in the early days of dark comedy, many critics were simply bowled over by the film's audacity ... yet *unlike* those early days, the reviewing majority embraced Fosse's fearlessness. *The Hollywood Reporter*'s Ron Pennington's overestimated the possibility for negative feedback in his lavish praise:

Gideon's monumental death finale, with O'Connor Flood (Ben Vereen) and Kate (Ann Reinking in veined bodystocking, right).

[*Jazz*] is going to be considered Fosse's masterpiece or a total disaster, depending on to whom you talk, but it is sure to stimulate a lot of controversy. Personally, I think it is a masterpiece and it is certainly one of the most original films ever made.[27]

For every critical crack about egotism, or squeamishness over the operating scene,[28] there are struggling attempts to describe what *Variety* called a "compelling film ... conveying [Fosse's] absorption with choreography and directing to the exclusion of almost everything else [to create] a number of stunning routines...."[29] Some *Jazz* reviewers credited Fosse with literally expanding the normal limitations of cinema. For instance, the *Los Angeles Times'* Charles Champlin wrote:

There is or was a school called action painting, in which the gesture—bold, spontaneous, personal, direct, uncorrectable—was everything. Films don't really lend themselves to bold personal gestures.... But, damn, that's what Bob Fosse has done to a fare-thee-well in *All That Jazz*, his explosion of energy, imagination, autobiography, choreography, fantasy and all-stops-out celebration of the possibilities of film ... *Jazz* reconfirms anybody's belief in the infinite possibilities of film.[30]

Champlin's essay even poetically rechristens Francois Truffaut's "profile film" *à la* biographical category, as a "spiritual autobiography," one of the many anti-genres addressed herein, sometimes to mask what the critic ultimately calls Fosse's ability with *Jazz* to create, "[f]rom first to last ... *dance macabre* with the idea, the possibility, the imminence of death."[31]

If the early 1960s had finally pulled cinematic dark comedy front and center for a singular belated recognition (if the establishment as enemy was fully recognized), by the late 1970s the genre seemed to permeate every pore of pictures, either directly, or in a postmodern fragmentation of anti-genre crossover bending. Fosse, more than any other filmmaker, had fully broken through to the other side. Fosse's inspired narcissism had suddenly given razzle-dazzle distraction to Pogo's expressive observation, "We have met the enemy and he is us." And dark comedy has neither been absent, nor the same, since.

Epilogue with Notes on
A Clockwork Orange (1971)

Do you think Stanley Kubrick ever gets depressed?
    —Joe Gideon (Roy Scheider) in *All That Jazz* (1979)

From the comic to the sublime, cinema has always had dark comedies. But the genre finally came into its own during the 1960s. Besides new dark comedies like Stanley Kubrick's *Dr. Strangelove or: How I Learned to Stop Worrying and Love the Bomb* (1964) and the re-issuing of previously underappreciated ones, like Charlie Chaplin's *The Great Dictator* (1940) and *Monsieur Verdoux* (1947), the genre was finally receiving the recognition which it deserved. Yet most of these examples smacked audiences right between the eyes with their mood, such as Chaplin's use of Hitler for humor. The full ambiguous blossoming of the genre would occur during the American 1970s, fueled in part by many of the factors delineated in the prologue, including TV's gutting of old school Hollywood, a betrayed trust in feel-good Capraesque people by modern McCarthy populism, New American Cinema cannibalizing the French New Wave, and the promise of Kennedy's New Frontier quickly collapsing … into the violent discord and distrust leading to Watergate.

If one had to focus on any one of these components and its impact on this 1970s dark comedy shift, one could cherry pick these French New Wave storytelling elements at odds with classic American cinema: anti-heroes instead of traditional admirable heroes, a slice-of-life and/or disjointed narrative over a linear one, and an ambiguous or negative conclusion versus a happy ending. Granted, these differences could, and did, play out in all genres. But each is particularly suited to key dark comedy themes: the omnipresence of death, the world's inherent absurdity, and man as beast. And while the French initially felt their cinematic other game plan necessitated eliminating stories from media, 1970s American dark comedies often enriched their films by drawing upon novels which had already embraced this anti-establishment trilogy of values, as well as filling in cinema adaptation questions.

In the 1970s, American dark comedy was suddenly controversial again because it was becoming so all-pervasive (a victim of its own perverse success) that it, paradoxically, was not always immediately obvious. How was this possible? After all, genres are forever morphing in new directions, but dark comedy revamping is often on steroids—always needing to ratchet up its "smash mouth" shock values. Consequently, the answer lies in social-political instability fueling a 1970s topsy-turvydom in which film categories suddenly went anti-genre rogue. The ultimate culmination of this misdirection movement was *All That Jazz* (1979), a musical about death, a quasi biography about an S.O.B., and an art house movie which equates truth with a final orgasm.

This development played directly into black humor's 1970s formula. A dark comedy like *Jazz* became more palatable and/or less directly criticized (if recognized in that category at all) by appearing to use other traditional genres as smoke screens. Yet, these quasi-covers quickly embellished the black humor by breaking their own norms and becoming a smorgasbord of anti-genres. Ironically, though evermore universal, this mainstreaming of dark comedy often flew under film classification radar.

As a brief addendum to this epilogue, a reader might assume that my excluding Kubrick's *A Clockwork Orange* (1971) was because it did not fit the new mask scenario—since it directly dovetails into old school dark comedy, like the obvious mushroom cloud conclusion to *Strangelove*. Yet one could gerrymander *Clockwork* into this new fragmented pastiche approach by saying it plays anti-genre games with science fiction, problem films (juvenile delinquency), and even soft porn.

The *real* explanation is simple, despite its post-apocalyptic garnishing of the once pioneering straightforward dark comedy norm. This text examines a new American dark comedy transition, with no time for a learning curve. Moreover, and most importantly, Kubrick, like Henry James before him, was an American expatriate in England, from where he seldom strayed for nearly the last forty years of his life. It was almost as if Kubrick was a pre–Civil War artist dismissing America as culturally irrelevant. A Europhile even before his early 1960s exit from the U.S., Kubrick's Europeanized Yank status disqualified the brilliant *Clockwork*. One could even double-down on the decision's legitimacy by noting that the movie is an adaptation of an ultra–British novel posing an ethically questionable science fiction solution to that country's late 1960s "skinhead" gang problem. (The basic sci-fi slant used is taking a current action and projecting its ultimate future result.) Regardless, *Clockwork* was shot in England with an English cast. Even then it was seen as British. For example, Vincent Canby's *New York Times* review described the picture as "essentially [a] British nightmare."[1]

In a project of this nature one simply must make choices, and the twelve focus films of this study seemed to represent the best 1970s broad spectrum of American anti-genre examples from which to draw. I am reminded of Andy Borowitz's book *The 50 Funniest American Writers: An Anthology of Humor from Mark Twain to The Onion* (2014). It is a solid addition to humor scholarship despite, from my vantage point, the surprising absence of Robert Benchley and Kurt Vonnegut.[2] Choices. It is never an easy task and someone's favorite is inevitably left out. Consequently, accept a moment of author contriteness if a reader has been thus offended. I am merely placing words in a row on paper better to explain, to the best of my abilities, a 1970s anti-genre dark comedy subterfuge.

My career has been devoted to humor research, with an inordinate amount of time devoted to dark comedy.[3] One could argue at this point in my studies the genre even represents a pair of bookends. That is, as a young professor in 1989 I was invited to lecture on the topic at the Sorbonne–University of Paris. In the summer of

Charlie Chaplin as the ladykiller title character of *Monsieur Verdoux* (1947).

2014 a similar privilege was afforded me when New York's Museum of Modern Art requested I speak on my award-winning latest book *Chaplin's War Trilogy: An Evolving Lens in Three Dark Comedies, 1918–1947.*[4]

What I hope has been gained from the book in hand goes beyond screenwriter Tara Ison's tongue-in-cheek crack about what she learned from *One Flew Over the Cuckoo's Nest* (1975): "Never to take medication offered to you in paper cups."[5] First, for years most people could only appreciate cinematic dark comedy in sequences, such as a critic being enchanted by the ballet globe scene in *The Great Dictator* (1940), without being capable of understanding and/or acknowledging the whole film as a legitimate genre. Second, in the 1960s' obvious black humor movies, this cemetery genre without graves was finally validated by critics and viewers. Yet American political and social unrest of the period immediately began to befog acceptance and/or recognition of the genre variations by the fragmented 1970s. Third, an era anchored in an anti-establishment ethos enriched and encouraged dark comedy while often initially camouflaging the black humor in a cloak of many anti-genre colors. This often resulted in the dark comedy becoming, in the parlance of Vonnegut's 1969 novel *Slaughterhouse-Five*, a calloused "and so it goes" acceptance of life's absurdity, an extension of an uncaring—or a nonexisting God—as in Beckett's *Waiting for Godot* (1953). For instance, Beckett scholars James and Elizabeth Knowlson have explained it thus: "There was 'no revolt at all' [one cannot revolt from nothingness] in his work ... he used the terms 'complete submission' and said that he was 'revolted [with life] but not revolting.'"[6]

For other dark comedy victims, such as *Catch-22*'s (1970) Yossarian (Alan Arkin), what started out as an attempted escape through feigned insanity ultimately resulted in actual insanity—a getaway of an entirely different order. (A variation of this occurs in the alleged happy ending of the anti-genre dark comedy *Birdman or (The Unexpected Virtue of Ignorance)*, 2013—which screenwriter Alejandro González Iñárritu has repeatedly said in interviews, both before and after winning his screenplay Oscar, was really a suicide). Sandwiched between the two is a similar close to Terry Gilliam's *Brazil* (1985). There is the dark humor escape of a questionable feigned insanity which also results in the ultimate vanishing act—the death of Jack Nicholson's Patrick "Mac" McMurphy in *One Flew Over the Cuckoo's Nest* (1975). The dark comedy anti-hero could always skirmish with the genre, as in *MASH* (1970) or *Harold and Maude* (1971) but this usually only resulted in a holding pattern. *MASH*'s Hawkeye (Donald Sutherland) and company merely escaped the chaos of war to re-enter the greater disconnect of life in general. And like another iconoclastic Korean vet (McMurphy), re-entry into civilian life will offer no sanctuary.

Harold and Maude is a poser anticipating yet another black humor evolution more common in the 21st century. Call it "dark comedy lite." Examples would include *Little Miss Sunshine* (2006), *Sunshine Cleaning* (2008), and *The Skeleton Twins* (2014)—blatant dark comedies which offer eleventh hour hope. Though this is a subject for another book, *Harold and Maude* could seem a precursor of sorts. Harold (But Cort) eventually seems in a better place but vibrantly happy life force Maude (Ruth Gordon) has arbitrarily taken her own life. How can one of cinema history's greatest *carpe diem* cheerleaders suddenly die a 180 swan dive death? The absurdity of that development makes as much sense as this random dark comedy Arni Barcka poetry line: "It is better to have loved and lost than to put linoleum in your living room."[7] Despite many additional *Harold and Maude* components discussed earlier, this 1970s picture still abides comfortably in gender-bending dark comedy.

The dark comedy fall guy can also play the idle time game, *à la Waiting for Godot*, by endless intellectual conjecture about life's significant "raised issues," as Woody Allen does in *Love and Death* (1975) and *Annie Hall* (1979). One might note Henry Miller's fondness for calling this absurd world "an air-conditioned nightmare." The abyss forever lingers, and there is the temptation that killing time might convert to the genre's ever popular killing of self. Thus, there is always the danger that Allen's alter ego could follow the path of Cormac McCarthy's 2006 play *The Sunset Limited*, about a nameless suicidal professor (which Tommy Lee Jones later adapted to small screen cable, 2011, as both the director and the academic). Moreover, even if Allen's personas sidestep self-murder, his *Annie Hall* thesis that "love fades" has dark comedy roots of absurdity reaching back to the meaning of Shakespeare's sonnets, which critic Glyn Maxwell expounds on: "Love doesn't alter, for if it alters it's not love."[8] And if the only certainty in life is change, the implication takes one back to "love fades."

The constant dumbing-down of society is also anticipated in the 1970s genre-crossing dark comedies with ciphers such as Peter Sellers' Chance in *Being There* (1979). Here is a life force no more aware than a dimming Alzheimer patient ... who might also be the new Jesus. One is reminded of the T.S. Eliot poem "The Hollow Men" (1925), with their heads "filled with straw" and in which the world "ends not with a bang but with a whimper," arguably the 20th century's most quoted line (and belief?), with the possible exception of Shakespeare's dark comedy's suicide-friendly Hamlet asking the eternal question, "To be or not to be...." In any case, a fate of a whimpering exit is the minimum destiny one could predict for *Waiting for Godot*'s duo of Estragon and Vladimir, a team so like Laurel and Hardy it merits repeating Stan Laurel's description of the film pair: "Two minds without a single thought."[9] Such honorably dense characters as Stan and Ollie, or Sellers' Chance, are how the "Theater of the Absurd" defines humanity. And as noted earlier, vaudevillian Bert Lahr (the *Wizard of Oz* lion, 1939) played Estragon opposite comic actor Tom Ewell (of *Seven Year Itch* fame) in an early *Waiting for Godot* production.

Eugene O'Neill's *The Iceman Cometh* (1939/1945), a precursor to the forever lingering Theater of the Absurd, had its pivotal character Hickey, the traveling salesman, played by former vaudevillian James Barton when it opened on 1946 Broadway. The 2015 restaging of the play at the Brooklyn Academy of Music cast madcap comedian of stage and screen Nathan Lane as Hickey. And as just suggested, as in *Waiting for Godot*, *The Iceman Cometh* also plays a waiting game, only the principals are now drunks in a 1912 Brooklyn bar. Hickey is the only outsider, whose periodic visits liven things up. Only, unlike the silence of *Godot*'s closing blackness, *Iceman* ends with a confessed murder, a suicide, and a statement of life's pointlessness. As Lane has observed: "O'Neill ... is asking you to hold hands and jump off the cliff with him, and he's asking you to do what at times seems almost impossible ... to go to the darkest place in your soul...."[10] If one were to return to Laurel and Hardy, the latter's signature line would be the most appropriate of observations: "Here's another fine mess you've gotten us into."

The casting of comics in these parts makes possible several key conditions. It underlines yet softens a vision of humanity as simpletons, by staging this human comedy with our favorite entertainment fools. Next, and most central to this study, it reinforces and/or simply demonstrates a variation of the anti-genre distraction principle. That is, by seeing a clown, the viewer does not immediately realize one has entered the world of unanswerable questions concerning our own mortality. Finally, since most beloved fools play at a sort of merry monotony, this encapsulates our own lives—often *sans* the "merry"—watching people kill time as we do the same.

Finally, the study's additional cornerstone films not otherwise briefly revisited in this epilogue, *Little Big Man* (1970), *Cabaret*, (1972), *Slaughterhouse-Five* (1972) and *Chinatown* (1974), all embrace in varying ways similar anti-genre facades. And their central characters then struggle with the same dark comedy demons just sketched. Jack Nicholson's *Chinatown* detective ultimately reaches the shattered man status with which *Catch-22*'s Yossarian begins. In *Cabaret*, Sally Bowles' (Liza Minnelli) metaphorical dance with Hitler's approaching apocalypse—all for narcissistic success in show business—is little different than Joe Gideon's blindly self-centered pirouette with death during the Vietnam War era. *Little Big Man*'s 121-year-old Jack Crabb (Dustin Hoffman), whose obsession with TV Westerns has been the catalyst for his telling what could be geriatric tall tales, is merely a variation of *Being There*'s Chance, whose only world is TV. And Billy Pilgrim's (Michael Sacks) random pinballing through *Slaughterhouse-Five*'s rudderless time travel hell, except for brief respites with a porn star companion (Valerie Perrine) on another planet's zoo, would seem to be a twisted amalgamation of all that has gone before ... and will continue endlessly. Regardless, one could say, for the astute viewer, modern dark comedy often uses anti-genres as sort of a Cubist-distraction of eventually seeing all sides simultaneously.

Since this text begins with a Brecht-like sculpture, Richard Dupont's "Going Around By Passing Through" (see the frontispiece), the idling away of life, or what passes for it, in distracting anti-genre circles, a painting reference summing-up seems appropriate. The work is Salvador Dali's disturbingly inspired melting clocks in "The Persistence of Memory" (1931). Art historian Robert Goff suggests, "The three melting watches symbolize the innate lack of meaning or reliability of the non-dreaming conscious world.... Each watch tells a different time [and] not by linear times."[11] Yossarian and company could not have said it any better.

Filmography

January 24, 1970—*MASH* (20th Century–Fox, 116 minutes). DIRECTOR: Robert Altman. SCREENPLAY: Ring Lardner, Jr., based on Richard Hooker's novel. STARS: Elliott Gould (Trapper John), Donald Sutherland (Hawkeye), Tom Skerritt (Duke), Sally Kellerman (Major "Hot Lips" O'Houlihan), Robert Duvall (Major Frank Burns), Roger Bowen (Colonel Blake), René Auberjonois (Father "Dago Red" Mulcahy), Gary Burghoff (Corporal "Radar" O'Reilly), Jo Ann Pflug (Lieutenant "Dish"), John Schuck (Captain "Painless" Waldowski), Bud Cort (Private Boone).

June 20, 1970—*Catch-22* (Paramount and Filmways, 121 minutes). DIRECTOR: Mike Nichols. SCREENPLAY: Buck Henry, based on Joseph Heller's novel. STARS: Alan Arkin (Captain Yossarian), Martin Balsam (Colonel Cathcart), Buck Henry (Colonel Korn), Art Garfunkel (Captain Nately), Martin Sheen (1st Lieutenant Dobbs), Jon Voight (1st Lieutenant Minderbinder), Jack Gilford (Dr. "Doc" Daneeka), Richard Benjamin (Major Danby), Anthony Perkins (Chaplain Captain A. T. Tappman), Bob Newhart (Major Major Major), Charles Grodin (Captain Aarfy Aardvark), Marcel Dalio (Old Man in Whorehouse), Gina Rovere (Nately's Whore), Orson Welles (Brigadier General Dreedle).

December 15, 1970—*Little Big Man* (National General–Cinema Center, 150 minutes). DIRECTOR: Arthur Penn. SCREENPLAY: Robert Klane, based on his novel. STARS: Dustin Hoffman (Jack Crabb), Chief Dan George (Old Lodge Skins), Faye Dunaway (Mrs. Pendrake), Martin Balsam (Mr. Merriweather), Richard Mulligan (General George Custer), Jeff Corey (Wild Bill Hickok), Aimée Eccles (Sunshine).

December 21, 1971—*Harold and Maude* (Paramount, 90 minutes). DIRECTOR: Hal Ashby. SCREENPLAY: Colin Higgins. STARS: Ruth Gordon (Maude), Bud Cort (Harold), Vivian Pickles (Mrs. Chasen), Charles Tyner (Uncle Victor), Ellen Geer (Sunshine Doré), Eric Christmas (priest), G. Wood (psychiatrist), Tom Skerritt (motorcycle officer).

February 14, 1972—*Cabaret* (ABC Pictures–Allied Artists, 124 minutes). DIRECTOR: Bob Fosse. SCREENPLAY: Jay Presson Allen, based on Christopher Isherwood's *The Berlin Stories* (1939), as well as two stage productions of the stories *Cabaret* (1966) and *I Am a Camera* (1951). STARS: Liza Minnelli (Sally Bowles), Michael York (Brian Roberts), Helmut Griem (Maximilian von Heune), Joel Grey (Master of Ceremonies), Fritz Wepper (Fritz Wendel), Marisa Berenson (Natalia Landauer), Elisabeth Neuman-Viertel (Fräulein Schneider).

March 23, 1972—*Slaughterhouse-Five* (Universal, 104 minutes). DIRECTOR: George Roy Hill. SCREENPLAY: Stephen Geller, based on Kurt Vonnegut's novel. STARS: Michael Sacks (Billy Pilgrim), Ron Liebman (Paul Lazzaro), Eugene Roche (Edgar Derby), Valerie Perrine (Montana Wildhack), Holly Near (Barbara Pilgrim).

June 21, 1974—*Chinatown* (Robert Evans–Paramount, 131 minutes). DIRECTOR: Roman Polanski. SCREENPLAY: Robert Towne. STARS: Jack Nicholson (J.J. Gittes), Faye Dunaway (Evelyn Mulwray), John Huston (Noah Cross), Perry Lopez (Escobar), John Hillerman (Yelburton), Darrell Zwerling (Hollis Mulwray), Diane Ladd (Ida Sessions), Roy Jensen (Mulvihill), Roman Polanski (Man with Knife), Richard Bakalyan (Loach), Joe Mantell (Walsh), Bruce Glover (Duffy).

June 11, 1975—*Love and Death* (Charles H. Joffe–United Artists, 85 minutes). DIRECTOR AND SCREENPLAY: Woody Allen. STARS: Woody Allen (Boris), Diane Keaton (Sonja), Frank Adu (Drill Sergeant), Georges Adet (Old Nehamkin), Harold Gould (Anton), James Tolkan (Napoleon), Olga Georges-Picot (Countess Alexandrovna).

November 20, 1975—*One Flew Over the Cuckoo's Nest* (Saul Zaentz–Michael Douglas–United Artists, 133 minutes). DIRECTOR: Milos Forman. SCREENPLAY: Lawrence Hauben, Bo Goldman, based on Ken Kesey's novel. STARS: Jack Nicholson (Randle McMurphy), Louise Fletcher (Nurse Ratched), Will Sampson ("Chief"

Bromden), Brad Dourif (Billy Bibbit), Danny DeVito (Martini), Christopher Lloyd (Max Taber).

April 21, 1977—*Annie Hall* (Charles H. Joffe-United Artists, 93 minutes). DIRECTOR: Woody Allen. SCREENPLAY: Woody Allen and Marshall Brickman. STARS: Woody Allen (Alvy "Max" Singer), Diane Keaton (Annie Hall), Tony Roberts (Rob), Carol Kane (Allison Portchnik), Paul Simon (Tony Lacy), Shelly Duvall (Pam), Christopher Walken (Duane Hall), Colleen De-whurst (Mrs. Hall), Mordecai Lawner (Alvy's father), Marshall McLuhan (himself).

December 20, 1979—*Being There* (Lorimar, 130 minutes). DIRECTOR: Hal Ashby. SCREENPLAY: Jerzy Kosinski and an uncredited Robert C. Jones, based on Kosinski's novella. STARS: Peter Sellers (Chance the Gardener, a.k.a. Chauncey Gardiner), Shirley MacLaine (Eve Rand), Melvyn Douglas (Ben Rand), Jack Warden (the president), Richard Dysart (Dr. Robert Al-lenby), Richard Basehart (U.S. Soviet ambassa-dor), Ruth Attaway (Louise).

December 20, 1979—*All That Jazz* (20th Cen-tury–Fox–Columbia, 123 minutes). DIRECTOR: Bob Fosse. SCREENPLAY: Bob Fosse and Robert Allan Arthur. STARS: Roy Scheider ("Joe" Gideon), Jessica Lange (Angelique, angel of death), Ann Reinking (Katie Jagger), Leland Palmer (Audrey Paris, Gideon's ex-wife), Cliff Corman (Davis Newman), Ben Vereen (O'Con-nor Flood), Erzsébet Földi (Michelle Gideon), Michael Toland (Dr. Ballinger), Deborah Geffner (Victoria Porter), John Lithgow (Lucas Sergeant).

Chapter Notes

Foreword

1. Molly Haskell, *Love and Other Infectious Diseases* (New York: Citadel Press, 1990), 84.
2. James Agee, *Agee on Film: Essays and Reviews by James Agee, Volume 1* (1958 rpt. New York: Grosset & Dunlap, 1972), back cover blurb/letter.

Preface

1. Will Cuppy, *How to Become Extinct* (Garden City, New York: Garden City Books, 1941), 165.
2. Dana Stevens, "Bookends," *New York Times*, March 8, 2015, Book Review section: 35.
3. Steve Martin, *Born Standing Up* (New York: Scribner, 2007), 3.

Prologue

1. Joseph Heller, *Catch–22* (1968; rpt. New York: Dell, 1961), 184.
2. Manny Farber, "White Elephant Art vs. Termite Art," *Film Culture*, Winter 1962/63, cover article.
3. See the author's extensive writing on the subject, especially *American Dark Comedy: Beyond Satire* (Westport, Connecticut: Greenwood Press, 1996).
4. Peter Biskind, *Easy Riders, Raging Bulls* (New York: Simon & Schuster, 1998).
5. For example, see Gerald Mast's (revised by Bruce F. Kawin), *A Short History of the Movies* (1971; rpt. New York: Macmillan, 1992), 434.
6. Quoted in William Kelleher Storey's *Writing History* (1996; rpt. New York: Oxford University Press, 2004), 1.
7. Jim Leach, "The Screwball Comedy," in *Film Genre: Theory and Criticism*, ed. Barry K. Grant (Austin: University of Texas, 1986), 75.
8. See the author's *American Dark Comedy: Beyond Satire* (Westport, Connecticut: Greenwood Press, 1996); *Parody as Film Genre: "Never Give a Saga an Equal Break"* (Westport, Connecticut: Greenwood Press, 1999); *Personality Comedians as Genre: Selected Players* (Westport, Connecticut: Greenwood Press, 1997); *Populism and the Capra Legacy* (Westport, Connecticut: Greenwood Press, 1995); *Romantic vs. Screwball Comedy: Charting the Difference* (Lanham, Maryland: Scarecrow Press, 2002), and *Screwball Comedy: A Genre of Madcap Romance* (Westport, Connecticut: Greenwood Press, 1986).
9. Paris talk: "Chaplin's Film Pioneer Status in Black or Macabre Humor," in *Charlie Chaplin: His Reflections in Modern Times*, ed. Adophe Nysenholic (New York:

Morton de Gryton, 1991); see the author's *Chaplin's War Trilogy: An Evolving Lens in Three Dark Comedies, 1918–1947* (Jefferson, North Carolina: McFarland, 2014). (Chosen by *Huntington Post* as one of the best film books of 2014.)
10. Sam Roberts, "Herald Price Fahringer, 87, Free-Speech Defender, Dies," *New York Times*, February 20, 2015, B-10.
11. William Styron, *Darkness Visible: A Memoir of Madness* (1990; rpt. New York: Vintage Books, 1992), 23.
12. See the author's *Carole Lombard: The Hoosier Tornado* (Indianapolis: Indiana Historical Society Press, 2003).
13. See the author's *Irene Dunne: First Lady of Hollywood* (Lanham, Maryland: Scarecrow Press, 2006).
14. Kurt Vonnegut, *A Man Without a Country* (New York: Seven Stories Press, 2005), 119.
15. Mel Gussow, "Stage: Ewell in Waiting for Godot," *New York Times*, July 29, 1971, 43.
16. Ibid.
17. Vonnegut, *A Man Without a Country*, 115.

Chapter 1

1. "'MASH' Appeal," *Entertainment Weekly*, March 1996, 106.
2. See the author's *The Marx Brothers: A Bio-Bibliography* (Westport, Connecticut: Greenwood Press, 1987); *Groucho & W. C. Fields: Huckster Comedians* (Jackson: University of Mississippi Press, 1994); *Leo McCarey: From Marx to McCarthy* (Lanham, Maryland: Scarecrow Press, 2005).
3. *MASH* review, *Variety*, January 21, 1970.
4. Pauline Kael, "Blessed Profanity," *The New Yorker*, January 24, 1970, in Kael's *Deeper Into the Movies* (Boston: Little, Brown, 1973). 95.
5. Cobbett Steinberg, *Reel Facts* (New York: Vintage Books, 1978), 352.
6. Judith M. Kass, *Robert Altman: American Innovator* (New York: Popular Library, 1978), 61.
7. Rick Lyman, "Robert Altman: Altman, Director With Daring, Dies at 81," *New York Times*, November 22, 2006, C-11.
8. Ibid.
9. Bob Hope and Linda Hope, *My Life in Jokes* (New York: Hyperion, 2003), 56.
10. Ibid., 84.
11. See the author's *Chaplin's War Trilogy: An Evolving Lens in Three Dark Comedies, 1918–1947* (Jefferson, North Carolina: McFarland, 2014).
12. Mitchell Zuckoff, *Robert Altman: The Oral Biography* (New York: Alfred A. Knopf, 2009), 287.

13. Daniel O'Brien, *Robert Altman: Hollywood Survivor* (New York: Continuum, 1995), 36.

14. Zuckoff, *Robert Altman: The Oral Biography*, 39, 50.

15. For example, see Danny Peary's *A Guide for the Film Fanatic* (New York: Simon & Schuster, 1986).

16. Richard Hooker (pseudonym for H. Richard Hornberger), *H.* (1968; rpt. New York: Harper, 2001), 195.

17. Gary Shteyngart, "Gary Shteyngart," *New York Times*, February 2, 2014, Book Review: 7.

18. Hooker, *MASH*, 30.

19. See the author's many works on Chaplin, such as his *Charlie Chaplin's A Bio-Bibliography* (Westport, Connecticut: Greenwood Press, 1983).

20. Hooker, *MASH*, 9.

21. Robert T. Self, *Robert Altman's Subliminal Reality* (Minneapolis: University of Minnesota Press, 2002), 33.

22. Robert Altman, "Rambling Screening Comments Before a Sneak Preview of *Thieves Like Us*," University of Iowa, 1973–1974 term (author's notes).

23. Hooker, *MASH*, 34.

24. David Sterritt, ed., *Robert Altman Interviews* (Jackson: University Press of Mississippi, 2000), 193.

25. Michael Thomas, "Flicks: A Movie Column," *Status*, April 1970.

26. Hooker, *MASH*, 126–127.

27. Ibid., 127.

28. Sterritt, *Robert Altman Interviews*, 15.

29. Kass, *Robert Altman: American Innovation*, 177.

30. Nick Tosches, *DINO: Living High in the Dirty Business of Dreams* (1992; rpt. New York: Dell, 1993), 325.

31. Will Cuppy, *How to Become Extinct* (1941; rpt. Garden City, New York: Garden City Books, 1951); also see the author's *Will Cuppy American Satirist: A Biography* (Jefferson, North Carolina: McFarland, 2013).

32. Tom Stoppard, *Rosencrantz & Gildenstern Are Dead* (New York: Grove Weidenfeld, 1967), 71–72.

33. See the author's *Laurel & Hardy: A Bio-Bibliography* (Westport, Connecticut: Greenwood Press, 1990).

34. Carl Sandburg, *Chicago Poems* (1916; rpt. New York: Dover, 2012), 33.

35. Bill Read, *The Days of Dylan Thomas* (New York: McGraw-Hill, 1964), 150.

36. Joseph Gelmis, "Donald Sutherland: *MASH* Notes," *Newsday*, July 27, 1970, 14-W.

37. Joseph Heller, *Catch-22* (1961; rpt. New York: Dell, 1968), 184.

38. "Matthew 10:30," in *The Living Bible* (Wheaton, Illinois: Tyndale House Publishers, 1971), 754.

39. Altman, "Rambling Screening Comments Before a Sneak Preview of *Thieves Like Us*."

40. Thomas Heggen and Joshua Logan, *Mr. Roberts: A Play* (New York: Random House, 1948), 159–160.

41. Thomas Heggen, *Mr. Roberts* (Boston: Houghton Mifflin, 1946), 218.

42. Robert Match, "Between Tears and Laughter," *New York Herald Tribune*, August 25, 1946, 7:4.

43. Kael, "Blessed Profanity," 93.

44. Peter Biskind, *Easy Riders, Raging Bulls* (New York: Simon & Schuster, 1998), 82.

45. Henry David Thoreau, *Walden and Other Writings of Henry David Thoreau*, ed. Brooks Atkinson (1854, *Walden*; rpt. New York: Modern Library, 1965), 7.

46. William Johnson, "*MASH*," *Film Quarterly*, Spring 1970, 41.

47. For example, see Roger Greenspun's "*MASH*,"

New York Times, January 26, 1970, 26; or Daniel O'Brien's *Robert Altman: American Survivor*, 37.

48. See the author's extensive writing on the subject, especially: *Populism and the Capra Legacy* (Westport, Connecticut: Greenwood Press, 1995), and *Mr. Deeds Goes to Yankee Stadium: Baseball Films in the Capra Tradition* (Jefferson, North Carolina: McFarland, 2004).

49. Hooker, *MASH*, 82, 83, 90.

50. Katie Arnold-Ratliff, "Stealth Maneuvers," *New York Times*, December 29, 2013, Book Review section: 9.

51. Sterritt, ed., *Robert Altman Interviews*, 198.

52. Owen Gleiberman, "Philip Seymour Hoffman: The Master," *Entertainment Weekly*, February 14, 2014, 37.

53. Besides the author's aforementioned McCary biography (footnote 2) see his *Screwball Comedy: A Genre of Madcap Romance* (Westport, Connecticut: Greenwood Press, 1986), and *Romantic vs. Screwball Comedy: Charting the Difference* (Lanham, Maryland: Scarecrow Press, 2002).

54. Ring Lardner, Jr., *I'd Hate Myself in the Morning: A Memoir* (New York: Thunder Mouth Press, 2000), 171.

55. "'*MASH*' Appeal," *Entertainment Weekly*, 106.

56. Greenspun, "*MASH*," *New York Times*.

57. Robert Altman voice-over, *MASH*, directed by Altman (1970; Twentieth Century–Fox Home Entertainment, 2004), DVD.

58. Sterritt, ed., *Robert Altman Interviews*.

59. Ring Lardner, Jr., covers blurb for Richard Hooker's *MASH* (1968, rpt. New York: Harper, 2001).

60. "*MASH*" review, *Booklist*, January 15, 1969, 537.

61. "Hooker, Richard (pseud). *MASH*," *Library Journal*, October 15, 1968, 3798.

62. "*MASH*" review, *Publishers Weekly*, August 5, 1968, 54.

63. Hooker, *MASH*, 34, 59, 65, 130, 61, 84, 82 (text quoting order).

64. Ring Lardner, Jr., *I'd Hate Myself In the Morning*, 160.

65. Hooker, *MASH*, 32–33.

66. Ibid., 39, 216.

67. "Hooker, Richard, *MASH*," *Kirkus Review*, August 15, 1968, 925.

68. Wes D. Gehring, Conversation with Robert Mugge, Ball State University (Muncie, Indiana), February 22, 2014.

69. Ring Lardner, Jr., *The Lardners: My Family Remembered* (New York: Harper & Row, 1976), 354.

70. Ibid., 329.

71. Arthur M. Schlesinger, Jr., "The Cold War," in *The National Experience: A History of the United States*, John M. Blum, ed. (New York: Harcourt Brace, 1968), 783.

72. See the author's *Joe E. Brown: Film Comedian and Baseball Buffoon* (Jefferson, North Carolina: McFarland, 2006).

73. Hooker, *MASH*, 31.

74. Ibid., 123.

75. "Prototype for Trapper John Character of *MASH*," *Chicago Tribune*, December 25, 1999, 2:11.

76. Bill O'Reilly and Martin Dugard, *Killing Kennedy: The End of Camelot* (New York: Henry Holt, 2012), 131.

77. Ibid., 132.

78. Vincent Canby, "Blood, Blasphemy and Laughs," *New York Times*, February 1, 1970, Section 2:1.

79. Joseph Morgenstern, "Bloody Funny," *Newsweek*, February 2, 1970, 83.

80. Ibid.

81. Tom Milne, *"MASH* [Review]," *Monthly Film Bulletin*, July 1970, 140.

82. William Johnson, *"MASH,"* 41.

Chapter 2

1. Adam J. Sorkin, ed., *Conversations with Joseph Heller* (Jackson: University Press of Mississippi, 1993), 97.

2. For more on Mike Nichols' air force joke, see: Joseph Gelmis' *The Film Director as Superstar* (Garden City, New York: Doubleday, 1970), 268.

3. Peter Biskind, *Easy Riders, Raging Bulls* (New York: Simon & Schuster, 1998), 81.

4. Joseph Heller, *Catch–22* (1961; rpt. New York: Dell, 1968), 206.

5. See the author's *Leo McCarey: From Marx to McCarthy* (Lanham, Maryland: Scarecrow Press, 2005).

6. Heller, *Catch–22*, 56.

7. Ibid., 177.

8. Ibid., 450.

9. Daniel Sandstrom, "Philip Roth Interview: My Life as a Writer," *New York Times,* March 16, 2014, Book Review section: 15.

10. Heller, *Catch–22*, 347.

11. Joseph Gelmis, *The Film Director as Superstar*, 274.

12. Ibid., 281.

13. Vincent Canby, "A Triumphant Catch," *New York Times*, June 28, 1970, Section 2:1.

14. Ibid.

15. John Mahoney, *"'Catch–22'* Brilliant Bits; Cynical and Bitterly Cold," *Hollywood Reporter*, June 5, 1970, 3.

16. See the author's "Will Cuppy: Factual Fun Sautéed with Satire," *TRACES of Indiana and Midwestern History*, Winter 2014, 5; also see Gehring's *Will Cuppy, American Satirist, A Biography* (Jefferson, North Carolina: McFarland, 2013).

17. Samuel Beckett, *Waiting for Godot* (1954; rpt. New York: Grove Press, 1989), 65–66.

18. John Lahr, *Notes on a Cowardly Lion* (1969; rpt. New York: Ballantine Books, 1970), 309.

19. Sorkin, ed., *Conversations with Joseph Heller*, 91.

20. Luis Buñuel, *My Last Sigh*, trans. Abigail Israel (1982; rpt. New York: Random House, 1984), 14.

21. Beckett, *Waiting for Godot*, 12.

22. Ibid., 62; also see the author's: *Laurel & Hardy: A Bio-Bibliography* (Westport, Connecticut: Greenwood Press, 1990), and the aforementioned *Leo McCarey: From Marx to McCarthy* (Lanham, Maryland: Scarecrow Press, 2005).

23. Kurt Vonnegut, *Slapstick* (New York: Delacorte Press/Semour Lawrence, 1976), dedication page, and page one.

24. Heller, *Catch–22*, 187.

25. H. Wayne Schuth, *Mike Nichols* (Boston: Twayne Publishers, 1978), 75.

26. Heller, *Catch–22*, 34.

27. Lord Alfred Tennyson, "Lady Clara Vere de Vere"; this frequently anthologized poem first appeared in Volume 1 of Tennyson's *Poems* (1842); see also *The Poems of Tennyson*, Christopher Ricks, ed. (London: Norton, 1969), 636–638.

28. Heller, *Catch–22*, 272.

29. Ibid., 427.

30. Will Cuppy, "The Aard-vark," in *How To Tell Your Friends from the Apes* (1931; rpt. New York: Signet Classics, 2005), 193–140.

31. George Orwell, *1984* (1949; rpt. New York: Signet Classics, 1961), 245.

32. Sorkin, ed., *Conversations with Joseph Heller*, 59.

33. Ibid., 95.

34. Richard G. Stern, "Bombs Away," *New York Times*, October 22, 1961.

35. Orville Prescott, "Books of the Times," *New York Times*, October 23, 1961.

36. Joseph Heller, *Now and Then* (New York: Random House, 1998), 213.

37. Howard Jacobson, "Introduction" (2005) to Joseph Heller's *Catch–22* (1962; rpt. London: Vintage, 2005), vi.

38. Canby, "A Triumphant 'Catch,'" and Mahoney, "'Catch–22' Brilliant Bits; Cynical and Bitterly Cold."

39. Joseph Morgenstern, "Into the Mad Blue Yonder," *Newsweek*, June 22, 1970, 81.

40. Canby, "A Triumphant 'Catch.'"

41. "Some Are More Yossarian Than Others," *Time*, June 15, 1970, 95.

42. Ibid.

43. Heller, *Now and Then*, 187.

44. Roger Ebert, *"Catch–22"* [review], *Chicago Sun-Times*, January 1, 1970.

45. Arthur D. Murphy, *"Catch–22"* [review], *Variety*, June 10, 1970.

46. Ibid.

47. Morgenstein, "Into the Mad Blue Yonder."

48. Ibid.

49. Anthony Lane, "After Darkness," *The New Yorker*, April 14, 2014, 87.

50. Erica Heller, *Yossarian Slept Here* (New York: Simon & Schuster, 2011), 95–96.

51. McCandlish Phillips, "Heller Pleased with 'Catch–22' Film," *New York Times*, June 19, 1970, 24.

52. Ibid.

53. *"Catch–22* Caliber," *Time*, January 26, 1970, 80.

54. Schuth, *Mike Nichols*, 159.

55. Susan Sackett, *Box Office Hits* (New York: Billboard Books, 1990), 213.

56. Adapted from the King James version of the *Bible*, Luke 12:48.

57. Ebert, *"Catch–22"* [review].

58. William Goldman, "Culture Hero," in his *The Season: A Candid Look at Broadway* (1969; rpt. New York: Limelight Editions, 1984), 263–268.

59. Barry Bearak, "Mismatch in the Bronx," *New York Times*, April 15, 2014, B-9.

60. Jacobson, "Introduction," vi.

61. Lahr, *Notes on a Cowardly Lion*, 296.

62. Donna Freydkin, "'Railway Man' Shares Tips to Stay on Track," *USA Today*, April 14, 2014, 1-D.

63. Voice-over narration, *8½*, directed by Federico Fellini (1963; Corinth Films, Criterion Collection, 1980) DVD.

64. Murphy, *"Catch–22"* [review].

65. "No Comparison," *The New Yorker*, June 27, 1970, 62.

66. Arthur Lubrow, "The Woman and the Giant (No Fable)," *New York Times*, April 13, 2014, Art & Leisure section: 24.

67. Ibid.

68. J. Dudley Andrew, *The Major Film Theories* (New York: Oxford University Press, 1976), 88.

69. Gelmis, *The Film Director as Superstar*, 269.

70. Bearak, "Mismatch in the Bronx," B-11.

Chapter 3

1. "Epic and Crumbcrusher," *The New Yorker*, December 26, 1970, 52.

2. Jan Aghed and Bernard Cohn, "Interview with Arthur Penn" (1971), in *Arthur Penn Interviews*, eds. Michael Chaiken and Paul Cronin (Jackson: University Press of Mississippi, 2008), 67.

3. Bob Thomas, "'Little Big Man': History Rewritten" (syndicated), *Newark Evening News*, August 8, 1969, 18.

4. Michel Delain, "The First Cheyenne Film Director," *L'Express*, April 5, 1971, in *Arthur Penn Interviews*, eds. Michael Chaiken and Paul Cronin, 76–77.

5. Joe Hyams, "The Western He Wanted to Do," *New York Herald Tribune*, March 26, 1961, Book Review, section: 23.

6. *Little Big Man*, *Films and Filming*, July 1971, 21.

7. John G. Cawelti, *The Six-Gun Mystique* (Bowling Green, Ohio: Bowling Green University Press, 1971).

8. Glenn Frankel, *The Searchers: The Making of an American Legend* (New York: Bloomsbury, 2013), 254.

9. Tim Brooks and Earle Marsh, *The Complete Directory to Prime Time Network TV Shows: 1946-Present* (New York: Ballantine Books, 1979), 13.

10. Mason Wiley and Damien Bona, *Inside Oscar* (1986; rpt. New York: Ballantine Books, 1993), 476–477.

11. John Gerber, "Lecture on Southwestern Humor," in "American Humor and Satire," University of Iowa class, 1975.

12. Walter Blair, *Native American Humor* (1937; rpt. San Francisco: Chandler Publishing, 1960), 62–101.

13. Thomas Berger, *Little Big Man* (1964; rpt. New York: Dial Press, 2005), 142.

14. Mark Twain, *Adventures of Huckleberry Finn* (1984; rpt. New York: Oxford University Press, 1996), 366.

15. Berger, *Little Big Man*, xxx–xxxi.

16. Johnson J. Hooper, *Simon Suggs' Adventures* (1867; rpt. Americus, Georgia: Americans Book, 1928), 12.

17. See the author's *Film Clowns of the Depression* (Jefferson, North Carolina: McFarland, 2007).

18. Berger, *Little Big Man*, 429.

19. Tom Miline, "Little Big Man," *Focus on Film*, Spring 1971, 4.

20. Thomas, "'Little Big Man': History Rewritten," 18.

21. Michael Chaiken and Paul Cronin, "A Summing Up," 2006, in *Arthur Penn Interviews*, eds. Chaiken and Cronin, 208.

22. Larry Cohen, "'Little Big Man' Sure to Do Well at the Box Office," *Hollywood Reporter*, December 16, 1970, 3.

23. Joseph Gelmis, "Impressive Mock Epic," *Newsday*, December 15, 1970, 7-A.

24. Mario Foglietti, "Conflicts of Conscience," *Revista del Cinematografo*, December 1971, in *Arthur Penn Interviews*, eds. Chaiken and Cronin, 86.

25. Berger, *Little Big Man*, 99.

26. Brooks Landon, "Introduction," in Thomas Berger's *Little Big Man* (1964; rpt. New York: Dial Press, 2005), xvi.

27. Todd McCarthy, *Pulp Fiction* review, *Variety*, May 23, 1994.

28. George P. Elliot, "Heap Forked Tongue," *New York Times*, October 11, 1964, Book Review section: 24.

29. Art Murphy, *Little Big Man*, *Variety*, December 16, 1970.

30. Michel Delain, "The First Cheyenne Film Director," *L' Express*, April 5, 1971, in *Arthur Penn Interview*, eds. Chaiken and Cronin, 77.

31. Milne, *Little Big Man*, 4.

32. See the author's *Groucho & W. C. Fields: Huckster Comedians* (Jackson: University Press of Mississippi, 1994).

33. Edgar Allan Poe, "Diddling Considered as One of the Exact Sciences," in *The Complete Tales and Poems of Edgar Allan Poe* (New York: Random House, 1938), 367, 369.

34. Susan Kuhlman, *Knave, Fool, and Genius: The Confidence Man as He Appears in Nineteenth Century American Fiction* (Chapel Hill: University of North Carolina Press, 1973), 6.

35. See the author's *Groucho & W. C. Fields: Huckster Comedians*.

36. Vincent Canby, "Dustin Hoffman Stars in 'Little Big Man,'" *New York Times*, December 15, 1970, 53.

37. P. D. Z., ["message of corporate menace"], "How the West Was Lost," *Newsweek*, December 21, 1970, 98, 100.

38. Shelley Benoit, "Little Big Man," *Show,* March 1971, 57.

39. John M. Blum, ed., *The National Experiences: A History of the United State* (1963; rpt. New York: Harcourt, Brace & World, 1968), 283.

40. James Russell Lowell, *The Biglow Papers* (1848; rpt. Philadelphia: Altemus, 1910), 150.

41. Christopher Isherwood, *Goodbye to Berlin* (1939, rpt. New York: ISIS, 1945), 3.

42. Gelmis, "Impressive Mock Epic," 7-A.

43. For example, see "Epic and Crumbcrusher," *The New Yorker*, December 26, 1970, 50.

44. Judy Klemesrud, "Dustin Calls Him Grandpa," *New York Times*, February 21, 1971.

45. Ibid.

46. Guy Braucourt, "Interview with Arthur Penn," *Cinema*, May 1971, in *Arthur Penn Interviews*, ed. Chaiken and Cronin, 83–84.

47. Jean-Dominique Bauby, *The Diving Bell and the Butterfly*, trans. Jeremony Leggatt (1996; rpt. New York: Vintage Books, 1997).

48. Berger, *Little Big Man*, 165.

49. Ibid., 193–194.

50. Ibid., 130.

51. "Epic and Crumbrusher," *The New Yorker*, 50.

52. See the author's *Forties Film Funnymen: The Decade's Great Comedians at Work in the Shadow of War* (Jefferson, North Carolina: McFarland, 2010).

53. *"Little Big Man," Films and Filming*, June 1971, 63.

54. Gelmis, "Impressive Mock Epic," 7-A.

55. "The Red and the White," *Time*, December 21, 1970, 57.

56. Ibid., 56.

57. Roger Ebert, *"Little Big Man"* [review], *Chicago Sun-Times*, January 1, 1970.

58. Pauline Kael, *Reeling* (New York: Warner Books, 1976), 415–416.

59. Cobbett Steinberg, *Reel Facts: The Movie Book of Records* (New York: Vintage Books, 1978), 352.

60. Ibid.

61. Jessica Van Heller, "Rising Out of the Ashes" (previously unpublished), in *Arthur Penn Interviews*, eds. Chaiken and Cronin, 93.

62. Ibid.

63. Jean-Pierre Coursodon (with Pierre Sauvage), *American Directors, Volume II* (New York: McGraw-Hill, 1983), 275.

64. Ibid., 265.

Chapter 4

1. Art Murphy, *"Harold and Maude"* [review], *Variety*, December 15, 1971, 18.

2. See James Russell Lowell's *The Biglow Papers* (1848; rpt. Philadelphia: Altemus, 1910).

3. See the author's *Screwball: A Genre of Madcap Romance* (Westport, Connecticut: Greenwood Press, 1986); *Romantic vs. Screwball Comedy: Charting the Difference* (Lanham, Maryland: Scarecrow Press, 2002).

4. Herbe Sterne, *I Married a Witch* review, *Rob Wagner's Script* (December 19, 1942), in *Selected Film Criticism*, 1941–50, ed. Anthony Slide (Metuchen, N.J.: Scarecrow Press, 1983), 85; Richard Schickel, *Cary Grant* (New York: Applause Books, 1999), 56.

5. Nick Dawson, *Being Hal Ashby: Life of a Hollywood Rebel* (2009; rpt. Lexington: University of Kentucky Press, 2011), 127.

6. See the author's "Laughter from the Dark Side," *USA Today Magazine*, March 2008, 53.

7. Jonathan Mirsky, "An Inconvenient Past," *New York Times*, May 25, 2014, Book Review: 21.

8. See the author's *The Marx Brothers: A Bio-Bibliography* (Westport, Connecticut: Greenwood Press, 1987), and *Groucho & W. C. Fields: Huckster Comedians* (Jackson: University Press of Mississippi, 1994).

9. "Bud Cort and John Alonzo," in the untitled *Harold and Maude* (1971) booklet for the Criterion Collection's Special DVD edition, 2012, 26.

10. See the author's *James Dean: Rebel with a Cause* (Indianapolis: Indiana Historical Society Press, 2005).

11. "Bud Cort and John Alonzo," 23–24.

12. Matt Zoller Seitz, "Life and How to Live It," in the untitled *Harold and Maude* (1971) booklet for the Criterion Collection's Special DVD edition, 2012, 7.

13. W. H. Auden, "Funeral Blues" (1938), in *The Columbia Anthology of Gay Literature*, ed. R. S. Fone (New York: Columbia University Press, 1998), 395.

14. Isabel O'Neill, "*Harold and Maude*," in *Magill's Survey of Cinema*, ed. Frank N. Magill (Englewood Cliffs, New Jersey: Salem Press, 1980), 718.

15. Colin Higgins, *Harold and Maude* (1971; rpt. New York: Avon Books, 1975), dedication page.

16. For example, see C. S. Lewis' *An Experiment in Criticism* (New York: Cambridge Press, 1961).

17. Francois Truffaut, *Hitchcock* (revised edition, New York: Simon & Schuster, 1983), 201 n.

18. Matt Zoller Seitz, "Life and How to Live It," 9.

19. Colin Higgins, *Harold and Maude*, 21–22.

20. "Bill Mahr in Concert," Murat Theatre at Old National Centre, Indianapolis, Indiana, May 31, 2014.

21. Nick Dawson, *Hal Ashby: Interviews* (Jackson: University Press of Mississippi, 2010), 21.

22. Nick Dawson, *Being Hal Ashby: Life of a Hollywood Rebel*, 65.

23. Nick Dawson, *Hal Ashby: Interviews*, 77.

24. Nick Dawson, *Being Hal Ashby: Life of a Hollywood Rebel*, 124–125.

25. "Bud Cort and John Alonzo," 19, 27.

26. Richard Meran Barsam, *Nonfiction Film: A Critical History* (New York: E. P. Dutton, 1973), 128.

27. Nick Dawson, *Being Hal Ashby: Life of Hollywood Rebel*, 72.

28. "Bud Cort and John Alonzo," 22.

29. *The AFI's 100 Years … 100 Laughs*, a CBS television special, first broadcast June 13, 2000.

30. *Harold and Maude* ad, *Village Voice*, December 23, 1971, 66.

31. Jerry Oster, "To Die in New York & Live in Minnesota," *New York Daily News*, June 9, 1974.

32. AlJean Harmetz, "Harold's Back and Maude's Got Him," *New York Times*, May 26, 1974, 1.

33. Ibid.

34. Henry Alford, "Minnesota Nice," *New York Times*, June 1, 2014, Book Review: 24.

35. Michael Shedlin, "Reviews: *Harold and Maude*," *Film Quarterly*, Fall 1973, 53.

36. AlJean Harmetz, "Harold's Back and Maude's Got Him," 12.

37. Pauline Kael, *5001 Nights at the Movies* (New York: Henry Holt, 1991), 319.

38. Leticia Kent, "A Boy of 20 and a Woman of 80…," *New York Times*, April 4, 1971, D-13.

39. Douglas Martin, "Tadeusz Rosewicz, Fierce Poetic Voice of Postwar Poland, Is Dead at 91," *New York Times*, May 21, 2014, B-17.

Chapter 5

1. Christopher Isherwood, *Goodbye to Berlin* (1939; rpt. New York: New Directions, 1986), 47.

2. Sam Wasson, *Fosse* (New York: Houghton Mifflin Harcourt, 2013), 260.

3. Joan Acocella, "Dancing in the Dark," *The New Yorker*, December 21, 1998, 103.

4. Isherwood, 67–68.

5. Ibid.

6. Linda Mitejewski, *Divine Decadence* (Princeton, New Jersey: Princeton University Press, 1992), 3–4.

7. Drew Bernard, "Life as a Long Rehearsal," *American Film*, November 1979, 28.

8. Peter Levinson, *Puttin' on the Ritz* (New York: St. Martin's Press, 2009), 32; also see the author's *"Mr. B" or Comforting Thoughts About the Bison: A Critical Biography of Robert Benchley* (Westport, Connecticut: Greenwood Press, 1992).

9. Levnison, *Puttin' on the Ritz*, 323.

10. Keith Garebian, *The Making of Cabaret* (New York: Oxford University Press, 2011), 144.

11. Kevin Boyd Grubb, *Razzle Dazzle: The Life and Work of Bob Fosse* (New York: St. Martin's Press, 1989), 146.

12. Leslie Taubman, "Cabaret," in *Magill's Survey of Cinema*, ed. Frank N. Magill (Englewood Cliffs, New Jersey: Salem Press, 1980), 267–270.

13. Garebian, *The Making of Cabaret*, 155.

14. Peter Buckley, "*Cabaret*: Peter Buckley Finds Bob Fosse's Experience More Divine Than Decadent," *Films and Filming*, August 1972, 46.

15. Stephen Farber, "*Cabaret* May Shock Kansas," *New York Times*, February 20, 1972, Section 2, 2.

16. Edith H. Walton, "Berlin on the Brink," *New York Times*, March 19, 1939, Book Review section: 23.

17. Alfred Kazi, "Leaves Under the Lindens," *New York Herald Tribune*, March 12, 1939, Section 9, 10.

18. Dorothy Thompson, "Revolution and Revelation, Hitler Model," *New York Times*, March 19, 1939, Section 9, 3.

19. Will Cuppy, "Mystery and Adventure [review column]: 'Lunacy Becomes Us,'" *New York Herald Tribune*, April 16, 1939, Section 9, 17.

20. Brooks Atkinson, "Insurgent Penmen," *New York Times*, April 9, 1939, Section 10, 1.

21. Christopher Isherwood, "Introduction," in *Goodbye to Berlin*, 1.

22. Mitezewski, *Divine Decadence*.

23. Wasson, *Fosse*, 287–288.

24. Ibid., 396.

25. Martin Gottfried, *All His Jazz* (New York: Bantam Books, 1990), 215.

26. Quoted in Mitezewski's *Divine Decadence*, 5.

27. Gottfried, *All His Jazz*, 339.

28. *The Tramp and the Dictator*, A Kevin Brownlow Documentary Film, BBC, 2001 (55 minutes).

29. Frank Capra, *Frank Capra: The Name Above the Title* (New York: Macmillan, 1971), 328–329.

30. Wasson, *Fosse*, 287.

31. A. O. Scott, "A War to End All Innocence," *New York Times*, June 22, 2014, Arts & Leisure: 1, 21.

32. Richard W. Sonnerfeldt, *Witness to Nuremberg* (2002; rpt. New York: Arcade Publishing, 2006), 30.

33. Isherwood, *Goodbye to Berlin*, 150.

34. Siegfried Kracauer, *From Caligary to Hitler: A Psychological History of the German Film* (1947; rpt. Princeton, New Jersey: Princeton Press, 1971).

35. Wasson, *Fosse*, 224.

36. Christopher Isherwood, *A Single Man* (1964; rpt. Minneapolis: University of Minnesota Press, 2001), 10–11.

37. Otto Friedrich, *Before the Deluge: A Portrait of Berlin in the 1920s* (1972; rpt. New York: HarperPerennial, 1995), 149.

38. Christopher Isherwood, "About This Book [Introduction]," in *The Berlin Stories* (1954; rpt. New York: New Directions Book, 2008), xvii.

39. Isherwood, *A Single Man*, 69.

40. Ibid., 70–72.

41. Christopher Isherwood, "The Berlin Stories" (1963), in *Isherwood on Writing*, ed. James J. Berg (Minneapolis: University of Minnesota Press, 2007), 164.

42. Mason Wiley and Damien Bona, *Inside Oscar* (1986; rpt. New York: Ballantine Books, 1993), 967–968; Cobbett Steinberg, *Reel Facts: The Movie Book of Records* (New York: Vintage Books, 1978), 352.

43. Buckley, "Peter Buckley Finds Bob Fosse's Experience More 'Divine Than Decadent,'" 45.

44. Art Murphy, "*Cabaret*" [review], *Variety*, February 16, 1972.

45. Gary Giddins, "'Cabaret' on Film," *Hollywood Reporter*, February 15, 1972, 3.

46. Roger Greenspun, "*Cabaret*," *New York Times*, February 14, 1972, 22.

47. Gottfried, *All His Jazz*, 228.

48. Vincent Canby, "'A Clockwork Orange' Dazzles the Senses and Mind," *New York Times*, December 20, 1971, 44.

49. Giddins, "'Cabaret' on Film," 3.

50. Jody K. Biehl, "In Berlin Life Is Still a Cabaret," *USA Today*, December 12, 2001, 10-D.

51. Anthony Burgess, "Author Has His Say on 'Clockwork' Film," *Los Angeles Times*, February 13, 1972, Calendar section: 1.

Chapter 6

1. Louise Sweeney, "Films: A Deeply Original Thinker," *Christian Science Monitor*, May 5, 1972.

2. Mentioned frequently in Kurt Vonnegut, Jr.'s *Slaughterhouse-Five* (1969; rpt. New York: Dell Book, 1974), an early notation being on page 22.

3. Ibid., 27.

4. Benjamin Moser, "Patriarch and Pariah," *New York Times*, July 6, 2014, Book Review section: 17.

5. Ibid.

6. Anthony Burgess, "Author Has His Say on 'Clockwork' Film," *Los Angeles Times*, February 13, 1972, Calendar section: 1.

7. Vonnegut, *Slaughterhouse-Five*, 86.

8. Andrew Horton, *The Films of George Roy Hill* (New York: Columbia University Press, 1984), 82.

9. Kurt Vonnegut. Jr., *Between Time and Timbuktu* (1972; rpt. New York: Delta, 1975), xv.

10. Louise Sweeny, "Films: A Deeply Original Thinker," *Christian Science Monitor*, May 5, 1972.

11. Leslie Jamison, "Bookends," *New York Times*, July 13, 2014, Book Review section: 27.

12. Kurt Anderson, "True to Character," *New York Times*, October 28, 2012, Book Review section: 27.

13. Vonnegut, *Slaughterhouse-Five*, 166.

14. William Wolf, "*Slaughterhouse-Five*" [review], *Cue* magazine, April 1, 1972.

15. Bettany Hughes, "School for a Scoundrel," *New York Times*, July 13, 2014, Book Review section: 12.

16. Horton, *The Films of George Roy Hill*, 94.

17. See the author's *Robert Wise: Shadowlands* (Indianapolis: Indiana Historical Society Press, 2012).

18. Many authors have referenced this conflict as the "good war," such as Stud Terkel's Pulitzer Prize–winning *The Good War: An Oral History of World War II* (1984).

19. Richard Whelan, "Introduction," in *Robert Capa*, Aperture editorial staff (New York: Aperture Foundation, 1996), 12.

20. See the author's *The Marx Brothers: A Bio-Bibliography* (Westport, Connecticut: Greenwood Press, 1987).

21. Gregory D. Sumner, *Unstuck in Time* (New York: Seven Stories Press, 2011), 127.

22. Dalton Trumbo, *Johnny Got His Gun* (1939; rpt. New York: Bantam Books, 1989), 115.

23. Shores, *George Roy Hill*, 54.

24. One naysayer, at least for Cassidy escaping, can be found in Lulu Parker Betensen's (as told to Dora Flack) *Butch Cassidy, My Brother*, with a foreword by Robert Redford (1975; rpt. New York: Penguin Books, 1976).

25. Ken Kesey, *One Flew Over the Cuckoo's Nest* (New York: Signet Books, 1962), 254.

26. Trumbo, *Johnny Got His Gun*, 126.

27. Dave Itzkoff, "A Master of Illusion Endures," *New York Times*, July 20, 2014, Arts & Leisure section: 12.

28. Kesey, *One Flew Over the Cuckoo's Nest*, 233.

29. Shores, *George Roy Hill*, 48.

30. George Carlin periodically used variations of this line in his stand-up act and guest spots on television.

31. Vonnegut, *Slaughterhouse-Five*, 215.

32. Vonnegut frequently voiced this opinion on the talk show circuit. He also alluded to this point following a speech he gave at Clowes Hall, Indianapolis, on April 27, 2007.

33. Sumner, *Unstuck in Time*, 144.

34. *The Making of Butch Cassidy and the Sundance Kid*, directed by Robert Crawford, and narrated by *Butch Cassidy* director George Ray Hill, 1969/1970 (42 minutes).

35. John Irving, *The World According to Garp* (New York: E. P. Dutton, 1978), 166–167.

36. *Dress to Kill*, directed by Lawrence Jordan, an Eddie Izzard concert filmed in San Francisco, 1998/1999 (114 minutes).

37. Anna Holmes, "Bookends," *New York Times*, July 27, 2014, Book Review section: 31.

38. Elizabeth Green, "(New Math) – (New Teaching) = Failure," *New York Times Magazine*, July 27, 2014, 24.

39. Kurt Vonnegut, *Timequake* (New York: G. P. Putnam's Sons, 1997), 64.

40. Kurt Vonnegut, *Kurt Vonnegut: Letters*, ed. Dan Wakefield (New York: Delacorte Press, 2012), 380, 381.

41. Ibid., 381.

42. Holmes, "Bookends."

43. Wolf, *"Slaughterhouse-Five"* [review].

44. John Simon, "In Praise of the Well-Made Film," *The New Leader*, May 15, 1972.

45. Arthur Knight, "Past and Future Merge in 'Slaughterhouse-Five,'" *Hollywood Reporter*, March 22, 1972.

46. Art Murphy, *"Slaughterhouse-Five"* [review], *Variety*, March 22, 1972.

47. Wolf, *"Slaughterhouse-Five"* [review].

48. Murphy, *"Slaughterhouse-Five"* [review].

49. Vincent Canby, "Time-Tripping with 'Slaughterhouse-Five,'" *New York Times*, March 23, 1972.

50. Jay Cocks, "Lost in Space," *Time*, April 10, 1972.

51. Robert Scholes, *"Slaughterhouse-Five"* [review], *New York Times*, April 6, 1969.

Chapter 7

1. *"Chinatown* Revisited: With Roman Polanski, Robert Evans, and Robert Towne," bonus feature on Paramount Pictures' 1990 video of the 1974 film (14 minutes).

2. Colin Higgins, *Harold and Maude* (1971; New York: Avon Books, 1975).

3. For example, Syd Fields' groundbreaking *Screenplay: The Foundation of Screenwriting* (1979; rpt. New York: Dell, 1994) uses lengthy excerpts from the *Chinatown* script, as well as devoting an entire chapter to the film—"The Setup." And David Trottier frequently references *Chinatown* in *The Screenwriter Bible* (1994; rpt. Los Angeles: Silman-James Press, 2010).

4. *"Chinatown* Revisited: With Roman Polanski, Robert Evans, and Robert Towne."

5. Ibid.

6. For a tongue-in-cheek look at both this character, and *Chinatown* in general, see author's *Film Classics Reclassified: A Shocking Spoof of Cinema* (Davenport, Iowa: Robin Vincent Publishing, 2001).

7. Raymond Chandler, *The Big Sleep* (1939; rpt. New York: Random House, 1976), 213.

8. Raymond Chandler, "The Simple Art of Murder" (1950), in an anthology of shorter pieces also entitled *The Simple Art of Murder* (New York: Random House, 1988), 18.

9. Gabriel Chevallie (trans. Malcolm Imrie), *Fear* (1930; rpt. New York: New Review Books, 2011), 18.

10. Chandler, *The Big Sleep*, 159.

11. Chandler, "The Simple Art of Murder," 18.

12. Ibid.

13. Chandler, *The Big Sleep*, 158.

14. Ibid., 155.

15. Raymond Chandler, *The Long Goodbye* (1953; rpt. New York: Random House, 1992), 151.

16. Dashiell Hammett, "A Man Called Spade," in *World's Great Detective Stories*, ed. Will Cuppy (New York: World Publishing, 1943), 53.

17. David Downing, *Jack Nicholson* (New York: Stein and Day, 1984), 112.

18. Joe Morgenstern, "Remember It, Jake, It's *Chinatown*," *Gentleman's Quarterly*, January 1990, 130.

19. Vincent Canby, "Polanski's 'Chinatown' Views Crime of '30s," *New York Times*, January 21, 1974, 26.

20. Paul Cronin, ed., *Roman Polanski Interviews* (Jackson: University Press of Mississippi, 2005), 62.

21. Fred Schruers, "The Rolling Stone Interview: Jack Nicholson," *Rolling Stone*, August 14, 1986, 49.

22. Roman Polanski, *Roman by Polanski* (New York: William Morrow, 1984), 346.

23. Ibid.

24. Martin Scorsese and Michael Henry Wilson, *A Personal Journey with Martin Scorsese Through American Movies* (New York: Miramax Books, 1997), 110.

25. Ibid., 108.

26. Robert Towne, *Chinatown*, Third Draft (Hollywood, California: Paramount, October 9, 1973), 100. (Collection of the author.)

27. Robert Goff, *The Essential Salvador Dali* (New York: Harry N. Abrams, 1998), 57.

28. "Queen of Fearless Comedy Dies at 81," *USA Today Weekend*, September 5–7, 2014, 1-A.

29. "Chinatown Revisited: With Roman Polanski, Robert Evans, and Robert Towne."

30. Michael Eaton, *Chinatown* (London: British Film Institute, 1997), 27.

31. Ambrose Bierce, *The Devil's Dictionary* (1911; rpt. New York: Dover Publications, 1958), 99.

32. Eaton, *Chinatown*, 31–32.

33. *Roman Polanski: Wanted and Desired*, a documentary by Marina Zenovich (HBO), 2008 (99 minutes).

34. Paul Cronin, ed., *Roman Polanski: Interviews*, 35.

35. Raymond Chandler, *The High Window* (1942; rpt. New York: Random House, 1992), 209.

36. Raymond Chandler, *Farewell My Lovely* (1940; rpt. New York: Random House, 1992), 292.

37. Raymond Chandler, *The Long Goodbye*, 280.

38. Eaton, *Chinatown*, 30.

39. Joseph Conrad, *Heart of Darkness* (1902; rpt. New York: Penguin Books, 1983), 121.

40. Lenny Robenstein, *"Chinatown,"* *Cineaste*, Vol. 6 #3 [1974], 38.

41. Art Murphy, *"Chinatown"* [review], *Variety*, June 19, 1974.

42. Joseph Gelmis, "Un-Sweet Dreams from 3 Paranoid Plots," *Newsday*, June 23, 1974, Part 2:11.

43. Gordon Gow, *"Chinatown"* [review], *Films and Filming*, October 1974, 38–39.

44. Roger Ebert, "Polanski's *Chinatown*: A Private Eye Movie That's Not Restricted to the Formula Plot," *Star Ledger*, August 4, 1974, Section 4: 1, 14.

45. Roger Ebert, *Chinatown* review, February 6, 2000, Gowatchit (http://gowatchit.com).

46. Peter Biskind, "The Low Road to *Chinatown*," *Premiere*, June 1994, 72.

Chapter 8

1. Eric Lax, *Woody Allen: A Biography* (New York: Alfred A. Knopf, 1991), 24.

2. David Sterritt (syndicated), "Woody Worries as He Directs," *Des Moines Register*, May 10, 1977, 1-B.

3. Lax, 25.

4. Marion Meade, *The Unruly Life of Woody Allen: A Biography* (New York: Scribner, 2000), 128.

5. Graham McCann, *Woody Allen: New Yorker* (1991; rpt. Cambridge, Massachusetts, 1992), 52.

6. Douglas J. Rowe (syndicated), "Allen's Life Take On Life Is Comic, Tragic," *Indianapolis Star*, March 25, 2005, E-5.

7. Meade, *The Unruly Life of Woody Allen: A Biography*, 125.

8. *Woody Allen on Woody Allen: Conversations with Stig Björkman* (1993; rpt. New York: Grover Press 1995), 210.

9. Woody Allen, "The Kugelmass Episode" (1977), in Allen's *Side Effects* (New York: Random House, 1980), 44.

10. Ibid., 55.

11. For example, Jeannie Williams' article, "Woody's Film Sparks Pulitzer Tiff," made the front page of *USA Today's Weekend Edition*, April 18–20, 1986.

12. Ibid.

13. See the author's *Personality Comedians as Genre: Selected Players* (Westport, Connecticut: Greenwood Press, 1997).

14. Robert Benchley, "Carnival Week in Sunny Las Los," in *The Treasurer's Report and Other Aspects of Community Singing* (New York: Grosset & Dunlap, 1930), 41; see also the author's *"Mr. B" or Comforting Thoughts About the Bison: A Critical Biography of Robert Benchley* (Westport, Connecticut: Greenwood Press, 1992).

15. Maurice Yacowar, *Loser Taken All: The Comic Art of Woody Allen* (New York: Frederick Ungar, 1979), 162.

16. "Marble Review: *Love and Death*," *Marble*, July–August 1975, 8.

17. Ibid.

18. Joseph Gelmis, "Movies: Silly and Serious," *Newsday*, June 11, 1975, Part 2:11A; also see the author's *Parody as Film Genre: "Never Give a Saga and Even Break"* (Westport, Connecticut: Greenwood Press, 1999).

19. Julian Patrick, general ed., *501 Great Writers* (New York: Quintessence, 2008), 184.

20. Ronald D. LeBlanc, "*Love and Death* and Food: Woody Allen's Comic Use of Gastronomy," in *The Films of Woody Allen in Critical Essays*, ed., Charles L. P. Silet (Lanham, Maryland: Scarecrow Press, 2006), 107.

21. Will Cuppy, *How to Become Extinct* (1941; rpt. Garden City, New York: Garden City Books, 1951), 109.

22. See the author's *Will Cuppy, American Satirist* (Jefferson, North Carolina: McFarland, 2013).

23. Yacowar, 163.

24. F. Scott Fitzgerald, *The Curious Case of Benjamin Button and other Jazz Age Stories*, ed. Patrick O' Donnell (1922; rpt. New York: Penguin Books, 1998), 341.

25. Stig Björkman, ed., *Woody Allen on Woody Allen* (New York: Grove Press, 1993), 50.

26. Béla Zombory-Moldován, *The Burning of the World*, trans. Peter Zombory-Moldován (New York: New York Review Books, 2014), 11, 13.

27. Penelop Gilliatt, "*Love and Death*" [review], excerpt from *The New Yorker*, in Douglas Brode's *Woody Allen: His Films and Career* (Secaucus, New Jersey: Citadel Press, 1985), 149.

28. Art Murphy, "*Love and Death*" [review], *Variety*, June 11, 1975.

29. Vincent Canby, "Love, Death, God, Sex, Suicide and Woody Allen," *New York Times*, June 22, 1975, Part 11:1.

30. Roger Ebert, "*Love and Death*" [review], *Chicago Sun Times*, January 1975, reproduced at http://www.rogerebert.com/reviews/love-and-death-1975.

31. Pauline Kael, quoted in Miles Palmer's *Woody Allen* (New York: Protheus, 1980), 79.

32. Richard Schickel, *Woody Allen: A Life in Film* (Chicago: Ivan R. Dee, 2003), 105.

33. Diane Jacobs, *... But We Need the Eggs: The Magic of Woody Allen* (New York: St. Martin's Press, 1982), 84.

34. Ibid.

35. LeBlanc, "*Love and Death* and Food: Woody Allen's Comic Use of Gastronomy," 100.

36. Nikola Gogal, "The Diary of a Madman" (1833–1834), trans Andrew R. MacAndrew, in *The Diary of a Madman and Other Stories* (New York: Signet Classic, 1960), 22.

37. Nikololai Gogal, "The Nose" (1836), trans. An-

drew R. MacAndrew, in *The Diary of a Madman and Other Stories* (New York: Signet Classics, 1960), 29.

38. Schickel, *Woody Allen: A Life in Film*, 106.

39. Roger Ebert, *Life Itself: A Memoir* (New York: Grand Central Publishing, 2011), 288–289.

Chapter 9

1. Duane Byrge, ed., *Private Screenings: Insiders Share a Century of Movie Moments* (Atlanta, Georgia: Turner Publishing, 1995), 77.

2. Ken Kesey, *One Flew Over the Cuckoo's Nest* (New York: Signet, 1962), 121- 122.

3. John C. Pratt, "Introduction" in Ken Kesey's *One Flew Over the Cuckoo's Nest: Text and Criticism*, ed. Pratt (1962; rpt. New York: Penguin Books, 1977), xii.

4. James Parker, "Bookends," *New York Times*, September 21, 2014, Book Review: 27.

5. See especially Charles Maland's "The Social Problem Film," in *Handbook of American Film Genres*, ed. Wes D. Gehring (Westport, Connecticut: Greenwood Press, 1988), 305–329.

6. John G. Cawelti, *The Six Gun Mystique* (Bowling Green, Ohio: Bowling Green University Press, 1971).

7. Mark Twain, *The Adventures of Huckleberry Finn* (1885; rpt. New York: Oxford University Press, 1996), 366.

8. A. O. Scott, "They're Buddies But as Coarse as the War Around Them," *New York Times*, October 17, 2014, C-10.

9. Herman Melville, *Billy Budd* (1924) in *Great Short Works* (New York: Harper & Row, 1966), 376.

10. James F. Jones, "Camus on Kafka and Melville: An Unpublished Letter" (1951), *French Review*, March 1998, 647.

11. See the author's *Groucho & W. C. Fields: Huckster Comedians* (Jackson: University Press of Mississippi, 1994).

12. Hennig Cohen, "Introduction to Herman Melville," in *The Confidence Man* (1857; rpt. New York: Holt, Rinehart and Winston, 1964), x.

13. Harrison Hayford, "Poe in The Confidence Man," in Hershel Parker's (ed.) study and text of Herman Melville's *The Confidence Man* (1857; rpt. New York: W.W. Norton, 353.

14. Herman Melville, "Letter to Friend Samuel Savage" (August 24, 1851) in *Correspondence: The Writings of Herman Melville, Vol. 14* (Chicago: Northwestern University Press and the Newberry Library, 1993), 203.

15. Herman Melville, *Moby-Dick* (1851; rpt. New York: Heritage Press, 1943), 96.

16. Clifton Fadiman, "Introduction," to Herman Melville's *Moby-Dick* (1851; rpt. New York: Heritage Press, 1943), viii.

17. Ibid., viii–ix.

18. Thomas J. Slater, *Milos Forman: A Bio-Bibliography* (Westport, Connecticut: Greenwood Press, 1987), 2.

19. Kesey, *One Flew Over the Cuckoo's Nest*, 31.

20. Eric Lichtblau, "In Cold War, U.S. Spy Agencies Used 1,000 Nazis," *New York Times*, October 27, 2014, 1-A.

21. For example, see Peter Hames' *The Czechoslovak New Wave* (1985; rpt. New York: Wallflower Press, 2005).

22. Roger Ebert, "*One Flew Over the Cuckoo's Nest*" [review], *Chicago Sun-Times*, 1975; tweaked and reproduced at: http://www.rogerebert.com/reviews/one-flew-over-the-cuckoos-nest-1975.

23. Ibid.

24. Charles Champlin, "Nicholson Hatches Gold Ego in Nest," *Los Angeles Times*, November 16, 1975, Calendar section: 1.

25. Arthur Knight, *"One Flew Over the Cuckoo's Nest"* [review], *Hollywood Reporter*, November 14, 1975, 3.

26. Colbert Steinberg, *Reel Facts: The Movie Book of Records* (New York: Vintage Books, 1978), 354.

27. Tom Wolfe, *The Electric Kool-Acid Test* (New York: Farrar, Straus and Giroux, 1968), 48.

28. Ibid., 103.

29. Ebert, *"One Flew Over the Cuckoo's Nest"* [review].

30. Emily Nussbaum, "Maine and Miami," *The New Yorker*, November 3, 2014, 101.

31. Kesey, *One Flew Over the Cuckoo's Nest*, 212.

32. Byrge, ed., *Private Screenings: Insiders Share a Century of Movie Moments*, 125–126.

33. Vincent Canby, "'Cuckoo's Nest'—A Sane Comedy About Psychotics," *New York Times,* November 23, 1975, Section 11:1.

34. Art Murphy, *"One Flew Over the Cuckoo's Nest"* [review], *Variety*, November 19, 1975.

35. Lisa Rogak, *Angry Optimist: The Life and Times of Jon Stewart* (New York: St. Martin's Press, 2014), 18.

36. John Cashman, "Laughter at Their Expense," *Newsday*, November 20, 1975, Part 2: A-8.

Chapter 10

1. Diane Keaton, *Then Again* (New York: Random House, 2011), 128.

2. Richard Schickel, *Woody Allen: A Life in Film* (Chicago: Ivan R. Dee, 2003), 7.

3. See the author's *Romantic vs. Screwball Comedy: Charting the Difference* (Lanham, Maryland: Scarecrow Press, 2002).

4. Robert W. Butler, "And She Lived Happily Ever After," *Kansas City Star*, June 28, 1993, D-5.

5. "Chilly Scenes of Winter," *New York Times*, November 7, 2014, C-18.

6. Among the author's writing on the comedian, especially see: *Charlie Chaplin: A Bio-Bibliography* (Westport, Connecticut: Greenwood Press, 1983).

7. Keaton, *Then Again*, 143.

8. Paul Mariani, "Reassembling the Dust," in *Biography as High Adventure*, ed. Stephen B. Oates (Amherst: University of Massachusetts Press, 1986), 104–123; Paul Murray Kendall, *The Art of Biography* (1965; rpt. New York: W. W. Norton, 1985), 130.

9. Frank E. Vandiver, "Biography as an Agent of Humanism," in *Biography as High Adventure*, ed. Stephen B. Oates, 61.

10. James Parker, "Bookends," *New York Times*, November 9, 2014, Book Review section: 7.

11. See the author's "Cinema's Favorite Crime of the Century," *USA Today Magazine*, September 2012, 58–62.

12. Charles Bukowski, *Love Is a Dog from Hell* (New York: HarperCollins, 1977).

13. Charles Bukowski, *Factotum* (1975; rpt. New York: HarperCollins, 2002), 129.

14. Blake Bailey, "Art Over Life," *New York Times*, November 16, 2014, Book Review section: 18.

15. [*David Brenner:*] *Live From The Venetian Hotel*, HBO: Brenner's fourth solo special, February 19, 2000, rebroadcast in 2014 as *David Brenner: Back with a Vengeance*.

16. Vincent Canby, "Woody Allen Is the American Bergman," *New York Times*, April 24, 1977, Section 11: 19.

17. Ibid.

18. Vincent Canby, "Somber Comedy," *New York Times*, April 21, 1977, C-22.

19. Penelope Gilliatt, "The Current Cinema: Woody at His Best Yet," *The New Yorker*, April 25, 1977, 136, 138.

20. Ibid.

21. Rudi Blesh, *Keation* (1966; rpt. New York: Collier Books, 1971), 215.

22. Tom Dardnis, *Keaton: The Man Who Wouldn't Lie Down* (New York: Scribner's, 1979), 120.

23. Ibid., 270.

24. See the author's *American Dark Comedy: Beyond Satire* (Westport, Connecticut: Greenwood Press, 1996.

25. *"Annie Hall"* [review], *Variety*, March 30, 1977.

26. Robert Hatch, "Films: [*Annie Hall*]," *Nation*, April 30, 1977, 540.

27. Foster Hirsch, *Love, Sex, Death and the Meaning of Life: Woody Allen's Comedies* (New York: McGraw-Hill, 1981), 85, 87.

28. Ibid., 40.

Chapter 11

1. Auberon Waugh, "The Last Thoughts of Peter Sellers," [London] *Sunday Telegraph*, July 27, 1980, 19.

2. Jerzy Kosinski, *Being There* (1979; rpt. New York: Grove Press, 1970), 8.

3. Francine Prose, "Bookends," *New York Times*, November 30, 2014, Book Review: 35.

4. Steve Allen, *Funny People* (New York: Stern and Day, 1981), 268.

5. Ibid., 266, 268; Steve Allen, *The Funny Men* (New York: Simon & Schuster, 1956).

6. Peter Evan, *Peter Sellers: The Mask Behind the Mask* (New York: Signet Book, 1980).

7. Ibid., 158.

8. See the author's *Personality Comedians as Genre: Selected Players* (Westport, Connecticut: Greenwood Press, 1997).

9. Philip Norman, *John Lennon: The Life* (New York: HarperCollins, 2008), 66.

10. John Lennon, "No Flies on Frank," in the omnibus collection *In His Own Write & A Spaniard in the Works* (1964; rpt. New York: Signet Books, 1965), 21.

11. Steve Turner, *A Hard Day's Write: The Stories Behind Every Beatles' Song* (New York: HarperPerennial, 1994), 186.

12. Ibid., 47.

13. Evans, *Peter Sellers: The Mask Behind the Mask*, 230.

14. See the author's *Charlie Chaplin: A Bio-Bibliography* (Westport, Connecticut: Greenwood Press, 1983); and *Film Clowns of the Depression: Twelve Defining Performances* (Jefferson, North Carolina: McFarland, 2007).

15. See the author's *Populism and the Capra Legacy* (Westport, Connecticut: Greenwood Press, 1995); and *Parody as Film Genres: "Never Give a Saga on Even Break"* (Westport, Connecticut: Greenwood Press, 1999).

16. Sinclair Lewis, *It Can't Happen Here* (1935; rpt. New York: Signet Classics, 1970).

17. See the author's *Mr. Deeds Goes to Yankee Stadium: Baseball Films in the Capra Tradition* (Jefferson, North Carolina: McFarland, 2004).

18. Kosinski, *Being There*, 140.

19. Ed Sikov, *Mr. Strangelove: A Biography of Peter Sellers* (New York: Hyperion, 2002), 364.

20. James Power, "Dialogue on Film: Hall Ashby," *American Film* (May 1980), in *Hal Ashby: Interviews*, ed. Nick Dawson (Jackson: University Press of Mississippi, 2010), 84–85.

21. Kosinski, *Being There*, 129.

22. Paul Muldoon, "I Do Not Like Publications of Letters," *New York Times*, December 14, 2014, Book Review Section: 16.

23. Maxwell Geismar, *Mark Twain: An American Prophet* (New York: McGraw-Hill, 1970), 226–227.

24. Mark Twain, *Adventures of Huckleberry Finn* (1876; rpt. New York: W. W. Norton, 1962), 7.

25. Mark Twain, "The Mysterious Stranger," in *The Complete Short Stories of Mark Twain*, ed. Charles Neider (1916; rpt. New York: Bantam Books, 1964), 679.

26. See the author's *Laurel & Hardy: A Bio-Bibliography* (Westport, Connecticut: Greenwood Press, 1990).

27. Roy Blount, Jr., "America's Original Superstar," *Time* magazine, July 14, 2008, 48.

28. See the author's *Will Cuppy, American Satirist: A Biography* (Jefferson, North Carolina: McFarland, 2013).

29. Sikov, *Mr. Strangelove: A Biography of Peter Sellers*, 356.

30. Kosinski, *Being There*, 70 (see also pages: 8, 33, 41, and 97).

31. Nick Dawson, *Being Hal Ashby: Life of a Hollywood Rebel* (2009; rpt. Lexington: University Press of Kentucky, 2011), 147.

32. Ibid., 203.

33. Jordon R. Young and Mike Bruns, "Hal Ashby: Satisfaction in Being There," from *Millimeter* (May 1980), in *Hal Ashby: Interviews*, ed. Dawson, 99.

34. Alexander Walker, *Peter Sellers* (New York: Macmillan, 1981), 263; Sikov, *Mr. Strangelove: A Biography of Peter Sellers*, 357.

35. Aljean Harmetz, "Kosinski's 'Being There' Will Star Peter Sellers," *New York Times*, February 14, 1979, C-8.

36. Ibid.

37. Louise Sweeney, "Jerry Kosinski," *Christian Science Monitor*, March 27, 1979, B-10.

38. The author addressed this same issue in the following biographies: *Leo McCarey: From Marx to McCarthy* (Lanham, Maryland: Scarecrow Press, 2005); and *Robert Wise: Shadowlands* (Indianapolis: Indiana Historical Society Press, 2012).

39. Mark Twain, *The Wit and Wisdom of Mark Twain*, ed. Paul Negri (Mineola, New York: Dover Publications, 1999), 27.

40. Mason Wiley and Damien Bona, *Inside Oscar*, ed. Gail MacCall (1986; rpt. New York: Ballantine Books, 1993), 581.

41. Bruce Webber, "Billie Whitelaw, 82 Longtime Beckett Muse," *New York Times*, December 25, 2014, A-23.

42. Waugh, "The Last Thoughts of Peter Sellers," 19.

43. Paul Hyman, "*Being There*" [review], *Box Office*, January 1, 1980.

44. Philip French, "*Being There*" [review], *London Observer*, July 13, 1980.

45. The quote is not attributed to Lincoln until *over* twenty years after his death. And even short catch-all quotations texts of the president, such as *Abraham Lincoln: Wisdom & Wit* (Mount Vernon, New York: Peter Pauper Press, 1965), ed. Louise Bachelder, neglect to include this axiom.

46. Valentine Cunningham, "Eden and Apocalypse," *London Times*, July 25, 1980, 842.

47. Ibid.

48. Janet Maslin, "Watching TV: Being There," *New York Times*, December 20, 1979, C-20.

49. "*Being There*" [review], *Nation*, January 22, 1980, 91.

50. James Parker, "Bookends," *New York Times*, September 21, 2014, Book Review section: 27.

51. Brian R. Bland, "'Being There' Sadly Reflects Life: Kosinski," *Chicago Sun-Times*, February 1, 1980, 53.

52. Harmetz, "Kosinski's 'Being There' Will Star Peter Sellers," C-8.

53. "Shirley Suffering a Fool Gladly," *New York Sunday News*, March 25, 1979, Section 3:10.

54. Kosinski, *Being There*, 5.

55. William Grimes, "Mark Strand Dies at 80; Poet Laureate Won Pulitzer," *New York Times*, November 30, 2014, 33.

Chapter 12

1. Vincent Canby, "*All That Jazz*" [review], *New York Times*, December 20, 1979, C-13.

2. Moira Hodgson, "When Bob Fosse's Art Imitates Life, It's Just 'All That Jazz,'" *New York Times*, December 30, 1979, D-15.

3. Bruce Williamson, "All That Fosse," *Playboy*, March 1980, 175.

4. Janet Maslin, "Sifting Flaws," *New York Times*, January 13, 1980, section D:13.

5. See the author's *Robert Wise: Shadowlands* (Indianapolis: Indiana Historical Society Press, 2012).

6. Kevin Boyd Grubb, *Razzle Dazzle: The Life and Work of Bob Fosse* (New York: St. Martin's Press, 1989), 217.

7. Hodgson, "When Bob Fosse's Art Imitates Life, It's Just 'All That Jazz,'" D-15.

8. Shirley MacLaine, *My Lucky Stars: A Hollywood Memoir* (New York: Bantam Books, 1995), 156.

9. Williamson, "All That Fosse," 250.

10. Martin Gottfried, *All His Jazz* (New York: Bantam Books, 1990), 352–353.

11. Sam Wasson, *Fosse* (New York: Houghton Mifflin Harcourt, 2013), 448.

12. Ibid., 461.

13. Gottfried, *All His Jazz*, 377.

14. Wasson, *Fosse*, 462–463.

15. Liesl Schillinger, "The Other Sister," *New York Times*, January 11, 2015, Book Review: 11.

16. Peter Viertel, *White Hunter, Black Heart* (Garden City, New York: Doubleday, 1953).

17. Douglas Martin, "Peter Viertel, 86, Author and Screenwriter," *New York Times*, November 6, 2007, C-20.

18. Nora Sayre, "Films: All That Jazz," *Nation*, January 1980.

19. Leon Wieseltier, "Among the Disrupted," *New York Times*, January 18, 2015, Book Review section: 1.

20. Williamson, "All That Fosse," 178.

21. Gottfried, "All His Jazz," 125.

22. Christopher Hitchens, *Mortality* (2012; rpt. New York: Hachette Book Group, 2014), 5.

23. Tom Stoppard, *Rosencrantz and Guildenstern Are Dead* (New York: Grove Weidenfield, 1967), 71–72.

24. See the author's "*Mr. B*" *or Comforting Thoughts About the Bison: A Critical Biography of Robert Benchley* (Westport, Connecticut: Greenwood Press, 1992), 133.

25. Tom Buckley, "Ann Reinking Plays Herself in 'All That Jazz,'" *New York Times*, January 4, 1980, C-10.

26. Canby, "*All That Jazz*" [review], C-13.

27. Ron Pennington, "*All That Jazz*" [review], *Hollywood Reporter*, December 12, 1979, 3.

28. Maslin, "Sifting Flaws."

29. Geri Bluerock, "*All That Jazz*" [review], *Variety*, December 12, 1979.

30. Charles Champlin, "'All That Jazz': Reliving Fosse's Fantasies," *Los Angeles Times*, December 16, 1979, Calendar section: 1, 53.

31. Ibid., 1.

Epilogue

1. Vincent Canby, "'A Clockwork Orange' Dazzles the Senses and Mind," *New York Times*, December 20, 1971, 44.

2. Andy Borowitz, *The 50 Funniest American Writers: An Anthology of Humor from Mark Twain to the Onion* (New York: Library of American Humor, 2014).

3. The majority of my 34 books are about comedy and/or comedy personalities, with many of them keying on black humor, from *American Dark Comedy: Beyond Satire* (Westport, Connecticut: Greenwood Press, 1996), to biographies about artists so inclined, such as *Groucho & W. C. Fields: Huckster Comedians* (Jackson: University Press of Mississippi, 1994), and *Will Cuppy, American Satirist* (Jefferson, North Carolina: McFarland, 2013).

4. My Paris talk was based upon the essay "Chaplin's Film Pioneer Status in Black or Macabre Humor," and was reprinted in *Charlie Chaplin: His Reflections in Modern Times*, ed. Adolphe Nysenholic (New York: Mouton de Gruyton, 1991); *Chaplin's War Trilogy: An Evolving Lens in Three Dark Comedies, 1918–1947* (Jefferson, North Carolina: McFarland, 2014).

5. See Tom Shone's "Film Schooled," in the *New York Times*, January 25, 2015, Book Review section: 11.

6. James and Elizabeth Knowlson, eds., *Beckett Remembering, Remembering Beckett: A Celebration* (2006; rpt. New York: Arcade Publishing, 2014), 137.

7. Dwight Gardner, "Poetic Voices Wrapped Tight in Its Shifting Politics," *New York Times*, January 28, 2015, C-1.

8. Glyn Maxwell, "Eternal Lines," *New York Times*, February 1, 2015, Book Review: 20.

9. See the author's *Laurel & Hardy: A Bio-Bibliography* (Westport, Connecticut: Greenwood Press, 1990).

10. Rob Weiner-Kendt, "There's Something Funny in this Saloon," *New York Times*, February 1, 2015, Theatre section: 1, 11.

11. Robert Goff, *The Essential Salvador Dali* (New York: Wonderland Press, 1998), 57.

Bibliography

Books

Allen, Steve. *Funny People*. New York: Stein and Day, 1981.

Andrew, J. Dudley *The Major Film Theories*. New York: Oxford University Press, 1976.

Barsam, Richard Meran. *Nonfiction Film: A Critical History*. New York: E. P. Dutton, 1973.

Bauby, Jean-Dominique. *The Diving Bell and the Butterfly*. Trans. Jeremy Leggart. 1996; rpt. New York: Vintage Books, 1997.

Beckett, Samuel. *Waiting for Godot*. 1955; rpt. New York: Grove, 1989.

Berger, Thomas. *Little Big Man*. 1964; rpt. New York: Dial Press, 2005.

Betensen, Lulu Parke (as told to Dora Flack). *Butch Cassidy, My Brother*. Foreword by Robert Redford. 1975; rpt. New York: Penguin Books, 1976.

Bierce, Ambrose. *The Devil's Dictionary*. 1911; rpt. New York: Dover Publications, 1958.

Biskind, Peter. *Easy Rider, Raging Bull*. New York: Simon & Schuster, 1998.

Björkman, Stig, ed. *Woody Allen on Woody Allen*. New York: Grove Press, 1993.

Blair, Walter. *Native American Humor*. 1937; rpt. San Francisco: Chandler Publishing, 1960.

Blesh, Rudi. *Keaton*. 1966; rpt. New York: Collier Books, 1971.

Blum, John M., ed. *The National Experience: A History of the United States*. 1963; rpt. New York: Harcourt, Brace & World, 1968.

Boehelder, Louise, ed. *Abraham Lincoln: Wit & Wisdom*. Mount Vernon, New York: Peter Pauper Press, 1965.

Borowitz, Andy. *The Fifty Funniest American Writers: An Anthology of Humor From Mark Twain To the Onion*. New York: Library of American Humor, 2014.

Brook, Tim, and Earle Marsh. *The Complete Directory to Prime Time Network TV Shows: 1946-Present*. New York: Ballantine Books, 1979.

Bukowski, Charles. *Factotum*. 1975; rpt. New York: HarperCollins, 2002.

_____. *Love Is a Dog from Hell*. New York: HarperCollins, 1977.

Buñuel, Luis. *My Last Sigh*. 1982; rpt. New York: Random House, 1984.

Byrge, Duane, ed. *Private Screenings: Insiders Share a Century of Movie Moments*. Atlanta, Georgia: Turner Publishing, 1995.

Capra, Frank. *Frank Capra: The Name Above the Title*. New York: Macmillan, 1971.

Cawelti, John G. *The Six Gun Mystique*. Bowling Green, Ohio: Bowling Green University Press, 1971.

Chandler, Raymond. *The Big Sleep*. 1939; rpt. New York: Random House, 1976.

_____. *Farewell My Lovely*. 1940; rpt. New York: Random House, 1992.

_____. *The High Window*. 1942; rpt. New York: Random House, 1992.

_____. *The Long Goodbye*. 1953; rpt. New York: Random House, 1992.

Chevallie, Gabiel, trans. Malcolm Imrie. *Fear*. 1930; rpt. New York: New Review Books, 2011.

Conrad, Joseph. *Heart of Darkness*. 1902; rpt. New York: Penguin Books, 1983.

Coursodon, Jean-Pierre (with Pierre Sauvage). *American Directors, Volume II*. New York: McGraw-Hill, 1983.

Cronin, Paul, ed. *Roman Polanski Interviews*, Jackson: University Press of Mississippi, 2005.

Cuppy, Will. *How to Become Extinct*. 1941; rpt. Garden City, New York: Garden City Books, 1951.

Dawson, Nick. *Being Hal Ashby: Life of a Hollywood Rebel*. 2009; rpt. Lexington: University of Kentucky Press, 2011.

_____. *Hal Ashby: Interviews*. Jackson: University Press of Mississippi, 2010.

Evans, Peter. *Peter Sellers: The Mask Behind the Mask*. New York: Signet Book, 1980.

Fields, Syd. *The Foundation of Screenwriting*. 1979; rpt. New York: Dell, 1994.

Fitzgerald, F. Scott. *The Curious Case of Benjamin Button and Other Jazz Age Stories*. Ed. Patrick O'Donnell. 1922; rpt. New York: Penguin Books, 1998.

Frankel, Glenn. *The Searches: The Making of an American Legend*. New York: Bloomsbury, 2013.

Friedrich, Otto. *Before the Deluge: A Portrait of Berlin in the 1920s.* New York: Harper & Row, 1972.

Gehring, Wes D. *American Dark Comedy: Beyond Satire.* Westport, Connecticut: Greenwood Press, 1996.

_____. *Charlie Chaplin: A Bio-Bibliography.* Westport, Connecticut: Greenwood Press, 1983.

_____. *Film Classics: Reclassified: A Shocking Spoof of Cinema.* Davenport, Iowa: Robin Vincent Publishing, 2001.

_____. *Film Clowns of the Depression.* Jefferson, North Carolina: McFarland, 2007.

_____. *Forties Film Funnymen: The Decade's Great Comedians at Work in the Shadow of War.* Jefferson, North Carolina: McFarland, 2010.

_____. *Groucho & W. C. Fields: Huckster Comedians.* Jackson: University Press of Mississippi, 1994.

_____. *James Dean: Rebel with a Cause.* Indianapolis: Indiana Historical Society Press, 2005.

_____. *Joe E. Brown: Film Comedian and Baseball Buffoon.* Jefferson, North Carolina: McFarland, 2006.

_____. *Laurel & Hardy: A Bio-Bibliography.* Westport, Connecticut: Greenwood Press, 1990.

_____. *Leo McCarey: From Marx to McCarthy.* Lanham, Maryland: Scarecrow Press, 2005.

_____. *The Marx Brothers: A Bio-Bibliography.* Westport, Connecticut: Greenwood Press, 1987.

_____. *"Mr. B," or Comforting Thoughts About the Bison: A Critical Biography of Robert Benchley.* Westport, Connecticut: Greenwood Press, 1992.

_____. *Mr. Deeds Goes to Yankee Stadium: Baseball Films in the Capra. Tradition.* Jefferson, North Carolina: McFarland, 2004.

_____. *Parody as Film Genre: "Never Give a Saga an Even Break."* Westport, Connecticut: Greenwood Press, 1999.

_____. *Personality Comedians: Selected Players.* Westport, Connecticut: Greenwood Press, 1997.

_____. *Populism and the Capra Legacy.* Westport, Connecticut: Greenwood Press, 1995.

_____. *Robert Wise: Shadowlands.* Indianapolis: Indiana Historical Society Press, 2012.

_____. *Romantic vs. Screwball Comedy: Charting the Difference.* Lanham, Maryland: Scarecrow Press, 2002.

_____. *Screwball Comedy: A Genre of Madcap Romance,* Westport, Connecticut: Greenwood Press, 1986.

_____. *Will Cuppy, American Satirist: A Biography.* Jefferson, North Carolina: McFarland, 2013.

Garebain, Keith. *The Making of Cabaret.* New York: Oxford University Press, 2011.

Gelmis, Joseph. *The Film Director as Superstar.* Garden City, New York: Doubleday, 1970.

Gismar, Maxwell. *Mark Twain: An American Prophet.* New York: McGraw-Hill, 1970.

Goff, Robert. *The Essential Salvador Dali.* New York: Wonderland Press, 1998.

Gottfried, Martin. *All His Jazz.* New York: Bantam Books, 1990.

Grubb, Kevin Boyd. *Razzle Dazzle: The Life and Work of Bob Fosse.* New York: St. Martin's Press, 1989.

Hames, Peter. *The Czechoslovak New Wave.* 1985; rpt. New York: Wallflower Press, 2005.

Heggen, Thomas. *Mr. Roberts.* Boston: Houghton Mifflin, 1946.

_____, and Joshua Logan. *Mr. Roberts: A Play.* New York: Random House, 1948.

Heller, Erica. *Yossarian Slept Here.* New York: Simon & Schuster, 2011.

Heller, Joseph. *Catch–22.* 1961; rpt. New York: Dell, 1968.

_____. *Now and Then.* New York: Random House, 1998.

Hirsch, Foster. *Love, Sex, Death and the Meaning of Life: Woody Allen's Comedies.* New York: McGraw-Hill, 1981.

Hitchens, Christopher. *Mortality.* 2012; rpt. New York: Hatchette Book Group, 2014.

Hooker, Richard (pseudonym for H. Richard Hornberger). *MASH.* 1968; rpt. New York: Harper, 2001.

Hooper, Johnson J. *Simon Suggs' Adventures.* 1967; rpt. Americus, Georgia: American Book, 1928.

Hope, Bob, and Linda Hope. *My Life in Jokes.* New York: Hyperion, 2003.

Horton, Andrew. *The Films of George Roy Hill.* New York: Columbia University Press, 1984.

Irving, John. *The World According to Garp.* New York: E. P. Dutton, 1978.

Isherwood, Christopher. *A Single Man.* 1964; rpt. Minneapolis: University of Minnesota Press, 2001.

_____. *Goodbye to Berlin* (Different Intro Material). 1939; rpt. New York: ISIS, 1943.

_____. *Goodbye to Berlin.* 1939; rpt. New York: New Directions, 1986.

Kael, Pauline. *5001 Nights at the Movies.* New York: Henry Holt, 1991.

_____. *Reeling.* New York: Warner Books, 1976.

Kass, Judith M. *Robert Altman: American Innovator.* New York: Popular Library, 1978.

Keaton, Diane. *Then Again.* New York: Random House, 2011.

Kendall, Paul Murray. *The Art of Biography.* 1965; rpt. New York: W. W. Norton, 1985.

Kesey, Ken. *One Flew Over the Cuckoo's Nest.* New York: Signet, 1962.

Kosinski, Jerzy. *Being There.* 1979; rpt. New York: Grove Press, 1970.

Knowlson, James, and Elizabeth. *Beckett Remembering, Remembering Becket.* 2006; rpt; New York: Arcade Publishing, 2014.

Kracauer, Siegfried. *From Caligary to Hitler: A*

Psychological History of the German Film. 1947; rpt. Princeton, New Jersey: Princeton Press, 1971.

Kulman, Susan. *Knave, Fool, and Genius: The Confidence Man as He Appears in Nineteenth Century American Fiction.* Chaplin Hill: University of North Carolina Press, 1973.

Lahr, John. *Notes on a Cowardly Lion.* 1969; rpt. New York: Ballantine Books, 1970.

Lardner, Ring, Jr. *I'd Hate Myself in the Morning: A Memoir.* New York: Thunder Mouth Press, 2000.

_____. *The Lardners: My Family.* New York: Harper & Row, 1976.

Lax, Eric. *Woody Allen: A Biography.* New York: Alfred A. Knopf, 1991.

Lewinson, Peter. *Puttin' on the Ritz.* New York: St. Martin's Press, 2009.

Lewis, C. S. *An Experiment in Criticism.* 1961; rpt. New York: Cambridge Press.

Lewis, Sinclair. *It Can't Happen Here.* 1935; rpt. New York; Signet Classics, 1970.

Lowell, James Russell. *The Biglow Papers.* 1848; rpt. Philadelphia: Altemus, 1910.

MacLaine, Shirley. *My Lucky Stars: A Hollywood Memoir.* New York: Bantam Books, 1995.

Mast, Gerald, and Brucet Kawin. *The Movies: A Short History.* Boston, Massachusetts: Allyn & Bacon, 1992.

McCann, Graham. *Woody Allen: New Yorker.* 1991; rpt. Cambridge, Massachusetts, 1992.

Meade, Marion. *The Unruly Life of Woody Allen: A Biography.* New York: Scribner, 2000.

Melville, Herman. *Billy Budd.* 1924. In *Great Short Works.* New York: Harper & Row, 1966.

_____. *Moby-Dick.* 1851; rpt. New York: Heritage Press, 1943.

Mitejewski, Linda. *Divine Decadence.* Princeton, New Jersey: Princeton University Press, 1992.

Norman, Philip. *John Lennon: The Life.* New York: HarperCollins, 2008.

O'Brien, Daniel. *Robert Altman: Hollywood Survivor.* New York: Continuum, 1995.

O'Reilly, Bill and Martin Dugard. *Killing Kennedy: The End of Camelot.* New York: Henry Holt, 2012.

Orwell, George. *1984.* 1949; rpt. New York: Signet Classics, 1961.

Palmer, Miles. *Woody Allen.* New York: Protheus, 1980.

Patrick, Julian, general ed. *501 Great Writers.* New York: Quintessence, 2008.

Peary, Danny. *A Guide for the Film Fanatic.* New York: Simon & Schuster, 1986.

Read, Bill. *The Days of Dylan Thomas.* New York: McGraw-Hill, 1964.

Rogak, Lisa. *Angry Optimist: The Life and Times of Jon Stewart.* New York: St. Martin's Press, 2014.

Sacket, Susan. *Box Office.* New York: Billboard Books, 1990.

Sandburg, Carl. *Chicago Poems.* 1916; rpt. New York: Dover, 1994.

Schickel, Richard. *Cary Grant.* New York: Applause Books, 1999.

_____. *Woody Allen: A Life in Film.* Chicago: Ivan R. Dee, 2003.

Schuth, Wayne, H. *Mike Nichols.* Boston: Twayne Publishers, 1978.

Scorsese, Martin, and Michael Henry Wilson. *A Personal Journey with Martin Scorsese Through American Movies.* New York: Miramax Books, 1997.

Self, Robert T. *Robert Altman's Subliminal Reality.* Minneapolis: University of Minnesota Press, 2002.

Shields, Charles J. *And So It Goes: Kurt Vonnegut: A Life.* New York: Henry Holt, 2011.

Sikov, Ed. *Mr. Strangelove: A Biography of Peter Sellers.* New York: Hyperion, 2002.

Slater, Thomas J. *Milos Forman: A Bio-Bibliography.* Westport, Connecticut: Greenwood Press, 1987.

Sonnerfeldt, Richard W. *Witness to Nuremberg.* 2002; rpt. New York: Arcade Publishing, 2006.

Sorkin, Adam J., ed. *Conversations with Joseph Heller.* Jackson: University Press of Mississippi, 1993.

Steinberg, Cobbett. *Reel Facts: The Movie Book of Records.* New York: Vintage Books, 1978.

Sterritt, David, ed. *Robert Altman Interviews.* Jackson: University Press of Mississippi, 2000.

Stoppard, Tom. *Rosencratz and Guildenstern Are Dead.* New York: Grove Weidenfeld, 1967.

Sumner, Gregory D. *Unstuck in Time.* New York: Seven Stories Press, 2011.

Styron, William. *Darkness Visible: A Memoir of Madness.* New York: Vintage Books, 1992.

Thomas, Bob. "'Little Big Man': History Rewritten" (syndicated). *Newark Evening News,* August 8, 1969, 8.

Thomas, Michael, "Flicks: A Movie Column." *Status,* April 1970.

Thoreau, Henry David. *Walden and Other Writings of Henry David Thoreau,* ed. Brooks, Atkinson. 1854; rpt. New York: Modern Library, 1965.

Tosches, Nick. *DINO: Living High in the Dirty Business of Dreams.* 1992; rpt. New York: Dell, 1993.

Town, Robert, *Chinatown,* Third Draft. Hollywood, California: Paramount, October 9, 1973; (Author's collection).

Trottier, David. *The Screenwriter Bible.* 1994; rpt. Los Angeles: Silman-James Press, 2010.

Truffaut, Francois. *Hitchcock* (revised edition). New York: Simon & Schuster, 1983.

Trumbo, Dalton. *Johnny Got His Gun.* 1939; rpt. New York: Bantam Books, 1989.

Twain, Mark. *Adventures of Huckleberry Finn.* 1984; rpt. New York: Oxford University Press, 1996.

_____. *The Wit and Wisdom of Mark Twain*, ed. Paul Negri. Mineola, New York: Drover Publications, 1999.

Viertel, Peter. *White Hunter, Black Heart*. Garden City, New York: Doubleday, 1953.

Vonnegut, Kurt. *Between Time and Timbuktu*. 1972; rpt. New York: Delta, 1975, xv.

_____. *A Man Without a Country*. New York: Seven Stories Press, 2005.

_____. *Slapstick*. New York Press: Delacorte Press/Semour Lawrence, 1970.

_____. *Slaughterhouse-Five*. 1969; rpt. New York: Dell Book, 1974.

_____. *Timequake*. New York Times: G. P. Putnam's Sons, 1997.

Walker, Alexander. *Peter Sellers*. New York: Macmillan, 1981.

Wasson, Sam. *Fosse*. New York: Houghton Mifflin Harcourt, 2013.

Wiley, Mason, and Damien Bona. *Inside Oscar*. 1986; rpt. New York: Ballantine Books, 1993.

Wolf, Tom. *The Electric Kool-Acid Test*. New York: Farrar, Straus and Giroux, 1968.

Woody Allen on Woody Allen: Conversation with Stig Björkman. 1993; rpt. New York: Grover Press, 1995.

Yacowar, Maurice. *Loser Take All: The Comic Act of Woody Allen*. New York: Frederick Ungar Publishing, 1979.

Zombory-Moldován, Béla. *The Burning of the World*. Trans. Peter Zombory-Moldován. New York: Review Books, 2014.

Zuckoff, Mitchell. *Robert Altman: The Oral Biography*. New York: Alfred A. Knopf, 2009.

Shorter Works

Acocella, Joan. "Dancing in the Dark." *The New Yorker*, December 21, 1998, 103.

Aghed, Jan, and Bernard Cohen. "Interview with Arthur Penn" (1970). In *Arthur Penn Interview*, eds. Michael Chaiken and Paul Cronin. Jackson: University Press of Mississippi, 2008.

Alfred, Henry. "Minnesota Nice." *New York Times*, June 1, 2014, Book Review: 24.

Allen, Woody. "The Kugelmass Episode: (1977)." In Allen's *Side Effects*. New York: Random House, 1980.

Altman, Robert. "Rambling Screening Comments Before a Sneak Preview of *Thieves Like Us*." University of Iowa, 1973–1974 (author's notes).

Anderson, Kurt. "True to Character." *New York Times*, October 28, 2012, Book Review: 27.

Annie Hall [Review]. *Variety*, March 30, 1977.

Arnold-Ratliff. "Stealth Maneuvers." *New York Times*, December 29, 2013. Book Review: 9.

Atkins, Brooks. "Insurgent Penmen." *New York Times*, April 9, 1939, section 10:1.

Auden, W. H. "Funeral Blues." 1938. In *The Columbia Anthology of Gay Literature*, ed. R. S. Fone. New York: Columbia University Press, 1998.

Bailey, Blake. "Art Over Life." *New York Times*, November 16, 2014, Book Review: 18.

Bearak, Barry. "Mismatch in the Bronx." *New York Times*, April 15, 2014, B-9.

Being There [Review]. *Nation*, January 22, 1980, 91.

Benchley, Robert. "Carnival Week in Sunny Las Los." In *The Treasurer's Report and Other Aspects of Community Singing*. New York: Grossett & Dunlap, 1930.

Benoit, Shelley. "Little Big Man." *Show*, March 1971, 57.

Bernard, Drew. "Life as a Long Rehearsal." *American Film*, November 1979, 28.

Biehl, Jody K. "In Berlin Life Is Still a Cabaret." *USA Today*, December 12, 2001, D-10.

Biskind, Peter. "The Low Road to Chinatown." *Premiere*, June 1994, 72.

Bland, Brian R. "'Being There' Sadly Reflects Life: Kosinski." *Chicago Sun-Times*, February 1, 1980, 53.

Blount, Roy, Jr. "America's Original Superstar." *Time*, July 14, 2008, 48.

Bluerock, Geri. "*All That Jazz*" [Review]. *Variety*, December 12, 1979.

Braucourt, Guy. "Interview with Arthur Marx." *Cinema*, May 1971. In *Arthur Penn Interviews*, eds. Michael Chaiken and Paul Cronin. Jackson: University Press of Mississippi, 2008.

Buckley, Peter. "Cabaret: Peter Buckley Finds Bob Fosse's Experience More Divine Than Decadent." *Films and Filming*, August 1972.

Buckley, Tom. "Ann Reinking Plays Herself in 'All That Jazz.'" *New York Times*, January 4, 1980, C-10.

"Bud Cort and John Alonzo." In the untitled *Harold and Maude* (1971) booklet for the Criterion Collection, Special Edition, 2012 DVD.

Burges, Anthony. "Author Has His Say on 'Clockwork' Film." *Los Angeles Times*, February 13, 1972, Calendar section: 1.

Butler, Robert W. "And She Lived Happily Ever After." *Kansas City Star*, June 28, 1993, D-5.

Canby, Vincent. "'A Clockwork Orange' Dazzles the Senses and Mind." *New York Times*, December 20, 1971, 44.

_____. "*All That Jazz*" [Review]. *New York Times*, December 20, 1979, C-13.

_____. "Blood, Blasphemy and Laughs." *New York Times*, February 1, 1970, section 2:1.

_____. "Cuckoo's Nest: A Sane Comedy About Psychotics." *New York Times*, November 23, 1975, section 11:1.

_____. "Dustin Hoffman Stars in 'Little Big Man.'" *New York Times*, December 15, 1970, 53.

_____. "Love, Death, God, Sex, Suicide and Woody Allen." *New York Times*, June 22, 1975, Part 11:1.

_____. "Polanski's 'Chinatown' Views Crime of the '30s." *New York Times*, January 21, 1974, 26.

_____. "Somber Comedy." *New York Times*, April 21, 1977, C-22.

_____. "Time-Tripping with 'Slaughterhouse-Five.'" *New York Times*, March 23, 1972.

_____. "A Triumphant Catch." *New York Times*, June 28, 1970, section 2:1.

_____. "Woody Allen Is the American Bergman." *New York Times*, April 24, 1977, section 11:19.

Cashman, John. "Laughter at Their Expense." *Newsday*, November 20, 1974, Part 2:A8.

"Catch–22." *Time*, January 26, 1970, 80.

Chaiken, Michael, and Paul Croncin. "A Summing Up." In *Arthur Penn Interviews*, ed. Michael Chaiken and Paul Crowin. Jackson: University Press of Mississippi.

Champlin, Charles. "'All That Jazz': Reliving Fosse's Fantasies." *Los Angeles Times*, December 16, 1979, Calendar section: 1, 53.

_____. "Nicholson Hatches Gold Ego in Nest." *Los Angeles Times*, November 16, 1975, Calendar section: 1.

Chandler, Raymond. "The Single Art of Murder" (1950). In a Chandler anthology of essays also entitled *The Single Art of Murder*. New York: Random House, 1988.

"Chilly Scenes of Winter." *New York Times*, November 7, 2014, C-18.

Cocks, Jay. "Lost in Space." *Time*, April 10, 1972.

Cohen, Hennig. "Introduction to Melville." In *The Confidence Man*, 1857; rpt. New York: Holt, Reinhart and Winston, 1964.

Cohen, Lavry. "'Little Big Man' Sure to Do Well at the Box Office." *Hollywood Reporter*, December 16, 1970, 3.

Cunningham, Valentine. "Eden and Apocalypse." *London Times*, July 25, 1980, 842.

Cuppy, Will. "The Aard-vark." In *How to Tell Your Friends from the Apes*. 1931, New York: Signet Classics, 2005.

_____. "Mystery and Adventure [review column]: 'Lunacy Becomes Us.'" *New York Herald Tribune*, April 16, 1939, section 9:17.

Dardis, Tom. *Keaton: The Man Who Wouldn't Lie Down*. New York: Scribner's, 1979.

Delain, Michel. "The First Cheyenne Film Director." In *L'Express*, April 5, 1971. In *Arthur Penn Interviews*, eds. Michael Chaiken and Paul Cronin. Jackson: University Press of Mississippi, 2008.

Downing, David. *Jack Nicholson*. New York: Stein and Day, 1984.

Eaton, Michael. *Chinatown*. London: British Film Institute, 1997.

Ebert, Roger. "*Catch–22*" [Review]. *Chicago Sun-Times*, June 1, 1970.

_____. "*Chinatown*" [Review]. Gowatchit (http://gowatch.com). February 6, 2000.

_____. "*Little Big Man*" [Review]. *Chicago Sun-Times*, January 1, 1970.

_____. "*Love and Death*" [Review]. *Chicago Sun-Times*, January 1975, reproduced at http://www.rogerbert.com/reviews/love-and-death-1975.

_____. "*One Flew Over the Cuckoo's Nest*" [Review]. *Chicago Sun-Times*, 1975; Tweaked/Reproduced at http://www.rogerbert.com/reviews/one-flew-over-the-cuckoos-nest-1975.

_____. "Polanski's Chinatown: A Private Eye Movie That's Not Restricted to the Formula Plot." *Star Ledger*, August 4, 1974, section 4:1, 14.

Elliot, George P. "Heaped Forked Tongue." *New York Times*, October 11, 1964, Book Review: 24.

"Epic and Crumbcrusher." *The New Yorker*, December 26, 1970, 52.

Fadiman, Clifton. "Introduction." In Herman Melville's *Moby-Dick*. 1851; rpt. New York: Heritage Press, 1943, viii.

Farber, Stephen. "*Cabaret* May Shock Kansas." *New York Times*, February 20, 1972, section 2:2.

Farber, Manny. "White Elephant Art vs. Termite Art." *Film Culture*, Winter 1962/63, cover article.

Foglietti, Mario. "Conflicts of Conscience." *Revista del cinematografo*. In *Arthur Penn Interviews*, ed. Michael Chaiken and Paul Cronin. Jackson: University Press of Mississippi, 2008.

French, Philip. "Being There" [Review]. *London Observer*, July 13, 1980.

Freydkin, Donna. "'Railway Man' Shares Tips to Stay on Track." *USA Today*, April 14, 2014, D-1.

Gardner, Dwight. "Poetic Voices Wrapped Tight in Its Shifting Politics." *New York Times*, January 28, 2015, C-1.

Gehring, Wes D. "Chaplin's Film Pioneer Status in Black or Macabre Humor." In *Charlie Chaplin: His Reflections in Modern Times*, ed. Adolphe Nysenholic. New York: Mouton de Gruyton, 1991.

_____. "Cinema's Favorite Crime of the Century." *USA Today* Magazine, September 2012, 58–62.

_____. Conversation with Robert Mugge. Ball State University (Muncie, Indiana), February 22, 2014.

_____. "Laughter from the Dark Side." *USA Today Magazine*, March 2008, 53.

_____. "Pandro S. Berman on Hollywood During the 1930s: An Interview." *Paper Cinema* (Boston), Issue Number One, 1976.

_____. "Will Cuppy: Factual Fun Sautéed with Satire." In *TRACES of Indiana and Midwestern History*, Winter 2014, 5.

Gelmis, Joseph. "Donald Sutherland: *MASH* Notes," *Newsday*, July 27, 1970, W-14.

_____. "Impressive Mock Epic." *Newsday*, December 15, 1970, A-7.

_____. "Movies: Silly and Serious." *Newsday*, July 11, 1975, Part 2: A-11.

_____. "Un-Sweet Dreams From 3 Paranoid Plots." *Newsday*, June 23, 1974, Part 2:11.

Gerber, John. "Lecture on Southwestern Humor." In *American Humor and Satire*. University of Iowa class, 1975.

Giddins, Gary. "'Cabaret' on Film." *Hollywood Reporter*, February 15, 1972, 3.

Gilliant, Penelope. "The Current Cinema: Woody at His Best Yet." *The New Yorker*, April 25, 1977, 136, 138.

_____. "Love and Death" [Review]. Excerpt from *The New Yorker*. In Douglas Brode's *Woody Allen: His Films and Career*. Secaucus, New Jersey: Citadel Press, 1985.

Gleiberman, Owen. "Philip Seymour Hoffman: The Master." *Entertainment Weekly*, February 14, 2014, 37.

Goldman, William. "Cultural Hero." In *The Season: A Candid Look at Broadway*, 1969; rpt. New York: Limelight Editions, 1984.

Gow, Gordon. "Chinatown" [review]. *Films and Filming*, October 1974, 38–39.

Green, Elizabeth. "(New Math) – (New Teaching) = Failure." *New York Times Magazine*, July 27, 2014, 24.

Greenspun, Roger. "MASH." *New York Times*, January 26, 1970, 26.

Grimes, William. "Mark Strand Dies at 80; Poet Laureate Won Pulitzer." *New York Times*, November 30, 2014, 33.

Hammett, Dashiell. "A Man Called Spade." In *World's Great Detective Stories*, ed. Will Cuppy. New York: World Publishing, 1943.

Harmetz, Aljean. "Harold's Back and Maude's Got Him." *New York Times*, May 26, 1974, 1.

_____. "Kosinski's 'Being There' Will Star Peter Sellers." *New York Times*, February 14, 1979, C-8.

Harold and Maude ad. *Village Voice*, December 23, 1971, 66.

Hatch, Robert. "Films: *Annie Hall*." *Nation*, April 30, 1977, 540.

Hayford Harrison. "Poe in The Confidence Man." In *The Confidence Man: His Masquerade*, ed. Hershel Parker. New York: W. W. Norton, 1971.

Heller, Jessica Van. "Rising Out of the Ashes" (previously unpublished). In *Arthur Penn Interviews*, eds. Michael Chaiken and Paul Cronin. Jackson: University Press, 2008.

Higgins, Colin. *Harold and Maude*. 1971; rpt. New York: Avon Books, 1975, dedication page.

Hodgson, Moira. "When Bob Fosse's Art Imitates Life, It's Just 'All That Jazz.'" *New York Times*, December 30, 1979, D-15.

Holmes, Anna. "Bookends." *New York Times*, July 27, 2014, Book Review section: 31.

Hooker, Richard. *MASH*. New York: Morrow, 1968.

Hughes, Bettany. "School for a Scoundrel." *New York Times*, July 13, 2014, Book Review: 12.

Hyams, Joe. "The Western He Wanted to Do." *New York Herald Tribune*, March 26, 1961, Book Review section: 23.

Hyman, Paul. "*Being There*" [Review]. *Box Office*, January 1, 1980.

Isherwood, Christopher. "About This Book" [Introduction]. In *The Berlin Stories*, 1954; rpt. New York: New Directions Books, 2008, xvii.

_____. "The Berlin Stories." 1963. In *Isherwood on Writing*, ed. James J. Berg. Minneapolis: University of Minnesota Press, 2007.

Itzkoff, Dave. "A Master of Illusion Endures." *New York Times*, July 20, 2014, Arts & Leisure: 12.

Jacobson, Howard. "Introduction." In Joseph Heller's *Catch–22*. 1962; rpt. London: Vintage, 2005, vi.

Jamison, Leslie. "Bookends." *New York Times*, July 13, 2014, Book Review section: 27.

Johnson, William. "*MASH*." *Film Quarterly*, Spring 1970, 41.

Jones, James F. "Camus on Kafka and Melville: An Unpublished Letter." 1951. *French Review*, March 1998, 647.

Kael, Pauline. "Blessed Profanity." *The New Yorker*, January 24, 1970. In Kael's *Deeper Into the Movies*. Boston: Little, Brown, 1973, 95.

Kazi, Alfred. "Leaves Under the Lindens." *New York Herald Tribune*, March 12, 1939, section 9:10.

Kent, Leticie. "A Boy of 20 and Woman of 80..." *New York Times*, April 4, 1971, D-13.

Klemesrud, Judy. "Dustin Calls Him Grandpa." *New York Times*, February 21, 1971.

Knight, Arthur. "*One Flew Over the Cuckoo's Nest*" [Review]. *Hollywood Reporter*, November 14, 1975, 3.

_____. "Past and Future Merge in *Slaughterhouse-Five*." *Hollywood Reporter*, March 22, 1972.

Landon, Brooks. "Introduction." In Thomas Berger's *Little Big Man*, 1964; rpt. New York: Dial Press, 2005, xvi.

Lane, Anthony. "After Darkness." *The New Yorker*, April 14, 2014, 87.

Lardner, Ring, Jr. Cover blurb for Richard Hooker's *MASH* (1968; rpt. New York: Harper, 2001).

LeBlanc, Ronald D. "*Love and Death* and Food: Woody Allen's Comic Use of Gastronomy." In *The Film's of Woody Allen in Critical Essays*, ed. Charles L. P. Silet. Lanham, Maryland: Scarecrow Press, 2006.

Lennon, John. "No Flies on Frank." The omnibus collection: *In His Own Write & A Spaniard In the Works*. 1964; rpt. New York: Signet Books, 1965.

Lichblau, Eric. "In Cold War, U.S. Spy Agencies Used 1,000 Nazis." *New York Times*, October 27, 2014, A-1.

Lubrow, Arthur. "The Woman and the Giant (No Fable)." *New York Times*, April 13, 2014, Arts and Leisure, section: 24.

Lyman, Rick. "Robert Altman: Altman, Director With Daring, Dies at 81." *New York Times*, November 22, 2006, C-11.

Mahoney, John. "'Catch–22' Brilliant Bits; Cynical and Bitterly Cold." *Hollywood Reporter*, June 5, 1970, 3.

Maland, Charles. "The Social Problem Film." In *Handbook of American Film Genres*, ed. Wes D. Gehring. Westport, Connecticut: Greenwood Press, 1988.

"Marble Review: *Love and Death*." *Marble*. July–August 1975, 8.

Mariani, Paul. "Reassembling the Dust." In *Biography as High Adventure*, ed. Stephen B. Oates. Amherst: University of Massachusetts Press, 1986.

Martin, Douglas. "Peter Viertel, 86, Author and Screenwriter." *New York Times*, November 6, 2007, C-20.

_____. "Tadeusz Rosewics, Fierce Poetic Voice of Postwar Poland, Is Dead at 91." *New York Times*, May 21, 2014, B-17.

"'MASH' Appeal." *Entertainment Weekly*. March 1996, 106.

"MASH" [Book Review]. *Booklist*. January 15, 1969, 537.

"MASH" [Book Review]. *Kirkus Review*. August 15, 1968, 925.

"MASH" [Book Review]. *Library Journal*, October 15, 1968.

"MASH" [Book Review]. *Publisher Weekly*, August 5, 1968, 54.

"MASH" [Review]. *Variety*. January 21, 1970.

Maslin, Janet. "Sifting Flaws." *New York Times*, January 13, 1980, section D:13.

_____. "Watching TV: Being There." *New York Times*, December 20, 1979, C-20.

Match, Robert. "Between Tears and Laughter." *New York Herald Tribune*, August 25, 1946, 7:4.

"Matthew 10:30." In *The Living Bible*. Wheaton, Illinois: Tyndale House, 1971.

Maxwell, Glyn. "Eternal Lines." *New York Times*, February 1, 2015, Book Review section: 20.

Melville, Herman. "Letter to Friend Samuel Savage" (August 24, 1851). In *The Correspondence: The Writing of Herman Melville, Vol. 14*. Chicago: Northwestern University Press and the Newberry Library, 1993.

Miline, Tom. "*Little Big Man*." *Focus on Films*, Spring 1971, 4.

_____. "*MASH* [Review]." *Monthly Film Bulletin*, July 1970, 140.

Mirsky, Jonathan. "An Inconvenient Past." *New York Times*, May 25, 2014, Book Review: 21.

Morganstern, Joseph. "Bloody Funny." *Newsweek*, February 2, 1970.

_____. "Into the Mad Blue Yonder." *Newsweek*, June 22, 1970, 81.

_____. "Remember It, Jake, It's Chinatown." *Gentleman's Quarterly*, January 1990, 130.

Moser, Benjamin. "Patriarch and Pariah." *New York Times*, July 6, 2014, Book Review section: 17.

Muldoon, Paul. "I Do Not Like Publications of Letters." *New York Times*, December 14, 2014, Book Review section: 16.

Murphy, Art. "*Cabaret*" [Review]. *Variety*, February 16, 1972.

_____. "*Catch–22*" [Review]. *Variety*, June 10, 1970.

_____. "*Harold and Maude*" [Review]. *Variety*, December 15, 1971, 18.

_____. "*Little Big Man*" [Review]. *Variety*, December 16, 1970.

_____. "*Love and Death*" [Review]. *Variety*, June 11, 1975.

_____. "*One Flew Over the Cuckoo's Nest* " [Review]. *Variety*, November 19, 1975.

_____. "*Slaughterhouse-Five*" [Review]. *Variety*, March 22, 1972.

Nussbaum, Emily. "Maine and Miami." *The New Yorker*, November 3, 2014, 101.

O'Neil, Isabel. "Harold and Maude." In *Magill's Survey of Cinema*, ed. Frank N. Magill. Englewood Cliffs, New Jersey: Salem Press, 1980.

Oster, Jerry. "To Die in New York & Live in Minnesota." *New York Daily News*, June 9, 1974.

Parker, James. "Bookends." *New York Times*, November 9, 2014, Book Review section: 7.

_____. "Bookends." *New York Times*, September 21, 2014, Book Review section: 27.

P. D. Z. [message of corporate menace]. "How the West Was Lost." *Newsweek*, December 21, 1970, 98, 100.

Pennington, Ron. "*All That Jazz*" [Review]. *Hollywood Reporter*, December 12, 1979, 3.

Poe, Edgar Allan. "Diddling Considered as One of the Exact Sciences." In *The Complete Tales and Poems of Edgar Allan Poe*. New York: Random House, 1938.

Power, James. "Dialogue on Film: Hal Ashby," *American Film* (May 1980). In *Hal Ashby: Interviews*, ed. Nick Dawson. Jackson: University Press of Mississippi, 2010.

Pratt, John C. "Introduction." In Ken Kesey's *One Flew Over the Cuckoo's Nest: Text and Criticism*, ed. Pratt. 1962; rpt. New York: Penguin Books, 1977, xii.

Prose, Frances. "Bookends." *New York Times*, February 22, 2015, Book Review: 35.

Prose, Francine. "Bookends." *New York Times*, November 30, 2014, Book Review: 35.

"Prototype for Trapper Character of *MASH*." *Chicago Tribune*, December 25, 1999, 2:11.

"Queen of Fearless Comedy Dies at 81." *USA Today Weekend*, September 5–7, 2014, A-1.

"The Red and the White." *Time*, December 21, 1970, 57.

Robenstein, Lenny. "*Chinatown*." *Cineaste*, vol. 6 #3 (1974), 38.

Rowe, Douglas J. (syndicated). "Allen's Life Take on Life Is Comic, Tragic." *Indianapolis Star*, March 25, 2005, E-5.

Sandstrom, Daniel. "Philip Roth Interview: My Life as a Writer." *New York Times*, March 16, 2014, Book Review section: 15.

Sayre, Nora. "Films: All That Jazz." *Nation*, January 1980.

Schillinger, Liesl. "The Other Sister." *New York Times*, January 11, 2015, Book Review section: 11.

Schlesinger, Arthur M. Jr. "The Cold War." In *The National Experience: A History of the United States*, John M. Blum, ed. New York: Harcourt Brace, 1968, 783.

Scholes, Robert. "*Slaughterhouse-Five*" [Review]. *New York Times*, April 6, 1969.

Schruers, Fred. "The Rolling Stone Interview: Jack Nicholson." *Rolling Stone*, August 14, 1986.

Scott, A. O. "A War to End All Innocence." *New York Times*, June 22, 2014.

_____. "They're Buddies but as Coarse as the War Around Them." *New York Times*, October 17, 2014, C-10.

Seitz, Matt Zoller. "Life and How to Live It." In the untitled *Harold and Maude* (1971) booklet for the Criterion Collection, Special Edition, 2012 DVD.

Shedlin, Michael. "*Harold and Maude*." *Film Quarterly*, Fall 1973, 53.

"Shirley Suffering a Foul Gladly." *New York Sunday News*, March 25, 1979, section 3:10.

Shone, Tom. "Film Schooled." *New York Times*, January 25, 2015.

Shteyngart, Gary. "Gary Shteyngart." *New York Times*, February 2, 2014. Book Review: 7.

Simon, John. "In Praise of the Well-Made Film." *The New Leader*, May 15, 1972.

"Some Are More Yossarian Than Others." *Time*, June 15, 1970, 95.

Sterne, Herbe. *I Married a Witch*, review, Rob Wagner's Script, December 19, 1942. In *Selected Criticism*, 1941–50, ed. Anthony Slide. Metuchen, New Jersey: Scarecrow Press.

Sterritt, David (syndicated). "Woody Worries As He Directs." *Des Moines Register*, May 10, 1977, B-1.

Storey, William Kelleher. *Writing History*. 1996; rpt. New York: Oxford University Press, 2004.

Sweeney, Louise. "Films: A Deeply Original Thinker." *Christian Science Monitor*, May 5, 1972.

Taubman, Leslie. "Cabaret." In *Magill's Survey of Cinema*, ed. Frank N. Magill. Englewood Cliffs, New Jersey: Salem Press, 1980.

Tennyson, Lord Alfred. "Lady Clara Vere de Vere." 1842. In *The Poems of Tennyson*, ed. Christopher Ricks, 1969.

Thomas, Dorothy. "Revolution and Revelation, Hitler Model." *New York Times*, March 19, 1939, section: 9:3.

Thomas, Michael. "Flicks: A Movie Column." *Status*, April 1970.

Turner, Steve. *A Hard Day's Write: The Story Behind Every Beatles Song*. New York: Harper-Perennial, 1994.

Twain, Mark. "The Mysterious Stranger." In *The Complete Short Stories of Mark Twain*, ed. Charles Neider. 1916; rpt. New York: Bantam Books, 1964.

Vonnegut, Kurt. "Clowes Hall Talk." Indianapolis, Indiana, April 27, 2007.

Walton, Edith H. "Berlin on the Brink." *New York Times*, March 19, 1939, Book Review section: 23.

Waugh, Auberon. "The Last thoughts of Peter Sellers." [London] *Sunday Telegraph*, July 27, 1980, 19.

Webber, Bruce. "Billie Whitelaw, 82, Longtime Beckett Muse." *New York Times*, December 23, 2014, A-23.

Weiner-Kendt. "There's Something Funny in This Saloon." *New York Times*, February 1, 2015, Theatre section: 1, 11.

Whelan, Richard. "Introduction." In *Robert Capa*, ed. staff Aperture. New York: Aperture Foundation, 1996.

Wieseltier, Leon. "Among the Disrupted." *New York Times*, January 18, 2015, Book Review section: 1.

Williams, Jeannie. "Woody's Film Sparks Pulitzer Tiff." *USA Today Weekend Edition*, April 18–20, 1986.

Williamson, Bruce. "All That Fosse." *Playboy*, March 1980, 175.

Wolf, William. "*Slaughterhouse-Five*" [Review]. *Cue* magazine, April 1, 1972.

Yardley, William. "Martin Sharp, 71, an Artist Who Sharpened Imagery of Rock." *New York Times*, December 7, 2013, B-12.

Young, Jordan R. and Mike Bruns. "Hal Ashby: Satisfaction in Being There," from *Millimeter* (May 1980). In *Hal Ashby Interviews*, ed. Nick Dawson. Jackson: University Press of Mississippi, 2010.

Zinoman, Jason. "Can Broadway Be Funny Again?" *New York Times*, February 22, 2015, Arts & Leisure section: 1, 14.

Documentaries and Concerts, Live and Filmed

The AFI's 100 Years ... 100 Laughs. CBS television special, first broadcast June 13, 2000.

"Bill Mahr in Concert." Murat Theatre at Old National Centre, Indianapolis, Indiana, May 31, 2014.

"*Chinatown* Revisited: With Roman Polanski, Robert Evans and Robert Towne." Bonus Feature on 1990 video of 1974's *Chinatown*, Paramount (14 minutes).

[David Brenner] Live from the Venetian Hotel. HBO: Brenner's fourth solo special, February 19, 2000, rebroadcast in 2014 as *David Brenner: Back with a Vengeance.*

Dressed to Kill (Eddie Izzard concert film). Directed by Lawrence Jordan. Vision Vidio, 1998/1999.

The Making of Butch Cassidy and the Sundance Kid. Directed by Robert Crawford. Narrated by Butch Cassidy director George Roy Hill. Robert L. Crawford Productions, 1969/1970 (42 minutes).

Robert Altman voice-over on *MASH* (1970). Directed by Altman. Twentieth Century–Fox Home Entertainment, 2004 DVD.

Roman Polanski: Wanted and Desired, A Documentary by Marina Zenovich. HBO, 2008 (99 minutes).

The Tramp and the Dictator. A Kevin Brownlow Documentary Film, BBC, 2001 (55 minutes).

Voice-over narration on *8½* (1963). Directed by Federico Fellini. Corinth Films, Criterion Collection, 1980 DVD.

Index

Numbers in **bold italics** indicate pages with photographs.

Adventures of Huckleberry Finn 56–57, 65, 157, 159, 191
Agee, James 1
All That Jazz 9, 98, 198–211, **200, 201, 202, 210**, 213, 214, 216
Allen, Steve 184–185
Allen, Woody 35, 79, 115, **141, 144, 150, 154**, 155, 161, **174**, 199, 216; *Annie Hall* and 169–183; as auteur 139, 146, 150, 152, 199; *Love and Death* and 139–154
Altman, Robert 7, 12–14, 17–30; as auteur 20–21, 23, 198, 34–35, 166, 198
Andalusion Dog 42, 129, 174
Anderson, Wes 79
Annie Hall **141, 144, 150, 154**, 169–183, **174**
Ashby, Hall: as auteur 80–**81**, 94, 194; *Being There* and 184, 189, 190, 191, 193, 196; as editor 73, 109, 194; *Harold and Maude* 68, 72–73, 75, 78–82, 84
Auden, W.H. 1, 78, 93

Babbittry 47, 116
"Bartleby the Scrivener" 163–165, 191
Beatles 17, 44–45, 105, 186, 190
Beckett, Samuel 9, 39, 40, 60, 67, 74, 131, 132, 137, 164, 175, 179, 182; *Being There* and 190, 191, 195, 215
Being There 184–197, **185, 189**, 216; walking on water conclusion 190, 191, 192, 194
Benchley, Robert 88, 142, 208, 214
Berger, Thomas 40, 53, 56, 57, 59–60, 62, 63, 64–65, 67
Bergman, Ingmar 139, 140, 141, 144, 148, 151, 203; Woody Allen and 173, 175, 178, 182
Berman, Gil 9
Billy Budd 161, 162
Birdman or (The Unexpected Virtue of Ignorance) 203, 215
Birdofredum, Sawin 62, 71
Biskind, Peter 6, 24, 138
Blair, Walter 56
Bonnie and Clyde 11, 24, 67, 115, 116
Brazil 43, 215
Brecht, Bertolt 4, 208, 217
Brenner, David 180
Brooks, Albert 8

Bukowski, Charles 179
Buñuel, Luis 15, 40, 42, 129, 174
Burgess, Anthony 103–104, 106–107, 121

Cabaret 40, 62, 86–104, **89, 90, 92, 95**, 217; George Grosz art and 100, 101; Holocaust and 87–88, 90, 92, 99
Camus, Albert 161
Carlin, George 116, 129; football vs. baseball and 25
Carroll, Lewis 78–79, 182
Catch-22 5, 22, 28, 34–52, **44, 51**, 73, 102, 180; doubling for dying boy and 42, 43, 47, 50; fantasy ending 43, 45–46, 48, 50, 51, 116, 157, 215
Catcher in the Rye 11, 12, 65–66, 157
Chandler, Raymond 123–125
Chaplin, Charlie **6**, 16, 18, 19, 76, 84, 143, 152, **214**; Bob Fosse and 88, 205; *The Great Dictator* and 6, 13, 66, 93, 116, 168, 213, 215; *Monsieur Verdoux* 32, 36, 39, 44, 66, 84, 213, 214
Cheyenne Autumn **54**–55
Chinatown 37, 81–82, 122–138, **130, 131, 137**, 217; "capable of anything" and 123, 126, 136; "Forget it Jake" and 122, 136; "As little as possible" and 122, 137; racism and 135–136
A Clockwork Orange 103–104, 106–107, 121, 214
Coen Brothers 75
The Confidence-Man 162
A Connecticut Yankee in King Arthur's Court 191
Cronkite, Walter 58
Cuban Missile Crisis 102, 116
Cuppy, Will 39, 45, 118; *How to Become Extinct* 3, 21, 93, 102, 119, 148; Kurt Vonnegut, suicide and 119, 153
"The Curious Case of Benjamin Button" 149

Dali, Salvador 42, 129, 174, 217
Dalio, Marcel 41, 62, 87, 88
"dark comedy lite" 75
Darkness Visible 8
Defending Your Life 8

The Diving Bell and the Butterfly and "locked-in syndrome" 64, 203
Dr. Strangelove or: How I Learned to Stop Worrying and Love the Bomb 6, 40, 43, 119, 165, 195, 213, 214
Dostoyevsky, Fyodor 146–147, 153; gambling 21
Dreyfus, Alfred 76, 80
Duck Soup 11, 13, 18, 42, 142
Dupont, Richard 4, 208

Ealing Studio 72
8 1/2 50, 204–205
Einstein, Albert 77
The Electric Kool-Aid Acid Test 166
The Enigma of Kaspar House 197
Eternal Sunshine of the Spotless Mind 203
Evans, Robert 134

Fahringer, Harold Price 8, 10
Farber, Manny 5
Faust 96–98
Fear 124
Fellini, Frederico 38, 204–205
Fields, W.C. 43
Finck, Werner 103–104
Firth, Colin 50
A Fish Called Wanda 72
Forman, Milos 157, 163, 164–167
Fosse, Bob **89, 200**; *All That Jazz* and 198–211, as auteur 93, 94, 95; *Cabaret* and 86, 88–92, 93, 94, 95, 96–99, 102–104; Charlie Chaplin and 88, 205
French New Wave 5, 6, 38, 46, 115, 213
From Caligari to Hitler: A Psychological History of the German Film 98
"Funeral Blues" 78

The Gatekeepers 113
Gerber, John 56
German Expressionism 96–98, 134
Gilliam, Terry 43, 215
Göering, Herman 96
Gogol, Nikolai 147, 150, 153, 160, 184
"Going Around By Passing Through" 4, 208
Good Morning, Vietnam 18

Goodbye to Berlin 40, 62, 86, 87, 92, 93, 99, 102
Grand Illusion 41, 76, 88, 110
The Great Dictator **6**, 13, 66, 93, 166, 168, 213, 215
Grosz, George 4, 99, ***100***, ***101***

Hammett, Dashiell 125
Harold and Maude 8, 68–85, ***69***, ***81***, ***83***, ***84***, 86, 161, 191, 195, 215; direct address 73–74; "Dreyfus Case" and 76, 80; Holocaust and 76, 80, 84–85
Heart of Darkness 137
Heathers 60
Heller, Joseph 34, 37, 40, 41, 42, 45, 46, 47, 50, 51, 52, 53, 67, 108; McCarthyism and 183; response to *Catch-22* adaption by 48; Vietnam views 46
Hellman, Lillian 31
Henry, Buck 34, 45, 48, 50, 51
Herzog, Werner 197
Higgins, Colin 68, 78–79, 80, 84, 122
Hill, George Roy 51, 105, 106–107, 109–110, 113, 114, 115, 118, 119, 120; as auteur 118
Hitchcock, Alfred 79, 138, 166, 199
Holocaust 54–55, 68, 76, 80, 84–85, 87–88, 90, 92, 99, 117, 160
Hooker, Richard 11, 16, 18, 19, 20, 26, 27, 28–32, 34, 183
Hope, Bob 12–13, 17, 55, 139–140, 143, 148, 150, 152, 153, 173, 185
Hopper, Edward 75
Howard, Ron 156
Huxley, Aldous 99–102

I Am a Camera 86, 87, 99
The Iceman Cometh 216
The Invention of Lying 114
Isherwood, Christopher 40, 62, 86, 87, 92, 93, 98, 99–104, 115–116
Izzard, Eddie 118–119

Johnny Got His Gun 7, 113

Kael, Pauline 11, 24, 66, 84, 85, 89, 152, 209
Kafka, Franz 37–38, 46, 115, 131, 161, 177, 178, 183
Kaufman, Charlie 203
Keaton, Buster 182
Keillor, Garrison 83
Kennedy, John F. 32, 94, 102, 176, 178, 213
Kesey, Ken 115, 155, 161, 162, 164, 165, 166, 167
Kind Hearts and Coronets 44
Korean War 11, 14, 15, 21, 34, 47, 53, 67, 80, 215
Kosinski, Jerry 184, 189, 190, 193, 194, 196, 197
Kubrick, Stanley 27, 103–104, 106–107, 108, 119, 195, 213, 214
"The Kugelmass Episode" 140–141

Lahr, Bert 9, 41, 50
Lang, Fritz 97–98, 134

Lardner, Ring, Jr. 11, 27, 28–31, 51
Lardner, Ring, Sr. 31
Leach, Jim 7
Leary, Timothy 94
Lennon, John 44–45, 177, 186, 190
Lewis, C.S. 79
Lewis, Sinclair 47, 116
Little Big Man 40, 50, 51, 53–67, ***54***, ***65***, 96, 102, 108, 111, 133, 217; Custer and 62–63, 64, 65, 80; My Lai Massacre and 56, 58
The Little Prince 209–210
"locked-in syndrome" 64, 203
Louis, C.K. 119
Love and Death 139–***154***, ***141***, ***144***, ***150***, 178, 199, 216
Lowell, James Russell 62, 71

M 97–98
Maher, Bill 80
A Man Without a Country 9
Martin, Steve 3, 9, 75–76, 143, 169
Marx Brothers 11, 13, 17, 18, 19, 77, 112, 142, 166, 186
MASH 7, 11–33, **14**, **26**, **32**, 34–35, 37, 40, 46, 47, 48, 50, 68, 73, 161, 165, 166, 199, 215; TV and 157
May, Elaine 48, **49**
McCartney, Paul 17, 105, 186, 190
McCarthyism 31, 46, 67, 93, 102, 115, 183, 187, 193, 197, 213
McLuhan, Marshall 179–180
Mein Kampf 92–93
Melville, Herman 157, 161, 162–163, 164, 191
Mister Roberts 23–24
Moby-Dick 157, 162
Monsieur Verdoux 32, 36, 39, 44, 66, 84, 213, **214**
Moulin Rouge (1952) 204
Mugge, Robert 3, 30
Murrow, Edward R. 7, 45, 102
My Lai Massacre 56, 58, 94
The Mysterious Stranger 190–191, 192, 195, 197
The Myth of Sisyphus 8, 108, 179

New England Yankee 62
Nicholas, Mike 22, 34–35, 37, 38, 39, 41, 42, 44, 47, 48–49, 50, 51, 52, 66
1984 45

On Death and Dying 205, 206, 207
One Flew Over the Cuckoo's Nest 115, 155–168, **156**, **159**, **160**, 215; *Little Big Man* and 155, 158, 159–160, 217
Orwell, George 45, 46

Penn, Arthur 40, 50, 53–54, 55–56, 57–60, 66, 67, 183
Pentagon Papers 94
Poe, Edgar Allan 61, 123
Pogo 24, 25, 38, 211
Polanski, Roman 125, 126, 127, 128, **130**, 133, 137, 138; as auteur 134

Rand, Ayn 192

Renior, Jean 41, 76, 88, 110, 164, 205
Rock, Chris 180
Rosencrantz and Guildenstern Are Dead 21, 41, 206
Roth, Philip 38, 208
Rozewicz, Tadeusa 84
Rules of the Game 205

Salinger, J.D. 11, 65–66
Sandburg, Carl 22, 205
Scarface (1932) 43
Schickel, Richard 188
Schlesinger, Arthur M., Jr. 31
The Seventh Seal 140–141, 142, 144
Shoulder Arms 13, 18, 19
A Single Man 98, 99–102, 115–116
Slaughterhouse-Five, or The Children's Crusade: A Duty Dance with Death 9, 11, 17, 51, 58, 96, 105–121, 189; *Catch-22* and 105, 112, 115, 116; *Little Big Man* and 96, 108, 111, 117, 217
Southwestern Humor 56–57, 61–62
Stoppard, Tom 21, 41
"Suicide Is Painless" 23
The Sunset Limited 216
Sweeny Todd: The Demon Barber of Fleet Street 26
Swift, Jonathan 32

Tarantino, Quentin 9, 58, 60
Thomas, Dylan 22
Thoreau, Henry David 24
Titus, Christopher 17
Tolstoy, Leo 153
Towne, Robert 122–123, 125, 126, 127, 130, 131, 132–135, 137, 138, 141
Truffaut, Francois 5, 56, 107, 211
The Truman Show 21
Trumbo, Dalton 7, 113, 115
Twain, Mark 10, 53, 56–57, 115, 190–192, 195, 197, 214
Unfaithfully Yours 8–9, 32

Van Druten, John 86, 99
Vietnam War 34, 46, 47, 53, 58, 62, 66–67, 68, 71, 72, 74, 78, 105, 147, 152; and the "American War" in Vietnam 92; *Cabaret* and 93, 94, 99; *MASH* and 11–33; self-immolation in *Harold and Maude* and 73
Vonnegut, Kurt 9, 10, 17, 32, 42, 57–58, 105, 106–107, 108–109, 115, 116, 117, 118, 119, 120, 158, 214; "and so it goes" and 53, 58, 107, 108, 109, 113, 114, 121, 164, 173, 215

Waiting for Godot 9, 39, 40, 41–42, 50, 74, 108, 132, 164, 175, 183, 191, 215, 216; Keaton and 182
Walter Mitty 9, 35, 150
Watergate 94, 126, 138, 165, 213
West, Nathanael 49, 177
Williams, Robin 9, 18, 118, 203
Wolfe, Thomas 166
The World According to Garp 107, 118